INSIDE SOCCER

INSIDE SOCCER

The Complete Book of Soccer for
Spectators, Players, and Coaches

Alex Yannis

McGraw-Hill Book Company

New York   St. Louis   San Francisco   Auckland   Bogotá   Hamburg
Johannesburg   London   Madrid   Mexico   Montreal   New Delhi
Panama   Paris   São Paulo   Singapore   Sydney   Tokyo   Toronto

Library of Congress Cataloging in Publication Data

Yannis, Alex, date.
  Inside soccer.
  Includes index.
  1. Soccer. 2. Soccer—United States. I. Title.
GV943.Y36   796.334   80-13287
ISBN 0-07-072244-7

1234567890   HDHD   89876543210

The editor for this book was Robert A. Rosenbaum, the designer was Elliot
Epstein, and the production supervisor was Sara L. Fliess. It was set in
Souvenir by The Clarinda Company.

Printed and bound by Halliday Lithograph.

*The material on pages 115–120 and 230–249 was reprinted with the kind permission
of FIFA.*

*For Joan, and all my folks in the
United States and Europe*

Contents

Foreword

No sport in the world generates more enthusiasm than soccer, and no one knows soccer like Alex Yannis.

Alex has played and coached the game all his life. He has covered the soccer scene for *The New York Times* for 13 years and has been a soccer journalist for more than 20 years. His understanding of the current scene is a product of all the years of watching soccer history unfold, from the days when soccer in the United States was little more than a dream to the current soccer explosion.

One of the most enlightening discussions is the extensive presentation of the sport in the United States at all levels, from the six-year-olds to the colleges to the Cosmos. Every aspect of the sport as it is played, coached, and watched — in all corners of the world — is covered with Alex's singular expertise and humor. The anecdotes about the game the world so dearly loves are the best I have read anywhere.

The book is filled with action photographs that capture the excitement of soccer at its best. And the many diagrams will aid any reader in learning to play and watch the game.

The Appendixes, eight of them in all, are a miniature history of the sport that even the most finicky trivia buff will find satisfying. They include everything you need to know about soccer rules (both here and abroad, indoors and out), the Olympics competitions, champions in the Americas and in Europe, and the top twenty soccer nations and their national champions throughout history.

But perhaps the best thing about this book is the genuine affection evident on every page. It is a tribute to the sport and a generous gift to those of us who love soccer.

Franz Beckenbauer

Acknowledgments

My sincere thanks to the many who helped to make this book a reality, with special gratitude to Chuck Adams, Vince Casey, Rene Courte, Jerry Epstein, Dave Ferroni, Paul Gardner, Brian Glanville, Colin Jose, the Reverend John G. Maheras, Ursula Melendi, Thom Meredith, Arthur Pincus, Peppe Pinton, Steve Rankin, Steve Richards, Ted Rodriguez, Marcia Schallert, Jim Trecker, Hubert Vogelsinger, Paul Winfield, Phil Woosnam, and my wife, Joan.

The World of Soccer

In sidewalk cafes along the Champs Élysées, customers waited half an hour for café au lait. It took about as long for coffee and cognac to arrive on Rome's Via Venetto or Madrid's Gran Via. Customers waited longer on Rio de Janeiro's Avenue Copa Cabana for *Guarana*, and by the time you got a glass of ouzo or piece of baklava in Constitution Square in Athens, you could have walked to the Acropolis and back. No one paid much attention to business on Sunday, June 25, 1978.

Blame it on the soccer game played in Buenos Aires that day between Argentina and the Netherlands. A television audience estimated at over 1 billion was watching, and when Argentina won the game, practically all of South America began a wild celebration. It was the World Cup final, the culmination of an extravaganza in which more than 100 nations take part every 4 years. When the World Cup Final is played, the whole world watches because soccer is king in 147 countries.

In recent years Americans have become wildly enthusiastic about soccer as more young people have taken up the game. American soccer has changed from a sport played mostly by recent immigrants to a sport in which millions participate across the country. Professional soccer games draw more fans each year, and boosters of American soccer are certain that the United States will soon be a serious contender for the World Cup.

Factories in the United States might not close in order to allow their employees to watch a soccer game on television, and the Supreme Court might never postpone a session for that reason. But in 1978 in Iran, where the experts once saw only a slight potential for the growth of soccer, the Shah rescheduled the program of his court for the duration of the 25-day games when Iran reached the final round of the World Cup tournament.

Nor has soccer lost popularity in Europe. In 1974, the director of the Hamburg opera rescheduled a performance of Aïda so that it would not conflict with the West German–East German game, which the star tenor wanted to watch on television.

When kilted Scots in Frankfurt celebrated Scotland's scoreless tie with Brazil in a rowdy manner, British military police were flown in to help the local authorities. In the melee after the game, which was attended by Prime Minis-

(Top left) There's nothing like the excitement that accompanies World Cup competition. Here the crowd goes wild during the 1978 finals at River Plate Stadium in Buenos Aires. (George Tiedemann)

(Top right) In the final game of the 1978 World Cup competition, Argentine goalie Ubaldo Filliol (number 5, center) defends against Holland's Arie Haan (center, left). Other players from both teams crowd in on the play. The frenetic action is typical of soccer at its best. (UPI)

(Above) Argentina wins! Captain Daniel Passarella, balanced on the shoulders of his teammates, holds the coveted World Cup. (George Tiedemann)

ter Wilson, a burly Scot gave an American journalist a bear hug and yelled, "You see how it is, mate! It's Scotland that put the 'great' in Great Britain."

The effects of soccer are incomparable. After West Germany lost to England 4 to 2 in overtime of the final game of 1966, a despondent German student in London said good-bye to his friends and jumped to his death from a fourth-floor window.

Soccer is a game that can start or stop wars. Honduras and El Salvador declared war over a qualifying game for the 1970 World Cup tournament. Pelé stopped the war in Biafra temporarily in January 1969, when both sides wanted to see and talk with the world's greatest player.

Stories abound about soccer. A Frenchman in prison refused to be released because he wanted to continue playing for the prison soccer team. Shortly after the last of Hitler, Soviet soldiers and German prisoners cleared a pile of rubble from a parking lot and put on their soccer shorts. When the whistle blew, soldiers abandoned their posts and prisoners left their cells to watch. Almost 10 years later, in July 1954, a divided Germany was reunited briefly in celebrating West Germany's victory over Hungary in the World Cup final. The tide of joy and self-congratulation swept both sides of Berlin.

Then there was Rudi, son of a janitor in Vienna. One year he kept a pigeon on his roof, training and caring for it. On the day of an important soccer game tickets were almost impossible to get, and so Rudi was left at home while his family went to Hohe Warte Stadium. As soon as Rudi's father passed the turnstile, he asked for a return pass, explaining that he had forgotten to lock his bicycle. Instead of leaving the stadium, he went behind a pillar and opened his lunch basket. Away flew the pigeon, the return pass attached to its leg. An hour later Rudi was at the game.

Although soccer is popular everywhere, with essentially the same rules around the world, there are variations from country to country that reveal different styles of play and different attitudes, ideas, and emotions. Players, fans, and everyone else connected with soccer express their national characteristics inside the stadium. Latin Americans bring artistry and flexibility to the field. Their ball handling can be explosive at times, but it is always beautifully fluid. Russians and Germans are known for strength and determination. Spanish and Portuguese players display passion, improvisation, and flair.

In Great Britain, where the modern game began, teams employ a style of play that involves hard running, long punts by the goalkeepers on defense, and high kicks from the wings to the goalmouth area on offense. It's essentially a wide-open game. On the other hand, the Germans like to maintain control of the ball. They keep it on the ground, moving it gently from player to player. The Germans seem to have more freedom of movement and readiness to improvise.

The German game produces more goals, but according to an English coach, "It's too complicated, isn't it? There is too much individual play, too much slow stuff, a lot of buildup. Our fans would never go for this sort of thing. Our fans want a lot of action in front of the goal."

As the coach implied, fans make the game what it is in different countries, and soccer fans around the world are certainly not homogeneous. When the home team scores a goal in Germany, the stands explode in a rousing cheer, but Brazilian crowds often celebrate with pistols and fireworks. In South America, where demonstrations of emotion are acted out in grand style, water-filled moats or wire fences ring the field. The players are kept at a safe distance from the fans by tunnels that lead directly from locker rooms to playing fields.

Wherever emotions run high, there are people ready to exploit the situation. Soccer has been used by monarchs, emperors, dictators, and despots to enhance their personal prestige and the prestige of the state. In 1938 Mussolini capitalized on Italy's victory in the World Cup. He was photographed with his arms around the players, who were national heroes of the day, and the picture was on the breakfast table of every family in Italy the next morning.

Mussolini's use of soccer to gain popularity was nothing new. An emperor of China during the Han Dynasty staged soccer matches at the royal pavillion

(Below) Goal! Players and fans join in the celebration. Soccer inspires more intense and enthusiastic participation than just about any other sport. *(Jerry Liebman)*

(Bottom left) Teams from two of the world's great soccer countries, Brazil and Great Britain, met in the 1970 World Cup competition in Mexico. Here the incomparable Pelé takes a header as a teammate and four British players (in white) move in. Brazil won, 1–0. *(Pepsico International)*

(Bottom right) Fireworks tossed on the field by exuberant fans interrupt play in this 1978 game between France and Brazil. *(Sven Simon)*

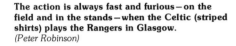

The action is always fast and furious — on the field and in the stands — when the Celtic (striped shirts) plays the Rangers in Glasgow.
(Peter Robinson)

to impress the court and foreign diplomats. Unfortunately for the losing team, its players were summarily beheaded after the game.

For over 70 years supporters of the Glasgow Rangers and Glasgow Celtic have made the game a theater for religious conflict. Rangers supporters are Protestant and Celtic fans are Catholic. Their rivalry, Irish in origin, is too deeply rooted ever to disappear despite the strict and courageous police methods used in recent years to mitigate the violence. When the two clubs meet at Celtic Park or Ibrox Park in Glasgow, policemen are stationed in the stands, where whiskey flows freely and the language is ferocious. If there are fewer than fifteeen arrests, the game is considered a quiet one.

Beginnings and Development

Soccer's roots go deep into the past, and the stories of its beginnings are numerous and varied. So many peoples claim to have discovered something similar to soccer that it would be fruitless to try to decide who invented the game, when, and where. The earliest reference to a game close to soccer comes from China in 1697 B.C. An emperor there is given credit for inventing a team game called *tsu-chu* that was played with the feet and a leather ball filled with cork and hair.

After all the early variations — from the Greek *episkyros* to the Roman *harpastum* — have been examined, a look at the origins and development of soccer reveals a strong English influence. Perhaps the Romans, who often borrowed from the Greeks, brought soccer to the British Isles, but it is far more likely that the natives were already playing their own version.

Their game was probably similar to what the Berbers of North Africa called *koura,* a game that was associated with agricultural fertility rites. In Berber games the ball represented the sun and was kicked ceremonially across planted fields. In other games the ball was the head of a sacrificed animal, with teams from neighboring villages competing to bury it in their fields.

In 1175 a monk named William Fitzstephen described in Latin how schoolboys in London played *ludus pilae* — a "game of ball" — after dinner on

Shrove Tuesday. Other records from that time indicate that an annual ritual game was played in Chester on Shrove Tuesday. Historians also refer to games at Derbyshire and at Corfe Castle in Dorset and Scone in Perthshire.

The games had become so popular by 1314 that King Edward II issued a proclamation banning them as frivolous distractions from work, worship, and warfare. In 1389 King Richard II banned the game because it interfered with archery. Subsequent monarchs confirmed Richard's laws, but in 1497 King James IV was given two *fut balles* as a present by his High Treasurer.

By the end of the fifteenth century the game had begun to be called *football.* Some students of soccer consider the origin of the term obvious—the ball was propelled by the foot, not the hand. Others say that the game was played *on foot,* unlike most ball games of the day, which were played on horseback. Common people did not own horses, and so football became the game of the working classes and students. Over the next several centuries football became the most popular game at English schools and universities.

In the seventeenth century football was played over vast areas, with the goals half a mile or more apart. As the game was played in a more organized

(Left) This sixteenth-century engraving from Italy shows two stalwart players pumping up an early version of a soccer ball. *(Radio Times Hulton Picture Library)*

(Bottom left) In Crowe Street, London, people played an enthusiastic if undisciplined type of football early in the eighteenth century. *(Radio Times Hulton Picture Library)*

(Bottom right) An 1868 English engraving, "Winter Amusements: Football," shows players at the line of scrimmage, some of them clutching battered shins and aching heads. Beginnings of the modern game are evident here, with a confined playing field and two clearly positioned goals, each guarded by a goalkeeper. *(Radio Times Hulton Picture Library)*

way—especially at the public schools, where the sons of the aristocracy and upper bourgeoisie were educated—the size of the field was shortened.

Another change that came with organization was the establishment of rules. Although the rules varied from place to place, their basic purpose was to lessen the violence that had come to be associated with football. One of the most famous events in the history of the game involved a violation of the rules. In 1823 a student at Rugby picked up the ball and carried it the length of the field. As stated on a plaque at the school, this "fine disregard for the rules of football" had the effect of "originating the distinctive feature of the rugby game."

In modern terms, that student opened a "can of worms." Some teams played rugby, others played football, and still others played something in between. Many of the rules were ignored, and in some areas violence returned to the playing field. Over the years two factions developed—pro- and anti-rugby. In 1846 men meeting at Cambridge University drafted a set of rules incorporating what they believed to be the best features of both games. However, running with the ball in hand was prohibited. No copy of these rules has survived, perhaps because they never gained wide acceptance.

In 1862 the anti-rugby group was given a boost when J. C. Thring published ten rules for what he called *The Simplest Game.* Since many believe these rules reflect football as it was then played, they are reprinted below.

In response to Thring or perhaps for their own reasons, representatives of eleven English football clubs met the next year in London to develop their own football organization. They met on October 26 at Freemason's Tavern, Great Queen Street, Lincoln's Inn Fields, and formed the London Football Association, which was in effect the English national association. They were well aware that there were two different games of football being played in England. After some wrangling, they published a set of rules that represented

J. C. THRING'S RULES FOR THE SIMPLEST GAME

1. A goal is scored whenever the ball is forced through the goal and under the bar, except it be thrown by the hand.

2. Hands may be used only to stop a ball and place it on the ground before the feet.

3. Kicks must be aimed only at the ball.

4. A player may not kick the ball whilst it is in the air.

5. No tripping up or heel kicking is allowed.

6. Whenever the ball is kicked beyond the side flags, it must be returned by the player who kicked it, from the spot where it passed the flag line, in a straight line towards the middle of the ground.

7. When a ball is kicked behind the line of goal, it shall be kicked off from that line by one of the side whose goal it is.

8. No player may stand within six paces of the kicker when he is kicking off.

9. A player is "out of play" immediately he is in front of the ball, and he must return behind the ball as soon as possible. If the ball be kicked by his own side past a player, he may not touch it, kick it nor advance until one of the other side has first kicked it or one of his own side, having followed it up, has been able, when in front of him, to kick it.

10. No charging is allowed when a player is out of play —i.e., immediately the ball is behind him.

THE LONDON FOOTBALL ASSOCIATION RULES

1. The maximum length of the ground shall be 200 yards; the maximum breadth shall be 100 yards; the length and breadth shall be marked off with flags; and the goals shall be defined by two upright posts, 8 yards apart, without any tape or bar across them.

2. The winners of the toss shall have the choice of goals. The game shall be commenced by a place-kick from the centre of the ground by the side losing the toss. The other side shall not approach within 10 yards of the ball until it is kicked off.

3. After a goal is won, the losing side shall kick off, and goals shall be changed.

4. A goal shall be won when the ball passes between the posts or over the space between the posts (at whatever height), not being thrown, knocked on, or carried.

5. When a ball is in touch, the first player who touches it shall throw it from the point on the boundary-line where it left the ground in a direction at right angles with the boundary-line, and it shall not be in play until it has touched the ground.

6. When a player has kicked the ball, any one of the same side who is nearer the opponents' goal-line is out of play, and may not touch the ball himself nor in any way whatever prevent any other player from doing so until the ball has been played; but no player is out of play when the ball is kicked from behind the goal-line.

7. In case the ball goes behind the goal-line, if a player on the same side to whom the goal belongs first touches the ball, one of his side shall be entitled to a free-kick from the goal-line at the point opposite the place where the ball shall be touched. If a player of the opposite side first touches the ball, one of his side shall be entitled to a free-kick (but at the goal only) from a point 15 yards from the goal-line opposite the place where the ball is touched; the opposing side shall stand behind the goal-line until he has had his kick.

8. If a player makes a fair catch, he shall be entitled to a free-kick, provided he claims it by making a mark with his heel at once; and in order to take such a kick he may go as far back as he pleases, and no player on the opposite side shall advance beyond his mark until he has kicked.

9. No player shall carry the ball.

10. Neither tripping nor hacking shall be allowed, and no player shall use his hands to hold or push an adversary.

11. A player shall not throw the ball or pass it to another with his hands.

12. No player shall take the ball from the ground with his hands while it is in play under any pretence whatever.

13. A player shall be allowed to throw the ball or pass it to another if he made a fair catch or catches the ball on the first bounce.

14. No player shall be allowed to wear projecting nails, iron plates or gutta percha on the soles or heels of his boots.

compromise between the two factions as shown above.

Rules 9 to 12 disallowed practices that had become common in rugby, causing a minority of the participants to withdraw from the coalition. According to some historians, the major issue was not the handling of the ball, but rule 10, which prohibited hacking. This practice, wherein "the players kick each others' shins without the least ceremony, and some of them are overthrown at the hazard of their limbs," was important to rugby enthusiasts. But this style of play soon proved to be too violent, and hacking was prohibited in rugby as well. By that time the use of the hands was firmly established in rugby, just as it was firmly prohibited in football, and so the two games continued to go their separate ways.

The modern term *soccer* has its origins in the Football Association meeting of 1863. The sport came to be called *association football,* then *association,*

(Top left) Artist's impression of the first game between England and Scotland in 1872. (Radio Times Hulton Picture Library)

(Top right) First game of the British Ladies' Football Club, played in 1895. (Mansell Collection)

(Above) Winners of the 1966 FA Cup, Everton, share the triumph with their fans. Left to right, Gordon West, Colin Harvey, Mike Trebilcock, Tommy Wright, Alex Young, and Manager Harry Catterick. (The Football Association)

and finally, in the schoolboy slang of the day—which added "er" to the ends of many words—*soccer*. In the non-English-speaking world, of course, the game was called *fútbol* or some other translation of the original *football*.

Except in the United States, soccer found greater acceptance than rugby, particularly in Europe and South America. Around 1870, Football Association rules were extended to Germany, and a team from Oxford University visited Germany in 1875, the first overseas tour by a soccer team. As a result of the tour several German universities took up the game.

The first game between national teams was held when England and Scotland met in 1872 in Glasgow. The idea for the game originated with the secretary of the Football Association, C. W. Alcock. England was the only country with a national association in 1872, but the game that year lead to the formation of the Scottish Football Association in 1873. Wales followed in 1876 and Ireland in 1880. English and Scottish teams played each other regularly after 1872, but it was not until 1882 that a uniform code of rules was established for this competition.

The English Football Association gained stature by deciding in 1871 to organize an open competition, the Football Association Challenge Cup (FA Cup), to be conducted on a knockout, or tournament, basis. The competition, another of Alcock's ideas, was an immediate success, and the FA Cup final is still the climax of the soccer season in England.

Since 1923 all FA Cup finals have been played at Wembley Stadium in London. The official attendance for the first final at Wembley was 126,047, including King George IV, but over 150,000 were actually inside the stadium to see Bolton Wanderers defeat West Ham United 2 to 0 in a game that has gone into soccer books as the *White Horse Final* because a policeman on a white horse helped control the fans.

In the early days of the English Football Association the players were amateurs. Many were gentlemen in the sporting tradition, averse to playing for money. In the 1880s this began to change, and by the turn of the century the professionals had eclipsed the amateurs—except for the Corinthians, the best and most famous of the amateur clubs.

The trend toward professionalism began in Darwen, Lancashire, of Manchester. The area was full of good, strong players and rabid fans; soon the best football in England was being played not by amateurs in London but by professionals in the northern counties. The public schools did not immediately notice this trend. They tried to destroy professionalism, but they failed and accepted the inevitable.

Most professionals in English soccer were Scots. The Scottish style of soccer—"combination" play, or passing the ball as well as dribbling—had been eagerly accepted throughout the British Isles after the national team of Scotland defeated England in 8 of 9 games between 1876 and 1885.

The professionals played a better brand of soccer, and the standards of the game were raised by their efforts. They also brought bigger crowds into the stadiums. In 1885 the FA Cup final attracted 12,500 fans. Ten years later 45,000 were in attendance, and in 1901 over 110,000 watched the game at the Crystal Palace Stadium in London. These were enormous crowds even by today's standards, but the price of admission to most games was quite low. The players were paid significantly less than their modern counterparts. The maximum salary for professionals around 1900 was 9 pounds a week, and it stayed about the same until after World War II.

Professional play did not come to the Continent until 1924, when it was introduced in Austria, but it made rapid progress. Soon professionalism was widely accepted not only in Europe but in South America. The rest of the world continued to follow the English lead; just as in England, the last group in each nation to accept the professionals was the governing body of the sport.

The International Organization of Soccer

Soccer's widening popularity and professionalism in Europe and South America did not really interest the British. They maintained that foreigners could play the game but would never play it as well.

Perhaps the British thought they were also superior in administrative and promotional matters. When a meeting was held in Paris in 1904 to discuss the founding of an international soccer organization, the British stayed home. The seven nations that sent representatives to the conference—Belgium, Denmark, France, the Netherlands, Spain, Sweden, and Switzerland—did quite well without the British. They founded the Fédération Internationale de Football Association (FIFA), which has remained the worldwide governing body of soccer to the present day.

Two years later the national associations of England, Ireland, Scotland, and Wales joined FIFA under the condition that the British International Board would be responsible for the rules of soccer. This understanding remains in effect today, but the relationship between the British and FIFA has been stormy for most of the twentieth century.

After World War I the British wanted Germany and her former allies Austria and Hungary banned from world soccer. In 1920, after failing to gain support for this stand, the British resigned from FIFA. They returned in 1924 but resigned again in 1928 after a policy dispute about the running of the Olympic tournament. They did not join FIFA again until after World War II.

With or without the British, FIFA flourished from the start, filling a significant need as soccer spread around the world. There could be no meaningful international competition if teams in different countries played under different

The greatest number of professionals in the early days of English soccer came from Scotland. It was there that "combination play," which was eagerly accepted all over the world, originated. *(The Football Association)*

The first World Cup, named for FIFA leader Jules Rimet, was retired by Brazil after they won it for the third time in 1970. *(FIFA)*

rules. Every country now has an association that functions through affiliation with FIFA. No player of any age can participate in international competition unless he and his team are affiliated with the national association, which must be affiliated with FIFA.

The first president of FIFA was a Frenchman, Robert Guerin. He was succeeded by an English soccer official, D. B. Woolfall, who held office from 1906 to 1909. Jules Rimet took over in 1921 and remained president until 1954. During his 33 years in office, FIFA expanded worldwide, taking under its umbrella such soccer powers as Brazil, the Soviet Union, and Uruguay. After years of planning by Rimet and his colleagues, particularly Henri Delaunay, the first World Cup competition was staged by FIFA in 1930 with 13 countries participating.

Delaunay was secretary of the FIFA from 1919 until his death in 1956. With Rimet, for whom the World Cup was originally named, he was one of the most influential figures in the formative years of world soccer.

After Rimet's death at the age of 83, Rodolph William Seeldrayers, a Belgian, held office for 1 year. Arthur Drewry of England was president from 1956 to 1961. He was succeeded by Sir Stanley Rous, whose tenure lasted 13 years. After Rimet, Rous has been perhaps the most imposing leader of FIFA. His judgment, experience, and leadership as secretary of the English Football Association enabled him to guide FIFA to higher standards.

Rous lost the presidency to Dr. João Havelange of Brazil in 1974 after refusing to oust Taiwan in favor of China and because Havelange pledged to include 20 teams in the final round of the 1978 World Cup. Minutes after his election, Havelange announced that 20 countries would participate in the final round in Argentina in 1978 and 24 would go to Spain in 1982, with Africa and Asia providing most of the new entries.

However, 16 countries rather than 20 attended the 1978 final round in Argentina. For the 1982 tournament in Spain, FIFA's Organising Committee for the World Cup decided unanimously to increase the number to 24. At a meeting in the new FIFA facilities in Zurich, the committee decided that in addition to the host country and Argentina, the defending champion, there will be 13 countries from Europe, 3 from South America, and 2 each from Africa, Asia, and North and Central America and the Caribbean (CONCACAF). The committee's resolution will not necessarily affect World Cup tournaments after 1982.

Havelange staged a well-organized campaign. A successful trilingual lawyer, he campaigned for 3 years, visiting eighty-four countries before the 1974 election. He was returned to office unopposed in 1978.

The organization of the World Cup and Olympic tournaments represents only a small part of FIFA's responsibilities. Most of the organization's work is done through small groups.

One of the most important groups is the Executive Committee, which includes members from all parts of the world and which is responsible for coordinating all other FIFA committees. Another important group is the Referees' Committee, which makes certain that the interpretation of the rules is uniform throughout the world. This committee maintains a list of referees and is responsible for the selection of officials for all international games.

FIFA also has a Technical Committee, which is concerned with raising the standard of play throughout the world and spreading new techniques in training and skills. In recent years increased interest in the game in Iran, Japan, Tunisia, and the United States has broadened the scope of soccer considerably. FIFA organizes courses for coaches, administrators, referees, and players.

There are also Finance, World Cup, Medical, Amateur, Disciplinary, Press and Publications, Emergency, and Players' Status committees. The Players' Status Committee makes sure that member nations respect each other's reserve clauses and disciplinary measures. A player under suspension in one country, for example, is automatically suspended everywhere else.

If no settlement can be reached in a dispute between national organizations, FIFA takes over. Its power to enforce decisions is considerable; it can effectively suspend a player, a club, or even an entire league. All players are registered with their leagues and their national associations, which means they are registered with FIFA as well.

If a player moves to another country, he must present a certificate of transfer from his former football association stating that he is in good standing. Any player suspended by his national association becomes an outcast, turned away by any club he approaches anywhere in the world. People who have attempted to circumvent FIFA's rules have paid the penalty.

FIFA, with headquarters in Zurich, is the largest and most successful sporting organization in the world. In February 1980 FIFA had 147 nations as members; the United Nations had 152.

The World Cup

FIFA sponsors the most widely followed sports competition on earth—the World Cup. Held every 4 years, the competition attracts the avid attention of sports fans from 150 countries.

The first World Cup tournament was held in Uruguay in 1930, with the host country beating Argentina 4 to 2 in the final. Thirteen countries—not including England—competed, with the United States beating Paraguay and Belgium by 3 to 0 scores. It was an American, Bart McGhee, who scored the first goal in the World Cup. (The tournament's thousandth goal was scored by Rob Rensenbrink of the Netherlands in 1978.)

Italy staged and won the second World Cup in 1934, defeating Czechoslovakia 2 to 1 in overtime. The Italian victory was repeated in 1938, when they defeated Hungary 4 to 2 in Paris. The success of the Italians has been attributed to Vittorio Pozzo, the father of Italian soccer. Another great soccer power, Austria, did not compete in 1938. Not long before the tournament began, *Anschluss* had made Austria part of Nazi Germany.

Europe went to war in September 1939, and the World Cup competition was suspended for 12 years. In 1950 the games were held in Brazil partly because soccer stadiums in Europe were not rebuilt quickly after the war.

The Soviets and other Eastern European countries avoided the tournament for political reasons, but England competed for the first time. Having rejoined FIFA, *i maestri*, as the Italians called the English, decided to test themselves in World Cup competition. In perhaps the biggest upset in the history of the World Cup, the English were beaten 1 to 0 by the Americans in a first-round game.

Uruguay won that tournament 20 years after it had won the first, beating Brazil 2 to 1 in the final. For the Brazilians it was a big disappointment; before the game the question was not whether they would win, but how many goals they would score. An enormous crowd packed the barely finished Mar-

(Below) **Jules Rimet.** *(FIFA)*
(Bottom) **João Havelange.** *(FIFA)*

The United States World Cup team, 1934. From left to right: (front) Gold, Pietra, Lynch, Czerkiewicz, Lehman, Fiedler, Houlian; (rear) Gadsby, Nilson, Martinelli, Moorehouse, McLean, Dick, Donelli, Arnheim, Flori, Harker, Gallagher.

acana Stadium, but the slaughter never materialized because the Uruguyan defense of Obdulio Varela, Victor Andrade, and goalkeeper Roque Maspoli withstood the Brazilian onslaught.

Because FIFA was 50 years old in 1954 and because its headquarters have remained in Zurich, the tournament was set in Switzerland that year. The World Cup of 1954 is remembered as the tournament of mud, rain, and showers of goals — 140 of them.

If the outcome of the final game of 1950 was a shock, the outcome of the 1954 final was a cataclysm. Never in the history of the tournament had there been as clear a favorite as Hungary, which had an undefeated streak of 28 games over 4 years.

Hungary had already defeated all the European countries. The "Magic Magyars" had also beaten England 6 to 3 in London, which represented England's first loss to a foreign team on home soil. The English team traveled to Budapest 3 weeks before the tournament started, but instead of getting revenge they were defeated again, this time 7 to 1. In the final Hungary faced West Germany, whom they had defeated 8 to 3 in the first round.

Gustav Sebes, the Hungarian coach, gambled on the questionable fitness of one of his top players, Ferenc Puskás. In the early stages of the game, the Hungarians toyed with the West Germans as they had in the first round. They did not realize that Sepp Herberger, the fine German coach, had fielded his reserves in the first-round game, giving a false impression of his team's true strength. The Hungarians took a 2 to 0 lead after only 8 minutes, but in the end it was the fitness of the West Germans rather than the skill and artistry of the Hungarians that prevailed. Herberger's men came back in heavy rain to win 3 to 2.

The 1958 tournament in Sweden started without a clear favorite. Three key Hungarian players, Ferenc Puskás, Zoltan Czibor, and Sandor Kocsis, had defected during a South American tour shortly after the Hungarian uprising in 1956. The Germans had gone downhill, and the English had lost 5 to 0 to the Yugoslavs in Belgrade shortly before the tournament. The Soviets, who had won the Olympic tournament in 1956, were the dark horse, with two superstars in goalkeeper Lev Yashin and midfield captain Igor Netto.

It was Brazil, under coach Vincente Feola, which surprised the world. Brazil had so much depth that Feola did not field the same team twice successively. After Brazil played England to a scoreless tie, Feola made drastic changes by playing Vavá, Garrincha, and two new players from Santos — Zito and a 17-year-old forward named Edson Arantes do Nascimento whom they called Pelé. With Pelé emerging as a star, the Brazilians defeated Sweden 5 to 2 in the final. Before this, the World Cup had always been captured by a nation from the continent where the final round was played.

In World Cup history 1962 was not a vintage year. The favorite was Brazil because so many Brazilian players from 1958 were returning. They were all 4 years older, and Pelé, only 21, was already becoming a legend. But Pelé pulled a muscle in a scoreless tie with Czechoslovakia and was replaced by Amarildo. In the final against Czechoslovakia the Brazilians won 3 to 1, joining Uruguay and Italy as two-time winners of the Jules Rimet trophy. Even without Pelé and without the wizardry they displayed in 1958, Brazil was the best team.

The English finally won the World Cup in 1966, 103 years after they had established the rules of soccer. The Brazilians were eliminated early, failing to make the quarterfinals after Pelé had been kicked repeatedly by the Bulgarians, who were not cautioned by the referee. Under the coaching of Alf Ramsey, who was later knighted, and playing in Wembley Stadium, England edged West Germany 4 to 2 in overtime in the final.

Geoff Hurst scored 3 goals, 2 in the 30-minute overtime, a feat still unmatched. His first goal in overtime was controversial; the Germans claimed that the ball never crossed the line. The shot hit the underside of the crossbar and bounced down. Roger Hunt, one of the English players, stood in front of the German goal with arms raised, not troubling to apply the coup de grâce because he was sure the ball had crossed the line.

Mexico built new stadiums, including the magnificent Aztec Stadium, or Estadio Aztecca, in Mexico City, for the 1970 tournament. There was widespread concern before this tournament that rough play, so evident in 1966, would be even worse. FIFA decided that skillful, artistic, and creative players

Russian goalkeeper Lev Yashin leaps high into the air in a vain attempt to block a goal kicked by England's Kevan in 1958 World Cup game.
(Wide World)

like Pelé had to be protected, and the referees were instructed to clamp down on foul play.

England and Brazil met in the first round in a fascinating game in which Gordon Banks, the goalkeeper who was so instrumental in England's triumph in 1966, made the most spectacular save ever seen in a World Cup tournament.

About 10 minutes into the game, Carlos Alberto sent Jairzinho down the right wing with a good pass. Jairzinho beat the English left fullback, Terry Cooper, and then crossed the ball to the far post, where Pelé leaped high in the air and headed the ball powerfully just inside the post. Banks, who was guarding the near post, suddenly flung himself full length across the width of the goal to scoop the ball off the line and up and over the crossbar.

The Brazilians won the game 1 to 0 on a goal by Jairzinho after a pass from Pelé and went on to the final, where they demolished Italy 4 to 1. Carlos Alberto, who later came to New York to solidify the Cosmos defense, was captain of the Brazilian team. He scored the fourth goal after an exquisite pass by Pelé. It was a game of positive soccer and a fitting moment for the retirement of the Jules Rimet trophy. Having won it for the third time, Brazil took permanent possession.

The new trophy, officially called the FIFA World Cup, appeared first in West Germany in 1974. It was designed by an Italian sculptor, Silvio Gazzaniga, who explained his work this way: "The lines spring out of the base, rising in spirals, stretching out to receive the world. From the remarkable dynamic tensions of the compact body of the sculpture rise the figures of two athletes at the stirring moment of victory. In a flowing and spontaneous language, the work expresses the force and purity of sporting competition." FIFA announced that the trophy was solid 18-carat gold and had cost $20,000.

Money and politics made their unwelcome presence felt in the 1974 tournament. It was estimated that Brazil spent $4.5 million to defend the title, and players from the Netherlands almost did not make the trip because of squabbles over bonuses. The problem was settled when the Dutch players were guaranteed $24,000 each plus 70 percent of the profits made from the tournament by their national association.

A political controversy arose when the Soviets refused to play the Chileans in Santiago. Just before the two countries were to play a home-and-home preliminary series in September 1973, the Marxist government of Chile was overthrown and President Salvador Allende was killed. The Soviets would not play in Santiago, which they termed "a concentration camp," and requested that the series be shifted to a neutral country. FIFA refused, and the Soviet Union withdrew. Chile qualified for the tournament in West Germany but failed to advance to the second round.

Led by Franz Beckenbauer and Gerd Mueller, the West Germans reached the final, as did the talented team from the Netherlands led by Johan Cruyff. But the West Germans prevailed, winning 2 to 1 despite being down a goal after the first minute.

Without Johan Cruyff, who decided to abstain from the World Cup, the Dutch again reached the final in 1978 but again were losers, this time to Argentina, the host country. Despite the poor refereeing, it was not a bad tournament. The final was deservedly won by the only team that had committed itself to play an aggressive, nonstop game of attack throughout the tournament.

The finalists in the 1974 World Cup, West Germany and the Netherlands, met again in the 1978 competition. Here German goalkeeper Sepp Maier falls to the ground while deflecting the ball away from Dutch players Rob Rensenbrink and Ernie Brandts. *(UPI)*

The United States again failed to reach the final round, but so did 91 other nations, including England and the Soviet Union. One hundred seven member nations of FIFA applied to participate in the 1978 tournament, hoping to qualify for Argentina, but only 14 could make it because the host country and the defending champion qualify for the final round automatically. The others had to get through qualifying matches, which took place over a period of almost two years.

FIFA's main consideration in assigning countries to various groups is geographical. Guatemala, Costa Rica, El Salvador, and Panama, for example, were placed in one group in the North and Central America and the Caribbean region. The winner of this group met the winning teams from other groups in the region in order to determine the region's entry in the final round. Mexico represented the region, having won a round-robin tournament with Haiti, Canada, El Salvador, Surinan, and Guatemala, countries that had either won or finished in second place in earlier qualifying rounds.

Meanwhile, in Africa three rounds of preliminary elimination games produced three teams with equal records—Tunisia, Egypt, and Nigeria. All three then played a home-and-away series, with the winner qualifying for the worldwide tournament. Tunisia was Africa's sole representative in the final round in 1978. They played 9 games before going to Argentina; in contrast, Scotland played only 4 games, but they were against excellent teams from Czechoslovakia and Wales. In these preliminary rounds the matchups of the countries are determined by lot. The 16 countries that qualify for the final round are divided again by lot, into 4 groups—no geographical considerations here—with 4 countries seeded to head the groups.

The Olympics

Professionals have always dominated World Cup competition, but amateurs can win the laurels in the Olympic Games held every 4 years. Here too FIFA is the sponsor and organizer selecting the 16 nations that will compete in the final rounds. The preliminary tournaments involve between 80 and 90 countries and extend over 2 years. Matches are held around the world, with the final tournament conducted as part of the Summer Olympics.

Soccer was the pioneer team sport in the Olympics. The first winner was recorded in 1900—predictably, it was Great Britain. The second team sport given Olympic status was ice hockey, with its first competition during the Winter Olympics of 1904. In that same year Canada won the soccer competition. Great Britain came back to demonstrate its supremacy by winning in 1908 and 1912, but competition was suspended because of World War I.

Through the years the popularity of soccer around the world has helped amateur sports. In many countries part of the receipts from admission tickets and betting pools for soccer are used to support other, less-lucrative sports competitions. Revenues from betting pools financed the 1960 Olympic games in Rome.

Olympic soccer between the world wars was marked by a broadening of competition as more countries developed world-class teams. In 1920 the winner was Belgium, and in 1924 and 1928 the honors went to Uruguay. In 1932 there was no soccer competition in the Olympics, but 4 years later the title was won by the Italians, who also dominated World Cup play during this period.

Another important factor between the wars was the rapid expansion of professionalism. As Henri Delaunay declared in 1926: "Today international football can no longer be held within the confines of the Olympics; and many countries where professionalism is now recognized and organized cannot any longer be represented there by their best players." In 1930 the World Cup tournament was opened for the first time to both professionals and amateurs. Since that time interest in the Olympic soccer matches has declined relative to interest in the World Cup games.

Since the victory of Sweden in the 1948 Olympics, all the top medals have gone to teams from Eastern Europe. According to many observers, while the rest of the world plays by the rules and fields teams of amateurs, many Communist governments subsidize athletes. In the Eastern European countries a ministry of sport controls soccer, spending millions to develop stadiums, gymnasiums, and training facilities. These governments state that soccer players have regular jobs outside the team. But most soccer clubs in these countries are sponsored by government departments, especially the military, which attracts the country's best players with good salaries and preferential treatment. Clubs are also sponsored by industrial agencies. The Locomotive team in Sofia, for example, has as its major sponsor the Bulgarian Railways.

This is not to say that athletes should not be paid, and paid well, as they are in the West. But if athletes who play for pay in England are barred from the Olympics, athletes who follow the same route in the Soviet Union should also be barred. FIFA has failed to show the firmness here that it has demonstrated in other areas. The judgment of the amateur or professional status of players has often been left to the national associations or federations of the various member nations, and this decentralization has led to different interpretations of the same law in different parts of the world.

Despite disagreements about the eligibility of players and teams, the consensus is that Olympic soccer matches since the end of World War II have provided fans with exhibitions of first-class play. The Hungarians have dominated, winning the finals in 1952, 1964, and 1968.

Two great players go one-on-one in a European Cup game in 1977. Berti Vogts of Borussia Monchengladbach (in white) challenges Dynamo Kiev's Oleg Blokhin, who was European Player of the Year in 1975. *(Peter Robinson)*

The Real Madrid team, which was number one in European soccer in the late 1950s and early 1960s. From left to right: (front) Canario, Del Sol, di Stefano, Puskas, and Gento; (rear) Dominguez, Marquitos, Santamaria, Pachin, Vidal, and Zarraga. *(Galvez y Vega)*

Other International Competitions

To decentralize FIFA's activities and allow a measure of home rule, continental confederations have been formed. These groups oversee activities at the national and club levels in their respective continents. The European Cup, an annual competition involving the champions of each country in Europe, for example, is run by the Union of European Football Associations (UEFA), which was founded in 1954. The European Championship for the national teams of each country is also run by UEFA.

UEFA's equivalent in South America is CONMEBOL, which stands for Confederación Sudamericana de Fútbol, which was founded in 1916. The newest group is the Oceania Football Confederation, which is composed of 5 nations, including Australia. Asia and Africa have their own confederations, as do the countries in North and Central America and the Caribbean. This confederation, which includes the United States and Canada, is known as CONCACAF, which stands for Confederación Norte-Centroamericana y del Caribe de Fútbol.

All these confederations organize competitions for the individual clubs and national teams of their member countries. The competitions are organized and run by these confederations but must be conducted according to regulations set by FIFA.

The most successful of these competitions is the European Cup. This annual tournament was conceived by Gabriel Hanot, soccer editor of the French sports newspaper *L'Equipe*. In 1955 the top club in each of 18 European countries received an invitation from *L'Equipe*. Sixteen accepted with only Sparta-Prague and Moscow Dynamo declining. The games went so quickly and smoothly that FIFA immediately sanctioned the tournament, giving it the official title of the European Champion Clubs Cup, now known as the European Cup.

To avoid conflicts with regular league games on weekends, the home-and-away series of the European Cup took place at night in midweek. The first

(Top left) **Alfredo di Stefano exults after scoring a goal against Barcelona in the Spanish league.** *(Albero y Segovia)*

(Top right) **Playing for Santos, Brazil, Pelé tries to get one by the goalkeeper.** *(Pepsico International)*

tournament in 1956 was so successful that 22 clubs entered the second, in which Real Madrid repeated as champions. Real won the first 5 European Cup tournaments and must receive a great deal of credit for the success of the competition.

With a team that included Alfredo di Stéfano from Argentina, Raymond Kopa from France, Ferenc Puskás from Hungary, Didi from Brazil, José Santamaria from Uruguay, Francisco Gento, Hector Rial, and Luis del Sol, Real Madrid brought a new dimension to soccer at the club level. Everyone in the world wanted to see Real Madrid in the late 1950s, just as everyone wanted to see Santos of Brazil in the 1960s and early 1970s and the New York Cosmos later in the 1970s. The 1960 European Cup final, in which Real overwhelmed Eintracht Frankfurt of West Germany 7 to 3, was attended by 127,600 fans. The average attendance for all 52 matches that year was 53,000.

UEFA also has jurisdiction over the European Cup Winners Cup, a competition for the winners of the association cups in each member country. There is also the UEFA Cup, which started as an invitational tournament called the Fairs Cup and was first held in cities that staged trade fairs. The UEFA Cup has since been changed to include teams other than the champion and the winner of the association cup in each country. A special UEFA Cup committee selects the participating teams, usually teams that finish near the top in their national championships. More than one team can be selected from each nation.

There were 248 matches played in the three European competitions of the 1977—78 season, and 764 goals were scored. There were 153 victories at home and only 46 away; the rest were ties. (These won-lost figures do not include the final games for the European Cup and the European Cup Winners Cup, which were played on neutral grounds.)

The South American Confederation awards its Copa Libertadores annually. However, many celebrated South American clubs have avoided the competition because of the travel and the tendency of small clubs to try to beat them by foul play. The competition has been dominated by Argentine clubs;

Independiente captured the Copa Libertadores 4 consecutive years, 1972 through 1975.

Until Cruzeiro took the trophy in 1976, no Brazilian team had won it since Santos in 1963. Many South Americans believe that the Brazilians have never taken the competition seriously, although Santos certainly did in the early years (the competition began in 1960), winning the trophy in 1960 and 1962.

The Brazilians have failed to dominate this competition because their talent is divided among more than a dozen top clubs, making it difficult for one great club to emerge. On the other hand, Argentina has most of its talent concentrated in five or six clubs and Uruguay in one or two.

Competitions within Countries

In countries where soccer is the national pastime, there are usually two major competitions: the league championship and a cup competition that is open to every team under the auspices of the national association.

The race for the league championship involves not only the title in the first division—or major division or Division I—but also the titles in the lower divisions that exist at a national level in most countries.

In England there are 4 divisions with teams throughout the nation. The first division is the strongest, and the winner is considered the national champion, but games in the second division are often as exciting and attract as many fans. The beauty of this system is that some teams get promoted and others drop into a lower division each year.

In Italy, there is as much interest in the standings at the bottom of Division I as in the standings for the national title. The three teams that finish at the bottom of Division I are demoted to Division II. Thus, teams can go from Di-

The winner of the First Division in each country is considered the national champion. Thus, games in that division are always exciting and hard-fought. Here players from Florence (white shirts) play against Torino in the Italian League. *(Peter Robinson)*

vision I to Division III in 2 years and vice versa. Imagine the Yankees or the Dodgers, for example, being demoted to triple-A baseball!

Stadiums and Crowds

The British, who take credit for inventing soccer, have clubs that are more than 100 years old. As a result, the home grounds of most teams are in heavily populated areas where space is a problem. Many clubs have been unable to expand because their stadiums are surrounded by factories and houses. A small number of these clubs have been able to purchase adjoining sites. Everton, one of the top clubs, has unfortunately lost out in this respect.

Formed in 1878, Everton makes it home in Goodison Park, Liverpool. There are stands on three sides, but the seating suddenly ends where the rear of a church juts into the stadium. It was in this church that the club was established. Liverpool, formed in 1892, plays its home games at Anfield Road, which was Everton's home in 1884.

Before 1945 there were only two stadiums in Europe, both in Great Britain, that could accomodate more than 100,000. Wembley Stadium, which is privately owned and used only for international games and national competitions such as the FA Cup, is located in London. There is also Glasgow's Hampden Park, where 134,000 have been packed in for a game. In the last 30 years, however, several other countries have built larger modern stadiums.

Real Madrid built Estadio Santiago Bernabeu with funds from its supporters in 1943, and their archrivals Barcelona followed suit with Nou Camp. Many new stadiums have been built in Eastern European countries to match Rome's Olympic Stadium. The biggest are in the Soviet Union and Poland, but Budapest's Nep Stadion, with a capacity of 100,000, is one of the best in the world.

Nep Stadion is the only European facility that can be compared with American stadiums. It has a seat for almost everyone admitted to a game whereas most stadiums around the world have seats for only half the crowd. At many games the standees are packed into comparatively small areas where individual movement is almost impossible. The resultant pushing and shoving have often magnified minor fights and other incidents into riots. One reason why American soccer fans are more orderly than fans almost anywhere else is that every fan gets a seat.

Soccer's worst riot occurred in Lima in 1964 when the amateur teams of Argentina and Peru met in a qualifying game for the Olympic soccer tournament. The referee disallowed a goal by Peru, and a fight started in the standing section of Peru's national stadium. A fan leaped onto the field and tried to assault the referee, and another fan was beaten by the police. Angry fans junped over the barriers after bombarding the police with stones and bottles. When the police unleashed canisters of tear gas to restore order, a full-scale riot ensued. Many spectators were trampled to death in the rush toward the narrow exits, which were reportedly shut. The end result was 309 dead and about 1000 injured.

Brazil claims to have the world's greatest fans and it is true that Brazilians are soccer fanatics. The game is considered more than a recreational activity. To many Brazilians soccer is a religion.

"Soccer is everything to Brazilians," said Luiz Fernando de Lima, a writer for Journal do Brazil. "For a lot, it's the only thing. People live and die by the sport, not just at the pro level but in the sandlots as well. It's a social phenomenon. In the United States and Europe people have other ways of affirming themselves as people. In Brazil it is not like that. Kids in Brazil grow up with only a soccer ball in their mind."

Not everyone in Brazil can become a top-notch player, and so most Brazilians become avid fans. The Corinthians Club of São Paulo claims to have the most dedicated supporters, and no one argues the point. Where else would 5000 people agree to take a 51-hour bus trip over 2000 miles to see their team in a quarterfinal game?

Scottish fans are not far behind the Brazilians. When Glasgow Celtic or Glasgow Rangers visit Western European countries, it is not unusual for 5000 Scots to follow. When the Mets played the Orioles in the 1969 World Series, about 50 New Yorkers went to Baltimore.

(Top left) **East German fans got special permission to watch their national team play West Germany in the 1974 World Cup tournament at Volkspark Stadium, Hamburg. They ate together, stayed at the same hotel, and sat together at the game. Their team won, 1–0.**

(Top center) **Tear gas clears a section of the stadium at Lima, Peru, during a 1964 Olympic-qualifying match between the home country and Argentina. Later the violence grew worse, panic set in, and 309 fans died.** *(UPI)*

(Top right) **Playing for the Cosmos, Pelé lost his cool in a game against the Washington Diplomats and knocked out an opponent with a hook to the jaw.**

(Bottom left and right) **In this sequence Jim Fryatt of Philadelphia goes after a Los Angeles player who did not treat him kindly.** *(George Tiedemann)*

(Top left) **Romeo Benetti, one of Juventus's all-time greats, has won many games for his team.** *(Peter Robinson)*

(Top right) **When Brazilian players score, they let the world know how happy they are. And their fans raise the roof.** *(Peter Robinson)*

The Game in Europe

Europe and South America are soccer's most vibrant areas. Soccer has been played in most European countries since around 1890. Players, spectators, and adminstrators in Europe are drawn from every walk of life and every level of society.

Climate has played a dominant role in the variety of styles and seasons in Europe. Countries bordering the Mediterranean seldom experience severely cold weather. As a result, these countries start the season in early autumn, play through the winter, and conclude in late spring.

Colder countries in Northern and Central Europe start their season in the spring and play through to the fall, with soccer giving way to ice hockey and skiing in the winter. The Soviet Union, Sweden, Norway, and Finland fall into this category. The Hungarians have adopted the same season but have not adopted a winter sport.

Austria, Switzerland, Poland, and Czechoslovakia begin the season in early fall, take a 3-month break to avoid winter weather, and conclude the season in June. During the winter break many teams from these countries tour South America, Africa, and often the Far East.

The teams in some European countries play in all weather. British, German, Belgian, French, and Dutch players plow through mud and snow, concluding their season on fields almost completely stripped of grass.

Soccer in Europe has flourished in heavily populated areas. The best-paid players are with teams from large cities, and some of these cities have two big clubs that dominate soccer throughout the country. In Italy, for example, Milan, Rome, and Turin each have two strong and heavily supported teams. The best and most popular teams in Great Britain are in London, Liverpool, Manchester, and Glasgow.

The internal structure of the clubs in Europe varies greatly. Professional clubs in England are controlled by shareholders. In Spain and Portugal clubs are run along democratic lines; a soccer team in those countries usually constitutes one section of a giant sports club with facilities for sports from golf to tennis to water polo. Anyone can join these clubs for a small monthly subscription. Members can vote at all meetings, use all facilities, and obtain tickets at reduced prices.

The biggest club in Spain is Real Madrid, which has about 60,000 *SOCIOS,* or members. In addition to winning the European Cup in soccer several times, Real has captured the European basketball championship. Apart from soccer, the clubs support predominantly amateur sports; in the large multisport clubs, profits from soccer are often used to subsidize sports that are less popular.

In Italy several popular teams are helped financially by major companies. The best example is Juventus of Turin. The Fiat company, controlled by the Agnelli family, donates large sums to the club, one of the few in Italy that provides multisport activities. The facility for tennis at Juventus is so lavish that Italy often stages Davis Cup matches there. The majority of Italian clubs, however, exist on gate receipts and donations from many individuals.

Juventus's wealth was demonstrated in May 1968, when it paid approximately $985,000 to get Pietro Anastasi from Varese. Today such sums are not unusual. A club in England may spend over $750,000 for the right to sign a player from another English club. (The acquisition of Pelé by the Cosmos did not involve a transfer fee because Pelé was a free agent, but the Cosmos paid Bayern Munich close to $1 million for Franz Beckenbauer and then gave Beckenbauer approximately $1.8 million to play for 4 years.)

Many European teams finance their purchases of foreign stars with cash from the gate receipts. A comparatively unimportant game can bring in over 80,000 fans. There are other sources of income, including substantial bequests from wealthy fans but this practice is nearly unknown in England and the United States.

European clubs would be even better off if they could take a share of the money that is bet each week in Europe. Several European countries have followed the British example of weekly pools. About 10 million people many of whom lack the slightest understanding of soccer, bet millions on the games every week in England. People have won millions of dollars in England and in Italy, where Il Totocalcio is run by the Olympic committee. Thirty-five percent of the money wagered in Italy goes to amateur sports.

(Bottom left) **An old-fashioned English mudder between Leyton Orient and Chelsea in 1972. In front, Peter Osgood of Chelsea is flanked by Paul Harris and Peter Bennett of Orient, which won 3–2.** *(UPI)*

(Bottom right) **The snow failed to slow down this game between the American and Polish national teams, played in Poznan, Poland. From the left are Kmiecik, Jarcobczak, and Gorgon of Poland, and Roboostoff and Bob Smith of the United States.**

Looking at bikinis and playing soccer are the principal recreational activities on the Copacabana beach in Rio de Janeiro, with Sugar Loaf in the background. *(Peter Robinson)*

Countries such as West Germany, Switzerland, and Greece have made betting a government business venture by granting a monopoly to state-operated agencies. They use the huge profits to purchase and construct sports facilities. Unlike the American system, there is no "point-spread" betting in soccer. Bettors predict only the wins and ties, not the margins of victory.

Because people are so fond of betting, wagers on foreign games are often available in the offseason. The English, for example, spend the summer months forecasting the results of Australian games. In Greece, at least two Italian games are on the weekly schedule of thirteen. The prize money is divided among the winners; the fewer the winners, the better the take.

The Game in South America

Soccer is well-loved in South America, particularly in Brazil, Uruguay, and Argentina. The game's seeds were sown there in the 1980s by European railway builders, businessmen, and merchant seamen, who christened clubs with names like Everton of Chile and Barcelona of Ecuador. Before long, the game had developed a passionate following. In Uruguary for instance, they say, "Every country has its history, and Uruguay has its football." South American soccer has been dominated by the largest country, Brazil, but Uruguay, Argentina, Chile, and Peru have also played important roles.

There was a time when soccer was the only thing that mattered to most South Americans. Now the story is different. Players and fans are better educated. The next generation, with its higher educational potential, will stay in school longer and have more time to think about things other than soccer.

Top-notch teams can no longer afford to wait for players with potential to come to them; they will have to actively seek new talent. What's worse, these teams must compete with scouts from neighboring countries or even other continents. Many Argentines, in particular, have been lured overseas.

Teams that kept their stars have had to play exhibitions overseas to earn the money to pay them. Between 1947 and 1959, Brazilian teams played a total of 1727 games overseas. They won 917, lost 437, and drew 373.

South American players, particularly Brazilians, have only recently earned a little of the freedom enjoyed by their European counterparts. Until about 15 years ago, players were transferred without consent. They had to pay their own medical expenses, and many were not guaranteed any portion of the transfer fee.

Transfer fees are still lower than in England. A few Brazilian stars have changed teams for substantial sums, but average first-division players are usually transferred for nothing. Paulo Cesar was purchased from Botafogo by Flamengo for $310,000 in 1972. After the 1974 World Cup, he moved to France for twice that. At the same time, however, another Brazilian team exchanged three players for a bus because no money was available.

The gate receipts are not as substantial in South America. In Brazil the attendance record for a club game was set in 1963, when the local derby in Rio de Janeiro between Flamengo and Fluminense attracted 177,636 fans to Maracana Stadium. The gate receipts were about $125,000. When the Cosmos celebrated Franz Beckenbauer Day on May 21, 1978, they attracted 71,219, earning $393,000 for gate receipts in addition to their share from parking and concessions.

A soccer game in South America can be quite an experience. Many stadiums have no parking lots. At Maracana Stadium, for example, you park on the street, if you can find a spot. As soon as you turn the motor off, a self-styled *guardador*—"watcher"—will usually approach you. For a normal league game he charges 2 cruzeiros, about 25 cents. If you don't pay, you might return to a car with four flat tires.

You can buy a numbered box seat for $10 or $5, depending on location. Unreserved grandstand seats usually cost $2. The most popular ticket in

The national team of Argentina, World Cup winners in 1978. From left to right: (front) Gallego, Ardiles, Luque, Ortiz and Galvan; (rear) Pasarella, Bertoni, Olquin, Tarantini, Kempes and Fillol. *(George Tiedemann)*

After Pelé began to play in the North American Soccer League, the caliber of play and the game's popularity both increased. Since then, many other foreign stars have joined the NASL, including Johan Cruyff (in white), who led the Netherlands in the World Cup in 1974.

South American stadiums is the approximately 65-cent general admission. Children under 8 do not pay. If you go to an important game, get there several hours early and don't be surprised to find 100,000 people in the stadium 3 hours before the kickoff.

After the teams emerge from underground dressing rooms, the fans will cheer, throw confetti and firecrackers, and show their flags and pennants. Don't do anything. If you cheer for one team, you may find yourself in trouble. The grandstand is divided into two sections, one for the fans of each team, and you may be sitting in the wrong section. If you get carried away and then have to give up your seat, it's no great loss. It wasn't a seat anyway, just part of a row of concrete bleachers.

When the outcome of the game has become clear, the fans of the winning team begin drumming a samba beat and singing, *"Ay, ay, ay, ay, Esta cherado ahora,"* which means, "It's almost over."

Several fans may have a heart attack during the game, and one may even die. You will read about it in the newspapers the next day. The fan who died will be identified by name and as a supporter of a particular team. You may also read that the President was at the game and sent a congratulatory telegram to the family of the deceased because their team won.

The Game in North and Central America

The soccer confederation in North and Central America and the Caribbean (CONCACAF) has 23 member nations, including the United States, Canada, and Mexico. By world soccer standards this region is underdeveloped except for Mexico. But the United States and Canada have taken to soccer and with the emergence of Cuba the CONCACAF region may produce two or three powerhouse teams in the near future. The United States in particular, with its limitless resources, can make this an important region in the world of soccer.

In 1913 the United States became the first country in this region to join FIFA. Canada did not become a member until 1948, 16 years after Cuba. Mexico joined in 1929 and has been the region's most prominent soccer nation ever since.

With a population of 51 million in 1978, Mexico had no fewer than 105,000 soccer teams. Canada, with a population of only 22 million in 1978, had 7900 teams according to the 1978 edition of FIFA's booklet of national associations. The United States was listed as having a population of 217 million and 1696 teams.

The Game in Asia, Africa, and Australia

Although the Asian Football Confederation was not founded until 1954, this highly organized body is thriving. Games between clubs from various countries and a competition for the national teams of all countries in the continent—the Asian Nations Cup—have been held for some time.

The continent's biggest impact on the World Cup came unexpectedly in 1966 in England, when North Korea reached the quarterfinals. The North Koreans had prepared for the tournament virtually in secrecy for 8 years, making no contact with Western European countries. China is expected eventually to achieve a similar feat.

Besides China, which appears ready to explode as the Soviets did in the 1950s, the biggest new power in Asia is Japan. Promoters used to have to beg Japanese fans to take free tickets, but now many league games and almost all exhibitions against foreign teams are sold out. When Santos first visited Japan with Pelé in the 1960s, approximately 10,000 fans turned out. When they returned to Japan in the early 1970s, 80,000 fans filled the stadium 2 hours before the kickoff.

Iran represented Asia at the 1978 World Cup in Argentina. It has also often been called on by the Asian Football Confederation to run the Asian Nations Cup. The Iranian Football Federation started in 1973; by 1978 it had grown from 12 teams to 23.

Israel represented Asia at the World Cup in 1970 and did poorly. Theoretically, all players in Israel are amateurs, and so good players like Mordechai Sphigler, who played with Pelé for the Cosmos in 1975, have left Israel for the high salaries paid in West Germany, France, and the United States.

India has not made an appearance in any soccer event of international significance. As a result, the All Indian Football Federation hired foreign coaches in 1976 to improve the level of Indian soccer.

Foreign coaches, particularly coaches from Eastern European countries, have improved soccer techniques in many African countries. However, there is usually little money to spare, and progress has been limited. In the more politically stable nations, governments have backed the growth of soccer by financing exhibition matches. In nations experiencing political unrest, however, the development of soccer has been relatively slow.

Soccer has been played in Africa since the early 1900s. The descendants of African slaves have produced a number of brilliant players in Brazil, and it should come as no surprise that the African continent is a good source of soccer talent. Standards are gradually improving, and players like Eusebio from Mozambique and Salif Keita from Mali have become famous in Europe.

There are two major drawbacks to the game in Africa: witchcraft and political antipathy. The Confédération Africaine de Football (African Football Confederation), established in 1956, has scheduled tournaments that were unseccessful because some countries refused to play against political rivals.

Several African nations, particularly Kenya, have repeatedly attempted to

A number of countries in Asia and the Middle East have hired European coaches and trainers to build up their national teams. Here Bill McGarry, an Englishman, works with Belchain Swalik of the Saudi Arabian team. *(Central Press)*

abolish witchcraft, but their efforts have had no more success than efforts to eliminate the spitball from baseball. Ultimatums forbidding spells and charms are issued to no avail.

In Kenya, where soccer is the national sport, no team considers itself complete without a witch doctor on the roster. Laborious precautions have been taken to protect the ball, the players, and the playing field from spells. The names of the starting players are generally withheld until game time, and some players grease their bodies with pig fat, a popular antidote to black magic. The pregame ritual involves inspection of the stadium, dressing rooms, and even the ball for evidence of sorcery.

Sharif Omar Abukar, a witch doctor in Nairobi claims that he has been consulted by 90 percent of the city's soccer teams. Players have told him that they saw two balls instead of one or snakes instead of the ball. Abukar relieves their anxieties by casting spells on the witch doctors employed by other teams.

Anything can happen when opposing witch doctors match strategies. A first-division game between two Tanzanian teams in Dar es Salaam was delayed for 45 minutes in 1973 because each club was afraid that the other team had hexed the ball. The referee finally settled the matter by carrying the ball onto the field with the teams holding on to it.

Witchcraft in soccer is difficult to spot. "It's not easy to detect what extraordinary things players take onto the field," according to Bartholomew Ogotu, secretary of the Football Association of Nairobi.

After Kenya, the black African nations that have had the most success are Zaire, Ghana, Cameroons, the Ivory Coast, and Zambia. Rhodesia's racially mixed team has appeared in the early qualifying stages of the World Cup in recent years without success. In South Africa the racial policies of the government have necessitated the formation of separate soccer organizations, a system that has not been successful. Several good South African players have competed or are now competing in the NASL. Derek Smethurst, Steve Wegerle, Mike Connell, Des Backos, Martin Cohen, Andries Maseko, Ken Mokgojoa, and Jomo Sono are just a few of the South Africans in the NASL.

The richer Arab countries to the north, such as Morocco and Tunisia, are better organized. Egypt entered the World Cup in 1934 but has shown little improvement since then. Morocco reached the final round in 1970 and certainly did not disgrace itself as Zaire did in 1974 in West Germany. Both Morocco and Zaire were coached in the World Cup by Blagojew Vidinic, a Yugoslav.

Recognition of Tunisia's achievement in reaching the final round of the 1978 World Cup came when one of its players, midfielder Dhial Tarak, was named African footballer of the year. Tunisia qualified for the trip to Argentina in 1978 by defeating Egypt 4 to 1 before 120,000 spectators in Tunis. Another great moment came in 1975 when the national team eliminated Algeria in the opening round of the tenth African Cup. Tunisia declared the day a national holiday, with the players receiving awards from government leaders.

Australia made its presence felt in 1974, when it qualified for the final round of the World Cup as the representative of Asia and Oceania. Australia granted citizenship to British players who were competing there at the time so that they could play for the national team. Coached by Rale Rasic, a Yugoslav, Australia lost 2 to 0 to East Germany and then 3 to 0 to West Germany, the eventual winner. The Australians performed well in their last game, a

Australia (in white shirts) lost to West Germany in one of the Final Round games of the 1974 World Cup competition.

scoreless tie against Chile. Soccer in Australia has been strongly influenced by English and Scottish players. There have been bitter conflicts between groups from Melbourne, Sydney, and Victoria. Under the able direction of Michael Weinstein and Sir Arthur T. George of the Australian Soccer Federation, a strong movement for unity has been in progress.

In an effort to expose Australians to the best possible competition, the government has spent a great deal of money inviting foreign teams such as Santos of Brazil, Manchester United of England, Dynamo of Moscow, and Ajax of Amsterdam to play exhibitions against Australian teams. The strongest teams in Australia are Sutherland, Western Suburbs, St. George, Safeway United, and Pan Hellenic.

New Zealand has also attempted to upgrade soccer by relying on imports from Great Britain, but the New Zealanders are several years behind. They continue to take greater pride in their all-black rugby team, one of the best in the world.

Country by Country – The Top Twenty

The top 20 soccer nations in the world have been elected for inclusion in this book on the basis of tradition; development of players, coaches, and systems; and general contribution to the game.

Argentina

Argentina is probably the top exporter of soccer players. Many go to Europe or to other South American nations. The partisan crowds and the vast majority of the players take the game almost too seriously at times. Nineteen of twenty-two players were ejected from a game in 1971.

The strongest teams in Argentina, which hosted and won the 1978 World Cup, are River Plate, Boca Juniors, Indepediente, Estudiantes, Huracan, and

(Top left) Lugue, Ardilles, and other members of the Argentinian team chase Scotland's Willie Johnston in a game in River Plate Stadium, Buenos Aires. (Peter Robinson)

(Top right) In the final game of the 1970 World Cup, Brazil whipped Mexico, 4–1, in Aztec Stadium, Mexico City. Here Pelé gets set for action. (Pepsico International)

Racing. British sailors introduced soccer into Argentina, but it was the massive influx of Italians in the early 1900s that produced the present-day game.

One story perhaps best illustrates the mentality of fans in Argentina. Angel Labruna—along with Alfredo di Stéfano, Mario Kempes and Omar Sivori—is one of the biggest names in the history of soccer in Argentina. Labruna, a forward, played in 1150 games before retiring at the age of 42. In his farewell game, he was sent off (ejected) by the referee and booed loudly by 80,000 fans.

Austria

Austria's inclusion here is due to Hugo Meisl, the son of a wealthy Jewish banker. Meisl brought Jimmy Hogan, a gifted English coach, to Vienna in 1912, and they formed a national team that became known around the world as the *Wunderteam.* The team featured exquisite control and short passes, which came to be known as the style of the Vienna school. Quite possibly, the *Wunderteam* was the best the world had ever seen. It reached its peak in 1931 and 1932, when it defeated Scotland 5 to 0, Germany 6 to 0, Switzerland 8 to 1, and Hungary 8 to 2.

Under Meisl's direction, Austrian soccer evolved a grace and artistry seldom equaled in the history of the game. Nevertheless, Austria did not defeat England until 1936 in Vienna.

Hugo Meisl spoke eight languages fluently and was a good friend of Vittorio Pozzo, another linguist and perhaps the greatest name in Italian soccer. Like Pozzo, Meisl had an affection for anything British. Meisl's passionate devotion to soccer infected his younger brother Willy, who became one of Europe's most respected soccer journalists.

Other prominent Austrian names in the world of soccer are Mathias Sindelar, Ernst Ocwirk, Gerhard Hanappi, and Rudi Hiden, the Viennese baker who kept goal so spectacularly for the *Wunderteam.* The strongest and most popular Austrian clubs have been Hakoah, Vienna, Rapid, Austria, and Admira.

Brazil

The size of Brazilian stadiums is only one indication of how big soccer is in the country that produced Pelé and many outstanding world-championship teams. Maracana, located in Rio de Janeiro, is the world's largest stadium, accommodating 220,000. Morumbi Stadium in São Paulo can hold 150,000 and there are at least four other stadiums that can each accommodate more than 100,000.

Part of the success of the game in Brazil is attributed to the Confederacão Brasileira de Desportos* (CBD), which was founded in 1916. São Paulo and Rio de Janeiro were the first two states with the resources to develop soccer. Because of the vastness of Brazil, which covers nearly half the continent, many states have their own leagues and competitions. In Brazil today there are approximately 25 federations affiliated with the CBD, representing about 500 leagues.

Soccer was introduced in Brazil in 1746 but was prohibited by the national council of São Paulo for "causing tumults and gathering vagabonds." It took 150 years for soccer to be accepted and practiced by Brazilian students, the sons of European parents, primarily English. Thus, "real football" was born on April 15, 1895, on the flat land of São Paulo. Born under the sign of Aries, soccer gained from that constellation the strength, audacity, movement, and energy which characterize it today.

The main rivalry in Brazil has always been between Rio and São Paulo, each with its own championship. Only recently has the huge state of Minas Gerais, long a major source of talent, begun to play an important role in Brazilian soccer. The most famous clubs in Brazil have been Flamengo, Santos, Fluminense, Botafogo, Vasco da Gama, Corinthians, and Cruzeiro.

Soccer in Brazil has been a source of propaganda for the government, providing the masses with national pride and involvement and helping them forget domestic poverty. Soccer has also fostered good relations with foreign countries.

Chile

As host of the World Cup in 1962, Chile finished a creditable third. Although an earthquake had shattered the country just 2 years earlier the finals were well organized. The effect on home attendance after the World Cup was astonishing.

The early 1970s were bad years for soccer. Luckily, the experiment of splitting Chile into provincial leagues and a metropolitan league in order to save money was abandoned. The country's morale was lifted when it qualified for the World Cup final round in 1974. The best-known Chilean clubs have been Colo Colo, named for an Indian hero, Universidad Católica, and Green Gross.

Czechoslovakia

Czechoslovakia has reached the World Cup final twice, losing on both occasions. They should have won in Rome in 1934, but lost to Italy 2 to 1 in overtime after the Italians had tied the game on a freak goal in regulation time. In Chile in 1962 they fell victim 3 to 1 to the wizardry of Brazil. Czechoslovakia captured the European Football Championship, formerly known as the European Nations Cup, in 1976.

Soccer in Czechoslovakia started, primarily in Prague, before World War I. Dukla Prague and Slovan Bratislava have been the most famous clubs. Frantisek Planica and Josef Masopust, who became Europe's player of the year in 1962, are the best-known Czech players.

*Confederation of Brazilian Sports.

First Division play in England is as good as any in the world. In this 1971 game, Eddie Kelly of Arsenal scores a goal against the Crystal Palace goalkeeper, John Jackson, at right. *(UPI)*

England

Although England has done very poorly in the World Cup since its triumph in 1966, the English remain one of the world's strongest soccer nations. It was not until 1929 that an English team was defeated by a foreign club, and it was 90 years after the formation of the Football Association that the English were beaten on their own soil by Hungary in 1953. The English were the first to establish a set of rules for soccer.

In England soccer is what Bobby Charlton, one of its greatest players, has called a "poor man's game." A top first-division player may enjoy vacations in Majorca, write a weekly column for a national newspaper, and have a Jaguar in his driveway. There are few players in this category, however, and many of them are crossing the Atlantic.

Many English teams have achieved greatness. The top clubs have been Preston in the late nineteenth century, Aston Villa before World War I, Huddersfield in the 1920s, Arsenal in the 1930s, Newcastle in the early 1950s, Manchester United in the mid-1950s, Tottenham in the early 1960s, and Leeds and Liverpool in the 1970s. Other popular clubs include Chelsea, West Ham United, West Bromwich, Wolverhampton, Burnley, Everton, Nottingham Forest, and Manchester City.

Few countries in the world have produced players and coaches of the caliber of John Goodall, Charles Buchan, Bob Crompton, Dixie Dean, Stanley Mathews, Eddie Hapgood, Tom Finney, Bobby Moore, Billy Wright, Steve Bloomer, Tom Lawton, Duncan Edwards, Gordon Banks, Jimmy Greaves, Stan Mortensen, Bobby Charlton, Matt Busby, Herbert Chapman, Walter Winterbottom, Sir Alf Ramsey, Jimmy Hogan, and, of course, Sir Stanley Rous, president of FIFA for 13 years.

France

France became a member of FIFA at the charter meeting in 1904, even though a formal national federation was not founded in France until 1919, 6 years later than in the United States. The French sent two teams to the 1908 Olympics in London. An early president of FIFA and the man responsible for the World Cup was a Frenchman, Jules Rimet, and France hosted the World Cup very successfully in 1938.

After a magnificent offensive display in the 1958 World Cup games in Sweden, which earned them third place, the French went through a prolonged decline. Foreign coaches tried to train French players in techniques incompatible with their natural gifts. Players such as Raymond Kopa, Juste Fontain, and more recently Michel Platini have been the best-known French players. Fontain, born in Morocco, holds the record for the most goals scored in a World Cup tournament—13. He achieved the feat in Sweden in 1958. Reims, Racing, St. Etienne, and Nantes have been the most popular teams.

Hungary

In England one of the most popular sports books of the early 1950s was *Learn to Play the Hungarian Way*. It was prompted by the Magic Magyars' defeat of England on British soil. The Magyars were the overwhelming favorites in the 1954 World Cup final in Switzerland, but the Germans upset them.

Ferenc Puskás, Sandor Kocsis, Nandor Hideqkuti, and an administrator named Gustav Sebes became household words around the world in the 1950s. However, decline set in quickly with the Soviet takeover of Hungary later in the decade. The country's best players, including Puskás and Kocsis, defected. Flórian Albert and Ferenc Bene have been the best-known stars in more recent years. Ferencvaros, Vasas, Honvend, MTK, and Ujpest Dozsa have been the most famous clubs.

Italy

Soccer was introduced in Italy by a Torinese businessman in 1887. Genoa, which in 1978 was relegated to Division II, was the first organized club. Vittorio Pozzo, who studied in Switzerland and England, was the architect of Italian World Cup triumphs in 1934 in Italy and 1938 in France. As coach of Azzuri—the national team—Pozzo did more than any other person to develop soccer in Italy.

Born in Piedmont, near Turin, Pozzo preferred track and field to soccer. He was a promising middle-distance runner until a friend told him one day, "You are fast, but when you run you look foolish because you run with nothing in front of you. Come and see our game, we run after a ball."

Pozzo fell in love with soccer at first sight. After his graduation from the lyceum and gymnasium, his family sent him to Zurich to study languages. He went on to London but did not stay there long because, "There were too many Italians looking for one another and spending evenings together."

Pozzo's family lured him back with a round-trip ticket so that he might attend his sister's wedding. He never used the return half. Soon after his arrival in Italy, he was made secretary of the infant Italian Federation, discovering a first division that included "more clubs than there were weeks in the year"—64.

Although this situation may have produced a chaotic tournament, it was a strong indication that the growth of soccer in Italy had been remarkably swift. Pozzo attempted to cut the first-division clubs to 24, precipitating a split of the Italian Federation before the 1912 Olympic tournament.

After the split, most of the clubs that had resigned formed a new federation. The president of the new group asked Pozzo to take a team to Stockholm for the 1912 Olympic tournament. Thus Pozzo became *commissario tecnico*, or coach of the Italian national team, a job he was to hold on and off

The Italians play hard. This photo was taken during a game between Inter and Roma, two First Division teams. *(UPI)*

for the next 36 years. When he became *commissario tecnico* for the third time in 1929, his term lasted another 20 years. Pozzo never made money from soccer. A French journalist described him as "the poor captain of a company of millionaires."

Italy's triumph in the 1934 World Cup was a triumph of Pozzo's tactics and handling of players. "British players must be dealt with collectively," Pozzo once said, "Italians must always be dealt with as individuals." The players on the Italian national team were often the spoiled idols of local crowds, with little interest in soccer as a game.

Pozzo was severe yet paternal with his players, but he could be quite devious as well. A player who was unwilling to keep the ball on the ground would be told "You know, I've been thinking about that discussion we had. You were right, you *should* keep the ball on the ground." If two players hated each other, Pozzo would room them together and then ask, "Well, cannibals? Have you eaten each other yet?"

Italy retained the World Cup in 1938 in Paris, beating Hungary 4 to 2 in the final. Pozzo considered this team the best he had ever chosen for Italy, although he though the members of the 1934 team were individually superior.

The Italians have experienced disappointment as well as success in the World Cup, including losses to North Korea in 1966 and Chile in 1962.

Juventus, Inter-Milan, A. C. Milan, Torino, Roma, Fiorentina, and Napoli have been the most popular teams. After Pozzo, the most distinguished names in Italian soccer are Guiseppe Meazza, Silvio Piola, Giampero Boniperti, Dino Zoff, Giacinto Facchetti, Sandrino Mazzola, Gianni Rivera, and Luigi Riva. In an unforgettable tragedy, the entire Torino team was killed in an airplane crash in 1949.

Mexico

Mexico staged the 1970 World Cup and reached the quarterfinals before losing to Italy, a 1970 finalist. Since World War II Mexico has qualified every year for the final round of the World Cup, with the exception of 1974, when Haiti went to West Germany. Although the competition has been weak, the Mexicans have cultivated soccer very seriously.

The finest player produced in Mexico was goalkeeper Antonio Carbajal, who played in 5 World Cup tournaments. The most powerful and popular teams have been Club America, Toluca, Guadalajara, Monterrey, and Universidad de Mexico. Estadio Azteca in Mexico City is the largest stadium in the country, with a capacity of 108,499.

The Netherlands

Soccer had an early start in the Netherlands, but a professional league was not established until 1954. Before 1954 the Royal Netherlands Football Association barred professionalism with exasperating rigidity, and many of the country's stars emigrated, usually to Spain, Italy, or France. Several clubs, led by Fortuna '54, formed an association, preparing the way for great clubs like Ajax of Amsterdam and Feijeñoord of Rotterdam.

Feijenoord captured the European Cup in 1970 and Ajax in 1971, 1972, and 1973. The national team had not done much before 1971, failing to qualify for the World Cup tournaments of 1950, 1954, 1958, 1962, 1966, and 1970. In 1974 the Dutch finished second and impressed fans around the world with their style and system of play.

With Rinus Michels, who joined the NASL in 1979, as the coach, the Dutch played what soccer writers termed *total soccer* because 10 players attacked when in possession and defended when possession was lost. The Dutch qualified for the 1978 World Cup but had to play without Johan Cruyff, the heralded captain of the 1974 national team. Besides Cruyff, Faas Wilkes has been the most graceful and surprisingly productive forward produced by the Dutch. After Ajax and Feijenoord, PSV Eindhoven and FC Twente have been the most successful clubs.

Peru

Like Chile, Peru has emulated Brazilian soccer. Despite the emigration of a large number of players, Peru has always been able to put together a strong national team. They performed well in the 1970 World Cup before losing to Brazil 4 to 2, and they also made the final round in 1978 in Argentina.

Alianza, Sporting Cristal, and Universitario have been the most popular teams. Teófilo Cubillas, twice named South American player of the year, and Hugo Sotil are the most popular players.

Poland

Although there are fine stadiums in Warsaw and Katowice and soccer is popular in Poland, the Polish national team did not qualify for the final round of the World Cup between 1938 and 1970. Poland was not a factor in international soccer until 1968, when Gornik advanced in the European Cup. The national team won the gold medal at the 1972 Olympics in Munich and qualified for the 1974 World Cup by eliminating England and Wales.

At the 1974 World Cup in West Germany, the Poles defeated Brazil in a match for third place after losing to West Germany, the eventual winner, in the semifinals. The Poles made it to the finals again in 1978, eliminating Portugal, Denmark, and Cyprus. Kazimierz Deyna, Wlodzimierz Lubanski, Jan Tomaszewski, and Gregor Lato, the leading scorer in the 1974 World Cup tournament, have been the Polish leading players. Legia, Gornik, Ruch, and Slask have been the most popular teams.

Scotland

It seems Scotland has always played its best soccer against England. Scotland has a wealth of talent, and it is surprising that the country has not done better in the World Cup. They qualified in 1974 and 1978 but didn't get far.

Soccer in Scotland has been characterized by an intense rivalry between the Catholic "Greens" of Celtic and the Protestant "Blues" of the Rangers. Under the coaching of Jock Stein in 1967, Celtic became the first British team to win the European Cup.

One of Scotland's legendary players was Patsy Gallagher, who, like another favorite, Charlie Tully, was an Irishman. Alex James, Alex Jackson, Alan Morton, Billy Steel, Jim Baxter, Dennis Law, and Billy Bremner have been just a few of the heroes of Scottish soccer.

The Soviet Union

The Sharnock family of England formed the first Russian soccer team at its cotton mills in Orekhovo-Zuyevo in 1887. After the national team was beaten

16 to 0 by Germany in the 1912 Olympic tournament, the Russians made no further contact with the world game until 1945, when the famous and talented Moscow Dynamo team was sent to England. Despite Dynamo's successful tour, the Soviets withdrew again until 1952, when they sent a team to the Olympics in Helsinki. In an extraordinary series with Yogoslavia, they tied 5 to 5 and lost the replay 3 to 1. They came back stronger 4 years later to win the Olympic tournament in Melbourne.

In their first appearance in the World Cup tournament in 1958, the Soviets qualified for the finals. They reached the quarterfinals by beating England 1 to 0 but were later eliminated by Sweden, the host. They qualified in 1962, 1966, and 1970, but failed in 1978, eliminated by Hungary.

The tendency in recent years has been to shift good players from Moscow to the provinces. As a result, Dynamo Kiev emerged as a power and at one time represented the Soviets as the national team. Besides Moscow Dynamo and Dynamo Kiev, Torpedo of Moscow and Ararat Erevan have been the most popular clubs. Lev Yashin, Igor Netto, and Oleg Blokhin are the nation's best-known players.

Spain

Soccer in Spain has been dominated by Real Madrid and its arch rival Barcelona. Many of the greatest players on Spanish teams have been foreigners, which partly explains the country's secondary role in the World Cup. Spain qualified for the 1978 tournament in Argentina but failed to reach the final round in 1954, 1958, 1970, and 1974. Spain was eliminated in the first round in 1962 and 1966.

Ricardo Zamora, a goalkeeper, was Spain's first legendary player. With his knee pads, black gloves, and flat cap, Zamora, who died in 1978, was as famous in the 1920s as the matador Juan Belmonte. Barcelona's most famous player has been Johan Cruyff of the Netherlands, and Mario Kempes of Argentina has performed for Valencia. Luis Suarez was born in Spain but left Barcelona for Inter-Milan in Italy. Other popular teams in Spain have been Atlético Madrid, Atlético Bilbao, and Valencia. Santiago Bernabeu (New Chamartin) Stadium in Madrid, with a capacity of 101,663, is one of the best in the world.

Sweden

Sweden won the gold medal in the 1948 Olympics in London. Two years later in the World Cup in Brazil, they finished third behind Uruguay and Brazil. Sweden qualified for the final round in 1970, 1974, and 1978. Sweden's greatest soccer achievement came in 1958 when they hosted the World Cup and reached the final before losing to Brazil, led by a 17-year-old Pelé. Much of the credit for Sweden's improvement goes to a little-known English coach, George Raynor, who arrived in Sweden in 1948.

Sweden has produced a number of good players, but many have played abroad, particularly in Italy, because Sweden is strictly an "amateur" soccer nation. Gunnar Nordhal and his brothers Knut and Bertil played in Italy, as Gunnar Gren, Nils Liedholm, and Kurt Hamrin. The most popular teams in Sweden have been Malmoe, IFK Gothenburg, AIK Stockholm, Norrkoeping, and Djurgaarden.

Uruguay

A national organization was formed in 1900, but it was not until the late 1920s that soccer blossomed in Uruguay. Outstanding teams, highly trained and virtually professional, won the Olympic games of 1924 and 1928. In 1930, the centenary of the country's independence, Uruguay staged and won the first World Cup tournament. For a country of under 3 million inhabitants, Uruguay has had a remarkable record in the World Cup, winning it a second time in 1950 by beating host Brazil 2 to 1 in the final.

Domestically the game has been dominated by Nacional and Penarol, and the league race has often been postponed to allow these teams to tour.

The emigration of the country's best players has caused the players who remain to strike for higher pay. Juan Schiaffino, Alcides Ghiggia, Obdulio Varela, Victor Andrade, and Roque Maspoli have been the country's outstanding players.

West Germany

A form of soccer is said to have been played in Germany by English school-boys as early as 1865. The Germans sent a team to the 1912 Olympic tournament in Stockholm, where a forward named Fuchs set a long-standing international record by scoring 10 goals against the Soviet Union. The game grew swiftly after World War I. After World War II, East Germany and West Germany formed separate associations.

German teams were not readmitted to the World Cup until 1954, when West Germany won under the leadership of coach Sepp Herberger. The West Germans have reached the final round ever since. They repeated as World Cup champions in Munich in 1974.

In the 1960s West Germany finally abandoned the regional format for their leagues and formed the national *Bundesliga*. This has been one of the strongest and most successful leagues in the world, with such powerful teams as Bayern Munich, Borussia Moechengladbach, FC Cologne, Schalke 04,

(Bottom left) Berti Vogts of Borussia Monchengladbach, a star of the German national team for years. *(Sven Simon)*

(Bottom right) Yugoslavia is a major exporter of playing talent. Goalkeeper Enver Maric, shown here in a match between Yugoslavia and Wales, is one of several Yugoslavs in the Bundesliga. *(AP)*

Eintracht Frankfurt, and Hamburg SV. Bayern Munich captured the European Cup 3 years in a row—1974, 1975, and 1976. They were led by Franz Beckenbauer, who is the biggest name in the history of German soccer after Sepp Herberger. Uwe Seeler, Helmut Shoen, Fritz Walter, Gerd Mueller, Gunther Netzer, Berti Vogts, Sepp Maier, Hennes Weisweiler, and Dettmar Cramer are Germany's best-known coaches and players.

Yugoslavia

Immediately after the Yugoslav Football Association was founded in 1919, the country's national team plunged into international competition. Within a decade the Yugoslavs were good enough to defeat Brazil and reach the semifinals of the first World Cup in Uruguay in 1930. They did not qualify for the final round again until 1950, although they edged England 2 to 1 in Belgrade in 1939. The 1950 World Cup team that went to Brazil was immensely talented, as was the team that finished second in the 1952 Olympic tournament. The Yugoslavs were second to the Soviets in the 1956 Olympic tournament but prevailed in 1960.

Red Star of Belgrade, Dynamo Zagreb, Partizan, and Hajduk Split have been the country's most famous teams. Rajko Mitic, Stefan Bobek, Zlatko Chaicowski, Vladimir Beara, Dragan Dzajic, Branco Zebec, Bernard Vukas, and Dragoslav Sekularac have excelled as players and coaches. In recent years Yugoslavia has been a good supplier of players to the NASL.

The Professional Scene in the United States

The world's most popular sport officially arrived in the United States on Father's Day, June 19, 1977. On that sunny Sunday the New York Cosmos, a team that had once played an exhibition game before 98 fans, attracted a crowd of 62,394 to Giants Stadium.

"When soccer's history in the United States is written," said Kurt Lamm, executive secretary of the USSF "June 19, 1977, will be Day One."

The record-breaking crowd saw Pelé score all the goals in the Cosmos' 3 to 1 victory over the Tampa Bay Rowdies, one of their most bitter rivals. A week later, 57,191 fans cheered the Cosmos to a 5 to 2 triumph over Los Angeles.

However, many close observers of soccer think that July 6, 1977, was the real turning point. For a game against the San Jose Earthquakes that had to be played without an injured Pelé, the Cosmos drew 31,875.

"That was the key," said Steve Ross, chairman of the board of Warner Communications, the conglomerate that owns the Cosmos. "The key was when we drew 31,000 on July 6 against a mediocre team on a rainy night when the Yankees were postponed and our game was on delayed home television."

Why did all these fans come to Giants Stadium? Sports reporters wisecracked that of the 62,394 Father's Day fans, 60,000 were illegal aliens and the rest were Americans who thought soccer was a form of harness racing.

Later that year, when over 76,000 fans paid to see the Cosmos in a rainy playoff game against Rochester, I left the air-conditioned press box at Giants Stadium to find out what kind of people had filled the stands. I remembered an exhibition game between two foreign teams some years ago at Randalls Island. After a disputed call by the referee, many of the fans stormed onto the field. Pleas by the announcer proved fruitless, and 35 minutes later the game had not resumed.

(Top) **Giants Stadium in New Jersey, filled with a capacity crowd for the 1978 championship game between the Cosmos and the Tampa Bay Rowdies.**

(Above) **Soccer fans come in all shapes and ages. This section of the crowd at a Cosmos game is typical of the people who have become soccer enthusiasts in recent years.** *(Jerry Liebman)*

"Please clear the field, please clear the field," the voice kept repeating over the public-address system, but no one responded. Suddenly, a voice announced something in Spanish, and the field was immediately vacated.

"What did he say?" I asked a Spanish-speaking colleague who could not hide his amusement.

"He said that if they don't clear the field immediately, he will call the Immigration Department."

While recalling that incident, I checked out section 132, directly under the press box. I heard some foreign languages, but most fans were speaking English. It was the same in section 108, but in section 236 in the mezzanine I didn't hear a word of any foreign language. The stands were filled mostly with families and young people.

I spoke briefly with an usher in section 132. "Soccer fans don't get drunk like in football," he told me. "It's mostly kids with their parents who come to the soccer games. Football is mostly adults. There are quite a few foreigners here, but most of the fans are Americans."

Professional soccer has succeeded in the United States because of its appeal to a new generation, its innovative marketing that emphasizes the family, its organization and guidance by a commissioner and staff who learned from the mistakes of others, and its good fortune in having at the right time, Edson Arantes do Nascimento, the man known as Pelé.

It is only natural for a generation that has taken to natural foods to like soccer. Young people are looking for a sport to call their own, and soccer reflects many facets of contemporary American society. There is more freedom and opportunity for individual creativity than in many other sports. Everyone can touch the ball and do his own thing.

The younger generation has grasped the essence of soccer: continuity. A good professional player lives about 3 seconds into the future, always a part of the constant flow of the game. In the eyes of the younger generation, baseball players do nothing most of the time, and football is slowed down by huddles, timeouts, and 2-minute warnings. As Joey Cox of Middletown, New Jersey, told me, "Soccer moves. It moves all the time, and you move with it."

The Early Days

It has taken American professional soccer quite a while to realize that the future lies with the young. A league formed in the 1920s enjoyed some success, but mostly among foreign-born Americans. The successor of this league, the American Soccer League, (ASL) is still in operation but constantly changes teams each season.

"The oldest professional league," as the ASL likes to be called, continued the philosophy of its predecessor. Founded in 1933, the ASL placed emphasis on attracting ethnic groups and utilizing players from overseas.

In 1960 the International Soccer League (ISL) was founded and organized by Bill Cox, once the owner of baseball's Philadelphia Phillies. The new league was composed of foreign teams, with a single American all-star squad competing for a short time during the summer.

Cox started the league after realizing that good foreign teams could draw large crowds in New York. Teams like Manchester United, Real Madrid, Celtic, and Rapid-Vienna had had highly successful visits to the United States.

Instead of staging exhibition games, Cox had the teams compete for the championship of the ISL. This venture, however, did nothing to familiarize Americans with soccer. Teams came from overseas, picked up holiday money by playing in double-headers, and went home, perhaps to return the next year and repeat the routine.

The Beginning of the NASL

In 1965, despite the fact that most Americans knew little or nothing about soccer, three different groups decided to form new professional leagues. They

Veteran Players All-Star Team, American Soccer League, 1966. From left to right: (front) Paul Gioia, Jackie Hynes, John Boulos, Chico Manteiga, Sol Eisner, and Joe Boyle; (rear) Werner Meith, Richie Miller, Ceasar De Rostaing, Gene Olaff, Bert Anderson, George Barr, Walter Bahr, and Ray Fernandez.

were presumably motivated by the value of baseball and football franchises, many of which had been purchased for a few thousand and were worth millions by 1965.

In the fall of 1965 the three groups of investors journeyed to New York to request permission from the national governing body, the United States Soccer Football Association (USSFA)—now the United States Soccer Federation (USSF)—to form professional leagues.

To operate effectively, a league must have the blessing of the national governing body. Without this approval, leagues would have no legal status with FIFA or with teams, players, and other leagues throughout the world. Therefore, without the sanction of the USSFA, the proposed teams would not be able to compete against teams outside the United States, and players would be reluctant to join an outlaw league.

Because American soccer was still run by teams that emphasized specific ethnic groups, the sport was dominated by foreign-born Americans. These men were dedicated to soccer and devoted their spare time to the governing body. Most of them strongly resisted the idea of becoming Americanized and knew little of big business and big money.

When they received applications from the three groups of investors, they decided to sanction only one. They appointed a committee to study the applications, look into the background of the applicants, and decide which group should be accepted and under what conditions.

The committee's conditions shocked the prospective owners. The committee recommended that each franchise be required to pay the USSFA $25,000 plus a percentage of gate and television receipts. The committee, composed of a German, a Rumanian, and a Scotsman, had decided that the USSFA should not miss the opportunity to augment its finances after so many years of poverty.

Each of the three groups gave signs of willingness to abide by these conditions, but the lawyers for the prospective leagues discovered that the ASL was paying the USSFA just $25 a year, with nothing required of the teams beyond registration fees for players.

The groups refused to pay the $25,000 per franchise. The committee then suggested that the three groups unite to form one strong organization, but the investors rejected that idea immediately.

The committee's recommendation was approved at the annual USSFA convention in San Francisco in July 1966. The committee met again and decided that the group headed by Jack Kent Cooke and called the North American Soccer League (NASL) should be sanctioned by the USSFA—Cooke's group had agreed to their terms.

The other two groups, which had declined to merge, did just that before the convention was concluded. They formed the National Professional Soccer League (NPSL) with teams in 10 cities, told the USSFA they were ready to accept its conditions, and produced a check for $250,000.

However, Cooke's group already had a contract with the USSFA for the exclusive* rights to operate a nationwide professional league. It seemed that

---

*Under the terms of the agreement, the ASL was permitted to operate only in six states in the Northeast, but in 1975 the ASL petitioned to go nationwide in 1976. The governing body asked each ASL franchise to pay $25,000, the same as the NASL franchises. The ASL agreed to pay for each new franchise but not for existing franchises. As a result, a lawsuit was filed by the ASL against the USSFA. The suit is still pending.

the NPSL was dead and that the sanctioned NASL would have the vast American market to itself.

The officials of the NPSL on August 23, 1966 announced that their league would operate without the sanction of the USSFA and would start operations the following April, a year before the sanctioned league. Television signed a 10-year contract with the league, perhaps not understanding the problems of an unrecognized league.

For the NPSL to present high-quality soccer, it would have to seek foreign players. However, no established player would risk being banned for life by playing in a league that FIFA considered an outlaw. Despite this threat, a steady stream of players did arrive on American shores, eager to play with NPSL clubs. The caliber of the players, however, did not live up to the claims of the NPSL's press releases.

There was no television contract for the sanctioned league, which had already changed its name to the United Soccer Association (USA). To keep up with the NPSL, the USA had to accelerate its kickoff by a year.

Since there can be no league without a commissioner, both groups moved quickly to find their Pete Rozelle. The USA was the first to make an appointment to their $75,000 post. They chose Dick Walsh, a baseball administrator. One of Walsh's first statements to the press was, "I don't even know what a soccer ball looks like." Not to be outdone, the NPSL also came up with a man who knew nothing about soccer: Ken Macker, a publisher of newspapers in the Philippines.

This is not a practice session, but a league game between the Los Angeles Toros and the Atlanta Chiefs in 1967. Only the spectators are missing.

The First Season

Both leagues started to operate in 1967, with the NPSL importing 179 players, often with their wives and children, to form the nucleus of its 10 franchises. The USA followed another route, importing 12 entire foreign teams to represent 12 American cities.

Cerro of Uruguay, for example, represented New York as the New York Skyliners. New York was the nation's strongest supporter of Italian soccer, but the only Italian team the league could get for New York had finished in last place, and USA officials felt it would be an insult to Italian fans.

The teams representing USA cities in 1967 were: Boston — Shamrock Rovers of Ireland, Chicago-Cagliari of Italy, Cleveland-Stoke City of England, Dallas-Dundee United of Scotland, Detroit-Glendoran of Northern Ireland, Houston-Bangu of Brazil, Los Angeles-Wolverhamptom of England, New York-Cerro of Uruguay, San Francisco-ADO of the Netherlands, Toronto-Hibernian of Scotland, Vancouver-Sunderland of England, and Washington-Aberdeen of Scotland.

The USA staged a preseason invitational tournament to kick off the campaign. A game in Houston attracted 33,351 to the Astrodome, and games in Washington, D.C., and Los Angeles attracted over 20,000 fans each. Even though it rained at 3 of the first 4 games, the 6 exhibitions attracted a total of 108,352 spectators, an encouraging sign for the USA.

In the regular season, however, when each team played 6 home games and 6 away games, attendance was dismal. When Boston visited Detroit, for example, 648 people showed up, and only 853 fans came to San Francisco to see their team defeat Boston 4 to 3.

Most of the NPSL teams had players from several different countries, making communication difficult. There were 179 players imported from 38 countries. Chicago led the league with 11 nationalities, followed closely by New York with 8. A few years after playing for the New York Generals in the NPSL, Micky Ashe, an English player, said at Eintract Oval in Astoria, New York, "I finally realized why I was not getting any passes from the two chaps from Argentina who played with me. I was calling 'Mas,' 'Plas,' and 'Plas,' 'Mas.' I had the two blokes mixed up."

John Rooney, owner of the NPSL team in Philadelphia, wondered about "the final translation of the coach's talk," which was given in English, Spanish, and German. John Best, who later played in Dallas, coached at Seattle, and became general manager of Vancouver, played for the Philadelphia Spartans. Best remembered a player with the Spartans in 1967 who claimed that he could speak any language after living a few weeks in a country. Midway through the season an airline stewardess asked this player his name and he replied, "Coca-Cola."

The NPSL's language problems were minor compared with its attendance woes. With franchises in Atlanta, Baltimore, Chicago, Los Angeles, New York, Oakland, Philadelphia, Pittsburgh, St. Louis, and Toronto, the NPSL's 159 regular-season games attracted 775,846 fans, an average of less than 5000 per game. Oakland became the champion of the NPSL, and Washington triumphed in the USA, which averaged close to 8000 fans per game in its short season.

Led by wealthy investors such as Lamar Hunt, some teams lost close to $1 million the first year. This prompted a USSFA official to say that if teams in the leagues continued to lose a million a year, Hunt would have to file for bankruptcy in 150 years. The jokes stopped when the aptly named Pittsburgh Phantoms vanished after their first year in the NPSL. The owners of both leagues were convinced that something had to be done, particularly after the accountants had finished comparing revenues with expenses.

The Leagues Merge

A merger was strongly encouraged by the USSFA at the urgent direction of FIFA, which grew restless after being named as a defendant in an $18 million lawsuit filed by the NPSL. The suit charged the USSFA, all member clubs of the USA, and FIFA with conspiring to drive the NPSL out of professional soccer. FIFA handed the USSFA an ultimatum to either settle the lawsuit or face suspension.

The USSFA did its best to encourage the merger, but it took 4 months to work out the details. Finally, the merger was achieved in January 1968 at the Waldorf Astoria Hotel in New York. The offspring of the merged leagues was to be called the Professional Soccer League. A day later the 17-team organization renamed itself the North American Soccer League (NASL).

The NASL started the 1968 season with weekly telecasts over a national network. The commissioners of the original leagues were now commissioners of the Eastern and Western conferences. There were predictions of opening-day crowds over 20,000 in several cities, but the largest attendance was 11,000 in Atlanta.

The smallest was 1400 in Dallas, which had sent its team on a world tour before the season. The Tornado played 45 games on that tour and won only 10. In their first season in the NASL, Lamar Hunt's team won 2, lost 26, and tied 4, a league record that may never be broken. Chicago's record of attract-

Lots of action on the field, but none in the grand-stand, at this 1968 game between the Chicago Mustangs and the Toronto Falcons.

ing only 336 fans to a game that year will also be hard to beat.

After the season was over and Atlanta had defeated San Diego for the ti-tle, the NASL started to crumble. Franchises were swimming in red ink, and many rushed for the exits. People wondered how so many millionaires could be mistaken at the same time.

The owners had vowed to stay in the game and face the consequences, but that vow was easily broken. Of the 17 franchises that operated in 1968, only 5 were left in 1969. Only Atlanta, Baltimore, Dallas, Kansas City, and St. Louis were able to put up $150,000 performance bonds for 1969. The New York Generals were the last to fold, preceded by Boston, Chicago, Cleveland, Detroit, Houston, Los Angeles, Oakland, San Diego, Toronto, Vancouver, and Washington.

The NASL failed largely because the general public knew so little about soccer. The same was true of the people who worked for the league and those who covered soccer for newspapers, radio, and television. Writers covered up their lack of knowledge by dwelling on the size of the crowd and the state of the field. They described soccer as "clumsy basketball played with the feet" and "hockey on the rocks."

Media coverage of soccer still stresses statistics. Assists in soccer were in-vented in the United States, and shots on goal and saves by the goalkeepers must have been borrowed from hockey. To give journalists more to write about, the Dallas Tornado come up with the most outlandish statistic: "box penetrations" which indicates the number of times each team reaches the penalty area.

It is easier for a writer to dwell on statistics handed out by a publicist than to analyze the game and tell readers how a team played and why. The news media are important for the education of the public, but they must be careful in their judgments and avoid telling the public that something is good when it is actually mediocre. Honesty must prevail, but honesty requires knowledge.

The 5 remaining teams bravely made plans for the 1969 season. Phil Woosnam, who led the Atlanta Chiefs to the championship and was named coach of the year in 1968, became the league's executive director. However, the total collapse of the NASL was narrowly avoided through the single-handed efforts of Lamar Hunt. There were rumors that Hunt subsidized 4 of the franchises. Woosnam unequivocally states that Hunt was responsible for the survival of professional soccer and its subsequent emergence.

"The main reason we stayed alive," Woosnam says, "was the presence of Lamar Hunt. He gave the league credibility. People knew who Lamar Hunt was and that he would not stay with a league he didn't believe had a future in the United States."

Hunt is also widely credited with salvaging the American Football League. As owner of the Kansas City Chiefs, Hunt lost close to a $1 million in a season, but he stayed with it and proved that the league could work. His World Championship Tennis has also been a growing force in sports. Potential investors could see that Hunt was a believer in soccer and follow his lead.

"Phil and everybody else in the league give me too much credit," Lamar Hunt said as we watched a game between the Dallas Tornado and the Cosmos at Yankee Stadium in 1976. "Phil Woosnam is the guy who really kept it alive. He went out and knocked on doors. I just gave the league a little stability because of my involvement in other sports."

Hunt looked at the crowd that was beginning to fill the stands and said, "I always felt that if soccer was so big in the rest of the world, it had to catch on here sooner or later. Besides, I am a sucker for the entertainment industry. I think Pelé and soccer are show business. People came here tonight to see Pelé, to see a show."

The 5 teams made it through the 1969 season, each playing 16 games. Kansas City was declared the champion on the basis of its 110 points. Atlanta was second with 109 points, followed by Dallas with 82 points, St. Louis with

This is not a sandlot soccer game, but the 1970 championship match between Rochester and Washington at Catholic University's field.

47, and Baltimore with 42. The point-scoring system that year was 6 points for a victory, 3 points for a tie, and 1 point for each goal up to a maximum of 3 per team per game.

By 1970 Baltimore had folded and Rochester and Washington had joined the league. Coincidentally, these two expansion teams won their divisions and then met in a 2-game, total-goal playoff.

The first game was played in Rochester, with the home-team Lancers winning 3 to 0. The second was played at the home of the Darts, the stadium at Catholic University in Washington, D.C. Lamar Hunt presented Carlos Metidieri of the Lancers with a trophy for leading the league in scoring. Actually, Metidieri shared the scoring title with Kirk Apostolidis of Dallas, but Apostolidis had left for Greece before the championship series.

After he presented the trophy to Metidieri, I approached Hunt and asked what he was doing in the boondocks. I didn't know what I was doing there either. My colleagues in the press box, most of them from the Washington area, thought *The New York Times* was crazy to send me to cover the game. I was ashamed to tell them I had attended on my own.

"We are in the boondocks today," Lamar Hunt answered back. "But we will be in the big stadiums with a lot of people in the near future. You can be sure of that because I am going to stay with soccer until I lose my last T-shirt. Right now we are going through 2 or 3 years of marginal operation, but we are going to be a big-time league with a lot of franchises."

Washington defeated Rochester 3 to 1, but the Lancers won the championship on the basis of a 4 to 3 advantage in total goals.

I ran into two other men at Catholic University that afternoon who sounded very much like Lamar Hunt. They were the owners of the Lancers, a team that a year before had been in the ASL, playing in cornfields much less professional than Catholic University's stadium. Charles A. Schiano and Pat V. Dinolfo are lawyers from Rochester and great soccer fans. They told me when I first met them that Rochester would be the Green Bay of soccer one day.

That almost happened in 1977 when the Cosmos came to Rochester to play a nationally televised game for the Atlantic Conference title. I sat in the press box at Holleder Stadium and watched the crowd overflow the 20,000-seat facility. The public-address system kept reminding the fans to "squeeze" so that more could be accommodated. Charlie Schiano was directing operations with a walkie-talkie; when he gave the signal for the Lancers to be introduced, tears rolled down his cheeks.

The Lancermania that hit Rochester in 1977 can be attributed largely to the efforts of Schiano and Dinolfo. A third partner, Bernie Rodin, bought 20 percent of the Lancers for $400,000 in 1978. There were rumors that Rodin, a millionaire, wanted to raise the value of his investment by moving the Lancers to another city, but he told me at the end of the 1978 season that he did not want to be another Walter O'Malley. A native of Brooklyn, Rodin did not want to take a club away from its fans as O'Malley had done with the Brooklyn Dodgers.

With the addition of the New York Cosmos, Montreal Olympiques, and Toronto Metros and the loss of the Kansas City Spurs, the league had 8 teams in 1971. Carlos Metidieri won the scoring title again, but the Dallas Tornado won the championship under the leadership of Ron Newman, edging Atlanta in a 3-game series.

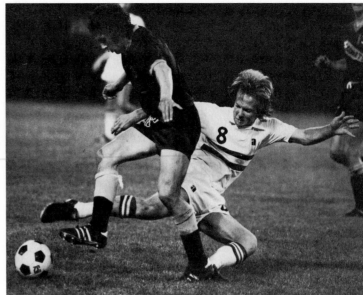

(Top left) **Randy Horton (16) and Cosmos teammate Joe Fink (12) seem to be fighting over the ball while defender Winston Earle moves in to boot it away. As a climax to the play, Horton scored a goal.** *(George Tiedemann)*

(Top right) **One of the few Americans in the NASL during the early 1970s, Stan Startzell (white jersey) was a lot happier playing for the Philadelphia Atoms than he was as a Cosmos benchwarmer during his rookie season.** *(George Tiedemann)*

Years of Progress

In 1972, for the first time, the composition of the league remained almost unaltered. The only change was Washington's move to Miami. Randy Horton, a bearded giant from Bermuda, led the Cosmos to their first championship. The league's most vauable player in 1972, Horton had tremendous ability in the air. With his size and his spectacular diving and twisting headers, Horton was one of the most feared players in the league. He combined soccer with studies at Rutgers, where he earned a master's degree in economics, and he is now an educator in Bermuda.

Like the rest of the Cosmos, Horton earned barely enough to pay for a cheeseburger and a couple of beers at the Cosmos' favorite nightspot near Hofstra University. (The Cosmos had moved to Hofstra after a disastrous 1971 season at Yankee Stadium.) Why did the players even bother?

"You have to understand why we are doing this," Horton said after a victory on a rainy Saturday night before fewer than 1000 fans. "We are not doing it for the groupies because there are no groupies in soccer. And we are certainly not doing it for the money. We are just a bunch of crazy dudes who love to play this game."

Yet progress was being made. The average attendance rose to 5000—not much by the standards of professional football, but enough to give everyone connected with the NASL hope for the future. More important, 1972 was a turning point in the movement to change soccer's ethnic image and join the American sports mainstream.

A collegiate draft was instituted by the NASL, which passed a rule requiring each team to have 2 American or Canadian citizens on the roster. Although all the teams complied, very few took the next logical step of letting the Americans play. As Stan Startzell, an all-American from the University of Pennsylvania, said after sitting on the bench in 1972 as a rookie with the Cosmos, "We were token Americans. It was a joke."

One prominent exception to this system was the St. Louis Stars. They were fortunate in having a surplus of local talent and an owner, Robert R. Hermann, who believed in encouraging American players. St. Louis had been a hotbed of soccer for many years mostly because of the Catholic Youth Organization, which had been cultivating the sport in its parishes since 1902.

One local boy who made good with the Stars was Pat McBride, who played from 1967 to 1976. He later became coach of Merrimack Community College in St. Louis, guiding them to a national title in his first 2 years. The other natives of St. Louis who played with the Stars were Larry Hausman, whose career ran from 1968 to 1976, and Al Trost, who was captain of the United States national team and is still playing as a professional. Other St. Louis players from that era are still involved in soccer, mostly as high school coaches.

These men and others like them proved that Americans could hold their own in the NASL. In 1972 the Stars went all the way to the finals, losing the championship to the Cosmos on a penalty kick with only 4 minutes left in the game. That was quite a night at Hofstra University. A rainstorm turned the Astroturf field into a swimming pool, and players had a difficult time remaining upright.

Bob Hermann had owned the franchise in St. Louis for 11 years before moving it to Anaheim, California, in 1978. Hermann has been one of the outstanding boosters of American soccer; in 1974 he was able to boast that his club's roster was composed totally of American players. As a tribute to Hermann's dedication to soccer, the award for the college player of the year has been named for him.

The First American Stars

The presence of one young man, Kyle Rote, Jr., made 1973 an important year for American soccer. Drafted by the Dallas Tornado, Rote was already known to Texans through his father, a star football player with Southern Methodist University and the New York Giants. Skeptics said that Lamar Hunt had drafted Rote for publicity, but Rote not only became rookie of the year in 1973 but also was the first native American to lead the league in scoring. He accumulated 30 points, 1 more than Warren Archibald, a Miami player from Trinidad.

After winning the Superstars television competition three times, Rote neglected soccer and fell practically into obscurity in the NASL. The skeptics said, "We told you so," but the tenacious and talented forward returned and raised his game to higher standards in 1977 and 1978. He played out his option in 1978 and signed with Houston for a reported $375,000 for 3 years.

Rote started playing soccer to condition himself for football when he was 17, too old (supposedly) to develop soccer skills. After spending his freshman year at Oklahoma State on a football scholarship, Rote transferred to the University of the South at Sewanee, Tennessee, to play soccer. He set a school-scoring record in 1971 with 17 goals and 7 assists in 12 games. By 1979 he had started in 6 games for the U.S. national team. He has already written two books on soccer, has done television commentary, and has also studied theology and law.

Rote never pretends to be something he is not. He told me once that the use of his name and Pelé's in the same sentence represented poor juxtaposition. People apparently do not think so because Rote endorses seven products, films television commercials, and is tremendously popular as a speaker.

Another significant event in 1973 was the granting of a franchise to the

Kyle Rote, Jr., gave soccer in the United States a shot in the arm in 1973 when he became the first American-born player to lead the NASL in scoring. The Dallas Tornado star (in white) achieved his record despite being closely marked by some of the best defenders in the league.

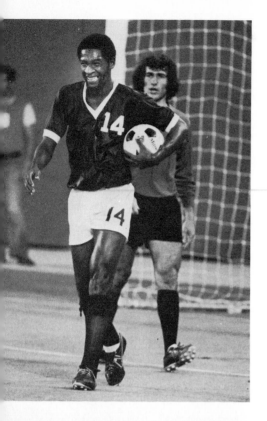

Selvis Figaro of the Miami Toros looks pleased at a referee's decision in this 1973 game between the Toros and the Philadelphia Atoms. *(George Tiedemann)*

Playing for the Cosmos in 1976, Bobby Smith goes up against another talented American player, Miro Rys of Chicago. (Rys later died in an automobile accident.) *(Bill Smith)*

Philadelphia Atoms, the only new team that year. Its owner was Tom McCloskey, a good friend whom Lamar Hunt had convinced that soccer was the coming sport. Because McCloskey wanted to keep close ties with Hunt, hoping for his help in securing a franchise in the National Football League, McCloskey put up $25,000 for the soccer franchise.

McCloskey's philosophy for the Philadelphia Atoms was to create an American image that he could sell to the public. He started by hiring as coach a former all-American soccer player and college coach, Al Miller. As American as apple pie and as colorful as a rainbow, Miller had established Hartwick College in Oneonta, New York, as a soccer powerhouse.

As the expansion team in 1973, the Atoms had the first pick in the collegiate draft. Miller put it to good use by selecting Bob Rigby. Rigby was an all-American goalkeeper at East Stroudsburg State College, where he was coached by Dr. John McKeon, who had also coached Miller. Rigby was born in Ridley Park, a suburb of Philadelphia. He started playing soccer when he was 12, but he played football for 3 years in school because his father had played football.

"I was the center who hikes the ball and gets obliterated," Rigby said years later. "I got the living hell beat out of me. I realized that to play football I had to be a freak, and I was not big. I was just an average American kid. I got into soccer after the football season in the winter, and in the spring I played in the local amateur league. I was the kind of kid who played all kinds of sports all the time. When I got to college, I was the only freshman ever to be on the varsity soccer team."

The day of the 1973 draft, Rigby told me over the telephone from the Atoms' office, "Right now I am willing to play professional soccer for nothing. The money will come later, when soccer becomes a major sport." Miller and the Atoms loved that attitude, which is why they drafted Bobby Smith as well.

Smith, a native of Trenton, was known in the Philadelphia area as an all-American forward at Rider College. Coach Miller loved Smith's fighting spirit and decided to make him a fullback. Smith proved Miller right when he made the league's all-star squad, one of 9 Atoms to do so in 1973. In 1976 both Smith and Rigby joined the Cosmos and Pelé.

The Atoms did everything right from beginning to end in 1973, including winning the league title. Miller used dramatics to prod the Atoms to play beyond their ability. When the Atoms were losing a game at halftime, the players went into the locker room expecting Miller to raise hell. Instead, the coach sat on the bench silently reading the newspapers, which had given the Atoms plenty of publicity. Just before the second half, Miller stood up, tore the newspapers into shreds, and said, "Here is what I think of your newspaper clippings. If you guys learned to play soccer as well as you read, maybe you'd be getting the job done out there."

The Atoms won that game and went on to take the championship in style, beating Kyle Rote's team 2 to 0 in Dallas. Bob Rigby made the cover of *Sports Illustrated*, and the Atoms made soccer go in Philadelphia.

There were other encouraging signs in 1973. Miami attracted new owners, who had interests in the Miami Dolphins football team. With John Young as coach, Miami stunned the NASL by selling 2400 season tickets. The average attendance in the league climbed to 6290. Kyle Rote's presence in Dallas showed at the gate as attendance rose 86 percent over 1972 to an average of 7465.

In New York an American with the charismatic name of Joe Fink emerged, but his presence was not of the same magnitude as the presence of Rote or Rigby or Smith. An all-American out of New York University and a native of Ridgewood, New York, Fink came in second between Rote and Rigby in the voting for rookie of the year. But Fink did not get as much of a chance to play as the others. Although Fink scored 3 goals in his first game with the Cosmos, Gordon Bradley must have considered it a fluke because he benched Fink for the next game. Fink scored 11 goals in 14 games that year but had no assists, a sign that he was a goal scorer rather than a creator of opportunities. After the Cosmos signed Pelé and other foreign stars, Fink was traded to Tampa.

Other native players who broke into the NASL and did well in 1973 were Al Trost, Mike Seerey, John Carenza, Bil Straub, Dennis Vaninger, Charlie Duccilli, Lew Meehl, and Casey Bahr.

An interesting innovation that season was the change in the offside rule, an experiment that was undertaken with FIFA's permission. The new rule stated that a player could not be offside until he was within 35 yards of the opponents' goal. This rule and the awarding of bonus points for each goal encouraged teams to attack and score more.

The NASL lost Atlanta and Montreal after the 1973 season, but in December the league made its big move, expanding to the West Coast.

The Biggest Kick Forward

Despite the loss of Montreal and Atlanta, by 1974 the league began to show signs of stability. The NASL had become a hot but still highly speculative property, and cities had to sell themselves to the league. The Executive and Expansion committees felt that the NASL was again ready to expand nationwide. As a result, 8 new franchises were granted – Los Angeles, San Jose, Seattle, Baltimore, Boston, Denver, Vancouver, and Washington. Four of these franchises – Baltimore, Denver, Vancouver, and Washington – failed at the turnstiles, averaging between 3500 and 5500 fans, which would have been great in 1970 or 1971, but wasn't good enough in 1974.

The other newcomers, however, finished in the top 6 in attendance. In fact, the San Jose Earthquakes and the Seattle Sounders broke the previous attendance mark of 129,236 set by Kansas City in 1968. San Jose averaged 16,576 in 10 home games, and the Sounders averaged 13,495, including 7 consecutive sellouts at the end of the year.

With as many as 10 Canadian citizens in their starting lineup, the Vancouver Whitecaps established soccer in that city, averaging 10,098 in their first season. Boston, a sports-minded city, also did well, averaging 9642. These figures were not quite enough to keep these clubs out of the red, but they represented a step in that direction.

Another new franchise, the Los Angeles Aztecs, captured the NASL title in an exciting game against the Miami Toros at the Orange Bowl. The Aztecs won 4 to 3 in a nationally televised contest that was settled by the league's new tiebreaker procedure – penalty kicks. Believing that American sports fans prefer a winner, the NASL introduced the following system: When a game ended in a tie, the teams alternated taking 5 penalty kicks each, with the team that converted the most winning the game.

The NASL changed the procedure in 1975 to allow for 15 minutes of

THE PROFESSIONAL SCENE
IN THE UNITED STATES

Even in 1974 there still were many empty seats in the stands. The action of the field, however, was often top-notch. In this sequence Joe Fink (12) of the Cosmos scores against Miami in a thriller at Downing Stadium, Randalls Island, New York. *(George Tiedemann)*

Most of the players were non-Americans in this match between the Los Angeles Aztecs and the Chicago Sting. *(Bill Smith)*

sudden-death overtime divided into two 7½-minute periods. If no one scored in the overtime, penalty kicks were taken. The procedure was again changed in 1977, when the shootout replaced the penalty kicks. Now if teams remain tied after 2 periods of sudden-death overtime, 5 players from each team go one-on-one with the opposing goalkeeper. The teams alternate, and each player has 5 seconds to shoot. There are no restrictions on movement for the shooter or goalkeeper. Should the shootout end in a tie, it continues on a sudden-death basis.

Many soccer purists oppose this manipulation of the rules, but the NASL has persevered with the changes, claiming that a tie game is, as some fans claim, like "kissing your sister."

The Washington Diplomats made news in a thoroughly negative fashion in 1974 when they played the Philadelphia Atoms at Robert F. Kennedy Stadium. When the few members of the press covering the game chuckled at the official attendance figure of 3325, Diplomats' publicist Debbie Goldstein agreed that the crowd seemed smaller. A few minutes later Goldstein was the team's ex-publicist. Another administrator of the Diplomats later threatened to revoke Leonard Shapiro's press credentials for reporting the incident in *The Washington Post.*

Another feature of the 1974 season was a switch in playing sites for the New York Cosmos. After 2 years of struggling for an identity at Hofstra University, the Cosmos moved to Downing Stadium on Randalls Island, which is under the Triborough Bridge linking Manhattan, the Bronx, and Queens, a place almost as bleak as their record of 6 victories and 14 losses that year. An unsuccessful team playing in an unattractive stadium, the Cosmos drew an average of 3600. That changed for the Cosmos a year later when a Brazilian named Edson Arantes do Nascimento arrived in the United States.

Peter Osgood of the Philadelphia Atoms seems to be telling Jimmy Steele of Washington that he doesn't want to play before empty seats. *(John Paul Ruplenas)*

One of the greatest players of all time, Pelé never lost his enthusiasm for the game and was thrilled by each goal he scored. (Pepsico International)

When Pelé scored his thousandth goal at Rio's Maracana Stadium, the fans joined in the celebration. In his 22-year career, "The King" scored 1281 goals in 1363 games. (Pepsico International)

The Missionary

Throughout the world, Edson Arantes do Nascimento is better known than Joe Namath, Wilt Chamberlain, or even Pete Rose. When the word *soccer* comes up in crossword puzzles, the clue is often "Pelé's game" because Pelé has become a synonym for soccer.

According to Phil Woosnam and Clive Toye, the man who ran the Cosmos from their beginning until he joined Chicago in 1977, Pelé had been in the plans of the NASL since 1969. That year Woosnam and Toye sat daydreaming in the league's one-room office in Atlanta. Woosnam was the commissioner and Toye was director of administration and information. However, it was not until 1974, Toye's fourth year as general manager of the Cosmos, that Pelé was contacted seriously about coming to the United States.

I was in West Germany in 1974 to cover the World Cup for *The New York Times*. Pelé was there to give interviews to reporters from around the world as a representative of Pepsi-Cola. He had declined to play for Brazil and was planning to retire from soccer in October of that year. Pelé was not as good on the field as in his younger days, but he still showed flashes of genius that could be matched only by Johan Cruyff and Franz Beckenbauer, the undisputed stars of the 1974 World Cup.

Those were busy days for Pelé, but I finally got a chance to interview him. Professor Julio Mazzei, his inseparable friend and adviser, was there as translator, along with Pelé's wife, Rose, and a representative of Pepsi-Cola. We chatted for a while, and then I asked Pelé whether he had ever thought of coming to the United States. He answered very carefully that he was aware that soccer was becoming popular in the United States but certainly it would be a long time before American soccer was on a par with soccer in the rest of the world.

Later that day I had lunch with Clive Toye, who had flown in from New York. We met in the press center in Frankfurt's Intercontinental Hotel, where he was greeting many old friends from his days on the *London Daily Express*.

"Clive Toye should be your Secretary of State," one English reporter remarked. "He knows more people than Henry Kissinger." Indeed, Toye, who bears some resemblance to Charles Laughton, is known around the world.

One reason Toye had come to Frankfurt was to talk to a few players about signing with the Cosmos. He was particularly interested in Dragan Dzajic, the outside left of the Yugoslavian national team. Toye said that the Yugoslavs wanted $1 million for Dzajic, and if the Cosmos had that kind of money to spend for players, they'd go after Pelé.

I took Toye's remark in Frankfurt as mere speculation. A few months later in his tiny office in New York, Toye chose his words carefully in speaking about Pelé. I had gone to him with solid information about his secret trips to see Pelé, and I wanted confirmation. Toye categorically denied everything. I couldn't blame him because he had once come close to a deal with Georgie Best, but Best had backed out at the last minute.

The only thing Toye would tell me was, "If I had the information you do, I would have the lead story for the *Daily Express*." I told him that *The New York Times* was not the *Daily Express*, and I had to confirm my information. I returned to my office and told the sports editor, Jim Tuite, that Toye would not confirm what I had been told on the phone from Athens, Brussels, and London that day.

"I've got to get it from the horse's mouth," I told Tuite, "and I think I know where the horse is." The horse, I had been told by friends, was probably in Zagreb, Yugoslavia. I made two phone calls to Zagreb, to Pelé and to Mazzei. Steve Tyno, the head of the copy desk, kidded me about the company money I was spending on phone calls.

The phone rang at about seven o'clock, and one of the copy boys told me I had a collect call from some place called Zagreb. It was 1 A.M. Yugoslavian time, and the call was from Professor Mazzei. "Yes, Alex," Mazzei said loudly. "It's true that Pelé is coming to New York. If he signs, it will be for a lot of money."

I briefed Jim Tuite on the new development, but he had already laid out the first edition. "Let's run a two-column box," he suggested. That meant no more than 200 words for a story that would be on the front page of many newspapers outside the United States.

Pelé came to New York as a guest of the Cosmos on May 28, 1975. He was taken by helicopter to Randalls Island for the kickoff of a game against the Vancouver Whitecaps. On June 10 Pelé signed a 3-year contract for several million dollars, and on June 15 he played his first game with the Cosmos, a Sunday afternoon exhibition against the Dallas Tornado and Kyle Rote, Jr. The signing of the contract at the fashionable 21 Club in New York was covered by the world press, which also covered Pelé's first game with the Cosmos, a 2 to 2 tie, in which he got the tying goal on a spectacular twisting header.

Sitting to my immediate left in the press box at Randalls Island was Mike Hughes, sports editor of United Press International. To my right was Dave Anderson, a columnist for *The New York Times*. When Pelé scored, Hughes turned to us and said, "Son of a gun, he can still do it!" Commenting in his column about Pelé playing at Downing Stadium on Randalls Island—known to reporters as "Drowning Stadium on Vandals Island"—Anderson wrote, "It was like putting Nureyev in a Times Square joint."

The arrival of Pelé proved to be everything that Toye, the Cosmos, and the NASL had hoped for in terms of soccer exposure. Suddenly, the press box was crowded with sportwriters, including many who knew little about soccer. Paul Gardner, one of the best and most knowledgeable soccer writers in the country, often teased reporters, telling them Pelé was pronounced, "*Peel*, as in oranges and eggs."

Soon Pelé's name, and naturally the Cosmos' name, appeared in almost every magazine in the country. The Brazilian star did tricks with a soccer ball on the "Johnny Carson Show" and later showed President Ford how to handle the ball. His ability to attract crowds was unique. There were sellouts in New York, Boston, San Jose, Seattle, and St. Louis, and 35,620 gathered at Robert F. Kennedy Stadium to watch the same Diplomats that had attracted 3325 fans a year before.

The millions the Cosmos invested in Pelé appeared to be paying off. Everywhere he played, the Cosmos got half the gate receipts above the average of the opposing team. The Diplomats, for example, averaged about 5000 fans, which meant that the Cosmos earned a share of the revenue from about 30,000 tickets.

The Cosmos received a set fee for exhibitions, as had Santos when Pelé played for them. The Cosmos never revealed the fee, but Pelé once re-

Prof. Julio Mazzei, who came to the Cosmos with Pelé, became the team's technical director in 1979. *(Jerry Liebman)*

Pelé's appearance at the Cosmos–Vancouver game in 1975 marked a turning point for pro soccer in the United States. Less than three weeks later he was in uniform, and the crowds flocked to see him play. *(AP)*

Edson Arantes do Nascimento was noted not only for his brilliance as a player, but for his warmth toward the fans, especially the young-sters. A few days before his retirement tribute in 1977 at Giants Stadium, which capped a sensa-tional season during which he led the Cosmos to the championship, Pelé said, "God is very nice to me. Now I can die." *(Jerry Liebman)*

The Tampa Bay Rowdies won the NASL champi-onship in 1975 thanks largely to the scoring punch of Clyde Best. Shown here shielding the ball from Ron Davies of Los Angeles, Best was traded to Portland in 1977. *(Julian Baum)*

marked, "The Cosmos will make more money in 2 years from exhibition games than Santos made in 12 years." Reportedly, the fee was $25,000. No wonder Pelé played so often even when injured. An indication of the state of soccer finances at the time is that some teams did not pay the Cosmos until 1977 for games in 1975. (For exhibition games in 1978, the Cosmos set the fee at $50,000.)

The NASL had grown to 20 teams for the 1975 season, 3 more than in 1968. Chicago, Hartford, Portland, San Antonio, and Tampa Bay were the new franchises. The phenomenon of an expansion team winning the title was repeated in 1975 when the Tampa Bay Rowdies won the championship under the coaching of Eddie Firmani, a South African who had played in the Italian and English leagues.

Tampa Bay won the championship game, now called the Soccer Bowl, by defeating Portland in a marvelous exhibition of skill by such players as Stew-art Scullion, Stewart Jump, Derek Smethurst, and Clyde Best, another native of Bermuda, who was as gigantic as Randy Horton.

Best had played for West Ham United of the English League (he was the only black first-division player in England at the time) before joining the Rowdies in 1975. He was later traded to Portland along with Stewart Scul-lion. Despite his size, Best has been one of the most elusive forwards in the league. For 2 years with the Rowdies, Best was a menace to the Cosmos, particularly in the air. He scored the second goal in the 2 to 0 championship victory over Portland in 1975 after Arsene Auguste, a native of Haiti, had given the Rowdies the lead.

Even with Pelé the Cosmos did not do very well in 1975, finishing third in their division with a record of 10 victories and 12 losses. But they did well at the gate, primarily because of Pelé, and in 1976 they returned to a refurbished Yankee Stadium, their home during 1971.

The NASL after Pelé

The league stayed with 20 teams in 1976, the only changes being the moves of Baltimore to San Diego and Denver to Minnesota. Pelé's presence and an increased cash flow encouraged other stars to join the NASL that year. Georgie Best signed with Los Angeles, Bobby Moore joined San Antonio, John Kowalik went back to Chicago after 9 years in Europe, Rodney Marsh starred in Tampa, and Giorgio Chinaglia came to the Cosmos.

All these well-known players helped the league go over 2 million in attendance for the first time. To be precise, 2,481,000 fans attended NASL games in 1976; 5 years earlier the total had been under 400,000. The Cosmos in particular drew record crowds wherever they traveled. An exhibition game in Seattle broke all attendance records for American soccer when 58,128 fans showed up.

An interesting rivalry developed between the Cosmos, who won 16 of 24 games and finished second in their division, and Tampa Bay, the first-place team. The Rowdies humiliated the Cosmos and Pelé in their first meeting in 1976, beating them 5 to 1 in a nationally televised game at Tampa on June 6. The Rowdies came to Yankee Stadium on July 14 determined to win again, and they got off to an early 3 to 1 lead. But the Cosmos did not quit; in what many believe was the most memorable game in the history of the NASL, they came back to win 5 to 4.

Tampa Bay got its revenge in the playoffs, beating New York 3 to 1. The Rowdies were then shocked 2 to 0 in Tampa by Toronto, a team that went on to defeat Minnesota 3 to 0 in the Soccer Bowl in Seattle's Kingdome.

The Cosmos—Rowdies rivalry continued into the 1977 season. Despite the presence of their new star from West Germany, Franz Beckenbauer, the Cosmos lost 4 to 2 to the Rowdies in Tampa on May 29. A few weeks later

Georgie Best, European player of the year in 1968, signed with Los Angeles in 1976. Other stars who crossed the Atlantic in that year were Rodney Marsh, the "clown prince of English soccer" who joined Tampa Bay, and Giorgio Chinaglia (in white), who shifted his talents from Lazio of Rome to the Cosmos. *(Julian Baum, Mike Minardi, Jerry Liebman)*

(Top left) In 1977 another giant in world soccer became a Cosmo. Franz Beckenbauer of Bayern Munich provided the edge the Cosmos needed to get them the NASL championship that year. (Richard Pilling)

(Top right) There were six expansion teams in the NASL in 1978, among them the Memphis Rogues and the Philadelphia Fury.

in their new home at Giants Stadium in the New Jersey Meadowlands — just across the Hudson River from Manhattan — the Cosmos got their revenge 3 to 1 before 62,394 fans.

The attendance record for a soccer game in the U.S. and Canada was broken that year when 77,691 watched the August 14 playoff game between the Fort Lauderdale Strikers and the Cosmos. New York won 8 to 3 and then went on to beat Rochester and reach the championship game in Portland against the Seattle Sounders. Goals by Steve Hunt and Giorgio Chinaglia helped defeat the Sounders 2 to 1 and added the North American championship to Pelé's glorious career. With this victory the Cosmos became the first team to win the NASL title twice.

Although 1977 was a successful year for the Cosmos, it was also a time of turmoil. The team's presidency and coaching positions changed hands. Clive Toye, who was credited with building the Cosmos, was the first to fall, replaced by recording executive Ahmet Ertegun, the brother of Nesuhi Ertegun, the chairman of the board. Three weeks later Gordon Bradley became vice-president of personnel and Eddie Firmani took over as coach. Bradley's firing as coach was termed a promotion. The championship and the large crowds made many fans forget these two architects of the Cosmos.

Pelé had already "retired" several times before joining the Cosmos. Now his American contract had run out, and it seemed a good time to retire for good. Pelé completed his mission in Portland's dingy Civic Stadium. He cried in the arms of his wife and the arms of his friends and teammates. Perhaps he cried the loudest when he saw Gordon Bradley in the shower. The two men embraced and kissed, and then both began to cry uncontrollably. Bradley managed to say that he was pleased for Pelé.

"You brought soccer to America and you are leaving it as a champion," Bradley told Pelé between expressions of happiness.

"God is very nice to me," Pelé responded. "My mission is finished. Now I can die."

Encouraged by the success of the Cosmos in 1977, the NASL expanded to 24 teams in 1978. Several franchises relocated: Connecticut to Oakland,

Hawaii to Tulsa, Las Vegas to San Diego, and St. Louis to Anaheim. With these moves and expansion into Colorado, Detroit, Houston, Memphis, New England, and Philadelphia, the league was able to reach ten new markets. By the end of 1978 season, several franchises had relocated or changed ownership. Commissioner Phil Woosnam indicated firmly that no further expansion was in sight; the league's ultimate goal for 1979 was consolidation.

With Pelé watching from the sidelines, the Cosmos—as expected—remained champions in 1978. The championship game was played at Giants Stadium and attracted a crowd of 74,901, more than twice the attendance at Portland in 1977. The Tampa Bay Rowdies provided the opposition, but the game turned out rather dull, with the Cosmos winning 3 to 1. The Cosmos were never seriously threatened by the Rowdies, who played without the injured Rodney Marsh. Dennis Tueart, an English winger of immeasurable ability, scored twice, and Giorgio Chinaglia scored the other goal. Mirandinha tallied the lone goal for the Rowdies.

The same 24 franchises operated in 1979, with Colorado relocating to Atlanta and Oakland to Edmonton, both under new ownership. The caliber of play got progressively better and so did the attendance, which showed a 9 percent increase over 1978 as the league averaged slightly over 14,000 per game in the regular season. The Cosmos again led in the numbers in the stands, but it was not their year on the field. In fact, the champions of 1977 and 1978 didn't even reach the championship game, which again was played at Giants Stadium in the New Jersey Meadowlands. The Vancouver Whitecaps eliminated the Cosmos in the final of the National Conference and went on to win Soccer Bowl—79 by edging the Tampa Bay Rowdies 2 to 1. For the Rowdies it was the second disappointing Soccer Bowl appearance in a row. It was also Rodney Marsh's last official game in the NASL. Trevor Whymark's 2 goals for the Whitecaps crashed Marsh's dream of ending his playing career as a champion.

The Marketing of Soccer

A scantily clad "Indian princess" named Sherry Sundance rode a horse back and forth alongside Central Expressway, just a corner kick from the office of the Dallas Tornado. She claimed to be performing an ancient tribal ritual to keep it from raining on the next Tornado game. "If it rains," she told the curious, "everyone in the stadium gets free tickets to the next game."

A few days later, everyone who walked through the gate was handed a lucky number and a Howard Hughes "will." To make it more authentic, they found a parachutist named Howard Hughes, who jumped into the stadium at halftime and announced the winning number over a cordless microphone as he landed.

A week after President Ford threw out the first ball of the 1976 baseball season at Ranger Stadium in nearby Arlington, the Tornado announced that the foremost representative of the Republican party would kick out the first ball at their next game. Sure enough, the Tornado brought out an elephant to kick the ball!

The man responsible for these promotions was Dick Berg. His ideas raised the average attendance at Tornado games from 4000 in 1975 to about 14,000 in 1976. Before joining Dallas, Berg had done wonders for the San Jose Earthquakes. He left Dallas in 1978 to join the Oakland Stompers and

Milan Mandaric, whom he had worked for in San Jose. The first gimmick Berg came up with in Oakland was signing Shep Messing, a goalkeeper with the Cosmos.

Berg and his ideas set the tempo for the selling of soccer to the American public. Berg had been director of promotions for the San Francisco 49ers of the National Football League for 4 years before joining the Earthquakes. He had never seen a soccer game, but he became a believer quickly.

"Selling a sport is like running a political campaign," Berg stated. "You knock on doors, pass out literature, and kiss a lot of babies. We at the Tornado try to get out among the public as much as we can so that the players become human beings, not just numbers to the fans. I call it the person-to-person approach."

Different promotions have been tried throughout the league. The Rochester Lancers launched one of the most illogical promotions when they invited Gina Lollabrigida to a Lancer game. They promoted her from many angles, but the only result was that the usual 5000 or so fans brought extra film to the redecorated Holleder Stadium that day.

Another attempt at promotion also did not turn out well. Bruce Thomas, owner of the Toronto Metros, announced toward the end of the season that he would give a dollar to the first 5000 children who came to the stadium, provided they cheered loudly for the home team. Realizing the negative implications of this scheme, Phil Woosnam spoke with Thomas, and the idea was squelched.

One factor that has helped sell soccer to the public and to advertisers is the involvement of women as players and spectators. Surveys by a few teams have shown that the male-female ratio at NASL games is about 60–40. Soccer had become a means for advertisers of women's products to reach potential customers through commercials in the electronic media and advertisements in the league's program, *Kick,* which raised advertising rates for the national section to approximately $11,000 per page in 1978.

The NASL also has its own marketing company, which sells many products decorated with team logos. The best-selling product, of course, is still the ball with the red, white, and blue stars that is made exclusively for the NASL.

The Tampa Bay Rowdies have been very successful in their promotions. The first franchise to utilize a large advertising budget, the Rowdies have been the model for virtually every new NASL team since 1975 and several teams that joined before 1975.

Marty Rotberg, director of marketing for the Rowdies, explained that management had decided to construct an identity for the team. According to Rotberg, who later joined the League's headquarters in New York, "The team supersedes any one person, as do most teams in the league. As years go by, players leave and players come, but you have to maintain the team image. Our image is emphasis on entertainment. We have taken the team and made it total entertainment package."

When George Strawbridge, a product of the Campbell Soup family, bought the Tampa franchise, one of the first things he and his minority partner Beau Rogers did was engage the McDonald and Little advertising agency of Atlanta. The agency became the key to the Rowdies' success. Strawbridge, who also owns racehorses, a freight airline, and a large piece of the Buffalo Sabres of the National Hockey League, almost made his first mistake by vetoing the team's name. The name had been thought up by the agency, but the team announced that a panel of judges had selected it from names sug-

The irrepressible Rodney Marsh was a willing participant in the promotional antics of the Tampa Bay cheerleading squad.

Lincoln Phillips of Baltimore, surrounded by some of his fans after a game. *(George Tiedemann)*

gested by local soccer fans. The name was catchy, but not as catchy as the team's slogan, "Soccer is a kick in the grass."

Other teams in the league imitated the Rowdies, hiring cheerleaders and announcers to motivate the crowds. But the Rowdies' cheerleaders, or "Wowdies," and their fans have yet to be equaled by those of any other NASL team.

The Minnesota Kicks followed Tampa's example of spending for advertising, but chose not to sell the team as an "entertainment package."

"We have tried to gear ourselves around the game itself," said vice-president Kent Kramer, who had played 9 years in the National Football League and was a member of the Minnesota Vikings at the Super Bowl in 1969. "We promote the game's international atmosphere. We tell people in commercials that a billion watched the last World Cup final, which is more people than saw the landing on the moon."

A large poster in the Kicks' office, a few miles from Bloomington's Metropolitan Stadium, which the Kicks share with the Vikings and Twins, displays the team's philosophy. The poster shows a worn-out NASL ball. The top of the poster reads, "In 1976, Minnesota joined the world." At the bottom are the words "Minnesota Kicks."

The gimmicks pioneered by the Rowdies have had some success in other cities. In Memphis, for example, I sat in the press box at the Liberty Bowl on May 24, 1978, and thought I was at Tampa Stadium. The introductions of the various players and the announcements during the game were exact copies of what I'd heard in Tampa.

Teams in the NASL try to attract fans by means of uniforms with fringes, fight songs, tailgate parties, disco contests, and cheerleading sections. In one stadium a wedding took place at halftime. These "frills" show up at stadiums from Fort Lauderdale to Seattle to New York.

Pleasing the fans and attracting the uninitiated have been two paramount goals of NASL franchises in recent years. This means playing in comfortable stadiums and keeping ticket prices down. The Cosmos, for example, announced during a game against Toronto on July 26, 1978, that they would not raise ticket prices for the next season. The announcement drew more cheers than each goal the Cosmos scored to win 3 to 1 before 50,178 fans.

The NASL franchises that have enjoyed lasting success have all made the quality of soccer their top priority. Seattle, Tampa Bay, New York, Detroit,

(Top) Gordon Bradley.
(Center) Noel Cantwell.
(Bottom) Eddie Firmani.

New England, Vancouver, Portland, Dallas, and others have achieved success by fielding higher-quality players and better coaches.

The NASL's Best Coaches

Players and coaches come and go. Some have left their mark on the NASL, and others have left when nobody was looking. The sudden emergence of the professional game in 1967 brought several well-known coaches and players to the United States, but most departed quietly after the 1968 season. In those early days the top players and coaches were men like Hungary's Ferenc Puskás, Mexico's Salvador Reyes, West Germany's Horst Szysmaniak, Brazil's Vava, Hungary's Ladislao Kubala, and England's Dennis Viollet and Phil Woosnam. Only Woosnam and Viollet are still involved in soccer in the United States.

The following have been the NASL's best coaches over the years.

GORDON BRADLEY   Bradley signed his first professional contract at age 16 as a player with Sunderland, his home-town club in England. Bradley came to the United States in 1967 as a player and assistant coach of the New York Generals and later worked in Canada and in New York's semiprofessional leagues. He coached the newly formed Cosmos from 1971 until 1977, when he moved to the Washington Diplomats. Bradley is recognized as an outstanding recruiter and developer of talent. He is perhaps the best-liked coach in the league, a man without enemies.

NOEL CANTWELL   Born in Ireland, he played about 300 games for London's West Ham United before being sold to Manchester United in 1960 for a record fee of 30,000 pounds. He led Manchester United, or the "Red Devils," to the FA Cup final in 1963. He began his coaching career in 1968 at Coventry City and has also coached Peterborough United. Cantwell was named England's coach of the year in 1975. He joined the New England Tea Men, an expansion team, in 1978 and led them to a division title that year. His first impression of the collegiate draft was, "It looks like the stock exchange."

EDWIN (EDDIE) FIRMANI   Born in South Africa of English and Italian parents, Firmani was a star forward and goal scorer in the Italian League and played for Charlton of the English League. He came to the United States in 1975 to coach the Tampa Bay Rowdies, who took the NASL crown that year. He was named NASL coach of the year in 1976. Firmani became coach of the Cosmos in July 1977 and led them to the championship. A shrewd tactician and psychologist, he is very candid with his players.

TERRY FISHER   A native of Pennsylvania, Fisher became the youngest head coach in professional sports when he took over the Los Angeles Aztecs in 1975 at the age of 25. He had previously coached at Whittier College and UCLA. Under his leadership, the Aztecs earned a playoff berth 3 years in a row. A second-string player in college, he is living proof that a good coach doesn't have to be a good player. In 1978 Fisher moved to San Jose to coach the Earthquakes.

BILL FOULKES   After 18 years as an indestructible defender for Manchester United, Foulkes came to the United States in 1975 despite offers to coach in England, Austria, and New Zealand. He coached the Chicago Sting for 2 years and then moved to Tulsa. Foulkes had played for the famed "Busby Babes" that captured the English championship in 1956 and 1957. He was aboard the Manchester United team plane that crashed in Munich in 1958, killing eight members of the team, three team officials, and eight sportswriters. Matt Busby survived the crash, as did Dennis Viollet, who has coached the Baltimore Bays and Washington Diplomats.

KEN FURPHY   Not a very successful player, Furphy worked his way up in English coaching circles. He coached Workington in the fourth division and Sheffield United in the first division for 12 years. He spent half a season with the Cosmos in 1976, his first year in the United States, and coached Team America in the Bicentennial tournament. After a stint in England, he returned to the United States to coach the Detroit Express in 1978. He is known as a good tactician and developer of young players.

JIM GABRIEL   A native of Scotland, he was a star player with Everton and Southampton of the English first division for 12 years. Gabriel came to the United States in 1974 to play with the Seattle Sounders and assist the coach, John Best. When Best moved to Vancouver as general manager in 1977, Gabriel became coach of the Sounders. They played in the championship game that year, losing to Pelé and the Cosmos. Like Gordon Bradley, Gabriel is known as a man without enemies.

FREDDIE GOODWIN   Goodwin played for Manchester United and Leeds United of the English first division and was also a professional cricket player. He came to the United States as coach of the New York Generals in 1967; after 2 years he returned to England to coach Brighton and Birmingham City. Goodwin returned to the United States in 1976 and assembled the Minnesota Kicks 2 months before the start of the season. Under his guidance, the Kicks reached the championship game but lost to Toronto. In 1977 he became president of the Kicks, the only coach to also hold the presidency of an NASL franchise.

GORDON JAGO   A native of England, Jago played as a defender. Jago was in charge of England's youth team and was a member of the English Football Coaching Staff. He came to the United States in 1967 to coach the Baltimore Bays and then helped Phil Woosnam coach the American national team in the qualifying games for the 1970 World Cup. He later returned to England and helped the Queens Park Rangers get promoted from the second division to the first division. He became Tampa Bay's coach in 1978. Jago is a strong candidate for the best soccer coach in the United States in the last 15 years.

RINUS MICHELS   Michels was the first coach of real international stature to join the NASL. His acquisition by the Los Angeles Aztecs after the 1978 season was considered as significant a step as the signing of Pelé and Franz Beckenbauer. A native of the Netherlands, Michels established Ajax of Amsterdam as a world soccer power and then took the Dutch national team to the World Cup final in 1974. Johan Cruyff played for Michels with Ajax, the Dutch national team, and Barcelona.

Freddie Goodwin.

(Top) Al Miller.
(Center) Ron Newman.
(Bottom) Hubert Vogelsinger.

AL MILLER   Miller is the only native American to coach an NASL team to a championship. An all-American player at East Stroudsburg State College, Miller coached at New Paltz and Hartwick colleges. In his rookie year in the NASL, Miller led the expansion Philadelphia Atoms to the 1973 title and was selected as coach of the year. After 3 years with the Atoms, Miller coached the Dallas Tornado. He has coached the American national team several times. An advocate of Americanization, Miller has always fielded teams with a good number of native players.

RON NEWMAN   Newman left Portsmouth of the English League to play for Atlanta in 1967. He became coach of Dallas in 1969. He was referred to as "soccer's ambassador" for his work in expanding the youth program in Dallas from 300 participants in 1968 to over 50,000 in 1975. He is the only coach to have won championships in the NASL and the ASL—with the Dallas Tornado in 1971 and the Los Angeles Skyhawks in 1976, respectively. In 1977, his first year at Fort Lauderdale, he was named coach of the year when the Strikers broke a league record by winning 19 regular-season games.

DRAGAN POPOVIC   A premier midfielder in Yugoslavia, Popovic came to the United States to play for St. Louis in 1967. He moved to Canada to coach the White Eagles of the National Soccer League (NSL). In his rookie year as coach, his team lost only once in 35 games en route to the Canadian title. He became coach of the Rochester Lancers in 1976. Because of suspensions, he has paid more fines and coached more games from the stands than any other NASL coach.

HUBERT VOGELSINGER   In his first 5 years as coach in the NASL, Vogelsinger managed to start 4 teams from scratch. He had spent 5 years as a first-division player in his native Austria before coming to the United States in 1963. He coached at Brandeis and Yale from 1966 to 1974, when he joined the NASL as coach of Boston. When Boston was suspended he moved to Hawaii for a year and then to San Diego. The author of several articles and books on soccer, Vogelsinger knows how to get the most from his players.

TONY WAITERS   A goalkeeper with Blackpool of the English League, he coached briefly for Liverpool, Coventry, and Plymouth before joining Vancouver in 1977. He is an offense-minded coach, and his teams play the English style of long crosses in front of the opposition's goal. He was voted NASL coach of the year in 1978.

The Players

The quality of play in a league depends on the quality of the players. In its first 10 years of operation the NASL relied heavily on foreign players of the caliber found in the third and fourth divisions of the English League. These were not high-quality players, and most were over 30 years old.

Pelé joined the NASL, and others followed. But Pelé was 34 when he came to the Cosmos, and he had lost perhaps more than half a step. Still, Pelé often displayed the brilliance of his days with Brazil's national team and with Santos. It was Pelé's presence and the salaries offered by the owners that encouraged others to play for the NASL at the peak of their careers.

Giorgio Chinaglia, a towering center forward who was both worshiped and hated in Italy because of his personal success and the failure of the Italian national team, was the first world-class player in his prime to join the NASL. Despite missing 5 games in 1976, his first season, Chinaglia led the league in scoring. The former star of Lazio and the Italian national team scored 9 goals in 6 playoff games, including the winning goal for the Cosmos in the 1977 championship game. In 1978 Chinaglia scored 34 goals, breaking John Kowalik's 1968 regular-season record of 30 goals.

When Franz Beckenbauer came to the United States to play for the NASL in May 1977, the Cosmos not only obtained the captain of World Cup champion West Germany and a two-time European footballer of the year—they got the best player in the world. With Bobby Moore of England playing in San Antonio, the NASL had two captains of World Cup champion teams. A month later the league obtained a third in Carlos Alberto, the captain of Brazil in 1970, who signed with the Cosmos.

Gordon Banks, goalkeeper for the English national team when Moore was captain, joined the NASL in 1977 and led the Fort Lauderdale Strikers to the best regular-season record in the league. Moore and Banks faded in 1978, and Moore played only briefly with the Seattle Sounders toward the end of the season.

Georgie Best, one of the most exciting players in soccer, and Rodney Marsh joined the NASL in 1976, bringing showmanship and arrogance to the league. Marsh, the "clown prince" of English soccer, has been an attraction in Tampa. There was talk that the colorful and temperamental Marsh would leave the Rowdies in 1978, but he stayed and had his best NASL season, proving that he can play as well as anyone when he wants to. He scored several deciding goals, including the goal that sent the Rowdies to the championship game in 1978.

Another player who joined the league in 1976 was Eusebio, a star and leading goal scorer with Portugal in the 1966 World Cup tournament. A native of Mozambique, Eusebio left Boston to lead Toronto to the championship in 1976.

Alan Ball, another hero of England's World Cup team in 1966, joined the league as a player and became a player-coach in 1978. Ball silenced the critics by playing superbly and leading his team to the playoffs when its chances seemed poor. With help from Johnny Giles and Peter Osgood, two other English stars, Ball almost created a miracle in Philadelphia.

Three other well-established players joined the NASL in 1978. Dennis Tueart, an Englishman, and Vladislav Bogicevic, a Yugoslav, joined the Cosmos. Trevor Francis, another Englishman in his prime, joined Detroit. In 1979 the Cosmos bought Johan Neeskens, Francisco Marinho, and Wim Rijsbergen, while Fort Lauderdale raised eyebrows by purchasing Gerd Mueller and Teofillo Cubbilas. Another well-known player, Oscar of Brazil, was bought by the Cosmos in 1980.

Other foreign players who had instrumental roles in raising the league's caliber of play were Clyde Best, John Best, Jeff Bourne, Paul Cannell, David Clements, Mike Connell, Charlie Cooke, Kenny Cooper, Steve David, Mike England, Mike Flanagan, Charlie George, Kevin Hector, Gordon Hill, Jozsef Horvath, Carlos Metidieri, Ilija Mitic, Willie Morgan, Patrick (Ace) Ntsoelengoe, Stewart Scullion, Derek Smethurst, Jomo Sono, Wolfgang Sünholz, Derek Trevis, and Alan Willey.

There were few Americans and Canadians in the NASL in the early days, but as the league grew, so did the number of North American players. How-

(Below) Eusebio.

(Bottom) Mike Flanagan joined New England on loan as an unknown in 1978, promptly scored 30 goals during the season, and returned to England, where he was placed on the transfer market for $14 million.

(Left) Dennis Tueart, shown saluting the crowd after scoring against Rochester, was a menace to NASL defenses in his two years with the Cosmos. He returned to Manchester City in 1980. *(Steve Hale)*

(Right) Paul Cannell, shown here in a Diplomats uniform before he left Washington, is famous for his antics on the field. *(John Paul Ruplenas)*

ever, many older North American players had trouble holding their own in the NASL and ended their careers in the ASL. But the younger players did well, and the players coming through the collegiate ranks have been even better. "The younger they are, the better they are," foreign coaches say about North Americans.

Among the American and Canadian citizens who have done well in the NASL are:

Sonny Askew   Washington

Gary Ayre   Vancouver, New York, Portland

Chris Bahr   Philadelphia

Matt Bahr   Colorado, Tulsa

Boris Bandov   San Jose, Seattle, Tampa Bay, New York

Barry Barto   Montreal, Philadelphia, Fort Lauderdale

Tony Bellinger   Dallas

Sam Bick   Minnesota, San Diego

Zeljko Bilecki   Toronto, Tampa Bay

Jack Brand   Toronto, Rochester, New York, Tulsa, Seattle

David Brcic   New York

Brian Budd   Vancouver, Colorado, Toronto

Ringo Cantillo   Tampa Bay, New England

Chris J. Carenza   San Antonio, Hawaii

John Carenza   St. Louis

Peter Chandler   Hartford, Connecticut, Tampa Bay

Tony Chursky   Seattle, Chicago, Toronto

Joey Clarke   St. Louis, California

Neil Cohen   Dallas, San Jose, Tulsa

Dan Counce   Boston, San Antonio, Hawaii, California

Tony Crudo   Tampa Bay

Ricky Davis   New York

Arthur (Buzz) Demling   San Jose

Mark Demling   San Jose, San Diego

Dave D'Errico   Seattle, Minnesota, New England, Rochester

Angelo DiBernardo   Los Angeles, New York

Don Droege   Rochester, Washington

Winston DuBose   Tampa Bay

Kevin Eagan   Tampa Bay, New York, Tulsa

Gary Etherington   New York, Los Angeles

Pat Fidelia   Philadelphia

Joe Fink   New York, Tampa Bay, Houston

Mike Flater   Denver, Minnesota, Oakland, Portland

Santiago Formoso   Hartford, Connecticut, New York, Los Angeles

Colin Fowles   Tampa Bay, Fort Lauderdale

Tom Galati   Philadelphia, Las Vegas

Brian Gant   Vancouver, Portland

Randy Garber   Tampa Bay, Los Angeles, Washington

Billy Gazonas   Tulsa

Gene Geimer   St. Louis, Chicago

Alan Hamlyn   Atlanta, Miami, Fort Lauderdale

Larry Hausman   Chicago, St. Louis

All the Dallas Tornado players in this photo are native Americans. Shown playing against the Cosmos are, from left, Neil Cohen, Steve Pecher, Tony Bellinger, and Glenn Myernick.
(Ed Clough)

Mani Hernandez   San Jose

John Houska   Memphis

Larry Hulcer   Los Angeles, New York

Paul Hunter   New York, Detroit

Robert Iarusci   Toronto, New York, Washington

Mike Ivanow   San Jose, Seattle

Dave Jokerst   St. Louis, California

John Kerr   Detroit, New York, Washington

Robert Lenarduzzi   Vancouver

Tino Lettieri   Minnesota

Hank Liotart   Seattle, Portland

Mark Liveric   New York, San Jose, Washington, Oakland

Alain Maca   Miami, Washington

Greg Makowski   Colorado, Atlanta, Seattle

John Mason   Los Angeles

Bob Matteson   St. Louis

Arnold Mauser   Hartford, Tampa Bay, Vancouver, Colorado, Atlanta, Fort Lauderdale

Alan Mayer   Baltimore, San Diego, Las Vegas

Jim McAlister   Seattle, Toronto

Pat McBride   St. Louis

Mike McLenaghen   Minnesota, Toronto

Charlie McCully   Boston, New York, Hartford

Henry McCully   New York Hartford, Connecticut, Memphis

Wes McLeod   Tampa Bay

Nicky Megaloudis   Houston

Shep Messing   New York Boston, Oakland, Rochester

Ane Mihailovich   Los Angeles, Washington

Bill Mishalow   Los Angeles

Johnny Moore   San Jose, Oakland

Mark Moran   Minnesota

Tommy Mulroy   Miami

Glenn Myernick   Dallas

George Nanchoff   Fort Lauderdale

Louie Nanchoff   Colorado, Atlanta

Art Napolitano   Houston

Bill Nutall   Miami

Bob O'Leary   St. Louis, California

Les (Buzz) Parsons   Vancouver

Steve Pecher   Dallas

Fred Pereira   Fort Lauderdale, Connecticut, Colorado, Atlanta

Jim Pollihan   Rochester

Steve Ralbovsky   Chicago, Colorado, Tulsa, Fort Lauderdale

Gary Rensing   St. Louis, California

Craig Reynolds   Rochester

Bob Rigby   Philadelphia, New York, Los Angeles

Archie Roboostoff   San Jose, San Diego, Portland, Oakland

Peter Roe   Toronto

Kyle Rote, Jr.   Dallas, Houston

Werner Roth   New York

Willy Roy   Kansas City, St. Louis

Steve Ryan   San Jose

Miro Rys   Chicago, Los Angeles

Frantz St. Lot   Tampa Bay, Memphis

Bill Sautter   Tulsa

Mike Seerey   Miami, St. Louis

Branko Segota   Rochester

Peter Short   Philadelphia, Rochester, Dallas, Vancouver, Denver, Minnesota

Alex Skotarek   Chicago, Tulsa

Bob Smith   Philadelphia, New York, San Diego

Bob Stetler   Tampa Bay, Washington

Bill Straub   Montreal, Philadelphia

John Stremlau   Dallas, St. Louis, Houston

Gene Strenicer   Toronto, Chicago

Stefan Szefer   Chicago

Van Taylor   Miami

Al Trost   St. Louis, California, Seattle

Roy Turner   Philadelphia, Toronto, Cleveland, Dallas

Bruce Twamley   Vancouver, New York, Minnesota, Oakland

Tim Twellman   Minnesota

Dennis Vaninger   St. Louis, Fort Lauderdale

Julie Veee   Los Angeles, San Jose, San Diego

Greg Villa   Minnesota, Tulsa, Fort Lauderdale

Gary Vogel   Minnesota

Doug Wark   Rochester, Tampa Bay, San Diego, Las Vegas, Chicago

Kevin Welsh   Hartford, New England

Roy Willner   Washington

Bruce Wilson   Vancouver, Chicago, New York

Dennis Wit   Baltimore, San Diego, Tampa Bay, New England

Ruby Ybarra   Los Angeles, Memphis

Indoor Soccer

There is nothing new about playing soccer indoors. It has been played that way for decades in Europe and South America, and indoor tournaments have been played by semiprofessional and amateur leagues in the United States for the last 20 years. More recently, collegiate, interscholastic, and even youth tournaments have been played indoors across North America.

NASL teams played indoor exhibition games in the winter of 1972–1973, and 3 regional tournaments were held in 1975. The winners of these regional events and a wild-card team participated in a championship tournament won by the San Jose Earthquakes. The NASL held a similar tournament in 1976, with the Tampa Bay Rowdies winning. After virtually no indoor action in 1977 and 1978, the NASL held its first regular season indoors in the winter of 1979–80, but with only 10 of its 24 teams participating. What prompted the NASL to go indoors on a regular-season basis was the success of the Major Indoor Soccer League in the winter of 1978–79.

The MISL kicked off its inaugural season on December 22, 1978, with 6 franchises—the New York Arrows, Cincinnati Kids, Cleveland Force, Houston

Panoramic view of an indoor game in the Major Indoor Soccer League played at the Nassau Coliseum, Long Island, New York. *(Harrison Funk)*

Summit, Philadelphia Fever, and Pittsburgh Spirit. The New York Arrows won the first title of the MISL, which grew to 10 teams for the 1979–80 season.

Injuries are common in the indoor game because referees have a tendency to allow body contact and crushing against the boards. Thus, indoor soccer often becomes a game of force rather than skill. Because of the frequency of injuries, the NASL has had difficulty getting its top players to perform indoors. The stars in particular have stayed away from indoor soccer.

The pro version of indoor soccer is played on a carpet of artificial turf laid over the hockey rink of an indoor arena. As in hockey, there are 6 players on a team, substitutions are made in batches, there is a penalty box, the ball is played off the boards, and there is a blue line.

The biggest difference between indoor and outdoor soccer can be seen in the play of the goalkeeper. Outdoors, the goalkeeper protects a goal 8 yards wide by 8 feet high. He must have a highly developed sense of positional play because he can advance 18 yards forward and still touch the ball with his hands. He is likely to spend a good deal of time jumping to collect or punch away high balls that reach the area immediately in front of him, and he ignores anything that goes wide.

Indoors, the goal in the NASL is 6 feet 6 inches high and 12 feet wide, almost like a hockey goal (see diagram at right). The goalkeeper does no jumping but must make saves on shots that go wide to prevent the ball from

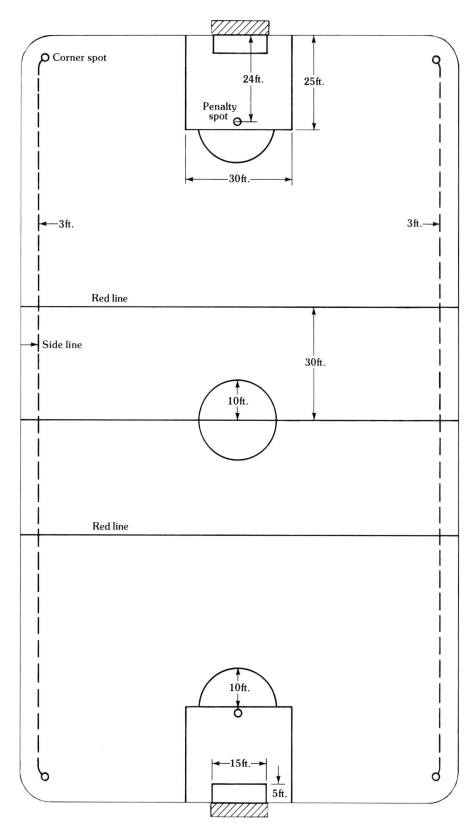

Corner spot

24 ft.

25 ft.

Penalty
spot

30 ft.

3 ft.

3 ft.

Red line

Side line

30 ft.

10 ft.

Red line

10 ft.

15 ft.

5 ft.

**Diagram of an indoor playing area
in the NASL. Size of the field is
close to that of a hockey court.
Teams consist of a goalkeeper,
two defenders, a midfielder, and
two forwards.**

bouncing straight back off the boards. It is possible for a goalkeeper who is weak in the air and therefore suspect in outdoor soccer to be a star performer in the indoor version.

There is no offside rule in indoor soccer (see the NASL rules for indoor soccer), but there is a rule against a 3-zone pass (when the ball moves forward over 2 yellow lines without being touched by a defender).

There is definitely more scoring in the indoor game, which consists of four 15-minute periods and sudden death in case of a tie. The abundance of goals has silenced many of the critics of low-scoring outdoor soccer. The NASL televised several indoor games in the mid-1970s, hoping to familiarize the American public with the game in order to attract more fans to outdoor soccer.

Soccer purists have never liked the indoor game. Many might be converted if appropriate rules changes and strict refereeing kept the bully-boys out of the game. If this should occur, however, indoor soccer might lose the advocates of the "physical" game.

There are also collegiate and interscholastic indoor games, usually played with 7 players on a side and without boards around the playing area. When the ball goes out of bounds on the sidelines, a throw-in takes place instead of the kick-in employed in the pros. Colleges and high schools that host tournaments usually set their own rules, but the rules must be reasonably similar to the rules of outdoor soccer.

The Amateur Scene in the United States

The world's most popular sport is at last becoming an important part of the American scene. Soccer is no longer a second-class citizen, neglected and misunderstood. It is now accepted and played by Americans of all ages, regardless of sex, color, or creed. Teams are now composed of groups ranging from scruffy 6-year-olds to 40-year-old financial analysts, doctors, lawyers, and sellers of insurance. Even homemakers have formed their own leagues and teams.

Soccer has become American, but it still has quite a way to go. However, when a child's first present is a soccer ball, one must wonder how far soccer is behind baseball and other American sports.

Pelé's game became American in the most American of ways, starting as an immigrant and gradually taking its place in our society. Soccer has needed something like 100 years to gain acceptance, but it has succeeded.

Soccer—or *football,* as it was called in the early days—has been played in the United States for over 200 years. The early colonists brought the game from England. In seventeenth-century Boston the violent aspects of the sport were deplored, and a fine was decreed for anyone caught playing it. Football continued to be played in other parts of the country, particularly among college students.

The first intercollegiate game was played between Princeton and Rutgers in New Jersey. When these colleges opposed each other for the first time in November 1869, they used rules that were a modification of the 1863 rules published by the London Football Association. In other words, the game that marked the beginning of intercollegiate football was actually a game of soccer. It was not the soccer of today, but soccer as it was played at the time, when the rules permitted the use of hands to catch or stop the ball. Running with the ball in hand was not permitted.

Following the English lead, soccer in the United States took two separate forms. Princeton, Rutgers, Columbia, Yale, and other colleges played an

The many faces of amateur soccer in the United States. From women's leagues in Southern California to the semiprofessional Cosmopolitan League in New York, from youngsters playing in a big league stadium to Ivy Leaguers giving their all in the Brown-Harvard game, millions of Americans are playing soccer. *(Julian Baum, Richard Pilling)*

American version of British Association football, or soccer, which was primarily a kicking game. At a convention in New York in 1873, uniform rules for soccer were adopted.

However, the most prestigious institution, Harvard, played a carrying game that strongly resembled British rugby. The year 1876 became important for both soccer and football when the athletes at Princeton decided that rugby was the better game. They met with representatives from Harvard and other colleges at Springfield, Massachusetts, and voted to adopt the English Rugby Union rules and form a league. Thus began the career of American football. The rest of the country tended to follow the Eastern schools, and the handling-catching game, rather than the kicking game, became the American standard.

Soccer took second place to its offspring, football, at the colleges that were then the centers of American sport. Baseball, football, and basketball went through periods of great expansion in later years, but soccer kept to itself.

The most popular game in the world was almost unheard of in large areas of the United States. Why? Aside from the choice to play collegiate rugby rather than soccer, it is difficult to find the reason.

Despite setbacks, soccer was too good to languish in obscurity, and many colleges could still field excellent teams. More important, soccer was widely played in industrial and port cities, especially in the Northeast. The teams were composed of immigrants from Europe, and most native Americans ignored the game. But the immigrants founded teams and leagues that formed the backbone of American soccer and still exist, although in different form, today.

By 1913 soccer had grown to the point where it became necessary to form a national governing body, the United States Football Association (USFA). The name was later changed to the United States Soccer Football Association (USSFA), and the group is currently known as the United States Soccer Federation (USSF). The first president of this organized group, G. Randolph Manning, served for 2 years. Manning was a doctor who apparently paid little attention to soccer. Unfortunately, he set the standard for his successors, and the national governing body is still directed by a part-time president.

Only during the 1970s has the game started to expand. There are several interrelated reasons for this. Recent presidents of the USSF have discouraged the former pattern of ethnic teams. In 1976 the strongest semiprofessional league in the country, the German-American Football Association, changed its name to the Cosmopolitan League. The league's philosophy was overhauled as well. Teams began to recruit young Americans rather than older Europeans.

"We had been fighting for this for a long time" said league president Harry Saunders, who was instrumental in changing that philosophy. "We had to convince a lot of people that the future of the game is with the American player and not with the 40-year-old from Germany or Greece or Yugoslavia. I hope other leagues will follow our example."

Perhaps the major impetus behind amateur soccer's new look has been the enormous success of the professionals. Pelé helped raise the Cosmos'

The 1928 U.S. Olympic soccer team. From left to right: (top) Lyons, Kane, Findlay, Cronin, and Gallagher; (middle) Ryan, Murphy, Duffer, Schroeder, Cooper, Smith, and Kuentner; (front) Rudge, Littley, Aikens, Carrol, and Deal.

"Everybody get ready to head the ball!" Practice session at a soccer workout for boys.

average home attendance figures from 4000 per game in early 1975 to 47,000 per game in 1978. Kyle Rote, Jr., became a national celebrity in less time than that. The message was not lost on the boosters of amateur soccer: Give American fans world-class players, heroes they can cheer for, and they'll cross the turnstiles in unprecedented numbers.

Yet the boom is not all at the top. In fact, soccer's growing strength in the United States is primarily due to the involvement of young Americans, especially those not yet in high school.

Youth Soccer

Younger children often fall in love with soccer at first sight. They don't have to get in a huddle or wait for someone to throw them a baseball. The soccer ball moves all the time, and they love to chase it and kick it.

Youngsters who play soccer have also spread the word, explaining to their parents what the sport is all about. And parents, who love to run up and down the sidelines yelling instructions and encouragement, are falling for soccer without realizing that they are being unfaithful to the traditional American sports. As a parent in the New York suburbs said while watching a Little League baseball game, "I find myself disliking baseball more and more. It's so slow. I wish the soccer season would start soon."

In some places the recent growth of soccer has been astonishing. In 1971, the Cosmos' first year, for example, a soccer program was started in suburban Massapequa, New York. At first there were 25 teams, but the number increased to 104 in 1975 and 170 in 1977. Rockville Centre, another suburb of New York, started with 1 team in 1972 and expanded to 50 in 1977. A youth program was started in Ramapo in 1977 with 350 boys and girls—920 participated a year later.

California was the first state to systematically cultivate soccer at the youth level. The American Youth Soccer Organization (AYSO) was founded in 1964 in Torrance by Hans Sterlie, with help from Ted McLean, Steve Erdos, Bill Hughes, and Ralph Acosta. These men became involved in an organization whose unique concepts have had a considerable influence on the course of American soccer.

Sterlie, who has been the AYSO's executive director for many years, came up with the concept that "everyone plays" and enforced it strictly. Each player on a team had to play at least half the game, and this principle provided a base for the broad acceptance of the group's philosophies and objectives.

The AYSO started with just 9 teams. On March 3, 1978, Sterlie proudly announced that the AYSO had grown to 9000 teams in 21 states, with a registered membership of 165,000 players, representing an increase of 49,000 over 1977. On December 22, 1978, the AYSO announced that it had registered 205,000 players.

"There is no limit to the growth in sight," said Ron Ricklefs, president of the AYSO, in 1978. "We are preparing ourselves for the quarter of a million AYSO members expected to be registered by 1980."

In summer 1978, 50 teams representing regions throughout the United States gathered in southern California to compete in a tournament sponsored by Pepsi-Cola.

In 1974, 10 years after the founding of the AYSO, the USSF formed its own youth group, the United States Youth Soccer Association (USYSA). Under the direction of Don Greer, a vice-president of the USSF, both organizations are run by volunteers, although the AYSO also employs several individuals full-time. Despite the shortage of staff, the USYSA had registered approximately 350,000 players by the end of 1978. That number includes all players registered with associations and groups affiliated with the USSF.

Don Greer has probably done more than anybody else to promote youth soccer in the United States. A quiet person who becomes a dynamo when

(Bottom left) Several teams in the NASL schedule youth teams to play before the regular league games. In this scene at Giants Stadium, the boys are trying to emulate their heroes. Interest in the pro game has helped build up amateur soccer. (Richard Pilling)

(Bottom right) The joys of winning. Boys celebrate just like the pros after a triumph in a hard-played AYSO league game. (AYSO)

Heavy traffic in front of the goal was a feature of this well-played game in AYSO's older boys division. As the game's appeal widens, the players' skills improve. *(AYSO)*

Pelé's son, Edson, is having a grand time, with or without spectators, trying to get the ball past John Yannis at Giants Stadium.

speaking about soccer, Greer has mustered a great deal of support for his young organization. No one had helped more than Colin Green, who has been secretary of the USYSA.

Greer divided the United States into 4 regions, each directed by its own commissioner. All these commissioners have run their regions with determination and have achieved remarkable results. The current commissioners are: Region I (EAST), Tony Perez of West Babylon, New York; Region II (Midwest), John Hilske of Elkhorn, Nebraska; Region III (South), Jimmie Wofford of Dallas; and Region IV (West), Peter Jebens of Santa Rosa, California. There are also 8 subregional commissioners.

Both the AYSO and the USYSA share the same goal—encouraging

youngsters to play soccer. Two questions naturally arise: Why must there be two groups? Would it not make sense for them to merge? Observers prefer merger, and representatives of both organizations have discussed the idea.

Until the two groups merge many young players will not be able to reach their potential. Unless a league is affiliated with the USSF, its teams cannot participate in official interstate, national, and international competitions. Affiliation with the USSF automatically means recognition by FIFA, whose approval is needed for international tournaments at the national or club levels. Thus, teams registered with Greer's group can compete anywhere in the world, but others, including affiliates of the AYSO, cannot play even on a "friendly" basis.

Several youth teams have traveled long distances only to find that they could not play because they were not affiliated with the USSF. I remember the disappointment of a team of 10-year-olds from Rockland County, New York, who could not register for an indoor tournament on Long Island. They were lucky to find out before they started the 50-mile trip. A group from Ohio visited the Soviet Union only to discover that they couldn't play any games there. The Russians are not especially strict, but every member country must follow the rules of FIFA. Soccer is a game, but it is also a serious business, and no country wants to break the rules of the world governing body.

Another problem is that players in the AYSO cannot be chosen to represent their state or country on an all-star team. The AYSO has officially requested affiliation with the USSF, but no progress has been made.

During a discussion with Don Greer, I told him how much I admired the AYSO's philosophy of "everyone plays."

(Bottom left) **Practice makes perfect in learning the bicycle kick.** *(Harrison Funk)*

(Bottom right) **California has become soccer country in the past few years. These youngsters from San Diego have the form and grace that could make them professionals in the future.** *(Julian Baum)*

High school soccer coaches used to have to teach the fundamentals of the game to their inexperienced players. Today many youngsters learn the basic skills, such as heading, in youth leagues.

Games at the high school level often don't attract the crowds, but technique and enthusiasm of the players run high.

"I like the AYSO's philosophy myself," Greer said. "But it has to go a bit beyond that. This is a vast, complex country with different needs for different people. While the majority of young people would only be interested in playing soccer at what you may call the recreational level, which is very good and desirable, you must also create opportunities for those who want to play competitive soccer."

Despite the differences between the two groups, there are good prospects of cooperation in the next few years. Every other nation has a single body to govern soccer, and the United States should not be an exception. Without a unified administration of the game, the result is chaos.

Soccer in High Schools

Except at the youth level, nowhere has soccer's popularity increased more dramatically than at the interscholastic level. There were 1650 schools with soccer programs in 1963 and 2217 in 1971. The High School Federation (HSF), which makes surveys every 2 years, reported in 1976 that 4195 schools had boys' programs and 599 had girls' programs. Delaware, for instance, which had 5 scholastic programs in 1961, had 32 varsity programs in 1977.

According to Ron Gilbert, the coach at Brandywine High School in Delaware, the figures should be much higher because many schools do not answer the survey of the HSF.

"In the state of Colorado, for instance," Gilbert said in 1977, "the HSF does not list anyone. Do you know how many high school coaches I know from Colorado?"

Gilbert went on to explain the trend toward soccer. He said: "Schools reduce emphasis on football and other sports and turn to soccer because of the costs. That is just one reason. The other reason is that the kids who played at the youth level put pressure on the schools to start varsity soccer programs."

The growing numbers of talented players at the interscholastic level and the youth level have changed many people's minds about the ability of the United States to produce enough good players for the collegiate and professional ranks. Because of the youth programs, interscholastic coaches like Ron Gilbert get players who already know the fundamentals. Gilbert said, "The kids who enter high school now are ready to play."

The main characteristic of high school games in the past was a lack of individual skills and tactics. American teenagers and collegians used to play a game of kick-and-run, which requires kickers and runners, not soccer players. But varsity programs have begun to emphasize improvement of individual skills and techniques and team tactics. By 1984 or 1985 players now participating at the scholastic level can be counted on to improve the game at the collegiate and professional levels.

The superintendent of schools in Dumont, New Jersey, was stunned in 1977 when 72 "fairly skilled players" tried out for the high school team. The superintendent recalled a year not long before when only 14 students had come out for the team, and they were "mostly the rejects of the football program."

William Patterson, athletic director of Lynbrook High School in New York, wants to correct a misunderstanding about soccer players at the scholastic level. "The story of kids playing soccer because they couldn't make it in football is no longer true," Patterson said. "There has been an increase in the number of good athletes attracted to soccer. I know that soccer has gained in popularity because schools that used to pay lip service to soccer have all of a sudden become competitive."

"Because of the professional input," said Lee Kenworthy, who was involved in soccer in Massachusetts for many years, "students in high school get involved in the game because they think there is a future. They have something to shoot for. Before, they didn't."

The high school season varies across the country. In the East, soccer is played in the fall. In the Midwest area around St. Louis, the season runs from late winter to early spring in most high schools. In California, according to Ernst Feinbusch, a long-time teacher, coach, and referee, most schools compete in the fall.

"High schools and everybody else play soccer all year round out here because of the climate," Feinbusch said. "In many regions the game is played at all levels throughout the year. It is not so good in the winter, though, because many participants in the winter come from other sports such as football, and it makes the game more physical rather than technical."

Regardless of the number of schools or players at the scholastic level, it is clear that better players are now competing. As Brad Jaworski, coach at Hicksville, New York, said, "I have learned that a soccer player is like someone who plays a musical instrument. He cannot be good unless he starts in junior high. And my players are all good."

Soccer in Colleges

At a teachers' convention in Nebraska in 1940, Branch Rickey, known for his involvement in baseball, made a curious prophecy. He told a shocked audience, "In 50 years soccer will supplant football as it is now played in college."

When someone in the back of the room asked Rickey which college he was referring to, everyone laughed, particularly those who knew that soccer at the college level had been "prospering" since 1873, the year soccer came close to being officially established as an intercollegiate sport.

In the nineteenth century soccer was a secondary sport at most — though not all — colleges. The college game became slightly more organized in 1905, when the Intercollegiate Soccer Association League was formed by Columbia, Cornell, Haverford, Pennsylvania, and Harvard. But the first national collegiate tournament did not take place until 1959.

The rules of collegiate soccer are significantly different from the rules currently used by the professionals. The colleges are playing under rules that were formulated decades ago by physical-education teachers. Many colleges employ 2 referees and no linesmen and have a timekeeper on the sidelines. Wholesale substitutions are permitted, with groups of players going in and out of the game almost at will.

The best professional and amateur soccer players play a different game than the American collegians. A young coach who was a member of the Soccer Rules Committee of the National Collegiate Athletic Association (NCAA) said at the Division I tournament in 1976, "I guess we will have to wait until some of these people retire before we can eliminate the 2-referee system and

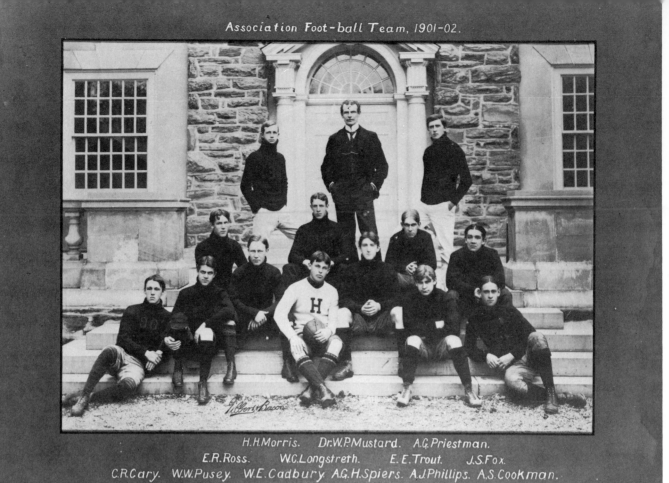

Association Foot-ball Team, 1901–02.

H.H.Morris.   Dr.W.P.Mustard.   A.G.Priestman.
E.R.Ross.   W.C.Longstreth.   E.E.Trout.   J.S.Fox.
C.R.Cary.   W.W.Pusey.   W.E.Cadbury.   A.G.H.Spiers.   A.J.Phillips.   A.S.Cookman.
R.M.Gummere. CAPTAIN.

They still called it Association Foot-ball at Haverford College, Pennsylvania, in 1901–1902.

a number of other silly things we have.''

St. Louis University has dominated collegiate soccer since the inception of the national tournament in 1959. The Billikens captured or shared 10 of the first 15 titles in Division I. To broaden competition and to make a place for smaller colleges, the NCAA instituted a Division II national tournament in 1972 and a Division III tournament in 1974. Until 1977, when the final game in Division I attracted 16,500 to the University of California at Berkeley, most tournaments had been played before a few thousand fans and had been financial failures.

Blame it on lack of promotion. The 1973 Division I tournament, for example, attracted only friends and relatives of the players. It was held in Miami as part of the Orange Bowl festivities. Instead of promoting its own tournament, the NCAA left it to the Orange Bowl Committee, which apparently forgot that the soccer tournament was part of the program.

It was felt that promotion would not have helped much because there were no soccer fans in Miami. The next year the tournament was held in St. Louis, a city considered to be the hotbed of American soccer. The popularity of soccer in St. Louis was taken for granted, however, and the tournament was again held before friends and relatives, even though St. Louis University was in the championship game.

Division I is usually divided into 6 regions, and each region selects 4 teams for the national tournament. Of the 24 teams that participate in the regionals, the winners in the Midwest and West advance automatically to the semifinals. The winners from New England, New York, the New Jersey-Delaware-Pennsylvania area, and the South compete in rotation to determine the other two semifinalists. In 1979 the NCAA divided Division I into 8 regions of 2 teams each and also awarded 3 at-large berths for the tournament.

For Divisions II and III the country is divided into 4 regions: New York-New England, New Jersey-Pennsylvania-South, Midwest, and West. All three national tournaments are usually held around the first week in December.

Despite organizational difficulties, soccer has grown remarkably at the college level. The NCAA cannot say exactly how many colleges participated in 1959, but they estimate the number at 160. In 1967 the NCAA was able to indicate for the first time exactly how many colleges played soccer: 277. The figure became ''approximate'' again in 1968, when there were about 300 of what the NCAA calls *sponsoring institutions*. In 1978, 459 colleges and universities had soccer programs. The National Association of Intercollegiate Athletics (NAIA) listed 196 schools that played soccer in 1978 and 126 junior colleges that maintained soccer programs.

Adult Amateur Soccer

It usually happens on Sunday, year-round in warmer areas but only in summer and fall in colder regions. Adults of all ages and from all walks of life bring their own uniforms and gather together for a game in the town park or high school field. The players put up the goals, mark the field, and change into uniforms in their cars. Some do not have uniforms—just a pair of sneakers, gym shorts, and a T-shirt.

This is a new American activity. It used to be restricted to people who could head the ball and do tricks with it impressing Americans who thought feet were made only for walking. But groups like Rainbow Soccer in North Carolina have set an example for several other leagues.

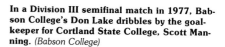

In a Division III semifinal match in 1977, Babson College's Don Lake dribbles by the goalkeeper for Cortland State College, Scott Manning. *(Babson College)*

Jeff Tipping of Hartwick College and Dave MacWilliams of Philadelphia Textile go after the ball in this Division I semifinal match. *(Ed Clough)*

(Left) Ray Williams scoots around Cathleen Heim in a Rainbow League game, where everybody plays and has a wonderful time.

(Right) These two women from California have no fear of the leather ball.

Rainbow Soccer offers people of all ages a chance to learn about soccer, teamwork, and the marvels of body control. Kip Ward, originator of this idea and soccer coach at the University of North Carolina, felt that everyone besides the standard "jock" is thwarted at an early age by the high degree of competition in sports. Ward therefore held a clinic for all age groups. About 40 people showed up for the first clinic and about 200 for the second. A year later there were 2500 people involved in the program, in which children play with 55-year-olds and teenagers.

Rainbow Soccer attempts to avoid the parental interference that often occurs in other sports. In one game, some overzealous parents were coaching from the sidelines. When their coaching took a negative turn, the referee stopped play and invited the parents onto the field to try to play better. The result was a better understanding of what the players were going through.

Ward maintains that a high level of competition is not necessary and can inhibit people who are trying to learn the game. He said, "In the safe environment of our program, people have the confidence to try things they would never have attempted otherwise. It is not competition and violence, after all, that win soccer games. It is skill, team play, fitness, and a basic understanding of the subtleties of the game."

Tony Balis was a student at the Fletcher Graduate School of Diplomacy in 1976 when he and Reuben Johnson, a Ph.D. candidate in urban affairs at Columbia University, played soccer in New York's Central Park with the American-Czechs. Balis recalled the first game he played for the now-defunct team: "A fight broke out and everyone started talking in a strange language. I tried hard not to act like an American."

Balis and Johnson, both Wesleyan alumni, conceived the idea of forming a team with former players from Amherst, Wesleyan, and Williams, the "Little Three." Their team became the Little Three Manhattan, and they now compete in the lowest division of the Cosmopolitan League. The accent is on having fun, and most of the fans are wives, girlfriends, and families.

Time will tell whether adults in the United States will ever become as addicted to soccer as is rock star Rod Stewart. An American reporter scheduled an interview with Stewart that proceeded like a typical celebrity interview until soccer came up. Stewart then whipped out a pen and started to diagram plays on the tablecloth.

He told the reporter and other listeners, "The Scots are the best football players in the world. Whenever there is a family reunion, playing football takes all our time. My parents are from Scotland, you see."

Stewart was so fired up about soccer that he could no longer hide his feelings. "I like football more than I like music or women," he confessed.

Women's Soccer

Their teams have names like the Moms, Audi Headers, Cisco's Kids, Picadillys, and Cyclones. Their uniforms are often pink and, in at least one instance in California, include a garter. They are women's teams, of course, composed of women who felt left out of the game Pelé calls beautiful.

These are women who felt bored watching their sons and daughters play on Saturday mornings and their husbands on Saturday afternoons. Now it is the women who are watched by their husbands and children. Some derive satisfaction from the competition, which is usually moderate. Some feel they don't have to prove anything to anyone and are out to have a good time, to "run and kick the hell out of the ball."

The profile of the woman soccer player is as varied as the profile of any other human being. Women players are wives, mothers, students, secretaries, nurses, dietitians, doctors, and attorneys. They ignore the bruises, sore muscles, and sprains. They don't care if their midriff feels like it's been separated from their pelvis as long as they can stop a shot from going into the goal and hear their sons and daughters yell, "Way to go, Mom!"

Women have found that soccer is physically demanding but rewarding. They are discovering that soccer helps them release aggression and that kicking the ball brings relief from tension. Ida Clements, who lives in Dallas, said, "I tell all my friends at work that I take out all my hostilities on the ball."

In recent years women's soccer has become most popular in Dallas and Seattle. There was a women's team in Dallas in 1973 called the Cyclones. Ida Clements recalled the team's first game: "It was against a bunch of disc jockeys. They were from a local radio station. But we had to play everyone, from boys' to mens' teams, that first season."

Nevertheless, the women's soccer movement caught on quickly, and 6 teams joined the first organized league in the Dallas area in spring 1975. There were soon 13 teams, and then 28 and 36. The last time they counted, they had 44 teams with exotic names like Lady Bugs, Peppermint Patties, Ms. Chiefs, and Redneck Mothers.

In Seattle women's soccer was founded in spring 1975. In only 2 years the number of teams escalated from practically none to 300. Tampa, Washington, D.C., and northern Virginia are other areas where women's soccer has caught on.

Grace and power are both important components of women's soccer, along with speed and hustle. *(Julian Baum)*

Janice O'Neal is a member of the Metropolitan Washington Women's Soccer League. She often leaves her four children at home and spends the afternoon chasing a soccer ball, sometimes in the mud, at West Potomac Park.

"I play to enjoy it," Mrs. O'Neal said. "It's fantastic. It's never dull." Marilyn Morrison, an attorney who competes in the same league said, "We want to win, but we don't let losing get in the way of having fun." Economist Susan Cobb added, "Soccer enables me to let off some steam. I am really relaxed afterwards."

Women are discovering that soccer is an equal-opportunity sport in which they play under the same rules as men. They have the same chance to excel as their husbands and boyfriends, who do not have a head start at the sport. And they can play until they are 50 or older.

The younger women, the ones still in school, are playing a larger role in soccer and other sports because of the Department of Health, Education, and Welfare's Title IX program. This program mandates mixed competition when comparable opportunities in a sport or athletic endeavor are not available to children of both sexes. A federal district court in Colorado ruled in 1977 that excluding a girl from a boys' team is unconstitutional if there is no girls' team in the sport.

Valerie Robin played freshman soccer in 1977 on the all-boys squad of Horace Greely High School in Chappaqua, New York; this was in direct contradiction to the regulations of the New York State Public High School Athletic Association. The principal allowed her to join the team after her parents sought help from civil-rights groups. Armed with a doctor's note attesting to her fitness, Valerie played with the boys and had an assist in her first game.

Because of similar cases, six women involved in soccer started a movement to form their own national association. In 1977 Alaina Jones, Candace Hogan, Wendy Cole, Cathy Currie, Lynn Berling, and Tina Klassen founded the National Women's Soccer Association (NWSA).

Alaina Jones, president and executive director of the NWSA, said that she had tried to find a place for women's soccer among the state associations under the USSF but had encountered a lack of enthusiasm. Before this she had formed the Women's Interstate Soccer Association (WISA), the first group for, by, and of women devoted to increasing opportunities for women in soccer.

"Women need a sense of community and encouragement in soccer," Jones said. "They need to know that there are opportunities to compete in soccer at all levels. They need information on how to get in touch with other teams. They need to know that there are opportunities to compete in soccer after high school and college."

The NWSA was established in order to:

1. Provide quality opportunities for women in soccer.

2. Assist in the organization of local, state, regional, national, and international women's soccer tournaments at both club and collegiate levels.

3. Provide intercollegiate soccer programs in conjunction with the Association for Intercollegiate Athletics for Women (AIAW).

4. Secure college scholarships in soccer for women.

5. Coordinate the development of professional women's soccer.

6. Provide accurate information on women's soccer and to establish a support center.

The Florida Suncoast Soccer League is one of very few leagues with a division for women. In 1977 the league maintained first and second divisions for men and a single division for women. Francisco Marcos, vice-president of the Tampa Bay Rowdies, coached a team called Cisco's Kids. A veteran of the soccer field, Marcos treated his players like athletes, not prima donnas.

"I've had girls break down and cry because they are not used to criticism," Marcos said. "I had to decide whether to treat them as players or

Teamwork moves the ball downfield in this AYSO league game. About 20 percent of AYSO's registered players are girls, with the numbers growing all the time. *(AYSO)*

women. They preferred I treat them as players. Relationships are strictly platonic. I can grab them or push them to stress a point without any sexual intentions. Many have discovered a whole new world and muscles they've never used before."

Patrick Keohane, who coaches the women's team at the University of California at Berkeley, pointed out one interesting aspect of women's soccer at the collegiate level: "Unlike the all-too-abbreviated men's season, we play on a year-round basis during the school year. We train from late September to January and play our conference season from the first of February to the end of May. The twist to what we are trying to do is to develop the woman player as a high-class soccer athlete, a serious, skilled, fit, intelligent competitor who can play exciting and entertaining soccer."

Keohane said that the collegiate conference for women in his region started in February 1977 and successfully incorporated 6 teams. The conference expanded to 12 teams for the 1978 season. All teams operated at the club level in 1978. The clubs were unfunded but were recognized by their universities and permitted to represent them.

A major reason for the success of soccer has been its acceptance by women. Women are not only playing soccer but attending soccer games as spectators. They are usually the ones who decide whether the family can afford to go. Women constitute a vast market, and it seems that North American Soccer League Marketing, Inc., is taking full advantage of it.

The involvement of women in soccer in the United States is not entirely contemporary. The late Alfreda Inglehart of Maryland taught the fundamentals of soccer to more than 1200 boys in Baltimore in the 1920s and 1930s. In 1951 Ms. Inglehart was elected to the Soccer Hall of Fame, formerly an all-male institution.

Semiprofessional Leagues

Semiprofessional leagues have existed in the United States for over 70 years. The teams have hyphenated names and are run by immigrants, men proud of a heritage which they want to maintain. Most of these men make a living in a variety of different jobs during the week, but on the weekends they get back to their roots on the playing field. To them, soccer has been, is, and always will be a non-American game.

Almost every Sunday from September to May, the prestige of the old country is put on the line. The strongest rivalries have been between teams of the same ethnic composition. A match between the Greek-Americans and the German-Hungarians is nothing compared to a game between the Greek-Americans and their compatriots on the Hellenic team. When I played for Hellenic in the late 1960s the Greek churches in Astoria were half empty on the Sundays when the two teams met.

I thought I'd seen the worst of these confrontations until I watched Dalmatinac meet Croatia. It was outrageous. While other teams were competing for superiority in soccer, they were battling for political supremacy.

Most of the semiprofessional leagues were formed to encourage ethnic groups to engage in their favorite avocation and thereby relive their experiences from the old country. These leagues are supported by dedicated people who scrimp to give generously to their clubs so that players can be paid

This photograph of a 1951 game in New York featuring the German-Hungarians captures the flavor and spirit of old-time semipro soccer. *(UPI)*

and shorts and jerseys cleaned. These people will pay $10 to see a game from Europe on closed-circuit television at 9:30 a.m. on a weekday. They are happy because they have something to live for and look forward to. They are soccer fans, and the feeling of belonging alleviates the problems of living in a foreign country.

I often watch these closed-circuit games, usually with my Italian-American friends. After the 1978 World Cup qualifying match between Italy and England (which Italy won), Luigi turned to us and exclaimed, "You know, guys, when the public announcer asked for a doctor at halftime, I felt like I was in Rome."

Semiprofessional leagues and teams may have been formed by immigrants for reasons like politics or regional rivalries from the old country, but they have also served another purpose—keeping the game alive.

The Greater Los Angeles League, the Cosmopolitan League in New York, and the National League in Chicago are the strongest semiprofessional leagues in the United States. The Greater Los Angeles League celebrated its seventy-fifth anniversary in 1978. The National League was formed in 1920, and the Cosmopolitan League began in 1923.

For years these leagues and several smaller leagues were supported strictly by immigrants. In recent years, however, the support, policy, and philosophy of these leagues have changed drastically. In the Cosmopolitan League each team must have a certain number of American citizens on its roster. The ethnic emphasis has diminished to such a degree that the New York Greek-Americans and Hellenic have merged. If you had mentioned to Greeks in the late 1960s that such a merger was feasible, they'd have rolled you up and used you for a soccer ball.

The Greek-Americans were the pride of the German-American League in the late 1960s. They are the only team to have won the United States Chal-

The Greek-American Team in the 1950s. From left to right: (rear) Coach Panagoulias (who became coach of the Greek National Team), Manousos, Gakis, Kambolis, Iosifidis, Hatjioannou, and Andreou; (front) Jordevic, Kosmidis, Hatzos, Vidalis, and Tsalouhidis. *(Carlo J. Ziliani)*

lenge Cup, also known as the Thomas Dewar Trophy, 3 consecutive times. With an exception or two, the team was composed solely of Greeks. But today, playing as the Astros—they were called Greek-Americans/Hellenic for a short time after the merger—the team has players of various nationalities, including Americans.

Spread over New York, New Jersey, Connecticut, and Pennsylvania, the Cosmopolitan League features almost nonstop competition. In addition to preseason games, the teams play approximately 20 games in each of the league's three divisions. There are postseason playoffs and several international games, and the league also conducts a rugged 8-week indoor campaign.

When the league played its indoor tournament over a decade ago in a small armory in New York, a fire broke out in the stands shortly before a crucial contest. Firemen arrived and ordered the fans and players to leave. The game continued while the fans fought the firemen, saying they'd leave only when the game was completed. An urgent appeal by league officials finally got the players to stop playing and the fans to leave the smoke-filled building.

For years one of the most attractive series of games in New York featured the league's all-star squad in competition with foreign teams. One of the most memorable games in this series occurred in 1955 when Kaiser-Lautern, with many members of the 1954 World Cup Champion West German national team, came to New York. The Germans were the overwhelming favorites, but the all-star squad won 1 to 0 before 20,000 fans.

The Israeli national team was the last noteworthy squad to meet New York's all-stars in the early 1970s. Foreign powerhouses such as Manchester United, Liverpool, the Polish national team, Hamburg, Frankfurt, and Hajduk Split of Yugoslavia have also played in New York against the league's all-stars.

In 1974, when the Cosmos were attracting about 3000 fans to games at Randalls Island, some officials of the German-American League believed that two or three of their teams could "beat the Cosmos on any given Sunday." You will not find anyone making such a statement now.

Do not, however, tell any immigrant group that the Cosmos or any other team in the NASL could hold their own against a first-division team back home. These groups think they know better than Franz Beckenbauer, who said in 1978, "Besides the Cosmos, Seattle, Minnesota, Tampa, and a couple of other teams in the NASL can do well in any league in Europe."

Many companies with large numbers of immigrant employees have formed soccer teams. A dominant force in the early days was the Bethlehem Steel Football Club, which was founded in 1914 and began to dominate the soccer scene immediately. Bethlehem Steel, composed of players from the steel mills, captured the United States Challenge Cup in 4 of the first 6 tournaments. Only about 300 fans came to the home games, but the team was a novelty on the road, where it drew over 20,000 to many games.

In that era it made sense for a company to sponsor a good soccer team. It helped keep the employees happy and staved off unions. It was also good publicity to have a company team play before large crowds. A few of the companies that fielded good teams were Bethlehem Steel, Indiana Flooring Company, Robbins Dry Dock, Todd Shipyards, and Morse Dry Dock. The teams took their names from the sponsoring companies.

Robbins Dry Dock Football Club of Brooklyn, New York, won the United States Challenge Cup in 1921. The Stix, Baer and Fuller Football Club of St. Louis won the cup in 1933 and 1934. Other successful teams of that era were Fall River F.C. of Fall River, Massachusetts; New Bedford F.C. of New Bedford, Massachusetts; and Hakoah All-Star F.C. of New York. Pawtucket of Rhode Island and the Brooklyn Hispano F.C. of New York dominated the scene in the 1940s. A number of these teams called themselves professional, but they were in effect semiprofessional.

Although soccer is not a highly organized sport, it has a definite structure that has been in place for many years. In semiprofessional soccer the key organizations are the state associations. All teams and leagues must be affiliated with the state associations and through them the USSF.

Soccer has come a long way in New York. The old German-American League used to play many of its games at Eintrach Oval, a dusty field in Queens that was a far cry from the Cosmos' new home ground, Giant's Stadium. In this 1960s game, Inter-Giuliana (dark jerseys) with star Peter Millar played New York Hungaria.
(Carlo J. Ziliani)

Depending on a state's size and the popularity of soccer in the area, there can be more than one association. New York, for example, has two state associations: the Southern New York State Soccer Association and the Northwestern New York State Soccer Football Association. (Many of these associations have the word *football* in their names, but more are following the example of the USSF and eliminating the word.)

A state association can have several leagues under its jurisdiction. The Illinois Soccer Association, for example, has the following affiliated leagues: National Soccer League, Chicago Latin American Soccer Association, Chicagoland Soccer League, Great Lakes Soccer League, and Western Illinois Soccer League.

According to statistics kept by the USSF, the California Soccer Association, the California Soccer Association South, the Colorado State Soccer Association, the North Texas State Soccer Association, the New Jersey State Soccer Association, and the Washington State Soccer Association have been growing at a fantastic rate as more semiprofessional leagues are organized in those areas. These new leagues have an entirely different image from the leagues in large cities. They are being formed by native-born Americans, and the games are meant to be watched by Americans.

The Unifying Force

Every soccer-playing country in the world has a national association that belongs to FIFA and is responsible for soccer within that country.

The birth of the governing body of soccer in the United States was by no means peaceful. It came about after a period in 1912 and 1913 during which a strong rivalry existed between two different organizations: the American Football Association (AFA) and the American Amateur Football Association (AAFA). Both organizations staked a claim to national recognition with the International Federation Congress in Stockholm in 1912.

Thomas W. Cahill of New York presented the case for the AAFA, which had as its nucleus the New York State Amateur Football Association League. The AFA controlled professional leagues and clubs in New Jersey, Philadelphia, and the New England states. Its cause was argued by F. J. Wall, secretary of the English Football Association, with which the AFA was affiliated. Wall claimed that it was essential for the national governing body to control the professionals.

After much discussion, the international body ruled that the two rival groups should attempt to form a single national body. Committees were appointed to iron out the difficulties, and the first meeting took place in New York on October 12, 1912. However, the AFA decided to discontinue negotiations.

Seeking additional strength, the AAFA then attracted the interest of the Football Association of Philadelphia, which agreed to join forces. Delegates from various associations around the country met in New York on April 5, 1913, and agreed to form the USFA. The new group was recognized by FIFA on August 15 as the governing body of soccer in the United States. (The name was changed to the USSFA in 1945 and to the USSF in 1974.)

With offices on the fortieth floor of the Empire State Building, the USSF is governed by a national commission consisting of a president, six vice-presidents, an executive secretary, and a treasurer. With the exception of the executive secretary, Kurt Lamm, the members of the national commission are rarely in the office; they are volunteers engaged in other occupations throughout the country.

One of the vice-presidential chairs goes to the commissioner of the NASL, and the other officers are elected at the federation's annual convention. All members of the commission except the NASL representative must be American citizens.

The USSF's constitution originally announced its aim as "supreme control of soccer football in the United States." In recent years the wording has been altered to eliminate "supreme control." The aim now is to "promote soccer in the United States."

The USSF promotes soccer in the United States in many ways. The Federation:

1. Serves as the central registering authority for players. Professionals are registered directly at $10 per player, amateurs at $2, and juniors under 18 at 50 cents. Players can also be registered indirectly through their state associations.

2. Attempts to enforce uniformity of rules throughout the country.

3. Organizes the three national competitions. Players must be registered with the USSF in order to compete.

4. Acts as the final arbitrator for disputes between clubs over registration or eligibility of players.

5. Selects coaches for the national teams and is in charge of all teams representing the United States at home and abroad.

6. Grants permission for international games between American and foreign teams. The federation gets approximately 5 percent of the gate receipts from every such game held in the United States.

Under the direction of the coach in charge of all national teams, the players who will represent the country are chosen through regional tryouts. Members of the USSF's coaching school, who reside throughout the nation, keep an eye on prospects. Coaches and scouts in the NASL can also notify the coach of the national teams of a good player. The national coach often

(Top) Gene Edwards, USSF President, and (above) Kurt Lamm, Secretary General of USSF.

(Left) A group of players of the U.S. national team, with Coach Walt Chyzowych at far left and two trainers. The players from left to right are: *(front)* Russell, L. Nanchoff, Liveric, Brcic, MacAlister, Etherington, and Davis; *(middle)* Ralbovsky, Bandov, Makowski, G. Nanchoff, Fowles, and Myernick; *(rear)* Pollihan, Trost, Droege, Mausser, Villa, and Pecher.

scouts NASL games and practices and keeps records of the progress of all prospects.

In recent years, the members of all national teams have assembled at least twice annually and have taken part in tournaments in the United States and abroad. In 1978, for the first time, a team of 15-year-olds and under traveled overseas to represent the United States in a tournament in France. As Gene Edwards, who was elected president of the USSF for a 4-year term in 1978, said about the 15-year-olds, "This may be the team to represent us in the World Cup in 1986."

In 1974 the USSF took an ambitious step by hiring Dettmar Cramer, a West German, as its first full-time coach. His job was to coach all the national teams in the United States, run a development program, and set up coaching schools across the country. Cramer had conducted coaching courses in over 70 countries, including the United States, while serving as a coach for FIFA for 7 years. The federation hired him, but it was reportedly the NASL that funded most of his $80,000 salary.

Cramer's tenure as national coach lasted only 5 months. The USSF had once again acted in an amateurish way by failing to actually sign him. When Cramer got a good offer from Germany, he took advantage of the lack of a binding contract and left the United States to coach Bayern Munich, one of West Germany's strongest teams. The USSF went to court, suing Cramer and Bayern Munich for several million dollars. But without Cramer's signature on a contract, the USSF had no case and was forced to withdraw the lawsuit.

Over a year went by before the USSF hired Walt Chyzowych, acknowledged as one of the best-qualified candidates for the job of national coach and director of coaching and development. Chyzowych was born in the Ukraine in 1937 and came to the United States when he was 7 years old. At Temple University he was an all-American in soccer and also played football and baseball. He made a name for himself as a soccer player at various levels

One of the mainstays of the great U.S. World Cup team in 1950 was Charlie Colombo. Known as "the one with gloves," he also played on U.S. Olympic teams. This photo was taken in Helsinki, Finland, during the game between Italy and the United States.

and was named to the American national team in 1964. He played for the national team for 3 years and also played professionally in Philadelphia. As soccer coach at the Philadelphia College of Textiles and Sciences, his record was 128 victories, 37 losses, and 13 ties.

Chyzowych is, aside from Cramer, the first coach to work full-time for the USSF. When he signed a 3-year contract on August 1, 1976, the national team had had 10 coaches in a span of 16 years, probably an international record. England, for example, has had about a dozen national-team coaches in its soccer history. Walter Winterbottom coached the national team of England and was director of the English coaching school for 16 years.

The American national team has had little to cheer about since its thrilling 1 to 0 victory over England in the 1950 World Cup finals in Brazil. When it wasn't Haiti or El Salvador that eliminated the United States in the Olympics and World Cup qualifying matches, it was Bermuda.

The Americans have often played important matches after only a few days of preparation. I remember practicing with the national team in 1973 on Long Island. The players assembled on Saturday afternoon, departed for overseas that night, and played a game the next day. Naturally, they lost 10 to 0 to a national team that had been preparing for 6 months.

Chyzowych wanted to change all that. "If we are going anywhere at the international level, whether it's the Olympic team, the youth team, or the World Cup team, we need to have some preparation time," he said.

The World Cup team, the most important American squad, had enough preparation for the qualifying matches of the 1978 World Cup but failed to qualify for the final round in Argentina. Playing in a group that included Mexico and Canada, the Americans finished in a deadlock with the Canadians at the end of the round-robin matches. The teams then met in a playoff on neutral soil. The game was played in Haiti, and the Americans lost 3 to 0 despite being heavily favored. The American national team exonerated itself a few months later by winning the Festival of the Americas tournament in New York.

The Festival of the Americas tournament was the first international tournament of any kind to be won by the Americans. The national team won all 3 games it played, scoring 8 goals against teams from Peru, Ecuador, and Colombia. Chyzowych's men performed very well, particularly against a Peruvian team that included Hugo Sotil and Teófilo Cubillas.

"We are becoming competent," Chyzowych said. "We proved that we can score. We've never won anything in the past and here we are today, winning a tournament and scoring 8 goals. It used to take us several years to score 8 goals."

In April 1978 Chyzowych took a group of players 20 years of age and under to Switzerland for an 8-nation tournament. The Americans won all 4 games by shutouts. The signs were so bright that former Secretary of State Henry Kissinger, a frequent visitor to Cosmos games, began to talk of having the USSF extend a bid to FIFA to allow the United States to host the World Cup in 1990.

As soccer becomes a big-time sport in the United States, it may become necessary for the USSF to be governed by individuals who devote full attention to the development and growth of the sport at all levels. The NASL may help in making this change. There has been some talk of dividing the USSF into two main headquarters—New York and Colorado. The office in New York would deal with all administrative matters, and the office in Colorado

Some teams and some individuals have done well for the United States in recent years. A key man on defense for Americans has been Bobby Smith, shown here in the Bicentennial tournament. *(George Tiedemann)*

would concentrate solely on the development of all national teams and the training of more coaches through the USSF's National Coaching School. It was estimated by Walt Chyzowych in 1977 that 10,000 federation-certified coaches were needed to meet the country's needs.

The USSF's *National Coaching School Directory of 1977–1978* lists 1384 certified coaches who are American citizens and 11 foreign coaches who have also been certified. Of the 1395 certified coaches listed, none is from the following states: Alaska, Arkansas, Idaho, Kansas, Mississippi, Montana, New Mexico, North Dakota, South Dakota, and Wyoming. Iowa, Louisiana, Tennessee, and West Virginia have one certified coach each. California leads with 298, and New York is next with 179.

Six or seven times a year the National Coaching School sends representatives across the country to set up courses. In 1978, for example, the school offered courses and awarded A, B, and C licenses to coaches from places like Wenham, Massachusetts; Lockport, Illinois; and Tacoma, Washington. The National Coaching School was instituted in 1970 but started to work constructively only after Walt Chyzowych became coach of the national teams and director of the school. Chyzowych said in April 1978 that he usually awards approximately 35 licenses at each 6-day session. The USSF's philosophy under Gene Edwards had been to produce more and better coaches who will produce more and better players.

National Competitions

Three national competitions are held annually under the auspices of the USSF. The United States Challenge Cup—also known as the Sir Thomas Dewar Trophy or the Open Cup—is open to semiprofessional and professional clubs across the country, although NASL teams have never participated. The National Amateur Cup is strictly for amateurs. The National Junior

Cup—or James P. McGuire Cup—is for amateur junior teams with players under 19 years of age.

The United States Challenge Cup is the most coveted prize. It is symbolic of soccer supremacy in the United States, but don't tell this to the NASL champion. The competition began in 1912, 1 year before the formation of the USFA. The trophy was donated by Thomas Dewar in London in 1912 to Thomas W. Cahill, secretary of the AAFA, which joined the USFA after the USFA had been recognized as the national governing body by the International Federation Congress at Copenhagen on August 15, 1913.

The trophy is solid silver with a player mounted on top and stands on a pedestal formed by four Corinthian pillars. It is 33 inches high. The Challenge Cup has not been dominated by any particular club. The Philadelphia Ukrainians and New York Greek-Americans have been the most successful Challenge Cup teams in the East in the last two decades, and Maccabee of Los Angeles has dominated in the West.

Like all national competitions, the Challenge Cup is held on a knockout basis—if you lose a game, you're out of the tournament. Teams have been charged a $100 entrance fee in recent years. About 130 teams from across the country participated about 10 years ago, when the entrance fee was $50, but in 1978 only 72 teams registered. Teams from California have dominated the competition lately, one indication that the Pacific Coast is slightly ahead of the rest of the country in soccer.

As the entrance fee has increased, so have the benefits. The USSF pays for half the cost of the semifinals and completely underwrites the grand final. John O. Best, a vice-president of the USSF, has been chairman of the competition for several years. He recently regretted the absence of teams from the NASL: "We have tried to get them to enter, since that would make the winner the true national champion, but so far they have shown little interest."

The National Amateur Cup was created during the 1922–23 season. Since then the competition has been dominated by Ponta Delgada of Massachusetts and Kutis of St. Louis. The Denver Kickers captured the trophy in both 1977 and 1978. There were 162 teams in the competition in 1976 but only 136 in 1978. USSF officials cite an increase in the entrance fee as the reason for this decrease. However, the USSF pays 50 percent of the traveling expenses of the visiting team in the final.

Matt Boxer, a vice-president of the USSF, has been the chairman of the National Amateur Cup for the past several years, and he aims for major status for the competition. Boxer said in 1977, "It has to be taken seriously by everybody, the teams as well as the state associations. To begin with, Amateur Cup games should be played on enclosed fields and given priority over other games."

Boxer, who lives in San Francisco, favored an even higher entrance fee for 1977. "A number of excellent teams do not enter because they cannot afford the traveling expenses," he said. With a higher entrance fee, he explained, the USSF could at least partially subsidize regional finals as well as the grand final.

The National Junior Cup—named the James P. McGuire Cup in honor of the late president of the USSF—has been contested since the 1934–35 season except during the war years of 1941–42 and 1943–44. The cup has been won most frequently by the Lighthouse Boys Club of Philadelphia. The trophy with the soccer ball on top was especially designed by the USSF. This competition, which is now run by Don Greer, Chairman of the USYSA, has

The United States Challenge Cup. From left to right, Kurt Lamm, Hugo Klein, and Richard Emmett. *(USSF)*

enjoyed a constant increase in the number of participating teams. There were 250 participants in 1974, 350 in 1976, and approximately 400 in 1978.

The USYSA subsidizes 50 percent of the travel expenses for regional finals and the grand final. Teams participate in this competition not only because of the low entrance fee. I was fortunate to witness the 1976 final held in Garden City, New York, between the Annandale Cavaliers of Virginia and Sparta of Chicago. Annandale won 3 to 0 on 3 goals by Gary Etherington, later to sign with the Cosmos as a 19-year-old. More fans came from Virginia that day than came to New York from Baltimore in 1969 to see the World Series.

This competition represents an exceptional opportunity for youth teams. Greer said at the 1976 final, "People are not sufficiently aware of the caliber of play in this competition. They are gradually realizing that some beautiful soccer is played by these teams. Any team that doesn't enter this competition is missing out on a wonderful opportunity."

The Annandale Cavaliers certainly took advantage of that opportunity in 1976—they had entered the competition for the first time that year. Entry blanks for teams that wish to participate in any of the three competitions are available at the offices of state soccer associations. The deadline for applications for the Challenge Cup and Amateur Cup is October 1, while the Junior Cup accepts applications as late as February 1. All three competitions are completed by the end of May.

American Heroes of the Past

Although the United States has never been a world power in soccer, some American players have distinguished themselves. Fortunately, there have been times of victory such as 1950, when the United States beat England in World Cup competition.

Many players who have achieved the highest honors and are most vividly remembered have been the native-born sons of immigrant parents. The first team composed entirely of Americans was the Kensingtons of St. Louis. They were members of the St. Louis Football Association, which was founded in the mid-1880s. The Kensingtons began to play competitively in 1890 and captured the league title that year, going through the entire season without allowing a goal.

Several players gained renown on a regional basis before 1910, but national heroes did not emerge until the 1920s and 1930s, when the American national team started to compete internationally in official tournaments such as the World Cup.

In a tiny office at the USSF headquarters in New York, a polite and gentle man has been keeping track of the early giants of American soccer and the members of the Soccer Hall of Fame. He is Julius G. Alonso, a member of the Hall of Fame who is known around the country as "Mr. American Soccer League."

"When we speak of the greatest American player of all time," Alonso said, "we think of Billy Gonsalves. He was a legend. For 6 years in a row he played with 5 different teams that won the Challenge Cup. He played for the World Cup team in 1930 and 1934. He was the best."

Gonsalves died a forgotten man in 1977, but his exploits fill the record books. He had once been offered a professional contract to play baseball, but

(Top) The Annandale Cavaliers of Virginia won the James P. McGuire Cup in 1976. Three players from this team made it into the professional ranks—Gary Etherington, Carl Strong, and Skip Germain.

(Above) Billy Gonsalves, in the later years of his career playing, is shown here (left). He died a forgotten man in 1977.

as Alonso put it, "Billy turned them down for soccer and $50 a week as a soccer player because he loved the game. Those were the days when a dollar was a dollar."

Gonsalves was born in Fall River, Massachusetts, in 1908, the seventh of eleven children. His parents were Portuguese, and "Big Billy" was their first child born in the United States. He lived in Kearney, New Jersey, at the time of his death.

Aldo T. (Buff) Donelli is the player most frequently mentioned by old-timers after Gonsalves. Born in Morgan, a small coal-mining town hear Pittsburgh, Donelli played with Gonsalves for the New York Americans. All the good teams in those days were semiprofessional but liked to call themselves professional.

Donelli got his nickname as a youngster because he always spoke and read about Buffalo Bill. Besides his heroics with the American World Cup team in 1934 in Italy, Donelli is known for his achievements in American football as coach of Duquesne University, the Pittsburgh Steelers, and Columbia University, which he led to the Ivy League title in 1961. In that year he was named coach of the year in the East.

Donelli made his mark in the 1934 World Cup. Mexico was the first opponent, and the Americans won, 4 to 2. Donelli scored all 4 goals for his team, a feat that is unmatched in the history of the World Cup. Not even Pelé has been able to score 4 goals in a game in the final round.

"The Buff could really pepper the goalkeepers with shots," Alonso said. "The funny thing is, though, that the goalkeeper was always picking the ball up from the back of the net."

After Gonsalves and Donelli, the best-known players from the past are the members of the American squad that defeated England 1 to 0 in the final round of the 1950 World Cup in Bello Horizonte, Brazil. The entire American team is enshrined in the Soccer Hall of Fame.

The game was played on June 27, 1950, before about 20,000 fans. Frank Borghi was in goal, with Harry Keough, Charlie Colombo, Joe Maca, Ed McIllveny, and Walter Bahr playing on defense. The forwards were Frank Wal-

The great U.S. World Cup team of 1950. From left to right: (front) Wallace, McIllveny, Pariani, Gaetjens, C. Souza, and E. Souza; (rear) Lyons, Maca, Colombo, Borghi, Keough, Bahr, and Jeffreys. *(USSF)*

lace, Gino Pariani, Joe Gaetjens, and the Souza brothers, John (Clarkie) and Eddie.

Bill Jeffrey, the coach, Joe Gaetjens, who scored the only goal, and Walter Giesler, the manager, are all dead. The others have gone their separate ways.

Frank Borghi is an undertaker in St. Louis. Harry Keough's oldest son, Ty, has been a member of the American national team and an all-American at St. Louis University, where Harry Keough has been soccer coach for the past several years and has won numerous NCAA titles.

Joe Maca is an interior decorator on Long Island. His son Alain was an all-American at Brockport State and the NASL's first draft choice in 1972. Ed McIllveny's whereabouts are unknown. He left for England not long after the game and may still be there. The English Football Association recently circulated inquiries about McIllveny to no avail.

Charlie Colombo is in the meat-packing business in St. Louis. Clarkie Souza is a mechanic for knitting machinery, and Eddie Souza is in construction-trucking in Rhode Island. Pariani and Wallace work and live in St. Louis.

Walter Bahr is the soccer coach at Pennsylvania State, where his sons Chris and Matt were all-Americans in soccer. Chris played with the NASL's Philadelphia Atoms in 1975 before concentrating on kicking field goals in the National Football League. Matt was also drafted by the NASL, and another son, Casey, played professional soccer and was a member of the American national team.

"It was a great thrill for me," Walter Bahr said of the 1950 game. "I had never been in anything like this in soccer. The team was a close, congenial group on and off the field. Individuals did not pair off into factions. We had a mission to perform. That, in my opinion, was the reason for our success."

Walter Giesler, who had served as president of the USSF, died during the Federation's sixtieth annual convention in 1976. He collapsed while delivering a speech extolling the World Cup team of 1950 and died 24 hours later. Born in St. Louis in 1910, Giesler was a driving force behind soccer in Missouri for 30 years. He coached the American team that played in the fourteenth Olympiad in London.

One of the most popular presidents of the USSF and a member of the Hall of Fame was Jimmy P. McGuire, who died in office on Thanksgiving Day in 1974 at the age of 64. McGuire had served on several FIFA committees and was widely respected throughout the world.

Several other great players deserve mention. Julius Alonso and other old-timers remembered Jack Rottenberg, the "grand old man" of soccer. Pete Renzulli, Archie Stark, Jimmy Mills, Jack Hynes, Sam Foulds, and Joe Barriskill were just a few of the names mentioned. (For a complete list of all the members of the Hall of Fame, refer to page .) Barriskill was secretary of the USSF for many years. He has attended every convention of the federation since its inception in 1913, a record which cannot be duplicated.

"I have enjoyed every convention, including the one in Alaska in 1973," Barriskill said in 1976 at a Cosmos game at Yankee Stadium. "I always said, 'Join the United States Federation and see the world.'"

Born in Belfast "about 90 years ago," Barriskill has fond memories of playing against Nelson Rockefeller when Rockefeller was left fullback at Dartmouth. Playing inside right with the Crescent Club, Barriskill jumped to head the ball and tangled with Rockefeller's foot. The tiny Irishman told Rockefeller to keep his foot on the ground, and Rockefeller replied, "Sissy!" The next time the ball came Barriskill's way, he was ready. He got underneath when Rockefeller when up for a header, causing Rockefeller to fall on his back. Barriskill then turned to his fallen opponent and said, "This is not a parlor game."

Although the soccer greats yearn for the good old days, they are also enthusiastic about the popularity the game has won in recent years. Soccer is not only attracting more spectators in the United States than ever before, it is also being played by millions of people of all ages. As a result, old-timers are often asked to kick the first ball to start games at all levels.

Forming a Team or League

Once you've learned something about soccer, you may want to start a team and form your own league. You may want to organize the children and adults you've seen kicking and heading soccer balls in the streets of your town, the fields of your village, or the schoolyards and parks of your city. The problem is that you don't know how to go about it.

First, get all the players together. If you have more than 22, form 2 teams because more players will want to join. If you want to organize a team but don't have the players, try approaching the local church groups, Boy Scouts, Girl Scouts, Y's, and recreational leagues. Try to interest schoolteachers. One day they will throw a soccer ball in the schoolyard or gym and ask their pupils to chase it.

Once you have the players, let them share the leadership by selecting a name for the team and choosing the captains and managers. Let the majority rule on the selection of uniform colors.

Now you need a place to practice and play. Look for the closest field or gym, and don't worry about equipment. Any kind of ball—even a basketball—can be used for practice in an emergency, and gym or tennis shoes are also all right. Although regular uniforms can be purchased later, you must require children to wear shinguards. Having coached young children, I can attest that the majority despise shinguards. Tell them that if the professionals wear them, so can they.

After you have the teams together, search for coaches and referees. Former soccer players or enthusiasts are best, but anyone can be taught through pamphlets from the USSF or sporting-goods stores.

"One thing you learn," said John Kicks, who organized a league in New Jersey that grew from 10 teams to 240, "is that you never turn down anyone who volunteers for anything."

"Women work harder than men," John Best, former coach of the Seattle Sounders and later general manager of the Vancouver Whitecaps, said about volunteers. "We have women referees and coaches."

For information on a constitution and bylaws for your league, write or call your state association. Describe the nature and purpose of your league and ask them to send sample constitutions and bylaws from similar leagues. After the league is organized, try to get publicity from local and neighborhood newspapers. This should help maintain the interest of your players and recruit new players from the area.

To conform with the regulations of the USSF, every player in organized and competitive soccer at the interstate, national, and international levels must be registered with that organization. This requirement has drawn criticism from people who simply want to form a league to play soccer for fun.

These people do not want to get involved with state associations, the national federation, or FIFA, thinking that there will be a charge for membership.

In a way this is true, but the assessments are modest. The fee for registration is $1 per player, of which half goes to the state association and half to the national federation. Most people interested in soccer feel that $1 per player is a fair price for membership in a state organization and subsequent affiliation with the USSF and FIFA.

Leagues affiliated with the USSF enjoy several privileges. Competitiveness and exposure can be enhanced by involvement in national tournaments like the United States Challenge Cup and the National Junior Cup. Uniformity of rules and low insurance rates ($2 rather than $4.60 per year for a 10-year-old) are two other advantages of affiliation.

Your league can have intramural programs or can sponsor "traveling" teams from your town. Traveling teams are normally all-star selections in various age brackets. Although the colors of the traveling team are always the same, intramural programs provide different colors for each team.

After your town has allocated a field, take the following steps to convert it for soccer. If your local recreation department or school authorities have not marked the field, don't be disappointed. It's easy to do, and the goalposts are not hard to put up.

If you are given a football field, don't turn it down. It's better than nothing. There are portable goalposts that can be put up and taken down when you desire. The nets cost about $25 and can be put up easily. To mark the field, use tape for Astroturf or lime, latex paint, or flour for grass.

If your town, village, or local educational authority is generous enough to provide a field designed for soccer, you are better off putting up permanent goalposts. Make them round for better safety, and paint them white so that they make better targets.

Learning
the Game

Soccer is among the simplest sports to understand, follow, and play at an elementary level. Yet there are millions of Americans who do not have the slightest idea of what the game is about.

Soccer is played by 2 teams that consist of 11 players each. The object of each team is to propel the ball into the other team's goal. In doing this, none of the players except the goalkeeper may use their hands or arms. Therefore they *kick*—anything from a 2-foot pass to a 50-yard punt—and *head*—propel the ball in the air with their heads. Although the actions of the players in the midst of an exciting, hard-fought game may seem random, each player has clear-cut and sharply defined responsibilities.

The goalkeeper's primary job is to make saves—to prevent the ball from entering the netted cage that is the goal. The goalkeeper wears a uniform of a different color so that he can be easily distinguished. He is the only player permitted to use his hands, but he may do so only in the penalty area in front of the goal.

The other 10 players are divided into three basic categories: defenders, midfielders, and forwards. The primary responsibility of the defenders is to prevent the opposition from getting into position to score. Midfielders help the defenders when the other team is on the attack and support the forwards when their team has possession. The objective of the forwards is to score. Most professional teams nowadays use 4 defenders, 3 midfielders, and 3 forwards in addition to the goalkeeper. The diagram on page 105 shows how two typical teams line up for the start of a game.

Having absorbed this information, the average person should be able to watch a soccer game—peewee or professional—and understand most of what happens. For complete comprehension and full enjoyment, it is helpful to know the rules, or *Laws of the Game.* In fact, soccer can best be explained at all levels in terms of its rules.

The rules are relatively simple and straightforward, and there are still only

In a confusing mass of arms and legs and hurtling bodies, it can be difficult for the fans in the stands to follow the action in a soccer game unless they understand the fundamentals of play.

17. If you can understand the infield-fly rule in baseball or recognize an ineligible receiver downfield in football, there is nothing in the soccer rules that you cannot comprehend. The rules apply to all matches—amateur or professional, senior or junior—throughout the world.

Because of the uniformity of rules, soccer is truly an international sport. The rules are laid down by FIFA, the governing body of soccer around the world, but a certain amount of flexibility is permitted.

American high schools and colleges differ from most teams around the world in their rules concerning substitutions, deployment of referees, and other facets of the game. FIFA also gave the NASL permission (through the USSF) to use a modified offside rule. In 1973 the NASL introduced an extra line running the width of the field 35 yards from each goal. This line marks the offside zone, replacing the midfield stripe. In games where an NASL team competes against a club from another nation, however, the standard rules apply. (For a complete explanation of offside, see Law XI.)

After nearly a hundred years of trial by experience, the laws now cover almost every event that might possibly happen during a game, but they are not unduly complicated. Clubhouse lawyers are not as active in soccer as in some other sports. To get a good idea of what soccer is all about, let us look at all 17 laws.*

Law I
The Field of Play

The entire first law concerns the playing field (see page 106), the condition of which is the responsibility of the home team. The dimensions of the playing field can vary, perhaps because the game was born in England, where the attitude toward certain formalities is casual. The playing field, or *pitch* as it is

*The complete laws and the decisions of the International Board, which has the power to amend or alter the laws, are printed in Appendix B. The changes that have been introduced in the United States at the professional, collegiate, and scholastic levels may also be found in Appendix B.

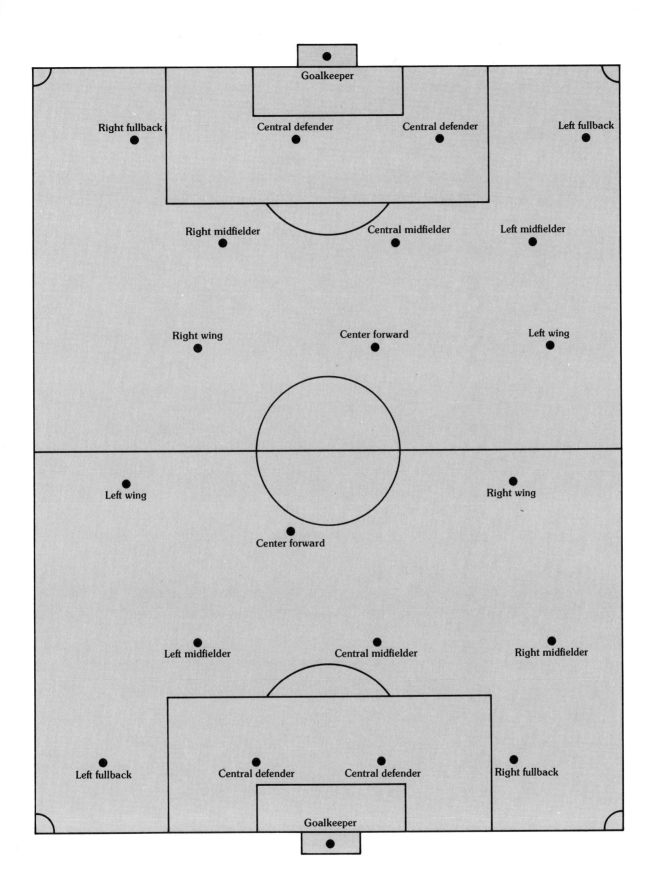

The starting lineup.

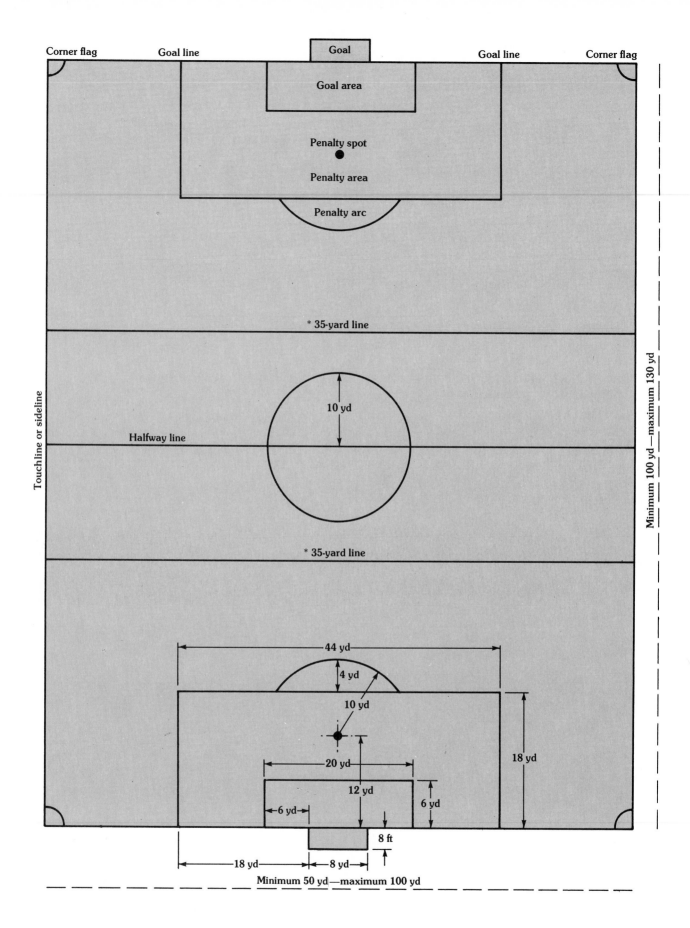

The field of play. (With the permission of FIFA, the NASL marks two extra lines on its fields, 35 yards in from each goal line. The lines can run the full width of the field, and the offside rule is applied only on the goal side of these two lines.)

called in England, can range from 100 to 130 yards in length and from 50 to 100 yards in width. However, length must always exceed width. A playing field 115 yards long and 75 yards wide is now generally considered the most desirable.

No variation is permitted in the size of the *goal*—8 feet high by 8 yards long—or the surrounding *penalty area,* which is 44 yards wide by 18 yards long and is nicknamed *the 18* or *the box.* Within this penalty area, 12 yards into the field from the midpoint of the goal, is the *penalty spot,* the point from which all penalty kicks (see Law XIV) are taken. During a penalty kick all players except the kicker and the goalkeeper are excluded from the penalty area and the *penalty arc*—the semicircle at the top of the penalty area, a radius of 10 yards from the penalty spot. This arc is not part of the penalty area; the only time it has any significance is during a penalty kick. The penalty area is important primarily because it is the only part of the field where the goalkeeper may use his hands and because fouls and misconduct in the penalty area result in a penalty kick, where there is a good chance that a goal will be scored.

Another marked-off section of the field is the *goal area*—the 6- by 20-yard space immediately in front of each goal. Goal kicks (see Law XVI) are taken within this area, which is also known as *the 6.* Corner kicks (Law XVII) are taken within the arcs at each corner of the field. The radius of these arcs is 1 yard from the corner point of the field.

In international soccer the *halfway line* in the center of the field serves as the guideline for offside (see Law XI). In the NASL 2 extra lines 35 yards from the opposing goal lines serve this purpose. In all circumstances the center circle (radius, 10 yards) marks off the area where opposing players may not be during a kickoff.

At each end of the field are goalposts that may be either round or square with nets that may be nylon or cotton. Goalposts and crossbars must be the same width, no more than 5 inches.

Law II
The Ball

The ball is spherical, and its outer casing must be made of leather or another approved material. The circumference of the ball can be no more than 28 inches and no less than 27 inches. The weight of the ball at the start of the game should be no more than 16 ounces and no less than 14 ounces. The pressure should be equal to 1 atmosphere, or 15 pounds per square inch (1 kilogram per square centimeter) at sea level. The ball should not be changed during the game unless authorized by the referee. In NASL games, there are many ball changes; the referee authorizes 3 or 4 balls before the game begins, and these are used throughout to speed up the game.

It is the duty of the home team to supply the ball, see that it is fully inflated, and make sure there are several other balls on hand in case something happens to the game ball.

Almost all soccer balls are now fitted with a valve, and they are a pleasure to make contact with. A few years ago balls were fitted with laces and players were reluctant to head them.

Old-timers love to tell the story about a center forward and two wingers who played for the national team of England. The center forward, a tall, husky man named Stan Mortensen, was superb at heading the ball from crosses

Soccer equipment has changed over the years. The ball with laces (below) was not as easy to head as is the modern ball (bottom).

by Stanley Matthews, perhaps the most gifted dribbler in soccer. (Matthews was later knighted for "services to football.") When Matthews retired and another winger, Tom Finney, took his place, Mortensen continued to score goals with his head. One day someone asked Mortensen whose crosses were better, Stanley Matthews' or Tom Finney's.

"Stan's," said Mortensen.

"Why?" he was asked.

"Because Stan crosses it with the laces facing the other way."

Law III
The Players

The rule states in part that a game "shall be played by two teams, each consisting of not more than eleven players, one of whom shall be the goalkeeper."

With the exception of the goalkeeper, Law III says nothing about the actual positions of the players. Years ago most teams played like a rugby team of today. The players ran around in bunches and tried to advance the ball by dribbling. When it was realized that a kicked ball traveled faster than a dribbled ball, the passing game came to life; players were gradually withdrawn from the pack to wait for passes. Someone had to cover the players waiting for the ball and create depth and coordination between defense and attack. Thus, fullbacks and halfbacks came into being.

Law III also deals with substitutions. There was a time when no substitutions were allowed in soccer, but this is no longer true. In most countries teams are allowed to make 2 substitutions during a game. Substitutions are made at the halfway line during a stoppage in the game. The referee must be informed of the proposed substitution before it is made. Most teams at the top level make changes at intermission and toward the end of the game. Substitutions are unlimited at the collegiate and interscholastic levels in the United States, where players are substituted freely, with the same players going in and out several times. A player who has been removed from a game at the professional level cannot reenter the game.

If a player is *sent off* (thrown out of the game) by the *referee* in accordance with Law XII, his team cannot replace him and must play a man short. Players are sent off for violent conduct or serious foul play and for using abusive language.

Law IV
Players' Equipment

The usual equipment consists of a jersey or shirt, shorts, stockings, and shoes or boots. The boots must conform to certain standards. The bars must be made of leather or rubber and must be transverse and flat, not less than one half inch in width and rounded at the corners. The studs must be made of leather, rubber, aluminum, plastic, or a similar material. They must be solid and not less than one half inch in diameter. Combined bars and studs can be used, provided that the bars and studs are used on the heels or soles do not project more than three-quarters of an inch.

Few soccer players devote enough time and attention to their shoes, but shoes can make an important contribution to the way an individual plays and should thus be purchased and maintained with care. Players should make

Playing through a hard-fought soccer game with only minimal substitutions can be exhausting for the players, even those who are in tiptop shape, like Art Welsh of San Jose. *(George Tiedemann)*

(Top left) **An excellent illustration of two different kinds of soccer shoes. Formoso (left) is wearing shoes with many small studs, which are effective on artificial turf. Bolota (right) is wearing shoes with fewer, larger studs, which are best for grass.** *(Jerry Liebman)*

(Top right) **Adi Dassler (far left) invented replaceable studs for soccer shoes and many other improvements in athletic equipment. His Adidas line is known throughout the world. Here he is shown with some of the members of the West German team that won the World Cup in 1954.**

(Bottom left) **Alan Mayer is the only goalkeeper in the NASL who wears a helmet. However, more and more goalies, especially at the interscholastic level, are now wearing some kind of protective equipment.** *(John W. Albino)*

(Bottom right) **A number of players young and old consider shinguards a pain in the leg. But many wear them, including pros like these playing in a game between the Chicago Sting and the Cosmos.** *(Jerry Liebman)*

sure of a comfortable fit, remembering that game shoes will most likely be worn over undersocks and thick stockings. Applying plenty of conditioner to the shoes—except to the top cap—will keep the leather soft and pliable. It is essential to remove all mud and dirt from soccer shoes after a match, even if this means washing the shoes. After being washed, the shoes must be allowed to dry slowly, not in front of a fire or near any other source of heat. If they dry too fast, the leather will probably crack.

Since comfort and service are the two main requirements for soccer boots, boots should not be laced too tightly or loosely. A well-laced boot will give support around the instep, where the main propelling force is applied.

Goalkeepers must wear jerseys or shirts of a different color from that of the other players. They are also permitted to wear long pants, hats to protect their eyes from the sun, and gloves. With permission a few goalkeepers wear special masks or helmets, especially at the interscholastic level. One NASL goalie who plays with a helmet is Alan Mayer of San Diego.

Shinguards should be worn by all players, especially the young and inexperienced. Many players complain that shinguards are quite uncomfortable but shinguards have prevented many injuries. Many players began to wear shinguards only after being injured. As many coaches of younger players have said, "If the likes of Pelé wear shinguards, so should everyone else."

Laws V and VI
Referees and Linesmen

In no other sport does a referee have as much power as in soccer, where he is even the timekeeper. Although there are linesmen patrolling the sidelines to enforce the throw-in and offside rules, the referee can ignore or overrule their calls. He is the boss, and many decisions in soccer rest on the "subjective opinion of the referee." Naturally, this can lead to arguments and even fights, but the referee's decision is final and must be respected by players and fans alike. In the vast majority of cases he is correct despite what fans may say about him the next day.

Most arguments in soccer are caused by ignorance of the laws. Many fans (and players) denounce an official's decisions because they do not understand the rules of play. The moral is: Do not argue with a referee unless you know what you are talking about, and even then wait until tempers haved cooled.

Soccer games throughout the world are governed by 1 referee, but in interscholastic and intercollegiate games in the United States there are 2 referees. However, in many years of watching soccer I have never seen a referee disagree with his partner, even if the one making the call was 50 yards from the play and the other was only a few feet away.

Another example of cooperation is the relationship between the referee and the linesmen. They must work together smoothly and never give the impression of disagreement. If the referee sometimes appears to ignore a linesman, it does not necessarily mean that he is not aware of what is going

(Left) The referee is master of the field, and his decision is final. Here referee Ken Burns lays down the law. *(Peter Robinson)*

(Right) Gordon Hill has been the best official in all the years that the NASL has been in existence. His method of verbally intimidating players is unique . . . and effective. *(George Tiedemann)*

on. It may simply mean that he disagrees with the linesman and is making the call himself. In their turn, linesmen must take their cue from the referee to avoid anticipating or contradicting his calls. Tempers flare quickly when fans or players see the officials disagreeing.

The referee's job begins even before the game starts. He is usually on the field well before a match to make sure that everything is in good order. The state of the grounds must be suitable. If the field is in a condition that might endanger the players, the referee can halt the proceedings. The linesmen are also on the field before the start of play, inspecting the nets to make sure that there are no holes and that they are properly pegged down. In the meantime, the referee checks the field's markings.

Nothing can be left to chance. In the 1974 World Cup final between West Germany and the Netherlands, the referee was John Taylor, an Englishman. Before the game, which was held in Munich's Olympic Stadium on Sunday, July 7, there was the usual confusion and excitement. Hundreds of photographers were running around. Officials from West Germany, the Netherlands, and FIFA were on hand, along with a band from Canada, a 2000-member choir, and of course both teams. Referee Taylor remained calm and took command of the situation without even blowing his whistle. He noticed that one of the corner flags was missing and stopped everything until it was replaced.

Once the game begins, it's up to the referee to maintain control. The best way to do this is to call all obvious infringements of the rules, especially at the beginning. If the players get the idea that anything goes, the match will degenerate into a brawl. However, many observers believe that the whistle should be used sparingly throughout the game, especially when minor infractions are involved. In games that are of only local importance, such as games between teams of youngsters, minor violations can be overlooked to maintain the even flow of play. There are also people who hold that if the referee is involved less in the game, fewer plays and calls will be disputed.

Most fans and players agree that the referee should use the whistle as little as possible in cases where the victim of the foul or infraction retains possession of the ball. The law states that the referee shall "refrain from penalizing in cases where he is satisfied that, by doing so, he would be giving an advantage to the offending team." Unfortunately, this rule is not always followed in professional games in the United States, and the situation is even more extreme in amateur and interscholastic competition. Many amateur officials appear to be unaware that such a rule exists, although continuing play is often the best way of punishing an aggressor whose primary aim in committing a foul was to stop the game.

Regardless of the individual referee's approach to the enforcement of the law, it is essential for him to be close to the center of the play throughout the game. The best way to distinguish victim from villain is to be an eyewitness to the event. That is why referees must be in top physical condition at all times. In most countries they are required to retire before the age of 50.

Nowhere is the referee's job more onerous than in international competition. Emotions run high, and language problems create many possibilities for misunderstanding and dispute. For games between national teams or clubs from different countries, the officials are usually selected from a neutral country unless the teams involved both approve the use of their own nations' officials. In all official games between national teams—such as World Club qualifying games—the referees are appointed by FIFA, which maintains a list of

(Top) The referee can tell anyone on the field to be quiet, even someone named Pele. (Pepsico International)

(Bottom) A referee cannot have an eyewitness view of the action unless he moves around the field quickly as the play shifts from side to side and end to end. (Jerry Liebman)

An NASL referee illustrating some of the most often used signals during a game. *(NASL Marketing)*

highly qualified international referees. In these qualifying games the referee and linesmen may all be from the same neutral nation. In the final round of the World Cup, however, the referee and linesmen must come from different countries. Thus in the game for third place between Poland and Brazil in the 1974 World Cup, the referee was from Italy, one linesman was from Iran, and one linesman was from England.

The referee uses a set of signals to communicate his decisions quickly and efficiently to the players and fans. If he whistles and raises his hand over his head, for example, he has awarded an indirect free kick. When his legs are together and his hands are near his ears, it means that a throw-in was executed improperly. (See diagram above for some signals used by the referee in professional games.)

Because referees occupy a key position in soccer, they must often bear the brunt of criticism from players, fans, and others involved in the game. Many referees have been manhandled, assaulted, and even beaten unmercifully; one or two have died as a result. However, there is no shortage of referees, and most perform better than one would expect. According to Gordon Hill, an articulate Englishman who many believe is the best referee the NASL has ever had, the referee has done his job well when he can leave the field unnoticed at the end of the game.

Laws VII and VIII
Duration of the Game and Start of Play

The standard soccer game consists of two 45-minute halves, unless the competing teams agree on some other limit. (Most high schools in America play four 12-minute periods.)

The clock does not stop when the referee calls an infraction or the ball goes out of bounds. Time is called, however, when a player is injured or a team makes a substitution. The referee signals for the clock to stop by crossing his arms in the shape of the letter X.

Before the start of the game, the referee and the captains of each team meet in the center of the field. After the traditional handshake, the referee tosses a coin for the captain of the visiting team to call. Whoever wins the toss can either choose his team's end or elect to kick off. On the rare occasions when the winner elects to kick off, the other team has the choice of ends. Generally, a captain has a definite preference about which goal to defend because of considerations such as wind direction and speed, position of the sun, slope of the field, and so on. When the choice of ends would bring no benefit to a team, a good captain will elect to kick off. Optimists regard this as the only kickoff they will have in any particular match because after a goal has been scored, the ball is put back into play by a member of the team that gave up the goal. Ends are changed at halftime and that kickoff is made by a player from the team that did not kick off at the start of the game.

The kickoff takes place at the center of the field, with the teams lined up in their respective halves. Players may not cross the line until the ball has been kicked because play begins at that moment and not with the referee's signal or whistle. The kickoff man, generally the center forward, must kick the ball into the opponents' half of the field and another player must touch it before he can play it again. Backward passes are not allowed at the kickoff. The ball must travel at least its own circumference (28 inches) before a second player can touch it. Failure to do so constitutes only a minor infringement, but it does occur at the youth level. The usual kickoff strategy is to make a short forward pass in order to retain possession and work the ball down to the opponents' goal as quickly as possible.

When extra time—such as sudden-death or regular overtime—must be played at the conclusion of regulation time, the whole starting procedure must be carried out afresh, with the captains again tossing a coin for the choice of ends and the kickoff.

Laws IX and X
Balls in and out of Play and Methods of Scoring

The ball is out of play when the *whole* ball has crossed the goal line or sideline on the ground or in the air. Similarly, a goal is scored when the *whole* ball has passed over the goal line "between the goal-posts and under the cross-bar."

When the ball crosses the sideline, it is put back into play by a throw-in (see Law XV) from a player of the team that did not touch the ball last before it went out of bounds. When a ball goes over the goal line after being touched by a player of the attacking team, it is put back into play by the defending team by means of a goal kick (Law XVI). If someone from the defending team is the last to touch the ball before it crosses the goal line, the attacking team puts it back in play by taking a corner kick (see Law XVII) from the side where the ball crossed the goal line.

Law XI
Offside

Soccer's most difficult rule is the offside rule, which says that a player is offside when he is closer to the opponents' goal line than the ball at the moment the ball is played unless:

1. He is in his own half of the field.

2. There are at least 2 opponents closer to their own goal line than he is.

3. The ball last touched an opponent or was last played by an opponent.

4. He received the ball directly from a goal kick, a corner kick, or a throw-in, or after it was dropped by the referee.

This law leads to the vast majority of arguments. It is the one law that *every player and spectator* should read carefully and study in all its implications. It should be distinguished from the offside rule in hockey, which is based on where the player is when he receives the puck. The deciding factor in soccer is not, as many people believe, where the player is when he receives the ball but where he *was* when the ball was last kicked by one of his teammates. Let us analyze each clause closely.

The law states that a player is offside when he is closer to his opponents' goal than to the ball at the moment the ball is played. Thus, if an attacker gives the ball to a teammate by means of a backward pass or a pass that runs exactly parallel to the goal line, the receiver of the ball cannot be offside (see Diagrams A and B at top of opposite page. See also other diagrams in connection with offside on pages 115 to 120.)

There are four important exceptions to this rule. A player is offside unless:

1. He is in his own half of the field. This is not a common occurrence, but it can happen to a forward if his opponents are throwing everything into the attack.

2. There are 2 opponents closer to their own goal line than he is. Until 1925 the law specified that 3 of his opponents had to be closer to the goal line, but a number of clever defenses caught forwards so often that the game tended to go far too slowly. The change in this law accelerated the tempo of the game and made offside decisions much easier for the referee.

3. The ball last touched an opponent or was last played by an opponent. This is very difficult to interpret in practice because in most cases a referee will blow the whistle a few seconds earlier to penalize the receiver for "interfering with the play."

A.—OFF-SIDE

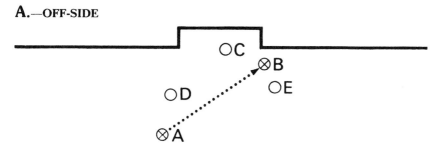

Clear pass to one of same side

A has run the ball up, and having **D** in front passes to **B**. **B** is off-side because he is in front of **A** and there are not two opponents between him and the goal-line when the ball is passed by **A**.

If **B** waits for **E** to fall back before he shoots, this will not put him on-side, because it does not alter his position with relation to **A** at the moment the ball was passed by **A**.

Some points in connection with offside.

NOTE

The players marked ⊗ are attacking the goal and those marked ○ are defending

Direction of movement of ball:

Direction of movement of player:

B.—NOT OFF-SIDE

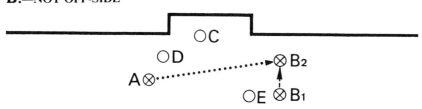

Clear pass to one of same side *(continued)*

A has run the ball up, and having **D** in front passes across the field. **B** runs from position **1** to position **2**. **B** is not off-side because at the moment the ball was passed by **A** he was not in front of the ball, and had two opponents between him and the goal-line.

C.—OFF-SIDE

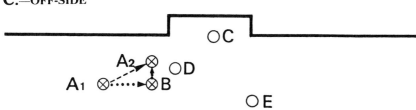

Clear pass to one of same side *(continued)*

A and **B** make a passing run up the wing. **A** passes the ball to **B** who cannot shoot because he has **D** in front. **A** then runs from position **1** to position **2** where he receives the ball from **B**. **A** is off-side because he is in front of the ball and he had not two opponents between him and the goal-line when the ball was played by **B**.

D.—OFF-SIDE

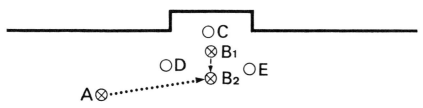

Running back for the ball

A centres the ball. **B** runs back from position **1** to position **2**, and then dribbles between **D** and **E** and scores. **B** is off-side because he is in front of the ball and he had not two opponents between him and the goal-line at the moment the ball was played by **A**.

E.—OFF SIDE

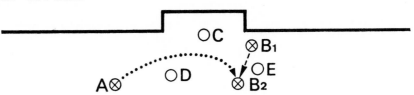

Running back for ball *(continued)*

A makes a high shot at goal, and the wind and screw carry the ball back. **B** runs from position **1** to position **2** and scores. **B** is off-side because he is in front of the ball and he had not two opponents between him and the goal-line at the moment the ball was played by **A**.

F.—OFF SIDE

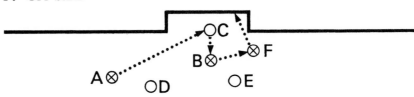

Shot at goal returned by goalkeeper C

A shoots at goal. The ball is played by **C** and **B** obtains possession, but slips and passes the ball to **F** who scores. **F** is off-side because he is in front of **B**, and when the ball was passed by **B** he had not two opponents between him and the goal-line.

G.—NOT OFF SIDE

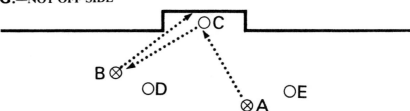

Shot at goal returned by goalkeeper *(continued)*

A shoots at goal. The ball is played out by **C** but **B** obtains possession and scores. **B** was in front of the ball and did not have two opponents between him and the goal-line when the ball was played by **A**, but he is not off-side because the ball has been last played by an opponent, **C**.

H.—OFF SIDE

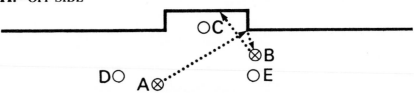

Ball rebounding from goal-posts or cross-bar

A shoots for goal and the ball rebounds from the goal-post into play. **B** secures the ball and scores. **B** is off-side because the ball is last played by **A**, a player of his own side, and when **A** played it **B** was in front of the ball and did not have two opponents between him and the goal-line.

I.—OFF SIDE

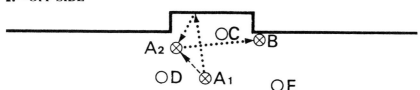

Ball rebounding from goal-posts or cross-bar *(continued)*

A shoots for goal and the ball rebounds from the cross-bar into play. **A** follows up from position **1** to position **2**, and then passes to **B** who has run up on the other side. **B** is off-side because the ball is last played by **A**, a player of his own side, and when **A** played it **B** was in front of the ball and did not have two opponents between him and the goal-line. If **A** had scored himself at the second attempt, instead of passing to **B**, it would have been a goal.

J.—NOT OFF SIDE

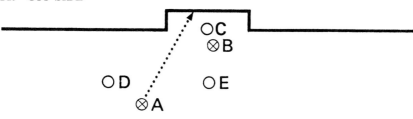

Ball touching an opponent

A shoots at goal. **D** runs from position **1** to position **2** to intercept the ball, but it glances off his foot to **B** who scores. **B** is not off-side because, although he is in front of the ball and has not two opponents between him and the goal-line the ball was last played by an opponent, **D**.

K.—OFF SIDE

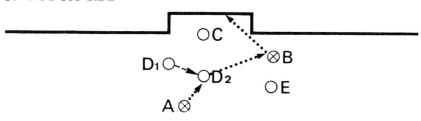

Obstructing the goalkeeper

A shoots for goal and scores. **B**, however, obstructs **C** so that he cannot get at the ball. The goal must be disallowed, because **B** is in an off-side position and may not touch the ball himself, nor in any way whatever interfere with an opponent.

L.—OFF SIDE

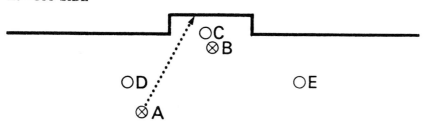

Obstructing the goalkeeper *(continued)*

A shoots for goal. **B** runs in while the ball is in transit and prevents **C** playing it properly. **B** is off-side because he is in front of **A** and has not two opponents between him and the goal-line when **A** plays the ball. When in this position **B** may not touch the ball himself, nor in any way whatever interfere with an opponent.

M.—OFF SIDE

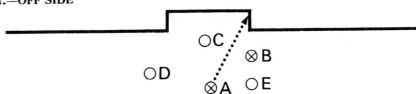

Obstructing an opponent other than the goalkeeper

A shoots for goal. **B** prevents **E** running in to intercept the ball. **B** is off-side because he is in front of **A** and has not two opponents between him and the goal-line when **A** plays the ball. When in this position **B** may not touch the ball himself, nor in any way whatever interfere with an opponent.

N.—OFF SIDE

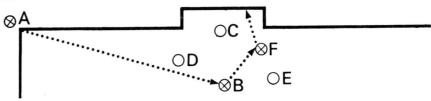

After a corner-kick

A takes a corner-kick and the ball goes to **B**. **B** shoots for goal and as the ball is passing through, **F** touches it. **F** is off-side because after the corner-kick has been taken the ball is last played by **B**, a player of his own side, and when **B** played it **F** was in front of the ball and had not two opponents between him and the goal-line.

O.—NOT OFF SIDE

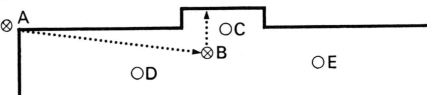

After a corner-kick (continued)

A takes a corner-kick and the ball goes to **B**, who puts it through goal. **B** has only one opponent between him and the goal-line, but he is not off-side because a player cannot be off-side from a corner-kick.

P.—NOT OFF SIDE

After a corner-kick (continued)

A takes a corner-kick and the ball glances off **D** and goes to **B**, who puts it through goal. **B** is not off-side because the ball was last played by an opponent, **D**.

Q.—NOT OFF SIDE

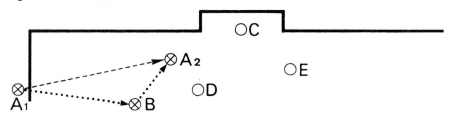

After a throw-in from the touch-line

A throws to **B** and then runs from touch-line to position **A2**. **B** passes the ball to **A** in position **2**. **A** is off-side because he is in front of the ball and has not two opponents between him and the goal-line when the ball is passed forward to him by **B**.

R.—OFF SIDE

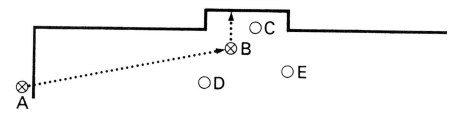

After a throw-in from the touch-line *(continued)*

A throws the ball to **B**. Although **B** is in front of the ball and has not two opponents between him and the goal line, he is not off-side because a player cannot be off-side from a throw-in.

S.—OFF SIDE

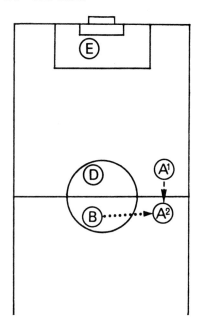

T.—NOT OFF SIDE

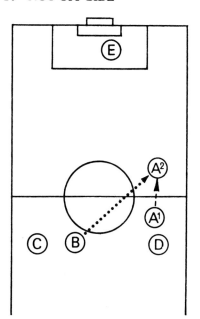

A player cannot put himself on-side by running back into his own half of the field of play

If **A** is in his opponents' half of the field of play, and is off-side in position when **B** last played the ball, he cannot put himself on-side by moving back into his own half of the field of play.

A player within his own half of the field of play is not off-side when he enters his opponents' half of the field of play

If **A** is in his own half of the field of play he is on-side, although he is in front of the ball and there are not two opponents nearer their own goal-line when **B** last played the ball. **A** is therefore not off-side when he enters his opponents' half of the field of play.

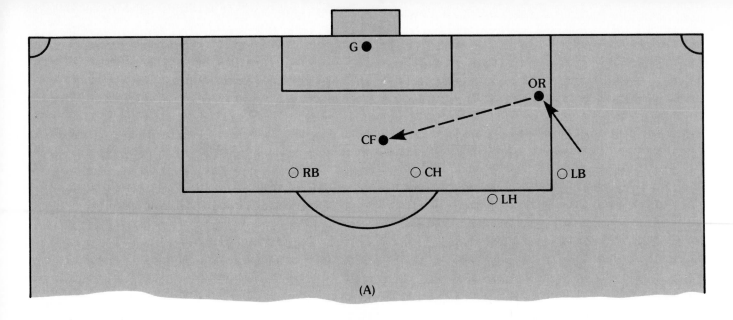

(A)

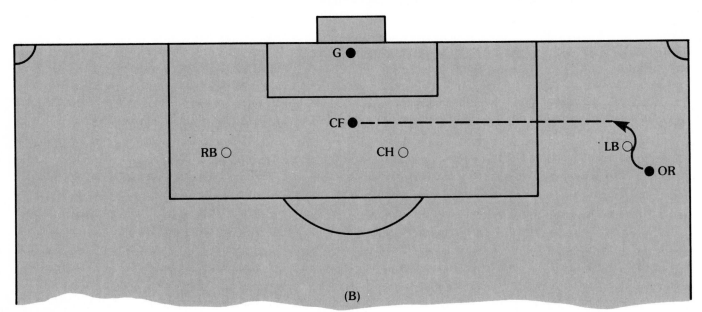

(B)

4. He received the ball:
   (a) Directly from a goal kick. This presupposes that unless the goalkeeper is an extremely powerful kicker, all the defenders have advanced into their opponents' half of the field, except, of course, the defending goalkeeper.
   (b) Directly from a corner kick. Since a corner kick must be taken from within 1 yard of the goal line, for all practical purposes such a kick is regarded as a square pass, parallel with the goal line. As shown above, no attacker can be offside if the ball is played exactly parallel to the goal line.
   (c) Directly from a throw-in. This makes an attacking throw-in more valuable because no attacker can be offside when the throw is taken.
   (d) After it was dropped by the referee. At certain times, such as when play has been suspended for an injury, the game is restarted by having the referee drop the ball between two op-

posing players. Players cannot be offside when the ball is dropped.

Bear in mind that a player should not be penalized unless he gains an advantage from being offside. Theoretically, if you find yourself offside, stand still and do not interfere in any way with the play. The word *theoretically* was used deliberately because in actual practice there are as many interpretations of the word *interfere* as there are referees.

Law XII
Fouls and Misconduct

Law XII deals with players who act illegally, whether intentionally or unintentionally, against other players. After an infringement, the referee awards the victim a free kick from the place where the infringement occurred. As explained in Law XIII, free kicks are divided into 2 types—direct and indirect—depending on the infraction. Goals can be scored from direct free kicks, but with indirect free kicks another player must touch or play the ball before a goal can be scored.

Direct free kicks are awarded for 9 *intentional* offenses against opposing players: kicking, tripping, jumping, charging in a violent manner, charging from behind, striking or attempting to strike, holding, pushing, and handling the ball.

If any of these intentional infringements are committed by the defending team inside its own penalty area, the opposing team is awarded a penalty kick (Law XIV), which is almost a sure goal. Thus, referees hesitate to award a penalty kick in questionable circumstances.

Indirect free kicks are given for more technical offenses such as: (1) playing in a manner the referee considers dangerous, such as charging the goal-

Two examples of dangerous play. *(George Tiedemann, Richard Pilling)*

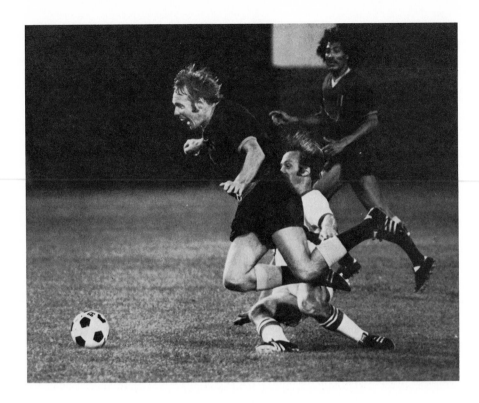

Tripping an opponent generally calls for a foul. *(George Tiedemann)*

keeper at the wrong time, (2) charging (shouldering an opponent) when the ball is not within playing distance, or (3) intentionally obstructing by running between the opponent and the ball.

To avoid misunderstandings and errors that could affect the outcome of a match, referees and players should have a thorough knowledge of all parts of Law XII. In addition, the referee has the difficult task of making an immediate decision about whether a foul is intentional. The ball may strike a player on the arm by chance; on such occasions a good referee will not blow the whistle because no unfair purpose was intended. (Players and spectators should note that the common cry of "Hands" applies to both hands and arms.)

Admirers of Pelé will not admit it, but he was a master at pretending he had been fouled intentionally when he had actually taken a dive. Pelé's teammates on the Cosmos often attempted to imitate his acting, but the good referees never took the bait; perhaps no one could really imitate Pelé.

There are two clauses in Law XII that deal specifically with cautioning the goalkeeper. One case occurs when the goalkeeper indulges in tactics which the referee feels are designed to hold up the game and waste time, giving an advantage to the goalkeeper's team. The other case occurs when the goalkeeper "takes more than 4 steps whilst holding, bouncing or throwing the ball in the air and catching it again without releasing it so that it is played by another player."

The second clause is constantly violated by goalkeepers and overlooked by referees, particularly at the higher levels of soccer. The only level where I have seen this law enforced regularly is in children's soccer, where the referee, very likely a graduate of a coaches' program, shows off his knowledge of the laws by penalizing this infringement.

Law XII also states that when a player has been guilty of certain offenses, he can be cautioned or ejected (thrown out) at the discretion of the referee.

When a referee displays a *yellow card* to a player, he is cautioning that

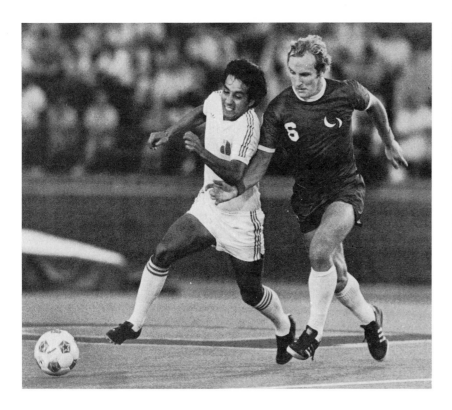

Two examples (top) of fair charging with the shoulder. In such cases a foul should not be called. *(George Tiedemann, John W. Albino)*

Some players admit their guilt quietly, as did Carlos Caszely of Chile during 1974 World Cup play (below left). Others, such as Dave Robb, formerly of the Tampa Bay Rowdies, react quite negatively (below right).

player. A yellow card is a warning that is usually shown when a player: (1) enters or leaves the playing field without permission, (2) persistently breaks the rules, (3) dissents by word or action from any decision by the referee, or (4) is guilty of ungentlemanly conduct. In addition to showing the yellow card, the referee awards an indirect free kick to the opposing team.

When a referee shows a *red card* to a player, the player is sent off automatically without further warning. A player is ejected from the game if he: (1) is guilty of violent or serious foul play, (2) uses foul or abusive language, or (3) persists in misconduct after having received a caution. A referee does not have to warn or caution a player before ejecting him.

Law XIII
Free Kick

As discussed in Law XII, a player is awarded a free kick if the opposing team violates certain rules. Depending on the offense, the free kick may be *direct* or *indirect*. Different procedures are followed depending on whether a free kick is taken inside or outside the penalty area.

When a player takes a free kick *outside* his own penalty area, all opposing players must stay at least 10 yards from the ball until it is in play—has traveled a distance equal to its circumference.

If a defending player moves within 10 yards of the ball before a free kick is taken, the referee will delay the kick until the player is properly positioned. Also, the ball must be stationary when a free kick is taken, and the kicker may not play the ball a second time until it has been touched or played by another player. If this rule is violated, an indirect free kick is taken by a player on the opposing team from the spot where the infringement occurred.

When a player takes a free kick *inside* his own penalty area, all opposing players must remain outside that area and no closer than 10 yards from the ball. The goalkeeper cannot "receive the ball into his hands, in order that he may thereafter kick it into play." He can of course deflect it or take other

Franz Beckenbauer executing a direct free kick from outside the penalty area and scoring the only goal in a game at Giants Stadium against Tulsa. *(Ed Clough)*

(Top) Goalkeeper Bob Rigby and all his teammates on the Philadelphia Atoms line up between the goalposts to form a human wall against an indirect free kick. (George Tiedeman)

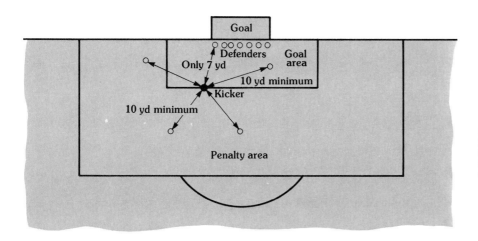

(Bottom) Diagram of a free kick taken fewer than 10 yards away from the goal. Except for the defenders on the goal line between the goalposts, all other defenders must be at least 10 yards away from the ball.

actions to keep it out of the goal.

When an indirect free kick is awarded against the defending team within its penalty area, it often takes place 7 or 8 yards from the goal. This makes it impossible for the defenders to remain at least 10 yards away from the ball, the traditional distance for a free kick.

In this case the defenders are permitted to stand on the goal line (see diagram above) between the goalposts. Since a goal cannot be scored directly—remember, it is an *indirect* kick—the kicker must make the awkward decision to either blast the ball into the wall of players, hoping that the ball will carom off someone into the net, or try to place the ball to an unmarked teammate so that he can shoot. Except for the defenders on the goal line between the goalposts, all other defenders must be at least 10 yards away from the ball.

Law XIV
Penalty Kick

As discussed in Law XII, a penalty kick is awarded to a player when the opposing team commits one of a number of specified violations in the penalty area. The kick itself is taken from the penalty spot 12 yards from the goal. At the time of the kick, all players must be within the field of play but outside the penalty area and at least 10 yards from the penalty spot. Until the ball is kicked, the goalkeeper must stand (without moving his feet) on the goal line between the goalposts. The ball must be kicked forward, and the kicker cannot play it a second time until it has been touched or played by another player. If a penalty kick is awarded in the last seconds before halftime or before the end of the game, the time of play is extended so that the kick can be taken.

Penalty kicks are not taken often. They represent a unique situation because only 2 players are involved—the kicker and the goalkeeper. Theoretically, the kicker has the advantage, but 1 out of every 4 penalty kicks is missed at the professional level. Still, if the kicker misses, he has committed an unforgivable error, and if the goalkeeper saves a penalty kick, he is feted as a hero.

The result of a match may well depend on a penalty kick, and it is important for players to learn this law in detail. Giorgio Chinaglia of the Cosmos once scored on a penalty kick but had to retake it because Dennis Tueart, a seasoned veteran, had moved into the penalty area before the kick was taken.

Law XV
Throw-in

The throw-in is the only play in soccer where a player other than the goalkeeper may use his hands. A throw-in takes place when the ball goes out of

Most penalty kicks result in goals, as in this game between Harvard and Brown.

Pelé displays the proper way of throwing the ball back into play after it has gone out of bounds on the sidelines. *(Pepsico International)*

bounds on the sidelines either on the ground or in the air. It is awarded against the team that last touched the ball before it went out of bounds. At the moment of delivering the ball, the thrower must face the field of play, and part of each foot must be on the sideline or the ground outside the sideline. The thrower must use both hands to hold the ball and must deliver it from behind and over his head.

There are a few points to remember about the throw-in. A goal cannot be scored directly from a throw-in. Also, players must learn to use both hands when making a throw-in. If one arm supplies all the power while the other merely guides the ball, it will be a foul throw and the ball will be awarded to the opposition. If an opposing player dances about or gesticulates in order to distract or impede the thrower, the referee will warn the offender.

Law XVI
Goal Kicks

When a ball that goes over the goal line has been last touched by the attacking team, the defenders are awarded a goal kick. The kick is taken from within the half of the goal area—the 20- by 6-yard box in front of the goal— closest to where the ball went out of bounds. The goal kick may be taken by any player including the goalkeeper. The ball is in play once it leaves the penalty area. The goal kick can be a short pass just outside the penalty area or a long kick downfield.

There are a few restrictions. The goalkeeper cannot "receive the ball into his hands from a goal-kick in order that he may thereafter kick it into play." The ball must be stationary when it is kicked, and the kicker cannot replay the ball until another player has touched it.

A goal kick is an opportunity to build an attack from the rear, but teams rarely take advantage of the chance. They usually have the kicker send the ball long downfield, thus putting their possession of the ball in jeopardy. There are teams with skillful defenders, however, who rarely kick the ball downfield. They rely on short, well-aimed passes that virtually guarantee their possession of the ball all the way downfield.

While a goal kick is being taken, the players of the opposing team must remain outside the penalty area. If the kicker touches the ball again before it has left the penalty area, the kick must be retaken. If the kicker touches the ball again after it has left the penalty area but before it has been touched or played by another player, an indirect free kick is awarded to the opposing team.

Law XVII
Corner Kick

A goal cannot be scored directly from a goal kick or throw-in, but it can be scored from a corner kick. A corner kick is awarded when a ball goes over the goal line after being last touched by a member of the defending team. The corner kick is taken from the corner closest to where the ball went over the goal line. The ball is placed within the corner area and must be kicked from that position. The corner flag cannot be removed while the kick is being taken, and players of the opposing team must be at least 10 yards from the ball until it is played.

There are two further points to note. The kicker is not allowed to play the ball a second time until someone else has touched it. And if the ball rebounds off the goalpost, the kicker is again not allowed to play it a second time. In either case a free kick will be awarded to the opposing team.

Corner kicks make for exciting plays, such as this action in a World Cup game in 1974 between West Germany and Australia.

Soccer Terminology

Soccer has its own special terminology. Several languages have made contributions, but English predominates. The player who guards the goal in soccer, for instance is called the *goalkeeper*. Another acceptable name is the *keeper,* short for *goalkeeper*. *Goalie* is also acceptable, but *goaltender* is definitely out. Another term that is often heard, particularly in interscholastic and youth games, is *offsides*. The word is *offside,* and it is singular.

ADVANTAGE   The situation in which play continues despite a foul because the victim or his teammate has retained possession of the ball.

BALANCE   The principle of defensive play that provides for defenders to be spread out over most of the width of the field to assure proper coverage of all vital space.

BICYCLE KICK   An over-the-head volley kick executed by swinging both feet high in the air.

BLOCK   To move in front of an opponent when the ball is within playing distance. This is not the same as *obstruction,* and a foul should not be called.

BOX   See *Penalty area*. It is sometimes called the *18-yard box* to distinguish it from the goal area, which is the 6-yard area directly in front of the goal.

CATENACCIO   The Italian word for chain. The term was used to describe the super defensive system devised by the Italians in the 1950s.

CAUTION   An official warning by the *referee* for a serious foul or unsportsmanlike conduct. The referee shows a yellow card to the player so that there can be no doubt that it is an official caution.

CENTER   To pass the ball from the side of the field into the penalty area.

CENTER BACK   A fullback who plays in the middle of the defense. His duty is usually to contain the opposing center forward, and he is also expected to assist the other fullbacks.

CENTER FORWARD   A forward who plays in the middle of the attack and is usually the spearhead of the attack. See also *Striker*.

CHARGE   To push an opponent off legally by shoulder-to-shoulder contact.

CHEST   To trap the ball or control it with the chest.

CHIP PASS   A method of lofting the ball by striking it sharply at the lowest point possible.

CLEARANCE   A throw or kick by the goalkeeper or a kick by a defender to get the ball away from the penalty area.

COMBINATION   (1) A play involving 2 or more players. (2) A series of passes and maneuvers.

CONTAIN   To limit the effectiveness of an opponent by restraining him and allowing him to operate only in the area you want.

CORNER KICK   A direct kick from the corner flag. It can be a short pass to a teammate or a long kick that reaches the goal area. The first is called a *short corner* and the second a *long corner*.

COUNTERATTACK   To initiate an attack immediately after dispossessing the opposition of the ball.

CROSS   See *Center*.

CUSHION   To soften the impact of the ball with the body, head, or feet to bring it under control.

DANGER ZONE   The space near the goal where a shot generally results in a goal.

DANGEROUS PLAY   Any action by a player that endangers the safety of another player. It is usually penalized by a direct free kick.

DEAD BALL   A ball not in play. A ball is not in play when it has wholly crossed the goal line or the sideline or when the game has been stopped by the referee. This does not mean that time has been called.

DEPTH   A synonym for *support* that refers to offensive as well as defensive play.

DRAW AN OPPONENT   To induce an opponent to leave his position or the player he is covering.

DRIBBLE   To advance the ball past opponents by using a series of short taps to move and control it.

DROP BALL   A ball dropped into play between two opposing players after a stoppage in the game for any reason other than the infringement of the laws.

EJECTION   Official dismissal from the game by the referee for flagrant violation of the laws or repeated violations following an earlier *Caution*. The referee shows a red card to the player, who must then leave the field. In most leagues ejection means suspension from one or more future games.

FAR POST   The goalpost farther from the player with the ball.

FIFA   Fédération Internationale de Football Association, the world governing body of soccer. Its headquarters are in Zurich, Switzerland.

FINAL TOUCH   See Finishing. The act of shooting or heading on goal or concluding an effort. Teams with finishing power can translate their efforts into goals.

FIRST-TIME   To pass or shoot on the player's first contact with the ball without first bringing it under control. See also *One-touch*.

FLICK PASS   A short, quick kick of the ball to a teammate.

FORWARD   An attacking player.

FOUL   Any infraction of the rules of soccer.

FREE KICK   A kick awarded when a member of the opposing team commits a foul. The ball is placed on the spot where the infraction occurred. All opposing players stand back at least 10 yards, and the team has a "free," or unhindered, kick at the ball. Free kicks can be direct or indirect. A *direct free kick* is awarded for more serious offenses, and it can be shot directly into goal. An *indirect free kick* is awarded for lesser fouls. In this case, at least 2 players including the player taking the kick must touch the ball before a goal can be scored.

FULLBACK   A defender.

GIVE-AND-GO   A pass to a teammate followed by a first-time return pass.

GOAL   (1) A goal is scored when the whole ball crosses the goal line between the goalposts and beneath the crossbar. A goal counts as 1 point for the attacking team, no matter which team puts it in. (2) The structure constituted by the goalposts and the crossbar.

GOAL AREA   The 6- by 20-yard area directly in front of the goal, from which all goal kicks are taken.

GOAL KICK   The kick awarded to the defending team whenever the ball has passed over the goal line after being last touched by an attacking player. The kick is taken within the half of the goal area closest to where the ball went over the goal line.

GOAL LINE   The line drawn at each end of the field of play.

HALFBACK   A midfield player.

HALF VOLLEY   A method of kicking the ball just as it hits the ground or starts to ascend after the bounce.

HALFWAY LINE   The line drawn in the middle of the field to divide it into halves.

HANDS   The foul committed when a player touches the ball with his hands or arms. The goalkeeper is allowed to use his hands within his penalty area.

HAT TRICK   The scoring of 3 goals by a player in a single game.

HEADING   To pass, score with, or control the ball by making contact with the head.

HOLD   To obstruct or hinder an opponent's movements by using the hands.

IMPROVISATION   The principle of play that allows players to adapt to any circumstance as it occurs.

INSIDE FORWARDS   The players positioned in the middle of the attacking line on either side of the center forward. There is an *inside right* and an *inside left*. In modern formations, the inside forwards and center forward are more commonly referred to as *strikers*.

INSWINGER   A cross or corner kick that curves toward the goal.

INTERCEPTION   The act of getting the ball before it reaches the intended receiver.

INTERNATIONAL   The title given to a player who has performed for his country's all-star or national team against foreign competition.

INTO TOUCH   A ball out of bounds.

JOCKEY   To contain an opponent, sometimes giving ground, while waiting for an opportunity to challenge for the ball.

KICKOFF   A place kick from the center of the field that is used to start play at the beginning of each half or period (in high schools) and restart the game after a goal has been scored.

LIBERO   The last man on defense in front of the goalkeeper. See also *Sweeper.*

LINESMEN   The two officials who assist the referee. They remain off the field of play on the sidelines.

LINKMEN   See *Midfielders.*

LOB   A high, soft kick taken on the volley that lifts the ball over the heads of the opponents.

MARK   To guard or shadow an opponent. This can be done tightly or loosely, depending on the tactics of a team.

MAN-TO-MAN   When a player marks a specific opponent.

MIDFIELDERS   The players positioned between the forward line and the defending back line whose job is primarily to link the two. They have both defending and attacking responsibilities and must be capable all-around players with a high level of fitness.

NEAR POST   The goalpost closer to the player with the ball.

OBSTRUCTION   To move into the path of an opponent when the ball is not within playing distance—a foul.

OFFSIDE   The foul committed when a player is closer to his opponent's goal line than is the ball at the moment the ball is played. For exceptions to this rule, see pages 114 and 120.

ONE-TOUCH   To pass the ball immediately without first controlling it. See also *First-time.*

ONE-TWO   See *Give-and-go.*

OUTSIDE PLAYERS   The right and left fullback, also the right and left wing.

OUTSWINGER   A corner kick or cross that curves or swings away from the goal.

OVERLAP   The attacking play a defender employs when he goes down the sideline past his own wing.

OWN GOAL   When a player accidentally puts the ball into his own goal. The goal is credited to the opposing team.

PASS   To move the ball from one player to another.

PENALTY   This word applies only to major infractions by the defending team inside its own penalty area that result in a penalty kick. It should never be used in connection with any other infraction or free-kick situation.

PENALTY ARC   An arc drawn around the penalty spot to keep all players 10 yards from the ball when a penalty kick is taken. It is not a part of the penalty area.

PENALTY AREA   The zone, 18 yards by 44 yards, in front of each goal.

PENALTY KICK   A direct free kick awarded when a foul is committed within the penalty area. It is taken from the penalty spot, with all players but the kicker and the defending goalkeeper outside the penalty area and 10 yards from the ball.

PENALTY SPOT   The spot 12 yards in front of the goal from which penalty kicks are taken.

PITCH   The field of play.

PLAYMAKER   A player who sets up scoring opportunities for his teammates.

READ THE GAME   To interpret the game or anticipate what will take place by watching a player or a specific situation.

REFEREE   The official in charge of the game. He is assisted by the linesmen but retains sole power of decision in all cases.

RESTART   To put the ball in play after a temporary stoppage.

RUNNING OFF THE BALL   (1) Getting into position when not in possession of the ball, (2) Continuous movement to escape close marking by an opponent.

SAVE   To stop an attempted goal by catching or deflecting the ball. It is usually done by the goalkeeper but can apply to any player.

SCISSORS KICK   See *Bicycle kick.*

SCREEN   To retain possession and protect the ball by keeping the body between the ball and an opponent.

SHIELD   To keep an opponent away from the ball by keeping yourself between him and the ball.

SHOOTOUT   The tie-breaking procedure used in NASL games when teams are tied after playing 2 sudden-death overtime periods. Five players from each team alternate in attempting to score, going up against the goalkeeper in a one-on-one situation.

SIDELINE   The line marking the boundary of the field on each side.

SKILL   The ability to perform a specific soccer technique such as dribbling or heading the ball.

SLIDING TACKLE   An attempt to kick the ball away from an opponent by sliding on the ground feet first and aiming at the ball.

SPACE   Open areas that can be exploited by the offense. *Deciding space* is in front of the goalmouth, and *important space* is on the flanks.

SQUARE PASS   A pass directly across the field to a teammate who is moving forward. It is often employed by a wing who is pinned on the sideline seeking the help of his halfback.

STOPPER   The defender who plays near or at the center of the fullback line.

STRIKER   The main attacking player; usually the center forward or the inside forwards.

STYLE OF PLAY   (1) The type of game—long or short passing, slow, determined, or aggressive that a team plays. (2) The placement of players on the field and the area of movement of each player.

SUDDEN DEATH   An extra period of play to break a tie, which ends when one team scores.

SUPPORT   To come from behind or alongside the man with the ball in order to establish numerical superiority around the ball. See also *Depth*.

SWEEPER   A defender who roams (usually) behind the fullbacks to pick up stray passes. See also *Libero*.

TACKLE   The skill of taking the ball from an opponent or causing him to lose control of it.

TECHNIQUE   The ability of a player to perform with the ball.

THROUGH-PASS   A pass through a group of opposing players to an onrushing teammate.

THROW-IN   An overhead throw from outside the sideline to put the ball back into play when it has crossed *into touch*. The ball is thrown with both hands over the head and both feet on the ground by a player from the team that did not last touch the ball before it went out.

TOUCHLINE   See *Sideline*.

TRAP   To control a ball with the feet, thighs, chest, or head.

TWO-ON-ONE   Two attacking players approaching one defender.

VOLLEY   To kick the ball while it is in flight.

WALL   A barrier of players positioned to assist the goalkeeper in his defense against free kicks near the goal.

WALL PASS   Interpassing between two teammates, with one acting as a rebounding wall to bypass an opponent.

WING   (1) The area of the field near the sidelines. (2) The outside right and outside left.

WORK RATE   The amount of running, both on and off the ball, by a player or team.

WORLD CUP   The world championship competition open to the national teams of all countries.

ZONE DEFENSE   A system in which each player has a designated area to protect.

5

Playing the Game

Because soccer is played with 22 players and 1 ball, the amount of time that each player has possession of the ball is minimal. Experts estimate that the average player will have the ball for approximately 3 minutes during an entire 90-minute game. A goalkeeper will probably have the ball less than that, and a midfielder more.

Each player must make the most of his possession of the ball and perform as efficiently as possible to help his team. Handling the ball in the course of a match, however, is only part of the total concept of how to play soccer.

A player's actions without the ball are as important as what he does when he has possession. Running without the ball, or off the ball, has become a vital part of modern soccer because it creates time and space for the player's teammates. In fact, the key terms in modern soccer are *time* and *space,* two words that are constantly on the lips of every coach and student of the game.

The more space a player has to work in, the more time he has to control a ball passed to him. With adequate space and time, he can play more effectively and generally make fewer errors that might result in losing the ball. Thus, time and space are interdependent. The more a player has of one, the more he has of the other. Attacking players in particular will note that the closer they get to the opposition's goal, the less space becomes available to them.

When they are on attack, players must utilize the space between and behind the defensive players. If the space is not there—if it is constantly being denied by the defense—an attacking player must create it by forcing a defender to move. This is where *running off the ball* becomes essential. If a forward makes a move, a defender's instinct is to follow. Although smart defenders quickly close the gap left by a teammate, that split second is really all that a skillful attacker needs to penetrate toward the goal.

One way of neutralizing an opponent and denying the defense enough time to set up is to accelerate the process of moving the ball from player to player. This can be achieved by touching the ball only once. This is called

(Top left) **The great English forward Bobby Charlton, quick to take advantage of just a little space between two opponents to move the ball toward the goal, in a 1967 match between England and Scotland.** *(Syndication International)*

(Top right) **Pelé loves to move the ball fast. Here he gets through an opening to receive a pass.**

one-touch, and it should be practiced in pairs and by the whole team in scrimmages. One-touch means that you have only one chance to touch the ball. It may involve stopping the ball for a teammate, pushing it a few feet or even inches or kicking it 50 yards downfield. Most of the time, however, one-touch is used in *give-and-go,* or *one-two,* situations where the exchange of a pass is necessary to get by an opponent.

One-touch soccer also serves as a means of changing the point of attack and moving the ball before defenders can adjust their positions. It is, therefore, the best means of creating space out of nothing. It is significant that the Brazilian national team has played one-touch soccer more effectively than any other world-class team. This has not happened accidentally; the Brazilians have mastered this skill by design and practice.

Perfection of one-touch enables a player to control the ball without looking down at it continuously. Playing the ball without looking at it allows you to observe what is occurring around you which in turn enables you to choose the best alternative of where and when to pass or move next. You can survey the playing field while handling the ball once you have gained confidence in your skills. Experience will also teach you what and whom to look for.

This chapter will show you how to develop individual skills and refine the rough edges of your ability to create time and space. It will also show you how to familiarize yourself with the ball, receive it from a teammate, control it, kick it, pass it, head it, beat an opponent with it, and take it away from an opponent.

The chapter will also describe the four major positions: *goalkeeper, defenders, midfielders,* and *forwards.* Fundamentals like stopping the ball and showing your friends how painless it can be to head the ball will also be covered.

Individual Skills

Running and Speed

Running is the most important element in soccer. To be an *effective* player, you must be able to run at a moderate or light pace for most of a game and run faster at certain times. Any weakness in a player's skill will be accentuated if the player lacks the ability to run at will.

Exercises to improve running and overall stamina are fairly simple and can be done individually or in a group. Trot around the field on your toes, inhaling through your nose and maintaining a body angle of about 70 degrees. Avoid kicking your heels too high or flapping or pumping your arms. Running in place is also a good exercise. Start slowly and work up to a fast rate.

Most professionals run an average of 3 miles before starting to kick the ball during practice in preseason or early in the season. Two miles should be light running (jogging or fast walking), and the other mile should be intensive running (sprints of about 50 yards or for periods no longer than 10 seconds). Some professionals go even further. Farrukh Quaraishi of the Tampa Bay Rowdies, a three-time all-American at Oneonta State College and the NASL's first draft choice in 1975, runs about 5 miles a day during the preseason.

Below the professional level, less running and more work with the ball are needed. (For further details, see Chapter 6, pages 183–194.) Players at all levels should practice the kind of running that occurs in a game—not just straightaway sprinting but unrhythmic, stop-and-go movements. To get yourself into shape, run slow, run fast, run sideways, run backwards, and then run a few steps and jump as high as you can. Repeat the jump a few steps later, pretending to head the ball. Practice your running techniques so that you can follow an opponent, lessen his efficiency, and restrain his capacity to create difficulties for your team.

Speed in soccer is much more than the ability to sprint. The simple talent of running quickly is an excellent weapon, but it is not sufficient in itself. There are players who can cover ground rapidly but have difficulty starting, stopping, or changing direction.

(Bottom left) **Steve David,** the top scorer in the NASL when he was with the Aztecs in 1977, has developed powerful leg muscles that make him a fast, steady runner. *(Julian Baum)*

(Bottom right) **Jim Fryatt** of the Atoms goes around an off-balance opponent. *(George Tiedemann)*

Quick starts and turns can be achieved by constant practice. Stand with your back to a line 8 yards away. Turn on a signal and get to the line as quickly as possible. Because you never know which way you may have to turn in a game, practice turning in both directions. You can practice quick turns with a friend. Ask your friend to run at you and make a break. Turn whichever way he breaks and try to catch him as quickly as possible. You can reverse roles after each sprint.

The easiest way to turn when a player is coming at you is to face him at an angle so that you can be on the half turn before he makes a break. When the opponent makes his approach, your arms should be hanging loose and you should be bending forward, ready to turn whichever way he does. If you position yourself properly, you may even force him to turn toward your favorite side or toward a space near the sideline where you can deal with him more easily.

There are players who are not and never will be great sprinters. The ability to sprint is a natural gift, but it can be improved. Stamina can be developed through hard and continuous training, and speed can be improved through the same kinds of exercises.

There are two other methods to improve your speed: (1) Have a friend stand next to you at midfield, facing the goal. Have another friend stand behind you and roll the ball toward the goal. As soon as you and the first friend see the ball, sprint after it. The first one to reach the ball becomes the attacker, and the other becomes the defender and tries to dispossess him.
(2) Stand on the starting line with a friend who has a ball at his feet. The moment your friend kicks the ball forward, sprint after it and try to stop it before it crosses a line 15 or 20 yards away.

Although you may never be a sprinter, you can still be a very fast player. If you can react quickly and anticipate situations during a game, you can often compensate for a deficiency in sprinting.

Ball Handling

Before you can outrun opponents, you must learn to master the ball. Nobody is born a baseball player, horseback rider, or soccer player. The skills that go with sports can be learned and perfected only by hours of devoted practice. To attain a natural ease in soccer, you must accustom yourself to the feel of the ball at your feet and learn how to keep it in constant motion on the ground. Here is an exercise that will help you do this naturally.

Stand with your feet about 15 inches apart and jump lightly from foot to foot, raising your feet only 4 inches off the ground and swinging your legs from side to side. Be careful not to swing your legs backward and forward—it must be from side to side. After you have done this several times and are accustomed to the motion, repeat the exercise with the ball between your feet (see diagram at left).

Tap the ball smoothly from foot to foot and keep it on the ground. Try to make your feet go up and come down in the same place each time, tapping the ball gently with the largest part of the inside of the foot and making contact 4 inches above the ground. Vary your speed, changing from fast to slow and back again. No matter how quickly or slowly you are performing the exercise, you can lose your rhythm if the ball is not tapped precisely right— too hard and the ball will get away, too light and you will not be able to maintain your rhythm.

The foot making contact with the ball should always be four inches off the ground. Raise and lower the foot in the same place; don't allow it to move backward or forward.

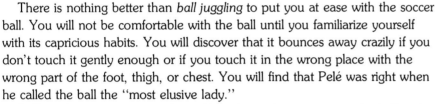

There is nothing better than *ball juggling* to put you at ease with the soccer ball. You will not be comfortable with the ball until you familiarize yourself with its capricious habits. You will discover that it bounces away crazily if you don't touch it gently enough or if you touch it in the wrong place with the wrong part of the foot, thigh, or chest. You will find that Pelé was right when he called the ball the "most elusive lady."

Ball juggling is an exercise that will teach you how to master the ball and make it obey your orders. The aim is to keep the ball in the air by touching it with the feet, knees, thighs, head, and every other part of the body except the hands and arms.

Start by juggling the ball with your feet (see diagram above). The first thing to learn is how to flick the ball into the air from the ground. Rest the sole of your foot on top of a ball approximately 12 inches in front of you. Draw your foot back, causing the ball to roll toward you. As the ball starts to move, plant your foot on the ground with your toes pressed down in the path of the ball. This will cause the ball to roll onto the front of your foot. When the center of the ball has passed over your toes, turn up your toes and make a forward movement. This will force the ball to rise slightly above the foot, actually putting the ball in the air.

After the ball is airborne, hit it in the center with the flat part of the top of your foot. If you hit it slightly off center, it will spin away from you. To avoid that, flex your ankle so that the toes are pulled upward toward the shin each time the ball is touched. The kicking foot should not touch the ground at this point, and you will have to hop on the supporting foot to maintain your balance. As soon as you feel at ease juggling with your better foot, try to use the other foot and then each foot in turn.

Once you feel comfortable juggling with your feet, kick the ball to about the height of your chest (see diagram on page 140). As the ball comes down, catch it on your thigh and continue to juggle with both thighs. Bounce the ball up and down, but don't let it bounce higher than your chest. The closer the ball remains, the more effective and attractive the juggling.

Juggling the ball with your head is not easy. Begin by throwing the ball about 1 foot in front of you and more than 2 feet above your head. As the

(*Top left*) **You can juggle the ball by using three or more parts of the body—for example, alternating among feet, thighs, and head. Move into this kind of juggling only after you feel comfortable alternating feet and thighs.**

(*Top right*) **When kicking for distance and power, stretch the kicking leg as far back as possible and keep your eyes on the ball, like Ian Anderson of the Tampa Bay Rowdies.**

ball drops, move directly underneath it, leaning your head back so that the ball bounces off the middle of the forehead. Don't be disappointed if you can't head it straight up to continue juggling from a stationary position; that will come with practice. For now you will be changing position to keep under the ball. When you become proficient with your feet, thighs, and head (see diagram above), you can start juggling with other parts of your body like the outside of your foot and shoulders.

Although players seldom get a chance to display juggling ability in a game, juggling is not a waste of time. You become familiar with every bounce and roll of the ball. You learn how to use every part of your body to control the ball. You learn how to keep your balance, keep your eyes on the ball, and judge how and where a ball must be touched.

Juggling is excellent practice that involves virtually all the ball-handling skills needed in a game. Each skill, however, must also be considered on its own, especially as it relates to a player's performance on the field.

Kicking

It is often said that soccer is a game of a foot and a ball. To be a good player, therefore, you must be able to kick the ball properly. Kicking serves three major functions: shooting, passing, and clearing the ball from your defensive end. Any part of the foot can be employed. You can use the instep for line drives, volleys, and half volleys; the inside and outside for passing the ball; and the heel for sending the ball backward. Kicking with toes should be avoided because it makes it extremely difficult to control the direction of the ball.

Although there are different ways of kicking a ball, you must master one fundamental method. The ordinary kick that goes straight forward and is performed with the instep is not simple. Too much theory would be confusing, but it is essential to understand the simplest method of kicking the ball accurately.

If the ball is stationary and the kick is being taken with the right foot, approach the ball so that the left (non-kicking) foot is alongside the ball (see photo at top right). Swing the kicking leg through, making contact with the instep as close to the ground as possible, and follow through to maintain the direction of the ball. The position of the non-kicking foot is important. If it is placed too far behind the ball, your body will incline backward at the moment of impact, sending the ball into the air. This is why so many shots from short distances go over the crossbar. If the non-kicking foot is placed beyond the stationary ball, you will drive the ball into the ground. This is why a ball kicked with force sometimes rolls only a short distance.

If the ball is on the move, which is usually the case, the non-kicking foot must be placed alongside the ball at the right moment. The secret of kicking a moving ball is to get your body into the same position you would use for a dead ball. Timing is the most important factor, and the only way to learn timing is through constant practice. A wall is your best partner for such practice because it returns the ball where you want it.

There are three basic rules for kicking: (1) Approach the ball with a regular stride. (2) Place the non-kicking foot in precisely the right place. (3) Concentrate on the swing of the leg in order to make contact with the proper part of the foot. Again, use the wall to test your progress.

Most players are right-footed. If you are a one-footed player, don't feel handicapped—there are several international stars who are one-footed. Your aim, however, should be to become equally good with both feet.

There are various ways of making your weak foot more proficient. I did it by practicing without a shoe on my favorite foot so that I was encouraged to use my weak—but protected—foot. Besides practicing to make your weak foot more proficient, never admit to yourself that one foot is different from the other. When kicking the ball against the wall, use both feet equally. You will soon notice an improvement in your weak foot, particularly if you realize that the problem is mostly mental.

When accuracy is more important than power, use the inside of the foot. (see diagram below). Most passes are made in this manner. You will be surprised how hard the ball can be struck with the inside of the foot.

Employ the *lofted kick* for distance and height (see diagram at top of page 142). Approach the ball from a slight angle and place the non-kicking foot between 6 and 9 inches to the side of and *behind* the ball. Allow the kicking foot a full swing with the knee bent. The key is the non-kicking foot, which must be behind the ball.

Most goals are scored with low drives, which keep the ball down and make it travel the fastest. When the non-kicking foot is precisely alongside the

The safest and most accurate method of passing the ball is with the inside of the foot. This is known as the push-pass. Notice how the kicking foot points outward after the kick is completed.

(Top) **Use the lofted kick when you want height and distance. What is important here is the position of the nonkicking foot: It must be *behind* the ball. Also, there must be a complete follow-through of the kicking foot.**

(Bottom left and right) **Dribbling means tapping the ball gently with the inside or the outside of the foot, like Graham Paddon . . . while keeping the ball under control, like Jomo Sono.**
(Richard Steinmetz; Jerry Liebman)

ball at the moment of impact, the knee of the kicking foot will be directly over the ball. Make contact with the center of the ball, keeping your toes pointed sharply downward. As the kick is made, straighten your knee and make a full follow-through.

The outside of the foot lacks power but is extremely useful for quick and deceptive passing; the ball can be flicked away at the end of what appears to be just another stride. Additional types of kicks are described in the sections on *passing* and *shooting*.

Control and Dribbling

In addition to running and kicking, soccer requires the ability to control the ball when you have possession. Control is the most important factor in the game, and learning perfect control is a never-ending process. Pelé, considered the world's greatest ball artist, once confessed that he learned more about control with every game. Ball control takes years to master, particularly for those who are not "born dribblers"—the privileged few who appear to run along as if the ball were tied to their laces.

Dribbling is essential for learning the general skill known as *ball control.* Dribbling doesn't mean kicking the ball several feet ahead and then racing after it. Rather, it entails nursing the ball along by a rapid series of gentle taps and pushes while keeping the head and shoulders well above the ball. There are occasions when you can kick the ball a few yards ahead and then sprint after it, but that doesn't constitute good dribbling.

Good dribbling is a combination of ball juggling on the ground, body movement, balance, acceleration, cleverness, and anticipation. To these qualities, great players like Sir Stanley Matthews, Georgie Best, Garrincha, and Pelé have added experience, confidence, and a special touch of magic.

As in basketball, dribbling is a technique of getting past your opponent by keeping the ball under control while making deceptive changes in direction and speed. This can be done in many ways, and a player should develop his own style. To be an effective dribbler, you must possess speed and quick reactions and develop a delicacy of touch in ball control. You must screen

Beating an opponent face to face is one of the most difficult things to do in soccer. Notice how Pelé approaches the ball. He keeps his eye on his rival's knees—the moment the man leans toward one side, Pelé goes the opposite way. *(Pepsico International)*

and shield the ball by placing yourself between the ball and the opponent. You must be able to work in confined space and face vigorous tackling. You must develop the ability to dodge and swerve.

Swerving consists of running in a wavy pattern instead of a straight line, occasionally placing one foot in front of the other. *Dodging* is similar, but it entails moving forward slowly and jumping literally from side to side. *Feinting,* of course, is pretending to run or pass in one direction and then going in another direction at the last possible moment. *Sidestepping* involves taking a pace to the left or right just as an opponent rushes in to take the ball away from you.

For some people these maneuvers are natural gifts, but they can be learned by almost anyone through practice. Try the moves first without the ball and then with the ball.

Your first practice in dribbling should consist of running and pushing the ball on the ground with soft kicks that allow you to keep close control of the ball. Do it in a straight line over a distance of about 20 yards until you have established a running rhythm and can play the ball with every other stride — with every other swing of one of your legs. The better you get at this, the faster you should run.

You can also try a change of pace. Accelerate suddenly, slow down, and then accelerate again. You will learn to adjust your touch of the ball to rapid changes in your running pace. Sudden changes of pace can deceive an opponent. A burst of acceleration can get you ahead of an opponent and gain a little extra space to pass the ball or get off a shot.

As was said earlier, dribbling skill is something you develop by yourself; it is not the kind of skill for which rules can be laid down. Dribbling is free-flowing and depends largely on improvisation. There are, nevertheless, three general rules about dribbling: (1) Use your body to shield and screen the ball. (2) Do not dribble too often or too long. (3) Do not spend endless hours trying to dribble with your weak foot instead of perfecting your strong foot.

Trapping

When the ball is passed to you, the more quickly you gain control of it — *trap* it — the more time and space you will have to pass, dribble, or shoot it. If you

The key to success in trapping the ball with any part of the body is to give way — that is, relax the muscles used at the moment you make contact with the ball.

Trapping the ball with the knees (left) is not recommended unless the field is very bumpy and a player is at the initial stages of making contact with the ball. At the right, Pelé demonstrates the proper way of trapping the ball with the chest. *(Pepsico International)*

don't trap the ball swiftly and surely, your opponent will be all over you, preventing you from doing anything productive with the ball.

After a perfect pass, the ball will come to you exactly where you want it. More often than not, however, the ball will come to you in an awkward way, either too high, too fast, or on the wrong side. Wherever or however the ball reaches you, absolute control with all parts of your body except the hands and arms is a must.

In situations of tight marking, you should be able to control the ball as soon as it comes to you, and it is as likely to come in the air as along the ground. Waiting for the ball to drop to your feet or waiting to establish a position where your favorite foot can be used can mean the loss of a split second, which may be all an opponent needs to get to the ball first.

The key to effective trapping is to treat the ball gently by relaxing the part of the body that is used to trap the ball. Try to develop your trapping skill until you can not only take pace off the ball in one delicate action but also direct the ball in the same motion to the exact spot that will set up your next move. When you show that you have already thought about your next move, you are showing that you are a good soccer player.

The most frequently used trap is made with the inside of the foot (see diagram at bottom of page 144). It is done by placing the foot slightly ahead of where you expect the ball to bounce. Keep your foot about 6 inches off the ground and meet the ball as it strikes the ground. The foot and the lower part of the leg should be inclined slightly over the top of the ball and must be relaxed enough to smother the upward bounce.

Trapping the ball with the outside of the foot involves the same principles. Meet the ball as it hits the ground and then lean the foot and lower leg over the ball to smother the bounce. If you have to reach for this trap, stretch your arms out for balance.

If the ball is falling so rapidly that you cannot get into position to trap it with the inside or outside of the foot, stretch your leg forward and trap the ball in front of you with the sole of the foot. Trap the ball as it hits the ground, using a relaxed ankle to smother the bounce.

The shin trap is popular with youngsters and players dealing with uneven surfaces. It is not one of soccer's most elegant moves, but all you want to do

Two of the world's greatest players, Johan Cruyff and Franz Beckenbauer, trap the ball with consistent skill. *(Peter Robinson; Jerry Liebman)*

is stop the ball any way you can. Press your legs together from the knees to the heels. Bend your knees sharply and lean forward from the waist, crouching over the ball. The ball is likely to bounce farther away than in other traps. Be ready to move in any direction to gain full control.

To trap the ball with your thigh, raise your leg with the knee bent and make contact with the flat part of the thigh high above the knee. To obtain cushioning, lower the thigh slightly and relax the muscles at the precise moment of impact. The ball should not rebound more than 5 inches before it drops to your feet.

As in the thigh trap, the key consideration in trapping with the chest is to make the ball bounce lightly off your body before it drops to the ground. Depending on the direction of the ball's approach, there are two ways of trapping it with the chest.

If the ball is dropping, stand with your feet parallel, but apart for good balance. Bend your knees and incline your body backward slightly from the waist up. As the ball arrives, spread your arms wide to avoid touching it with your hands and lean farther back. Breathe in deeply just before the ball arrives, puffing out your chest, and then breathe out sharply to hollow the chest as contact is made.

For a hard-hit ball that is rising or coming directly at you from a horizontal direction, stretch your arms straight down and knock the ball down toward your feet with the chest. You will be slightly airborne; when you come down with the ball, make sure you are in a well-balanced position to control it. Your legs should not be far apart when you hit the ground.

Trapping the ball on the run is not easy; it should be tried only after you have mastered all the basic techniques of trapping. When you are running to meet the ball, cushioning is no longer essential. You must control the forward movement of the ball so that it is kicked or bounced ahead of you to where you want it. Your run should not be interrupted by the trap. If the ball is not trapped just right, either you will stumble over it or someone else will get to it first. Don't expect to be able to choose your favorite method when you are trapping on the run.

Heading

To a novice the leather ball seems to weigh a ton. Your first thought is that heading the ball will cause discomfort and pain, and it will if you don't make contact correctly. Make sure to use the center of your forehead and hit the ball decisively rather than letting it hit you. Power and distance are accomplished by perfect timing and by getting as much weight behind the ball as possible.

Unlike kicking, which seems to come as naturally as walking to children, heading is an action that is anything but natural. Beginners are apprehensive and afraid of getting hurt by the ball, but their fears can be overcome.

Pick up a ball, hold it, and hit it with your forehead. Hit it lightly at first and then progressively harder. Be sure to make contact with the center of your forehead. This will show you that there is no pain involved when you head the ball properly.

If you blink your eyes every time you make contact, don't worry. It is a normal and involuntary act for the eyes to blink. However, you must keep your eyes open as long as possible or you may strike the ball improperly.

After you have hit the ball with your forehead several times, toss it a few inches in the air and make contact with your forehead as it drops (see diagram, page 148). Don't let it hit you. You are the one who does the hitting.

(Bottom left) Exceptionally talented players like Rodney Marsh employ all kinds of fancy ways to trap the ball.

(Bottom right) Three players jumping high in the air in front of the goal, trying to head the ball (top of photo) in this match between Scotland and Wales. *(Peter Robinson)*

Do not be discouraged if you instinctively close your eyes in the early stages of learning to head the ball. Sometimes even the pros do it, en masse. *(George Tiedeman)*

One point to remember in heading the ball is that you must hit the ball—do not wait for it to hit you. Keep your feet apart. Bend the knees slightly and arch your back; then, at the proper moment, whip your body forward and hit the ball with your forehead.

To head the ball with power from a stationary position, swing the upper half of your body forward, using your neck muscles to thrust your head at the ball. Your forehead must be positioned decisively downward at the moment of impact.

Once you have gained confidence in heading, learn to jump for the ball and head it in the direction you want it to go (see diagram at right). Don't stand still with both feet on the ground and wait for the ball. You'll never touch it because your opponent will jump and head it away from you.

The timing of your jump requires a great deal of practice. The taller player doesn't always win a heading duel because his opponent may time the jump better. The ability to *hover,* or stay in the air a split second longer, is one of the supreme skills of soccer.

If you have to jump to head the ball, jackknife your body in midair to produce a powerful swing. Jump early enough to be slightly higher than the ball before making contact. Kicking your legs behind you will help arch your back, enabling you to thrust your head forward with more power.

To achieve maximum height in a jump, push off from one leg while swinging the opposite knee upward for extra power. Swinging your arms up will add further momentum.

Your hands are instrumental in the diving header, which you can use for a waist-high ball that cannot be reached otherwise. You will probably be running at full speed, and so it is important to learn how to land properly after the dive. The key is to get both hands and arms down as quickly as possible before your body strikes the ground. Try it without the ball on a soft surface such as a mat. Be sure to relax as you strike the ground.

Passing

Accurate passing is a necessity at all levels of soccer. Nothing builds a team's confidence more rapidly than crisp, accurate passing. The art of passing is largely a matter of doing simple things quickly and well.

Soccer is a simple game that consists primarily of passing the ball back and forth, and so nothing should be treated more simply than passing. Don't become impatient and try to pass through a secure defense. If you become impatient, you will take uncalculated risks and reduce your team's efficiency. Remember that simple passes pay the largest dividends.

A pass is a link between two players—the passer and the receiver. The success of a pass depends on both players, and each should try to make the other's job easier. The passer should be aware of the movements of his prospective receivers and should pass the ball when one of them is in a good position to receive it or is moving into such a position. The receiver should always try to be available for a pass. If the potential receiver is not open, he should immediately move away from his opponent or run to an empty space.

Good passing requires accuracy and good judgment. Before you pass to a teammate on the move, you must assess his speed and the direction of

The key to getting power behind the ball when you jump to head it is to arch your body back, from the waist up. This helps to put weight behind your hit, and that means power.

movement of the opposing players. Concentration on accuracy and power can be wasted if your eyes are not on the ball during the act of kicking.

Like trapping and kicking, passing can be performed in various ways. For accuracy there is no better pass than the *push-pass*. The non-kicking foot is placed alongside the ball, with the toes pointing in the direction of the intended pass. The kicking foot is turned outward so that the inside of the foot faces forward. The ball is then pushed forward by the inside of the foot, with care being taken to strike the center of the ball.

Avoid relaxing the knee of the non-kicking foot or leaning backward at the time of the kick. These actions will cause the kicking foot to make contact too low, lifting the ball off the ground and weakening the pace of the pass. This method is known as the *push-pass* because the ball is not struck with significant power.

Another error that often occurs in the push-pass, or the pass with the inside of the foot, is the hanging toe. This happens when you fail to extend the ankle, making it almost impossible to establish contact at the arch. Most of the contact is made by the big toe, causing the ball to swerve to the side.

A common but more difficult modification of the push-pass involves stabbing rather than swinging the foot at the ball. You jab at the ball with a short, sharp action of the lower leg that sharply reduces the backswing and follow-through. This is used in passing on the run because it is an economical kick. The leg action is part of the running action, and so you kick the ball with hardly a break in stride.

Knowing when to hold the ball and when to pass requires instinct and anticipation, which must be developed through experience. Holding the ball too long can be as bad as not holding it long enough. The passer's aim is to deliver the ball the moment his teammate arrives in the most advantageous position to receive it. Needless to say, this is not always possible.

You must learn not only where, how, when, and to whom to pass but also how to pace the pass. You must hit the ball so that it arrives at a speed that can be easily controlled by the receiver.

Shooting

It has often been said that you cannot score unless you shoot, but there are coaches who know that this is only half the story. The location of shots is as important as their frequency.

Before Eddie Firmani became coach of the Cosmos, Pelé's teammates were taking volleys, half volleys, side volleys, curve shots, and even bicycle shots with their insteps and outsteps. In some games, the Cosmos took 35 or more shots and scored only 1 or 2 goals. Sometimes it seemed like the Cosmos were taking shots from the stadium parking lot.

To those who knew better, it was irritating to hear players and coaches say that the Cosmos were taking their shots and that sooner or later the shots would go in. However, they did not go in until Firmani arrived and curbed the number of shots.

"You don't shoot unless you have a chance to score," Firmani told his players the first day. He must have told Giorgio Chinaglia that if he hit the ball into the stands near the mezzanine again, he would have to fetch it.

Steve Hunt demonstrates the proper positioning of arms and legs in shooting with the right foot and with the left foot. His arm is stretched out for balance, and his kicking leg is pushed back as far as possible. This guarantees a perfect follow-through and, of course, plenty of punch behind the ball. In both cases his nonkicking foot is placed next to the ball. *(Jerry Liebman)*

```
 3        |         |  6
 4        |    1    |  7
          |_____|
 5        |    2    |  8
```

To practice shooting for accuracy, mark a wall as shown. First try shooting from 15 yards out, then go to 20, and so on. After you can hit numbers 1 and 2 with consistency, try the corners.

Chinaglia changed his philosophy and let the goalkeepers in the NASL fetch the ball from the back of the net.

Accuracy in shooting should be stressed before power. Players frequently shoot wildly and concentrate only on power. This is power out of control, and power out of control means inaccuracy.

The low shot is more difficult for a goalkeeper to handle than the shot in the air. Shots along the ground look less spectacular than those which hit the roof of the net, but low shots are likely to bump, skid, or stick, which can make stopping the shot more difficult.

There is one essential rule about scoring: It's not the way you score but whether you score. A ball put into the net with your nose, counts the same as a spectacular bicycle kick from the edge of the penalty area. Of all the skills in soccer, shooting requires the most practice because no other skill is more important.

Take a ball and a piece of chalk and find a wall. On the wall, mark a box the size of a goal; 8 yards wide by 8 feet high. Divide the box into 8 rectangles (see diagram above), and mark the rectangles 1 through 8 as shown. Place the ball about 12 yards away, choose a rectangle, and then try to shoot the ball into that particular spot. Repeat for another number, and so on. Go back to about 18 yards and try to hit each rectangle again.

Try to hit the numbers with various shots. Start by kicking a stationary ball with your instep. Then practice the more complicated task of shooting a moving ball, but do this only after you have mastered the technique of shooting a dead ball.

Try to *volley* the ball, which means to kick it while it's in the air. The volley kick or shot can be made in several ways, but the most popular method is to hit the ball with the full instep. The leg movement of the volley shot is made almost entirely from the knee.

The *half volley* is employed when the ball has bounced no more than an inch off the ground. The ball is struck with the full instep and with the toes pointing straight down. Because the ball is rising before the kick is made, the player should lean forward. The knee should be ahead of the ball to keep the ball from going upward.

The *side volley* requires a completely different technique. The non-kicking foot is placed much farther from the ball, and the kicking leg is swung sideways and kept fully stretched at the moment of impact. Unlike kicks where the body is over the ball, in this case the body leans away from the ball. Thus, for a side volley with the left foot, place your right leg about 30 inches to the right of the bouncing ball and swing your left foot sideways as you lean your body to the right. Because of the extensive swing of the leg and the twisting motion of the body, the side volley will become one of your most powerful shots.

The *bicycle kick,* or *scissors kick,* was invented by Leonidas, a Brazilian. It is an acrobatic action that calls for half a backward somersault in the air. The inevitable result is that you will land on your back. Trying to make that landing as soft as possible should be your first consideration. As you land, use your arms to cushion the fall. Try it without the ball first, on a soft surface.

The *curve shot,* or *banana kick,* is used when a clear shot on goal is impossible, as when a defensive wall has been set up to counter a direct free kick. A number of soccer players can curve a ball with their feet as effectively as a baseball pitcher can with his hand.

The ball is made to curve by giving it a spin as it is hit. This is done by making contact to the left or right of the center of the ball. Kicking the left side of the ball will result in a left-to-right curve, and kicking the right side will produce a right-to-left curve. Either the outside or the inside of the instep may be used for the curve shot. To curve the ball from left to right, a left-footed player uses the inside of the left instep and a right-footed player uses the outside of the right instep.

The skills and techniques discussed thus far are necessary for *every* player. There is another technique that all players should develop, although it is most useful to defenders.

Tackling

Tackling means taking the ball from your opponent, and it begins with the fundamental rules of defense. Position yourself between the goal and the at-

(Bottom left) **Giorgio Chinaglia gets off a scissors kick.** *(The Bergen Record)*

(Bottom right) **The Chinaglia again, demonstrating the perfect form in kicking a ball on the move with power.** *(Jerry Liebman)*

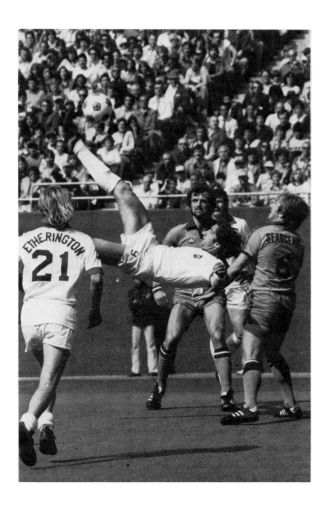

(Top left) **In a good tackle a player takes the ball away from an opponent without touching him. Here Roy Willner goes under Franz St. Lot.** *(John W. Albino)*

(Top right) **The idea of a sliding tackle is to knock the ball away from an opponent without committing a foul. If you make contact with the opponent more than with the ball, it can be costly, especially if the play is within your penalty area.** *(George Tiedemann)*

tacker to give yourself a good chance to intercept the ball. Limit the area in which your opponent can receive the ball. Mark closely enough to tackle the opponent as he receives the ball but not so closely that you will lose him if he moves away quickly.

In the *front-on tackle* your aim is to get solidly behind the ball and block it. The tackling foot, with as much weight behind it as possible, should make contact with the center of the ball. If you make contact with the upper part of the ball, your foot may slide over the ball and hit the opponent's shin, in which case you may be penalized for dangerous play. Keep your legs close together so that you can shift your weight quickly and easily.

In tackling from behind or from the side, the principle is the same. Make contact with the center of the ball, not the back of the legs of the player who is trying to screen the ball. Move in as close as you can and wait for an opportunity to knock the ball away. This should never be attempted out of range. It is impossible to put any strength into such a tackle, and it is easy for the player with the ball to sidestep the tackler.

Another type of tackle is the full-blooded, do-or-die attempt to dispossess an opponent who has the ball under full control. The main object is to block the ball firmly against your foot in the hope that your opponent will then stumble and overbalance. If you are able to approach from the side, you can, and should, combine a fair shoulder charge with your attempt to block the ball. If you can judge the charge so that it catches the opponent with his weight on the far foot, so much the better.

The *sliding tackle* is often used in desperate situations, and the aim is to kick the ball away from the attacker. If you can kick the ball away so that it goes to a teammate, that is a bonus. The sliding tackle must be perfectly timed because of the risk of missing the ball and perhaps tripping the attacker, which will result in a foul and a free kick against you. If you play the ball away before making contact with your opponent, there will be no foul. The sliding tackle represents one of a defender's greatest assets: the ability to reach, to stretch an extra inch for the ball, and cut off an attacker who has broken through on his own.

Quick recovery after an unsuccessful tackle is also a vital part of a defender's game. Too many young players rush in to tackle, overbalance and fall to the ground, and then remain on the ground for several seconds. However, the good back tackles warily and recovers rapidly when he is beaten.

Remember that leaning forward when you tackle gives you a more stable position, making it less likely that you will be knocked off balance. Except in the sliding tackle, try not to be caught with your legs spread out. Position your legs far enough apart for good balance but not so far apart that the ball can slip between them.

You can practice tackling with a teammate. Ask your friend to dribble a ball toward you and attempt to beat you. You must concentrate on keeping close to him, not letting him get past you, and forcing him to work the ball into an area that is convenient for you. Once you have him going in that direction, look for an opportunity to tackle.

Another good exercise is to move into an area about 20 yards square and play three-on-two. The 2 players are the defenders, who will learn the true value of teamwork. If they do not work together, they will have to do a lot of chasing. The 3 players on offense interpass the ball, keeping it within the area and away from the 2 defenders. The object is for the 2 defenders to work so that the ball is played into an area that gives them a chance of an interception or tackle. If one defender attacks the player with possession and pressures him into playing the ball, the second defender can anticipate, close in on the intended pass, and tackle as the receiving player attempts to gain control.

This is not an easy game because the player with possession can pass the ball to 2 players. The idea is for the defender applying immediate pressure to approach so that he not only makes the player with possession move in one direction but also cuts out one of the other attackers. The supporting defender positions himself to help cut out the same attacker while remaining close enough to the third attacker to intercept or tackle when the pass is made.

Beyond these techniques, the most important single factor in tackling is timing. In principle the tackle should be made at the first opportunity, just as the opponent is receiving the ball. At this time the opponent's concentration will be focused on controlling the ball, and so a quick, determined tackle before he has full control will often be successful.

Once your opponent has full control, you must hold off, slowing down his moves and trying to pressure him into an error such as dribbling the ball too far ahead. Once this occurs, you should go at the ball without hesitation and make a determined tackle. Remember that the less space you allow your opponent to operate in, the better off you are. That is one reason why you should always try to tempt the opponent to go toward the sideline.

Remember that a forward dislikes working against a defender who makes him bring the ball up close and is in no hurry to commit himself. Delay your tackle until the most convenient time—when the ball is temporarily out of control or within your reach because the opponent has failed to shield it correctly. A quick tackle at that point will make the job of dispossession successful.

Failure in your first tackle in a game will make you not only uncomfortable but also unsure of your ability. You may lose concentration and start passing the ball inaccurately and positioning yourself incorrectly. Thus, it is best to avoid spectacular tackles early on.

In your first encounter with the player you mark, you must think of "safety first" before gambling to impress your opponent or the fans. Your bench and

the fans who know the game will be impressed only when you offer the strongest and safest opposition and display absolute determination. Strength often undermines your opponent and makes him look for you instead of concentrating on controlling the ball. You must display strength within the limits of the rules, however, because a fierce tackle inside your penalty area will be costly.

When your opponent becomes aware of your strength, determination, and good judgment in tackling, his game will fall to lower standards and he will make errors. You can achieve this result by not allowing him time to recover after you have dispossessed him of the ball. Move away quickly and play the ball early.

Playing the Positions

Most of the skills discussed in the first part of this chapter can be applied to soccer at the highest level, where the majority of teams employ the concept of *total soccer*. This means that a player must be able to perform equally well in all parts of the field. For an attacker to play defense and a defender to be effective on offense, each must master additional skills. On the other hand, the more skilled a player becomes, the more specialized he tends to be.

The second part of this chapter will describe the individual positions— *goalkeepers, defenders, midfielders,* and *forwards*—in terms of the skills required for each position and how these skills may be employed in various situations.

Goalkeepers

Goalkeeping has changed drastically. The goalkeeper was once a purely defensive player, an acrobat who waited at the goal line to make spectacular efforts to prevent goals. The modern goalkeeper still represents the last link in the defensive unit, but his responsibilities are so diversified that he has become an additional fullback. Because the goalkeeper is the only one who sees the whole playing area, he often assumes the team's field generalship.

Like a catcher in baseball, the goalkeeper should always be talking and directing. He should be the commander in the penalty area, shouting to tell his teammates where to position themselves. Clever guidance will not only give his teammates confidence in his judgment but also limit the shooting opportunities for opposing forwards. The goalkeeper's directions should be given loudly and with authority. A silent or indecisive goalkeeper can create insurmountable problems for his teammates.

It is almost impossible to set hard-and-fast rules for the goalkeeper because he can never be sure of what is going to happen. Much of the goalkeeper's job is predicated on instinct, common sense, and agility. Nevertheless, the position demands mastery of basic soccer skills, a deep understanding of modern defense, and great mobility.

The goalkeeper has a chance to be a hero or a goat in *every* game. He can accomplish the former by relieving the defense through clever positioning, controlling the air immediately in front of his goal, making daring advances from his goal, and making brilliant dives in desperate situations, including a dive at the feet of a player coming at full speed.

A goalkeeper doesn't have to be very tall to play the position. Tony Chursky, Ken Cooper, and Kevin Keelan have been three of the best goalkeepers in the NASL, and they are all 5 feet 11 inches tall. Gordon Banks, one of the greatest of all time, is also 5 feet 11 inches tall. Alan Mayer, considered by many the best American-born goalkeeper in recent years, is exactly 6 feet tall.

However, an agile tall man has an advantage over a smaller man in reaching for the ball, especially on high crosses. A shorter goalkeeper is somewhat handicapped in controlling air attacks immediately in front of his goal, and his limited reach is evident when he fields a high ball or dives to make a save. On the other hand, tall goalkeepers are averse to going down for low shots, are often weak in diving, and are sometimes slow to regain their feet. They are also usually slower than the average player.

The first requirement for a goalkeeper is a natural ability to catch and handle the ball under all circumstances. Because the rules permit only one member of the team to touch the ball with his hands, the goalkeeper must make full use of this asset. Every goalkeeper observes certain principles and puts them into practice at every opportunity.

Whether standing, jumping, or diving, a goalkeeper must place his body behind the ball whenever he can. The ball may slip through his hands, but it will not get past his stomach or chest.

The goalkeeper must give with the force of the ball, never meeting it with straight arms, stiff hands, or a rigid body. He must also keep his eyes and attention exclusively on the ball until he has complete control. He must avoid such pitfalls as trying to catch the ball and move off at the same time.

Quick footwork enables the goalkeeper to make saves look easy. By using his feet, he gets into the right position and makes it appear that every shot has been fired straight at his chest. He must try to catch the ball rather than punch it away. Instead of allowing a corner kick against his team, he can be the originator of an attack.

A goalkeeper must work at fielding the ball from ground level to heights that require a full upward leap. Whenever possible he should bring his hands behind the ball as it arrives and draw it as quickly as he can to his chest or midsection.

Going down on the knee is the safest method of fielding a ground ball, especially when the goalkeeper has to move to the side. He maintains a moderate stride and bends down on the forward foot to form a barrier. Keeping his legs close together, he places his hands under the ball, scooping it up and trapping it securely against the chest. This is especially important when there is a possibility of an immediate challenge from an onrushing opponent.

A goalkeeper should avoid any kneeling position in which the knee sticks out toward the ball, which could cause the ball to bounce off the knee and out of control. The goalkeeper should also avoid being caught with his full weight on the kneeling leg because that can temporarily immobilize him in case of an unexpected bounce.

Sometimes, as in the case of a hard, low shot, it is a good idea to turn both feet sideways in the direction of the shot, bending down on one knee and facing the rest of the body toward the oncoming ball. The hands should be at ground level, backed up by the legs and in position to scoop up the ball and cuddle it securely into the body.

When a shot is directed at the midsection, the goalkeeper positions himself in line with the oncoming ball and catches it against the chest or waist. To catch a ball against the lower chest or stomach, the goalkeeper crouches with arms bent, elbows in, and fingers spread, ready to fling his forearms and hands around the ball at the moment of impact.

When the ball comes at the chest, the position is the same except that the elbows are slightly in front of the chest, not at the sides. By bending the elbows and shrugging the shoulders, the goalkeeper presents a deep chest cavity to accommodate the ball.

Instead of catching the ball with his hands on the sides of the ball, the goalkeeper sometimes places one hand on top of the ball and the other below. This technique is used when the goalkeeper jumps or dives sideways to grab the ball.

Knowing when to leave the line distinguishes very good goalkeepers from adequate goalkeepers. Basically, there are two reasons for the goalkeeper to leave the goal: to get the ball when it comes within range, and to narrow the angle when an opposing player has broken through and is about to shoot (see diagram at top of page 159).

The goalkeeper who hesitates in leaving the goal will not get the ball and his teammates will not know whether to cover him or go for the ball. The goalkeeper who is positive in his approach will leave nobody in doubt about his decisions. He will call to let his teammates know whether he wants them to clear the ball or clear his way and give him cover so that he can come off the line to get the ball.

After a goalkeeper has made the decision to come off the line, he must act with absolute determination to get to the ball. He must be ready to decide whether to catch it, punch it, or kick it away. If he is reasonably clear and in no danger of dropping a high ball, he should catch it. If he is not sure, he should punch the ball away, preferably toward the sideline and far enough so that it cannot be volleyed back to the goal.

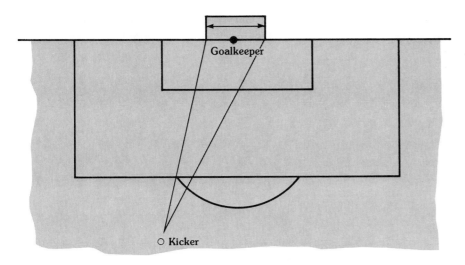

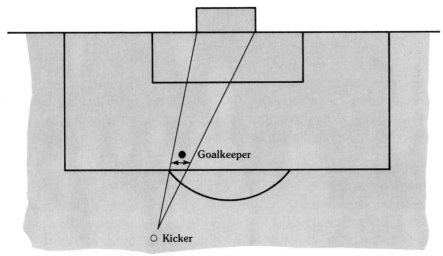

(Top) A goalkeeper can narrow the angle for the shooter simply by coming off his line.

(Bottom) David Harvey, goalkeeper for Leeds in the English First Division, punches the ball away from Alan Gilzean of Tottenham. *(UPI)*

(Top left) **Seen through the net, Phil Parkes of Vancouver makes a two-hand catch over his head.**

(Top right) **Bob Rigby dives for the ball.** *(George Tiedemann)*

A goalkeeper cannot be efficient in coming off the line to catch a high ball until he has mastered catching the ball over his head. Care must be taken when catching such a ball because the hands are not backed up by the body; if the ball slips through the goalkeeper's hands, he will have to gather it from the back of the net.

Practice catching the overhead ball with a friend, preferably another goalkeeper. Throw the ball to each other so that it arrives overhead, and catch and bring it to the chest before throwing it back. Get the feel of the ball. Make the catch while moving backwards, letting the ball drop slightly behind you and then stretching to get it and bring it forward and down to your chest with both hands.

Stand apart and throw the ball so that you get plenty of height and distance. Receive the ball high jumping off one foot, catching the ball at full stretch, and then bringing the ball down to your chest. You need all the height you can get to outstretch the jumping forwards in front of you, and so you should practice jumping as high as you can in this exercise.

Keep you eyes firmly fixed on the ball. Don't be fooled by the ball's initial path because if it's been last kicked by a player like Roberto Rivelino, Ramon Mifflin, or Johan Cruyff, it will dip, swerve, and spin in the air. Taking your eyes off the ball for a split second can prove fatal. Watch the ball right up to the moment it's in your hands. Cultivate the habit of bringing the ball down to the chest and holding it securely in case you are fairly charged and have to make a tumble.

One of the most thrilling sights in soccer is a goalkeeper in midair, traveling at top speed as he dives to make a save. A diving save is accomplished in much the same manner as catching a high ball, but the movement is on a horizontal line rather than a vertical line. When you dive for the ball, make certain to kick your legs upward so that you will land on the upper part of your body.

Positioning is an important feature of a goalkeeper's play. When a corner kick is taken, for example, your best place is on the line beside the far post because it is easier to move forward than backward. This also enables you to watch the ball and the players at the same time. You should have a good idea where everyone is so that when you have to punch the ball, you can punch it toward a teammate rather than an opponent.

When a winger cuts in to shoot, position yourself at the near end of the goal. However, you should be in the middle of the line for free kicks taken from the middle of the field. The actual distance a goalkeeper should stand in front of the goal depends on the individual. Some prefer to be several yards onto the field of play, a novice should remain on or near the line, where he can deal more easily with lobs.

Once you have full possession of the ball, you must throw it or kick it to a teammate. You must give this pass the same tactical consideration as any other pass made on the field. The ball must be thrown or kicked so that it can be easily controlled. How you should distribute the ball depends on the ability of your teammates and the tactics your team employs. It is useless to kick the ball downfield unless your team has forwards who can control such clearances, and it is dangerous to roll short passes to your fullbacks if they are not sharp or skillful enough to take advantage. Many goalkeepers kick the ball downfield because their coaches believe that the farther the ball is from the goal, the safer they are.

The best goalkeepers save all the shots that ought to be saved rather than making a brilliant save one moment and a mistake the next. A good team with an unsafe goalkeeper will lack confidence. A weak team with a good goalkeeper will gain confidence with every game and will be inspired to perform above its capabilities.

Goalkeeper Arnie Mausser displays good form in throwing the ball downfield. *(Richard Pilling)*

(Top left) Soccer has speeded up to such an extent that the slow defenders of the past would now be outclassed. Barry Barto (in white) shows that he can follow Warren Archibald, one of the fastest men in the NASL. *(George Tiedemann)*

(Top right) Werner Roth, here in the Cosmos' old uniform, has been one of the toughest central defenders in the NASL.

Defenders

When we speak of defenders, we refer primarily to the *fullbacks*, the last line of defense in front of the goalkeeper. The modern defensive system usually calls for 4 fullbacks—2 in the middle and 1 on each flank. The fullbacks in the middle will play either side by side or one in front of the other. In the latter situation, the front man normally acts as the *stopper* while the man behind acts as the *sweeper,* or *libero*.

In modern soccer the defenders do not have to be the tough, burly type that was common until the 1950s. Soccer has speeded up to such a degree that the slow and cumbersome players would now be outclassed. Defenders today must be able to move downfield on the attack. Forwards have become faster, quicker, and more skillful, and so the defenders have had to keep up with the times. In some instances they have become quite attack-oriented and dangerous to the opposing defenders.

The most important development in the use of defenders on offense is the increased use of the libero, the sweeper who patrols behind the main line of defense but also may join the attack. Thus the name *libero,* which means "free."

The most important duty of the sweeper is still defensive—to mop up all the loose balls that have been misplayed by teammates or opponents in and around the penalty area. The player who assumes this role is usually one of the most skilled on the team because misplaying the ball inside the penalty area can prove costly. For a further discussion of the libero in relation to defensive formations, see page 207.

To be valuable on defense, a player must be a good marker, a destroyer, someone who prevents other players from creating opportunities and scoring goals. To be a good marker, a fullback must establish a position: (1) between his opponent and the goal, (2) where he can see the opponent and the ball at all times without having to turn his head, and (3) close enough to an opponent to intercept a pass or make a tackle before the opponent has full control.

The defender should worry about the end result and not the method of destroying an offensive threat. Thus, a defender should be proficient at kicking and heading the ball from all angles and positions. Defenders often find themselves facing their own goal in which case a bicycle-kick clearance or backward header is necessary.

A defender must master all soccer techniques, continually adjust to the opponent's moves, and carry out his duties correctly when a successful move gives him possession of the ball at either end of the field.

Whatever the specific defensive structure of a team, there will be many occasions when a defender will have to face an attacker who will employ every imaginable move. The attacker will try to turn inside and outside until he finds a weakness and can exploit it. Thus, defenders must be fast, quick on the turn, good at tackling, good in the air, and able to recover quickly after they are beaten. Above all they must provide three basics: *pressure, cover,* and *balance.*

Pressure means delaying the player with the ball from taking any further action after his team has gained possession and your teammates have been caught out of position. The defender holds the player back in order to give his teammates time to set up.

One of the fullback's first duties is to work out a supportive relationship with the goalkeeper, who expects a certain amount of cover from his backs. Especially when the goalkeeper comes off his line, 1 or 2 defenders should fall back to cover for him. Many dramatic saves have been made by defenders this way.

One special covering assignment of a defender is to back up the goalkeeper on corner kicks. The standard procedure is to stand inside the near post, ready to take the goalkeeper's place in case he moves off the line. If the

Sam Bick knows that the defender must keep his eyes on the ball and never lose his concentration during a game. *(Fred Anderson)*

(Top left) **When under pressure on defense, even Franz Beckenbauer blasts the ball away in an attempt to give his team time to regroup.** *(Jerry Liebman)*

(Top right) **No one loves to overlap and go on attack better than Francisco Marinho, shown here in practice.**

goalkeeper cannot gather the ball after coming off the line, the defender can often head or kick the ball away while standing practically on the line.

Cover, or *support,* involves making sure that there is never a one-on-one situation. The defender must back up his teammate in case the teammate should lose the battle against a flashy forward.

Balance applies to the defender farthest from the ball. Your teammate closest to the player with possession will apply pressure and make it difficult for him to pass. Another teammate will cover him so that a one-on-one situation doesn't occur. You must take up a position which will balance the defense and protect against a through-pass.

If you gain possession in the crowded area in front of your goal, you will be challenged at once. Forget that the coach told you to always try to pass to a teammate. Your first thought must be to blast the ball away as quickly as possible, preferably out of bounds. This will give you and your teammates time to regroup and assume more favorable positions in the penalty area.

Soccer is a game of chances, and some chances are more risky than others. The consequences of defensive gambling can be especially severe, and so every defender must know how to control his urges and be constantly aware of his role and importance.

Many players find it difficult to adhere to the defensive principle of *control.* They have a tendency to grow overexcited and lose sight of defensive priorities. When they start to play soccer, youngsters are drawn to the ball like bees to honey, and all thoughts of defensive responsibilities are forsaken.

A defender should also develop an understanding with the goalkeeper about passing the ball back in tight situations. When you are chasing the ball backward toward your goal with opponents on your heels, it is often safest to push the ball back to the goalkeeper. This technique can also work to your advantage when you are not being challenged. If you survey the field and don't like what you see, it is a good idea to push the ball to the goalkeeper and position yourself to receive it back and restart the attack.

In order to attack, defenders must often *overlap* the attacking forwards. It is usually the outside fullbacks who overlap the wingers. Overlapping your winger is rather easy—you simply run into the space created ahead of him to receive the ball. The difficult part for most defenders comes next, when they must display offensive skills, use their imagination, and show variety in offensive thrusts.

A simple cross will be easily picked off by the opposing goalkeeper. You must practice crosses, putting enough spin on the ball to make it curve away from the goalkeeper. If a teammate is rushing in on the opposite side, you must place the ball over the goalkeeper and as closely to your teammate as possible. If you can cut into the middle by beating the man who comes your way and place yourself in a position for a shot on goal, you will create chaos in the opposing defense and open several options for yourself and your teammates.

A shot from a difficult angle should not be taken after the overlap unless the goalkeeper is screened. A cross directly to the goalkeeper or within his reach will create a quick counterattack while you are away from your defensive position. It's a good idea for the coach to designate a player to cover on defense when a fullback overlaps.

Midfielders

Along with the inside forwards, midfielders dictate the tempo of a game. They forestall the opposition's attack, slowing it down and giving their defense a chance to set up. And it is the midfielders who must often initiate and sustain an attack. As the front line of defense and the back line of attack, midfielders are a team's prime tacticians.

Working from defense to attack and from attack to defense, midfielders register the highest work rate on a team. They are long-distance runners rather than sprinters. Whether called *wing halves, halfbacks,* or *linkmen,* they must possess endurance, quick tackling moves, shrewd anticipation, excellent ball-handling skills, and accurate passing ability.

Without strong play from its midfielders, a team cannot control the center of the field, an area where many believe a game is won or lost. Advocates of this belief have increasingly emphasized the midfield and often use 4 players there. Consequently, the area has become crowded, with less room to operate in than in the glory days of the 1950s and earlier, when most teams employed just 2 midfielders. A number of South American teams still advocate using 2 midfielders, but few teams actually employ fewer than 3 midfielders.

Because they operate in a crowded area and with little time, midfielders must be exceptionally artistic ball handlers. Due to lack of time and space, a midfielder must have two or three alternate moves in mind before the ball reaches him.

Taking the ball away from an opponent is one thing; starting an attack in the other direction is another. Some teams are fortunate to have midfielders with both abilities but most teams have at least 1 offense-minded and 1 defense-minded midfielder.

The New England Tea Men had a player who did both for most of the 1978 season: Gerry Daly, a native of Dublin who played in the English first

(Top left) **Because many coaches believe that games are won or lost in midfield, it is an area that is often congested, as in this action from a 1976 game between Tampa Bay and Washington.**

(Top right) **Two midfielders, Vito Dimitrijevic and Fred Binney, gracefully battling for better positioning.** *(Richard Pilling)*

division before coming to the United States. I watched Daly in 3 games during which he stopped every attacking effort by the opposition and seemed to initiate and sustain attacks for the Tea Men. Daly was the "engine room" of New England's ship. He worked indefatigably, superbly complemented by Ringo Cantillo and Keith Weller.

When they are on the attack, midfielders must be careful to distribute the ball accurately and intelligently to the forwards. Quickness and speed (which are not the same thing) in moving the ball toward the opposing goal are the keys. Midfielders should remember that the shortest distance between two points is a straight line.

As a midfielder you must know where everyone is before the ball reaches you. If you see a teammate unmarked, pass the ball to him immediately. If you see a teammate running, pass the ball into the space in front of him but time the pass so that he can meet it without losing a stride.

If your forwards are covered and no one is running into an empty space, look for a little room ahead of you and attack quickly by yourself, preventing the defense from consolidating in front of you. A skillful midfielder who penetrates quickly gives the defense little time to assess the situation. Before the defense sets up, such a midfielder can penetrate into the penalty area and take a shot.

An attacking midfielder must try to move into the *danger zone* of the opposition as often as possible. You can create more problems for the opposing defense inside the penalty area than you can 35 yards away. What is important in offensive penentration is the time of your arrival inside the area.

If you have the ball, a lot of running off the ball by your teammates will draw off defenders and open avenues to the penalty area. If you are running off the ball, you should run convincingly and persuade the opponent that the ball will eventually come to you. If the ball is coming, time your run so that you arrive in the open space simultaneously with the ball. This will make it extremely difficult for an opponent to track you down.

Regardless of the success or failure of your offensive thrust, you must return immediately to the middle of the field, face the opponent's goal and be ready to defend. That will not be an easy task, particularly if you have just put the finishing touch on your team's offensive effort by shooting into the hands of the goalkeeper after a 30-yard run with the ball.

Franz Beckenbauer revealed the solution to this problem. He said that the easiest way for a midfielder to get back to the halfway line after an attack by his team is to have the attack result in a goal. That way the game can't continue until everyone is in position for the ensuing kickoff.

Defenders demand that midfielders slow down the opposition long enough for them to set up in the best way to thwart an attack. Defenders also demand that midfielders free themselves in a crowded area so that they will be available to receive the ball.

Forwards are a little more choosy about demanding support from the midfielders. They dislike being supported by midfielders on the side or in front of them; most forwards want the midfielders to support them from the rear. Forwards also demand that the midfielders deliver delicate, accurate passes at the right time and in particular circumstances.

Except during goal kicks taken by their team, midfielders are involved in all dead-ball situations anywhere on the field. They take part in all corner kicks at both ends of the field as well as free kicks and throw-ins, particularly on their side.

(Bottom left) Midfield is where the action is. The position for number 8 is inside forward, but in fact these players spend more time around the middle of the field, helping the defense when the ball is lost and supporting the attack when their team has possession of the ball. *(Richard Pilling)*

(Bottom right) Ramon Mifflin, a star of Peru's World Cup team in 1970 and of Santos, Brazil, joined the Cosmos later in his career and is considered one of the most imaginative midfielders in the NASL. According to one of his coaches, "he can make the ball sing and play music."

(Top left) **The greatest forward of them all, many fans say, is Pelé** *(Pepsico International)*

(Top right) **A winger should not hesitate to take on any defender face to face. Rich Reice, outside left, here in the uniform of the Philadelphia Fury, displays good form.** *(George Tiedemann)*

Forwards

Not long ago the forward line of a soccer team consisted of 2 *wings*, 2 *inside forwards*, and 1 *center forward.* Nowadays professional teams usually have only 3 players with primarily offensive responsibilities. The basis for choosing the attacking players, however, remains the same: The best scorer is usually chosen to play center forward, and the fastest players are selected to play on the wings.

Speed can take various forms in soccer. As a winger, you sometimes must employ the devastating 10-yard sprint and sometimes must sustain a fast run from a deep position to reach the opponent's penalty area.

A slow winger is a liability even if he can work the ball brilliantly near the sideline and cross it into the middle superbly. His slowness will prevent him from evading defenders and creating problems for the opposition. A slow winger enables a good opposing fullback to recover after being beaten.

Wingers were a vanishing species in the 1960s but reemerged triumphantly in the early 1970s, particularly in the 1974 World Cup tournament in West Germany. Perhaps the defense-minded coaches who crowd the middle and try to keep the scoring down have actually abetted the return of the wingers.

Wingers are now employed to open up tight defenses, or "stretch a defense." Patrolling the sidelines, the winger induces the fullback to move out to the flank and stay close to him. Naturally, as a fullback moves out to the flank, space is opened in the middle.

As a winger you must have the courage and confidence to take on anyone. You must be content to take bumps and knocks from highly skillful fullbacks who often resort to foul play. If you are a good winger, you will refuse to be put down. Use your skills, particularly along the sideline, to counteract brute force.

A good winger never approaches an opponent with a preconceived plan for eluding him. Do it instinctively with a wide variety of maneuvers. When your opponent shows signs of a weakness such as being slow in turning to the left, you should try at once to exploit that weakness.

Once you have beaten the fullback, you must move in quickly and do one of two things: continue down the sideline, drawing another defender, or cut in straight for the goal and try a shot. If you draw another defender, cut the ball back into the middle for a teammate or try to cross the ball beyond the far post and out of the goalkeeper's reach. This sets up a good opportunity for your teammate on the opposite flank. If you decide to take a shot, you should know how far you are from the goal and also know the goalkeeper's position. Gary Etherington, NASL rookie of the year in 1978, often said that in his years of development his biggest problem after beating an opponent was finding out where the goal was.

Wingers have again become an important factor in soccer. As a modern winger you must win the ball yourself with tackles and interceptions. Besides your offensive duties, you must help on defense, particularly when your fullback overlaps. You must also work closely with your inside forward.

Inside forwards could be spotted easily in the past but today's inside forwards may operate anywhere on the field. Pelé was an inside forward, but he could often be seen breaking up plays on defense.

The only way an inside forward can decide correctly whether to stay on attack or move back on defense is by being a computer. It takes an instant analysis of the whole situation. So an inside forward must be able to "read the flow" of the game at all times. He must be able to instantly interpret the movements of the player with the ball, anticipate the movements

George Best has been a headache to defenders for years. He is shown here slipping away from Bobby Moore, when the famous captain of the 1966 English team played for San Antonio and Best was with Los Angeles. *(Julian Baum)*

of that player's nearby teammates, and figure out what his own teammates will do.

Along with the midfielders, the inside forwards dictate the rhythm of the offensive game. They should be able not only to scheme and create but also to execute.

As a schemer and tactician, the inside forward must have a great deal of skill in manipulating the ball. Speed is one skill, but stamina is more important because a great deal of ground must be covered on attack and often on defense.

If an inside forward is entrusted with the role of a *striker,* with scoring goals as his primary task, he must have the speed of a center forward. Strikers are born, not made. Their responsibility is to achieve the ultimate—the scoring of goals. Strikers get the glory and the highest salaries, but they also suffer the most battered ankles, calves, and ribs.

Great modern strikers like Gerd Mueller of West Germany, Luigi Riva of Italy, Eusebio of Portugal, Jimmy Greaves of England, Alfredo di Stéfano and Mario Kempes of Argentina, and the NASL's own Giorgio Chinaglia, Mike Flanagan, Oscar Fabbiani, and Trevor Francis may have been born and not made, but *every* striker can increase his sharpness and effectiveness near the goal.

If you are a striker, most of the time your back will be facing the opposing goal and someone will always be breathing down your neck. When the ball comes, you must be able to protect it and then turn with it toward the goal. The closer you make the turn without losing control, the better.

You can cultivate this technique by having the ball come directly at you while a friend is on your heels trying to destroy what you are trying to create. The moment you make your turn, shoot the ball at a designated target. Do not practice this technique only a few times. The coach of my team once had

One of the classic inside forwards is Trevor Francis, who plays for the Detroit Express on loan from Nottingham Forest in England. Here he is battling Alex Skotarek. *(George Gellatly)*

They say strikers are born, not made. One of the all-time high scorers in the NASL is Giorgio Chinaglia, shown here on the ground after sending the ball toward the goal in a game between Lazio and Juventus in the Italian League.

the center forward work at this exercise for 4 hours.

You will not have time to control the ball the way you would like inside the penalty area, particularly in the 6-yard box. You must therefore hit the ball *first-time* no matter which direction it comes from. It helps if you can kick the ball effectively with either foot, and you must also be good in the air. When you head the ball to score, remember to put enough power behind the ball and try to head it downward and away from the goalkeeper.

If you have a reputation for scoring more goals than other strikers, someone will be assigned to keep an eye on you throughout the game. For this reason, you must vary your moves to elude your *marker*. The most ingenious maneuver becomes useless when employed too often.

You must also be prepared to vary your approach to running off the ball. You must run diagonally and laterally as well as penetrate the defense head-on. The timing of your runs is vital, particularly when you go after a through-ball early. A premature start will cause an offside, and a late start will allow an opponent to get to the ball first.

Whatever position you play, there are a few basic principles that apply. It is necessary to be in excellent physical condition so that you can run for most of the game. You must practice repeatedly the basic skills of soccer. You must learn to analyze a game and figure out how the play is going and what you can do—on the ball or off—to help your team.

6

Coaching the Game

A good coach is rare, and any club hates to lose one. In fact, the coach is generally the highest paid member of the team in the pro leagues.

A good coach evaluates players correctly, analyzes teams and games well, knows how to handle people, is an expert on tactics, keeps up to date on training methods, and never makes his training sessions boring.

Countries that require coaches to be highly educated have produced better teams in recent years. West Germany, Italy, and Spain, for example, require first-division coaches to have coaching diplomas. All three countries participated in the 1978 World Cup in Argentina. No similar demands are made of coaches in England and the United States, and both failed to qualify for the 1978 World Cup. Perhaps there is a lesson to be learned here.

To coach a first-division club in West Germany, a candidate must pass a 6-month course at the Sports High School of Cologne and receive a Football Teacher's Certificate. To keep the quality high, the West Germans admit only about 30 candidates per year. These lucky few must pay their own room and board for 6 months as well as a fee of about $1000. During this time, the prospective coaches are allowed to work with their local teams on weekends if they wish.

The toughest league in the world for coaches today is the NASL. Aside from the universal problem of winning—or not winning—several coaches in the United States have failed to bridge the gap between domestic and foreign players. Some coaches have also been unable to relate to and understand the American fan and the financial aspects of American sports franchising.

Nine of eighteen NASL franchises changed coaches in 1977. With the addition of 6 clubs in 1978, 15 coaches started the 1978 campaign in unfamiliar surroundings. At the end of that season 9 more coaches had been fired or had changed clubs.

Most coaches in the NASL have to do more than assemble a winning team. They must help develop soccer at the grass-roots level in their area by giving clinics and attending banquets almost every night of the year. In recent

Natural ability counts, but a good coach employs methods in practice that will help the players to develop themselves. What makes better players out of good ones is the ability to run a bit faster, to turn more quickly, and to be able to stop and go when it's least expected.

years a number of coaches have also acted as the team's traveling secretary.

Hubert Vogelsinger, one of the best coaches in the NASL, has performed all these duties at one time or another. A native of Austria who is now an American citizen, Vogelsinger coached at Yale before entering the pro ranks with Boston in 1975. He coached Boston to a division title in the team's first year by dealing with a wide range of personalities. In 1977 Vogelsinger started the franchise in Hawaii, and in 1978 he started the franchise in San Diego and took it to a division title. Vogelsinger has a knack of getting the most out of what he has, or has been given by the owners. "Coaching in the NASL," he says, "is like juggling hand grenades."

Team Preparation and Fitness

Contrary to what many coaches believe, soccer involves much more than the ability to kick a ball and run after it for the whole game. Soccer is a game of skills and techniques, fast running and slow running, and sudden bursts of energy—assets that can be acquired only through intensive training. For players to perform to their fullest, coaches must prepare them physically and mentally.

It is impossible to determine where physical fitness ends and mental fitness begins or know what influence the mind has on physical performance. It can, nevertheless, be stated with certainty that there is an influence and an interrelatedness between the mental and physical aspects of soccer.

An experienced coach uses exercises designed specifically for soccer. A conditioning exercise that does wonders for a baseball player or cyclist may not be good for a soccer player.

Players must have a thorough but light warm-up before they begin to train in earnest. The warm-up will loosen the body for the more strenuous exercises that follow. Weather conditions determine the duration of the warm-up period. At least 15 minutes should be devoted on a cold day, with the players wearing their warm-up sweat suits at first. On a warm day, 5 to 8 minutes is sufficient. The warm-up can consist of arm swinging, skipping, and jumping. A good way to organize the players is to have them line up around the circumference of the center circle, with the coach positioned in the middle.

When he formulates specific methods to achieve fitness, a coach must take into consideration the 4 factors that cause fatigue in a soccer player.

1. Running
2. Overcoming resistance
3. Physical contact
4. Mental concentration and tension

All *running* contributes to fatigue, but running at changing speeds is more tiring than even-paced running. Once he has started running, the hardest thing for a soccer player to do is not to continue to run, but rather to stop and turn.

Overcoming resistance represents the work a player must perform to move or stop moving. This may involve starting, stopping, jumping, or tackling.

There is plenty of *physical contact* in soccer, particularly in tackles and heading duels. A player will often collide with opponents and teammates; occasionally he will be struck painfully with the ball. Every time a player suffers such physical contact, a little more of his energy is sapped.

Students know that taking a test or writing to meet a deadline takes *mental concentration.* A top-notch player must deal with this kind of *tension* throughout the game. He must constantly assess each situation, analyze plays, and think of ways to outwit his opponent. This is in addition to the tension inherent in a player's desire to do well and his fear of failure, which can drain a player's energy more than anything else.

During a 90-minute pro game, players may cover a distance of 8 miles. One-fourth will be covered by running, and the rest will be taken at a slower pace—jogging or walking. An experienced coach will therefore have his players alternate running with short bursts of walking, jogging, running backward and forward, skipping sideways, and sprinting. Unrhythmic, or *interval,* running duplicates the type of activity a player encounters in a game. Here is a variation of interval running that many professional coaches use (see page 176).

(see page 176)

(Bottom left) **Physical contact, speed, and endurance are important in women's and girls soccer, just as in men's and boys' soccer.** *(AYSO)*

(Bottom right) **Sister Paola, reportedly the only nun to hold a coach's diploma in Italy, gives a pointer to two members of the Aquilotti (Little Eagles) soccer club.** *(UPI)*

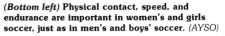

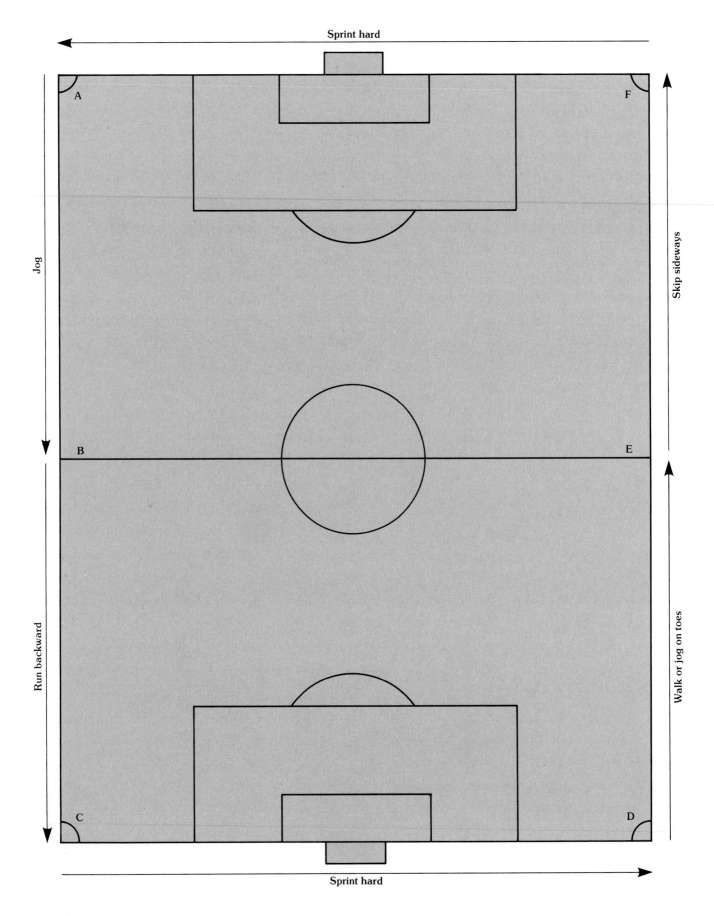

Interval running.

Jog from A to B. Run backward from B to C. From C to D, sprint as if you were running the 100-yard dash. From D to E, walk or jog slowly, using your toes. Skip sideways from E to F and sprint from F back to A. This sequence, repeated several times at each practice, will help players develop endurance and agility.

Another widely used exercise for endurance and speed is *shuttle running* (see below), which is very popular in South America. Professor Julio Mazzei, the best physical trainer in Brazil and the best to work in the NASL, came up with several excellent variations. When he trained Santos and Pelé, Mazzei often asked the players to bend and touch the ground every time they reached their destination and made the turn.

Stationary exercises should include push-ups, sit-ups, trunk twisting, alternate toe touching, jumping in place, groin stretching, and leg lifts.

To make practice more interesting, a good coach will include a number of exercises with the ball. These exercises should be performed by every player, including the goalkeeper. Each exercise should last about 20 seconds, with a break of 10 seconds between exercises.

1. With the feet together, jump backwards and forward over the ball. Then try jumping from side to side.

2. With the feet together, jump up and down while bouncing the ball with both hands.

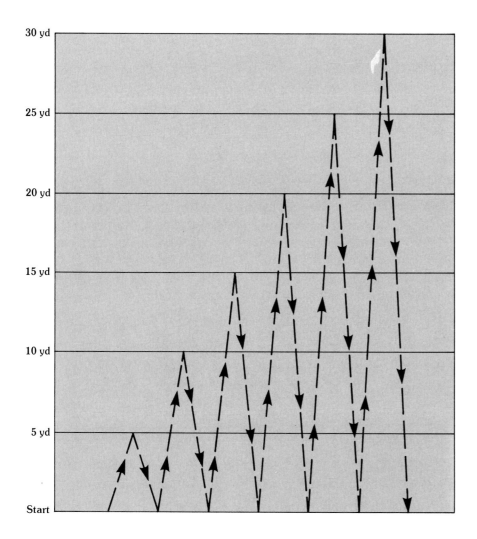

Shuttle running.

(Top) Slalom.

(Bottom) Pendulum ball.

3. Bounce the ball in front of you and alternately lift each leg over it.

4. Standing with the legs apart, throw the ball between your legs and up behind you. Turn quickly and trap the ball before it hits the ground.

5. From a standing position, throw the ball high into the air, sit down, and get back up. Try to control the ball before it hits the ground.

Variation in training routines helps prevent staleness, and so a coach should introduce variety whenever possible. A particularly effective routine is the *slalom* exercise (see diagram at left). The players should make their zigzags quickly and as close to the objects as possible. This is a bread-and-butter exercise that should not be overlooked.

The *pendulum ball* (see diagram below left) is a very useful piece of equipment. Players can use it to practice several techniques, especially heading and timing. A coach can devise many exercises with the pendulum ball, and the exercises can involve more than 1 player. For example, have 2 players try simultaneously to get the most jump headers. This is a good way to develop timing and learn how to get up for head balls in a crowd. The pendulum ball can also be used by goalkeepers to practice making saves.

Another effective routine is to have 2 players stand facing each other at markers about 20 yards apart. One player dribbles the ball toward the other, who runs to meet him. As they approach each other, the player with possession passes to the other player and they continue toward the markers, where they turn and repeat the exercise.

Pendulum balls are also an essential part of an obstacle course called the *obstacle-maze run* (see below). The course should not be shorter than 50 yards or longer than 100. This run is not recommended for players at the elementary level.

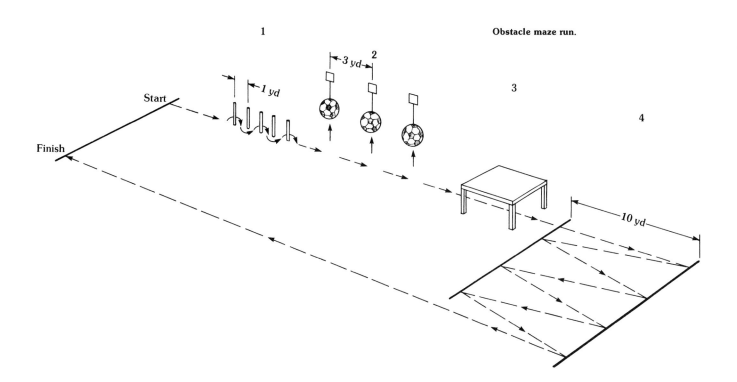

Obstacle maze run.

A player starts by sprinting to the first obstacle, where he must weave between stakes placed 1 yard apart. Next he comes to a set of 3 or 4 pendulum balls set 3 yards apart (the distance is important). The balls should be adjusted so that the player will have to jump to head each ball. The third obstacle should be a table or something similar for the player to crawl under. In the fourth and final segment, the player must do 3 shuttle runs before turning and sprinting back to the starting line. The shuttle runs should be 10 yards long.

Players can be brought to higher levels of fitness by working in accordance with the principle of *overload*, which entails doing a little more each week or at each training session. This principle can be applied to training in the following ways:

1. Increasing the number of repetitions of a given activity. If a player does five 40-yard runs, the coach can ask the player to do six 40-yard runs at the next practice.

2. Increasing the speed of the repetitions. If a player does the 5 runs in 10 seconds each, the coach can ask him to do them in less time.

3. Increasing the length of each repetition. The coach can ask a player to run 50 yards instead of 40.

4. Decreasing the rest period between repetitions. If a player has a rest period of 30 seconds after each 40-yard run, the coach can ask him to decrease the rest period to 20 seconds.

5. Increasing the load. The coach can ask a player to put weights in his pockets or wear weighted shoes.

Pressure training is one of the favorite methods used by pro coaches. It involves the running movements and techniques of an actual game, and the

Roberto Rivelino leads his Brazilian teammates in the slalom exercise without the ball.

Players should be trained to cope with stressful situations, such as this three-on-one battle for the ball in a game between Manchester United and Southampton for the 1976 English FA Cup. *(UPI)*

increased fitness which results is directly related to the needs of a game. The routine involves a controlled service of soccer balls to a player, who must reproduce one or more techniques in a situation that does not allow him to take his time. To get the best results from this routine, a coach will have 4 players, each with a ball, surround the player undergoing the exercise. The 4 players throw soccer balls at him in various ways, and he must return the balls. The objective of this exercise, which should not last more than 40 seconds, is to achieve intensive stress, with the quality of performance secondary. The routine must involve only techniques that the player in the middle has mastered. It is not advisable for unskilled players to undergo such training because they may wind up habitualizing their faults. It is a routine that helps a coach create better players out of good ones.

Early Training Sessions

At any level of play, the first few training sessions should be run at a slow, moderate pace. There should be only a little contact with the ball because physical fitness is the most important consideration. Most experienced players get out of shape during the offseason, and younger players may be having their first real experience of organized, competitive team sports. Thus, a period of adjustment is necessary for most players.

At the beginning of the season the coach may not be well acquainted with the players or their strengths and limitations. A coach of 10-year-olds has in all probability never seen most of the players before. A high school coach can generally do only a little advance programming because he does not have a clear idea of which players will be returning. A college coach has a more stable situation; besides his returning players, he will often have some rookies he has recruited. Pro coaches have the most control because all their players are under contract. Regardless of the circumstances, an experienced coach plans each training session the way a good professor outlines a syllabus and allots time to individual topics.

The first two or three practice sessions should have a moderate pace. A coach of 10-year-olds has probably never seen many of his or her players before, and as a result may not be aware of their strengths and limitations.

(Top right) Every coach must command the attention and respect of all players on the team. Here Brown University players crowd around Coach Cliff Stevenson for some advice and instruction. *(Ken Berkowitz)*

Organization and Programming

The programming for every training session must be based on the assumption that some segments of each session—and this applies to all levels—will not always produce the desired results. Throughout a season, however, a coach's program for all practice sessions should include:

1. A warm-up period
2. A running period
3. A period to work on skills individually and collectively
4. A period for games relevant to soccer
5. A discussion period
6. A scrimmage period

When you program practice sessions, remember that training is supposed to be hard work and that many exercises will become boring when repeated too often. Use a variety of exercises to stimulate the players' interest. There will be differences in the caliber of the players, especially at the interscholastic and youth levels. Instinctively, some coaches tend to give their lower-caliber players individual attention and neglect the higher-caliber players. Program your training sessions to include not only the needs of individual players but also the needs of the team.

An experienced coach determines what to teach on the basis of his players' previous performances. For maximum efficiency, a coach will establish progressive loads and rates, depending on the level at which he coaches. The running period should be about 6 minutes for 10-year-olds, for example, and as much as 30 minutes for professionals. Do not overlook the discussion period. A number of coaches make it the first order of business. The scrimmage period should come last because players like it the most. It leaves them with a pleasant and vivid memory of the training session.

Every coach—especially at the youth level—is a role model whose actions may be emulated by the players. If he is serious, the players will be serious; if he is prompt, the players will be prompt; and if he is lackadaisical in his preparation, the players will react in the same manner.

As the season progresses, more time should be spent on technique and tactics, which can be reinforced during the scrimmage period. A good coach never hesitates to stop a scrimmage and correct things that he feels are not being done properly. A coach who has prepared his players physically and technically in practice gives tactics top priority just before a game.

Since year-round soccer activity is unrealistic at the intercollegiate and collegiate levels (with the exception of the University of Connecticut, where coach Joe Morrone has soccer players work with the ball all year), coaches should encourage their players to participate in other sports. It is advisable to have players participate in these sports in alternate rather than consecutive seasons.

Good pro coaches also organize and program the activities of their players during the offseason. Rest is usually the best prescription for seasoned veterans who know how to maintain a high level of physical fitness in the offseason. But players who are not this experienced and younger players who need seasoning are often assigned by their coaches to leagues that compete in different seasons. Sometimes they are sent overseas for this purpose. Pat Fidelia of the Philadelphia Fury and Art Napolitano of the Houston Hurricane are examples; their coaches shipped them to England for action in the winter of 1979. Dave D'Errico and Bobby Smith, former members of the American national team, have also followed this route, playing in Ireland in the winter.

Coaches at the youth level should organize games in the offseason, whether in the fall, spring, or summer. Coaches who are unable to do this should tell their players at the last game that they should spend as much time with the ball as possible until the next season.

Scrimmages

As a former player and a current part-time coach, I can testify that on the first day of practice players of all ages love to get the ball, take shots at the goal, and then have a game. The coach must discourage this natural inclination. There is a time for everything, and full scrimmages or games should not take

The Cosmos made good use of one off-season period by traveling to mainland China to play some exhibition games and to encourage better relations between East and West.

place until the team is well into the training season. As has been mentioned, most players will not come to early practices in top shape or be ready for intense competition.

In early, controlled exercise routines, the coach can observe a player's physical condition and cut the exercise short if the player is overextending himself. In a game or full scrimmage, however, with 22 players on the field, the coach will not be able to look at each individual long enough to determine who is getting carried away. A player who does too much too soon is more prone to injury than a player who works into things gradually. This is not to say that practices should lag into a dull, boring routine. The coach should have a progressive program of training that includes the continual introduction of new exercises to keep the players interested and get them ready for actual play.

A team can have what I call *mini-games* after 4 or 5 training sessions, but the games should be held in a limited area and with a limited number of players. For example, a mini-game can be staged within the penalty area, with 5 players on each team. These scrimmages will be more effective if the coach imposes certain restrictions. For example, players can be required to touch the ball only once every time they make contact or use only the "weak" foot. This foot—the left foot in a "right-footed" player—can be indicated by having a sock rolled down on the appropriate ankle.

An experienced coach supervises and often participates in these miniscrimmages, which should be played without goalkeepers and should not last more than 15 minutes. However, the best coaches do not stay on the field when a full scrimmage takes place. They sit in the stands and observe while an assistant acts as referee.

The coach can then analyze the team and plan training techniques that will help overcome the weaknesses that are manifested in scrimmages. If the passing is sloppy, the coach may introduce routines in the next several training sessions that will emphasize passing. If the shooting is weak or inaccurate, the coach can ask his forwards to remain after practice and take shots against the goalkeeper. A coach with the ability to recognize the team's weaknesses has already solved half the problem.

Injuries

A coach must be on guard against injuries to the players. Fortunately, there are likely to be fewer injuries in soccer than in many other sports. According to Dr. Robert K. Kerlan, an orthopedic consultant with several pro teams in the Los Angeles area, "In soccer the players are hurt far less. In a soccer game you might not have even 1 injury, whereas in football there are at least 14 or 15 injuries a game."

From a questionnaire answered recently by 205 college and university soccer coaches, it was determined that the most common soccer injuries are, in this order: sprained ankles, pulled thigh muscles, bruised thighs or calves, knee problems, blisters, and shin splints. The injuries result most frequently from stretching or tearing of ligaments. Generally, the damage is to the lateral ligaments. Sprained ankles and pulled thigh muscles occur most frequently in early training sessions and are partially attributable to insufficient conditioning.

A coach can often tell the extent of injury by the player's initial reaction. At the top level, coaches have daily conferences with the team's trainers. Of course, most coaches at the amateur level do not have trainers to consult.

Although injuries may appear to be serious and painful at first, they usually turn out to be minor, as was the case with the Cosmos' Tony Picciano here in a game against Philadelphia. *(George Tiedemann)*

These coaches must learn as much as possible about the prevention and treatment of injuries.

Attack

Success on attack depends largely upon the creation and exploitation of space near the opponents' goal. Defenders have been taught not to yield any territory inside their penalty area and to pay particular attention to the space directly in front of the goal. That is the area attackers must penetrate in order to finish the team's offensive efforts.

It is difficult for an attacking team to create openings in front of an expertly defended goal, but it can be achieved through movement and maneuvering. No matter how good a defender is, he instinctively follows an attacker who decides to abandon an area and move to another spot. Expert defenders will quickly reoccupy the space vacated by their teammates. However, before that space is reclaimed by the defense, it is left unguarded, if only for a split second.

Except for the goalkeeper, each player in modern soccer must be ready to race forward. To combat overcrowded defenses, it is usually the forward players on attack who create space and the players immediately behind them who exploit it.

Depth is the first principle of successful attacking because it creates numerical superiority around the ball and gives the player with possession several opportunities to pass. No matter how tightly the forwards are marked by the opposing defense, one player will be free to either support his attacking teammates or put pressure on a defender and perhaps force him to misplay the ball. Also, the extra attacker can always entice a defender into vacating an area that the attacking team plans to exploit.

Mobility by the attackers can pose considerable tactical problems for the opposition. When attackers interchange positions, defenders often find themselves disorganized and without support. Attackers without the ball should make their runs *diagonally*. Diagonal runs establish better passing angles for

(Top left) Numerical superiority is important to a good attack. This goal by Tom Maresca of Hartwick College was scored in an NCAA tournament because the defenders were outnumbered. *(Ed Clongh)*

(Top right) A well-trained forward, Gary Etherington. *(Jerry Liebman)*

the player with possession and create gaps through which he can pass. Diagonal runs also discourage defenders from retreating to reduce the space behind them.

In certain situations, a coach will plan most of a team's running without the ball. A good coach tells his players where they should be when the ball is in a certain part of the field. If the right midfielder has the ball, for example, a good way to create space in the danger zone is to have the right wing go wide while the center forward retreats. This action will force 2 defenders to follow them. The coach tells the left wing to then make a diagonal run directly in front of the goal in order to meet the pass from the right midfielder.

A good coach can tell whether such a move will work after it's been attempted once or twice. If it does not work, the coach can switch wings, ask the center forward to go wide to the left instead of retreating, and have the right midfielder make a run with the ball and take a shot himself. The coach cannot give instructions on every play, but he can relay observations to the players at halftime or use that information to make the play work in the next game.

For a coach to do that, however, he must know the ability of the players. A good coach does not, for example, ask the left wing to make run after run when that player always gasps for air in the first half of the game. However, the worst thing a coach at the highest level can do is sit on the bench, watching things go wrong and doing nothing to correct the situation.

In the 1974 World Cup, Brazil tied Yugoslavia and Scotland at Wald Stadium in Frankfurt because the coach insisted on playing Jairzinho in the middle instead of on the right side. The coach, Mario Zagalo, also played

Roberto Rivelino, a gifted attacker, too far back, practically on the edge of Brazil's penalty area. As a result, the defending champions ended up in fourth place. This is what can happen when a coach fails to recognize the positions in which his players can be most effective.

When he plans offensive strategy, a coach must emphasize his team's strengths on attack and the opposition's weaknesses on defense. The strategy must be flexible so that the team can make an instant transition from attack to defense and vice versa. Speed is essential, particularly if the team relies heavily on counterattacks.

An experienced coach who emphasizes the *counterattack* will tell his players to immediately seek the open area, pass into the open area, use quick passing combinations, and try to strike instantly at the goal. Time is vital. Square passes or dribbling around the midfield area are time killers, and time is always the ally of defense. Thus, the attackers must exploit their opportunity as quickly as possible, which means that the attack must be prepared before possession is gained. Players no longer involved in regaining possession must put themselves into position to start the counterattack.

Counterattacks are usually employed as a last resort when the opposing defense is overcrowded and uses a sweeper. Many teams attempt to loosen such a defense by withdrawing their attackers and actually giving the opposing defenders the ball and allowing them to start an attack.

The plan here is to gain possession after the opposing defenders have come out of their territory. This often means that the midfield must be conceded in order to draw the opposing defenders farther from their nets. Needless to say, such a tactic should not be used against a team with experienced defenders who can take advantage of the room given for attack. The strategy can backfire, and it should be employed only by mature teams with players capable of taking the ball away from their opponents consistently.

An offensive strategy that provides for constant pressure on the opposing defense has the best potential. No matter how well organized a defense is and how disciplined the defenders are, the defenders will become anxious when subjected to the physical and psychological pressure of a constant attack. Defenders relax only when their team regains possession in a reasonable amount of time. The longer it takes for their team to get control of the ball, the less confident they become and the greater the risks they will be tempted to take.

Defense

Trends indicate that the defense of tomorrow will involve nearly all players regardless of position. A team will build a fort in front of its goal and attack en masse as soon as it gains possession. Thus, an experienced coach looks for defenders who can take the ball away from opponents and maintain cohesiveness with the midfield to create an attack.

A coach must formulate defensive tactics on the basis of each defender's ability to cover a player, cover for teammates, and cover space. Modern defenses are usually built in front of the goalkeeper, with 4 or 5 full-time defenders and 2 or 3 midfielders. The midfielders offer the first challenge to the attacking team so that the defenders will not be pulled out of position. When the opposition gets by the midfielders, the midfielders race to the aid of the defense and immediately fill any gaps. Midfield players, however, should

A well-coached team, like the players in white jerseys in this photo, tries to use speed and hustle to achieve numerical superiority at both ends of the field. Here the defenders have the edge, 5-4, and each offensive player is well marked. *(Jerry Liebman)*

be told that their primary responsibility on defense is to delay, stall, and retreat, giving the defenders time to set up.

A good coach will employ an extra player on defense if the right and left fullbacks have been getting beaten constantly by the opposing forwards and the whole defense has been getting caught *square,* or in a straight line in front of the goal.

Soccer involves a high degree of teamwork and requires "complete" players with a thorough understanding of the game. A defender cannot be expected to support the attack if his skills do not match the skills of the forwards. A coach must be aware that the process of developing complete players starts on the first day of practice. His entire training program should be creatively designed to produce players who can perform diverse duties anywhere on the field. A good coach also doesn't force specialization too soon. With a team of complete players, the coach can play either man-to-man or zone defense.

Man-to-man defense permits the coach to delegate specific assignments for various situations and match up with the opponents in terms of size, speed, and strength. Coaches often get more from defenders when they play man-to-man because pride in individual achievement is a strong motivation. Man-to-man can work well if the opposing coach does not allow his players to roam all over the field, which is exactly what an experienced coach will do when he believes in his players.

A coach can also have the team play a *zone defense,* which confines a player's defensive responsibilities to an area rather than to a particular opponent. A coach should use a zone defense if the players are young and inexperienced because it gives them more concrete guidelines and is easier to learn. He also should employ a zone defense if the defenders are slow and heavy and lack the mobility to stay close to the players they are marking. A zone defense is ideal on small fields because it reduces the area a defender has to cover as well as the width of the opposition's attack. An experienced coach who uses a zone defense may ask one player, preferably the best marker, to "follow" a particular player wherever he goes.

No player has been "followed" more often man-to-man than Pelé. Unfortunately, most players who were asked to shadow Pelé employed unlawful means and tried to get him kicked out of the game. Pelé was marked very closely, yet fairly, in a game against the former St. Louis Stars. Roger Verdi followed Pelé everywhere from the beginning of the game to the end. Midway through the second half, Pelé turned around to say something and almost bumped noses with Verdi, who was breathing over his shoulder.

"What did you tell Verdi?" I asked Pelé after the game.

"I told him it was time we went to the toilet," Pelé replied.

There are times when a star doesn't have to be shadowed. If the coach is smart enough to analyze the opposition's strategy correctly, he can sometimes find another method of making a player like Pelé completely ineffective.

Pelé was not shadowed in a 1977 game against the Dallas Tornado, led by Al Miller, the first American-born coach in the NASL. Miller had scouted the Cosmos and had come up with a plan to neutralize Pelé without putting a man on him. Instead, Miller put a man on one of Pelé's teammates, Ramon Mifflin. By neutralizing Mifflin, who originated every play before it reached Pelé, Miller cut off the danger at the source. The Cosmos scored only 1 goal that day, and it came from Bobby Smith, a defender. Smith's goal tied the contest, but the Cosmos lost in a shootout.

Whatever a coach's defensive strategy is, his players, especially the defenders, must know how to cope with free kicks and corner kicks. The closer to the goal a free kick is taken, the more immediate the danger is and the more alert the defenders, particularly the goalkeeper, should be. Organization and speed are of the utmost importance.

The best strategy is to form a human *wall*, or barrier, between the kicker and the goal, limiting the area of the goal into which the ball can be shot directly. An experienced coach designates in advance the 4 or 5 players who will form the wall. These courageous individuals should first be warned to

A good coach designates before the game starts the players who will form the wall when the team is penalized with a free kick, whether direct or indirect. *(Fred Anderson)*

Defending against a corner kick, the West Germans did an excellent job against the Australians in the 1974 World Cup tournament. Defense outnumbers the offense, 6-2.

guard the vulnerable parts of the body with their hands. Neck muscles should be tensed in case the ball must be headed.

The goalkeeper generally directs his teammates on the wall. From his position at the far post, where he can watch the ball until it is kicked, the goalkeeper directs the defenders to line up against a shot to the near post. The first man in line, the *anchor,* should stand at a point where the near post is lined up directly over his inside shoulder. He establishes himself at this spot, and then the others line up alongside him.

By giving these bits of advice, a coach helps the defense counter 3 of the 4 immediate dangers from a free kick: (1) a direct shot to the far post, (2) a direct shot to the near post, and (3) a chip shot to the far post. The fourth dangerous possibility is a chip shot over the wall and to the near post. If this happens, a defender should follow the opponent who is moving into the space behind the wall, and the goalkeeper should come off the line to gather the ball.

If the opposition elects to pass the ball *square,* the wall should move en masse as quickly as possible toward the ball. Most goals from free kicks are scored while the wall is still being set up or while the goalkeeper is out of position.

On corner kicks the defense must mark each opponent closely, especially the dangerous players. Opponents who are experts at heading the ball must be marked by the best-qualified defenders. Defenders must also be on the lookout for opposing defenders who come up when corner kicks are taken. Goals from corner kicks are usually scored because a defender failed to track down an attacker coming in late, failed to jump with the opponent, or was late in covering after the ball was played by someone other than the kicker.

Besides establishing a good training program, selecting the best players, and choosing the right tactics, a good coach must have the ability to motivate the players, resolve some of their personal problems, and recognize and remove their inhibitions. He has obligations to other coaches, the organization he represents, and the community. To his players he is a leader, a teacher, a parent, and a public-relations agent.

Although there is little difference in knowledge of soccer among coaches at the highest level, many achieve better results because of superior ability to communicate and motivate. Better players usually prevail, but the motivation a coach instills can make the difference when players of equal ability confront each other. Motivation can also overcome deficiencies and enable an inferior team to edge a superior opponent. The same team in the same circumstances will achieve different results with different coaches.

The intangible factor of personality can hamper or aid coach-player relationships. The successful coach understands every player so well that he can, with the greatest sincerity, motivate each to put out the best effort. Every line of communication between the players and the coach must be open at all times.

The ideal relationship promotes mutual respect and understanding as well as friendship. The experienced coach feels affection toward his players, and the players try to perform at a level that they know will please the coach.

A coach should set flexible, realistic goals for all the players. The players must know what is expected of them. Although a player rarely asks, he often wants to know not only how but also *why* specific steps are necessary. Players dedicate themselves to hard work much more readily when they have understood and accepted the necessity of executing a particular training routine.

A coach should make training routines and practice sessions as interesting

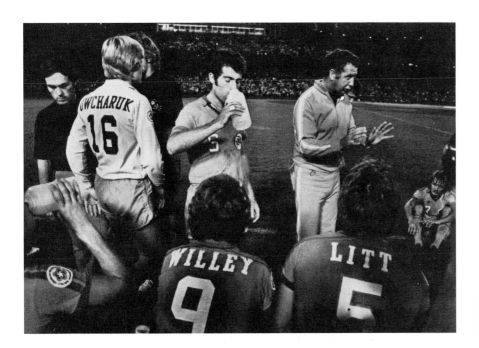

As a sudden-death overtime period is about to start, Coach Freddie Goodwin of the Minnesota Kicks tells his players to take it easy. This is not the time for the coach to show nervousness or to give confusing last-minute instructions.

and innovative as possible. This requires a great deal of planning and fore-thought on his part, but it results in more work from the players. Success should be praised to help enhance self-esteem. Valid criticism is necessary at times, but the more positive the coach, the better the team.

An experienced coach inspires the players to be totally involved in what happens on the field throughout the game. This requires concentration, and a coach can improve a player's concentration by organizing small-sided games such as those spoken of in the section on scrimmages. Lapses in concentration occur most frequently when a player begins to tire and when possession of the ball changes or play is stopped for a free kick or throw-in. Loss of concentration in a game is not intentional, and a coach can minimize it.

An experienced coach knows when to clown with the players and when to crack down heavily on the team comedian. One way to relax a player who has been in a slump is to encourage the team comedian to do his tricks. It is generally the better players who suddenly lose form and must learn how to relax, balance their emotions, and live philosophically. Enter the comedian, who tells slumping players, "You can always sell life insurance," or "Don't be depressed; you were never good, anyway."

Equipment

One reason soccer has become popular with directors of recreation programs and youth organizations, high school and college athletic directors, and parents is that little equipment is needed. Shorts and jerseys, shoes, socks, and a ball are all that a team needs. A high school superintendent in New Jersey said that he could outfit an entire soccer team for the cost of equipping one football player.

A coach should encourage every player to look sharp in uniform. There is truth in the adage, "The sharper a player looks, the sharper he will play." A coach must give plenty of thought to the way the team should be equipped. If the team cannot afford all the equipment he wants, the coach should at least encourage the players to wear clean uniforms of the right size.

NASL teams must tell the league what color uniforms they will wear at home. This avoids the confusion of having two teams turn up wearing the same uniform, which I have seen twice in games for youngsters under twelve. Most teams at that level have one set of uniforms that are not reversible. You can solve that problem by asking the home team to play in white T-shirts.

A good coach periodically reminds the players that their shoes are part of their feet and that both demand the closest attention. The players should be told often that their feet are the tools of their trade and should be bathed regularly. After washing their feet, players should dry them carefully between the toes to avoid athlete's foot.

The ball is another item worthy of a player's attention. A good leather ball is expensive (the last time I looked, it was $52), and if younger players are fortunate enough to own one, the coach should remind them to take care of it.

I read recently that a manufacturer was producing special shoes and balls designed to make ball control much easier. An experienced coach will remind the players that the only way to improve ball control is through practice, not by wearing certain shoes or eating certain cereals.

Coaching Youth

The major responsibility of coaches at this level is simply to provide every player with the opportunity to improve his or her skills while developing good sportsmanship, self-reliance, and teamwork. The emphasis should be on the joy of self-improvement through hard work and practice.

Every youth coach should follow the advice of the late Eli Marsh, who coached at Amherst College: "Always remember that the game is for the boys . . . don't ever let yourself think that the boys are for the game."

Part of a soccer coach's job is to organize practice sessions that will produce better players. This is best accomplished through drills that involve physical fitness, technique, and tactics at the same time. Ask your players to do something as simple as dribbling the ball within a limited area. Moving the ball and controlling it in a crowd is an excellent way to improve a player's technique of dribbling. Physical fitness is also improved by running with the ball. By trying to move into open space away from the crowd, a player improves the tactics he will employ in a game.

The teaching of techniques must be the highest priority of youth coaches. Scientific principles indicate that if the child never learns, the adult will not be able to execute. Experts say that if a player is not technically perfect at 16, he will never be. When teaching techniques such as trapping, dribbling, passing, shooting, tackling, and heading, a coach should use the following steps as a general guide:

1. Demonstrate the technique.

2. Explain the key teaching points briefly.

3. Organize the players into small groups.

It is a good idea for a coach to make a point by demonstrating the technique. Players of all ages pay more attention to practice than to theory.

4. Introduce the techniques under game conditions and make corrections.

It is important for the players to have a visual demonstration of specific techniques. No verbal instruction should be given at this point, and the demonstration should be performed by the coach. If you cannot perform a technique, don't even try. Find a more advanced player to demonstrate it for you.

After you have demonstrated and briefly explained a technique, organize the team into practice groups small enough to allow each player many chances for ball contact. Do not allow the players to scatter at random all over the field. If you want to practice heading, line the players up in 2 rows, facing each other about 7 or 8 yards apart. Have a player throw the ball and have his partner head it back. Allow at least 5 yards between each pair so that you can walk up and down and give individual attention where necessary.

You should then attempt to introduce the technique under game conditions. To teach dribbling, for instance, have your 2 best defenders mark you closely and get a third player to throw the ball at you. Control it the best way you can and then try to beat the defenders by dribbling past them. Convince the players that they should improve a specific technique for use in a game, not because you want them to. Do not overcoach. Allow the players more than one chance before you step in to make corrections. Elementary players can cope with only a limited number of corrections at one time.

When you teach techniques, increase the difficulty factor only when your players are ready. Do not set the standards too high or move ahead too quickly. You must build their confidence by having the players repeat a technique time and time again. Always try to give the players a sense of accomplishment and success.

The most rapid improvement in the players will come when each has his or her own ball to practice with. For a child to get the most joy out of soccer, ball control is essential. This can be achieved by constant repetition, with as much ball contact as possible. If your players' skills are low, 80 percent of the practice should be allotted to exercises with the ball.

A coach should teach and develop a young player gradually, employing methods commensurate with the player's ability. A general outline for coaching children of elementary school age is as follows.

In coaching a soccer team of 6-year-olds, the most important part of the phrase is "6-year-olds," not "soccer team." A child of this age can retain only a very limited number of instructions, and so you must be brief. To explain the proper technique of heading, you should discuss only the major points such as the contact area of the forehead.

Children in this age group like constant movement and have a limited span of attention. Keep the practice short, and simple, and let the children have fun.

You can encourage movement by employing soccer-related games. You can have a game of tag where the players attempt to touch someone with a soccer ball by passing it. Plenty of movement is also achieved in small-sided games, such as with 5 players on a side. This way the children can be active throughout the practice. There should be no competitive pressures and no full scrimmages utilizing the whole field until the last practice before a game. A team can dominate another team in a full scrimmage. When this happens, the goalkeeper and the defenders of the dominating team tend to lose concentration.

You should practice at least twice weekly, with each session lasting about 40 minutes. There should be little or no formal instruction at first. Children need the opportunity to get accustomed to the bounces the ball takes and time their approach to it. Brief formal instruction should be introduced after the third practice.

Seven-year-olds often lack the concept of team play. Like 6-year-olds, they have a tendency to crowd the ball. Therefore, it is better to form small groups for practice. They should scrimmage with 7 players on a side—a goalkeeper, 2 defenders, 2 midfielders, and 2 forwards. The scrimmage should consist of two 10-minute halves played on a field approximately 15 yards wide by 30 yards long. The markers for the goals should be approximately 3 yards apart.

These two ten-year-olds display the form and competitiveness that is beginning to develop among American players in this age group. (AYSO)

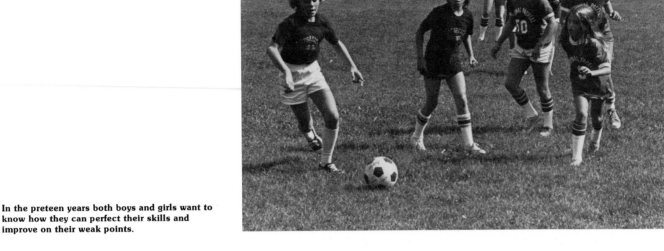

In the preteen years both boys and girls want to know how they can perfect their skills and improve on their weak points.

The pattern changes for coaching 8- and 9-year-olds. They have a great eagerness to learn, increase their experience, and challenge their skills. Your theme should be that it's more fun to play better, which means that the players must practice passing the ball with the inside of the foot, kicking with the instep, and trapping a rolling ball with the sole. The players should practice dribbling and heading with their feet on the ground. They should learn how to tackle with the sole of the foot and smother a bouncing ball. The scrimmages should be with 9 players on a side, using half the field, with the goals 3 yards wide.

The whole field should be used for scrimmages involving 10- and 11-year-olds. But before you engage them in a scrimmage, they should learn: (1) the basic positioning of attackers and defenders, (2) the basic rules of the game, (3) the basic forms of interpassing, (4) individual tactics like one-on-one, and (5) the basic tactics of team play. The goalkeeper should learn how to field low and medium-high balls.

Players in this age group are well balanced physically and mentally. They have a sensitivity for team performance, and they are daring, tough, and ready for action. It is important to provide them with enough chances to improve their techniques, but not so many that it will take the fun out of the game. This is the age where power, agility, speed, and endurance can be increased. Their scrimmages should take place twice a week, with two 25-minute halves on a full-size field.

Coaching Junior High School

Children in this age group (12 to 14) like to play as a team rather than practice technique. This is an age of physical change that produces difficulty with fine coordination. It is an age when the technical skills that were acquired earlier can be maintained and easily improved.

Skills practice at this age should be realistic. When a wing crosses the ball, for example, the ball should be crossed to the center forward to shoot into the goal. The same winger can learn in high school how to cross the ball beyond the reach of the goalkeeper to an onrushing teammate at the far post.

General endurance should be developed at this stage. The more universal the training here, the better the players' maximum performances will be later. The performances of children this age will be unsteady. Be patient. Depending upon the experience of the players, proceed with your program in a manner that ensures the development of good playing habits. Have plenty of two-on-one situations and ask the players to touch the ball twice *(two-touch)* in mini-games and scrimmages. Practice 3 days a week, about 1 hour each time. If you practice twice a week, make the sessions last 90 minutes each.

Coaching High School

Players in this age group (15 to 18) are very keen on individual technique, individual style of play, and team strategy. They derive satisfaction from working at routines that suit their style. In your instructions, emphasize the practical application of skills and techniques that are used in a game. Stress accuracy, speed, strength, and agility. This is the age when unorthodox kicks — scissor kicks, heel kicks, lobs, spins, and kicks with feints — should be worked at. It is also a good age for individual, group, and team tactics and special game situations. Collective attack and defense are also in order here. Goalkeepers should be taught positional play, including narrowing the angle and dead-ball situations.

A school team should practice 5 days a week during the season, devoting 90 minutes to each practice. A club or village team of similar age should practice 3 times a week. Players this age should compete in a maximum of 38 to 40 games a year, including playoff games.

(Bottom left) High school players are better trained than ever before. Here a student from Poly Prep in Brooklyn, New York, displays the proper form of passing the ball with the inside of his foot.

(Bottom right) Al Miller knows how to take a player aside and make a point, whether it is hard criticism or simply a piece of advice. Here the coach talks to Tom Galati at a tense moment during Philadelphia's 1973 championship season.

Coaching Techniques

Coaching during the game is usually more confusing than helpful to young players. Soccer is different from any other American game because once the soccer game starts, coaching should be confined to brief and specific reminders. You must prepare the team the week before a game. If the players are not prepared before a game, coaching them during that game will not help. There is no better coach than the game itself.

The game will also show a coach areas where improvement is needed. Proper analysis requires total concentration. You cannot concentrate on detecting your team's weaknesses if you keep running up and down the sidelines yelling at your players to move up or help on defense.

Telling your players what needs improvement is not enough; it is very important *how* you tell them. Young players can lose confidence, enthusiasm, and interest unless criticism is given constructively. Your aim is to improve the players' performance, not to discourage them. Individual mistakes can be mentioned briefly to the team as a whole, but individual criticism is much more effective on a one-to-one basis. Point out the positive to help build your team's confidence, and compliment the players often on their strong points.

A coach's responsibility is to give the players the opportunity to reach their maximum potential in physical, technical, and tactical performance. Here is a list of guidelines that will help you achieve this goal.

1. Before you try to improve the players' performance, try to improve your own. Coach yourself before you coach others.

2. Do your homework. Analyze the games and practice sessions. Prepare practice sessions and organize the team on and off the field.

3. Balance your practice. Too much and too little practice are equally bad for young players or professionals. The training sessions should take into account the players' age, physical and mental abilities, and needs.

4. Be flexible. It is a mistake to impose the same techniques on all players. Encourage each player to concentrate on individual weaknesses when training alone.

5. Don't confuse the youngsters with soccer terminology they don't understand. Use simple and specific explanations and demonstrate the point so they can see what you're talking about.

7

Watching the Game

Soccer is essentially a panoramic game. It is relatively easy to watch but difficult to assess because there is a great deal more to it than meets the eye. Unless you know what to look for and can recognize it when you see it, watching soccer all day long will not make you an expert.

There is a division of tasks in soccer. The goalkeeper's duties, for example, are by definition different from the duties of the center forward. The goalkeeper's job is to prevent goals, and the center forward's job is to score them at the other end of the field. Yet every player must be able to display the general skills of soccer and work as part of a team. For 11 people to work as a unit, however, a system of some sort is essential.

A system involves more than assigning players to various positions. A system of play, or *team formation,* is a recognizable order or organization of players on the field for the sole purpose of giving each player a clearly defined responsibility during the game. The players are of course allowed to improvise, making changes during the course of the game and adjusting to the problems posed by different opponents. Systems must be flexible so that they may be readily stretched or expanded without essential alteration.

There is no system that will enable a team to overcome inaccurate shooting or make a winner of a team whose players will not support each other. Nor is there any formation that will compensate for players who will not or cannot run. Soccer is the least static of games, making the concept of *positional play* difficult and complex.

Soccer Formations

In the early days, when towns and villages held games that often lasted several hours, soccer was known as the *dribbling game.* A player who got the ball dribbled it past as many opponents as he could, never thinking of passing it to a teammate. After the first player lost the ball, the player who got it

(Top) Soccer is a fast-moving game played on a large field. To get the most out of watching a game you should know what to look for and how to recognize it when you see it.

(Bottom) Talented as a dribbler and a passer, Rodney Marsh is one of the game's top players. Here he looks to go around defender O'Leary of the California Surf. (Julian Baum)

would start his own dribbling odyssey through enemy lines, hoping to get to the other end of town, which usually served as a goal. Soccer was definitely not a "team" sport, and it continued that way for a while, even after the duration of a game was limited and it was determined that only 11 team members could play at one time.

Even in those early days of individualistic play, soccer was an entertaining—if wild—game to watch. It became more interesting for both players and spectators when the idea of teamwork based on passing the ball was introduced. It is generally acknowledged that this occurred around 1860 and was started by the Scots. "Combination" play was introduced by the Scots in their first game against England, in Glasgow in 1872. Combination play was received enthusiastically by the rest of the soccer world and was soon utilized everywhere.

Teamwork and the art of accurate passing brought a gradual modification of the unbalanced formation used at that time. Teams played with a goalkeeper, 2 fullbacks, and 8 forwards for about 10 years after the Scotland–England game of 1872. To achieve a more equal distribution of players as the game opened up, first 1 forward and then 2 dropped back to become *halfbacks.* Eventually, 3 forwards withdrew to midfield, giving a team a goalkeeper, 2 fullbacks, 3 midfielders or halfbacks, and 5 forwards—thus the 2-3-5 formation.

Distribution within a formation always starts with the defense. The goalkeeper is not taken into account because his position has remained unchanged and it is assumed that everyone knows where he plays. The formation starts with the fullbacks, continues with the halfbacks, and ends with the forwards.

Because the 2-3-5 formation was the first drastic innovation in systems and tactics and remained the standard for nearly 50 years, it also provided the names for soccer positions. Despite later innovations in formations, the names of the positions have remained unchanged. The 2-3-5 formation is also called the *classic* formation and, for obvious reasons, the *pyramid* (see below).

The numbers next to the positions in the diagram were introduced in the late 1930s. Although they were designed primarily to identify the individual players, the numbers have come to be accepted as corresponding to posi-

The 2-3-5 formation, or pyramid, was the first of soccer's true formations.

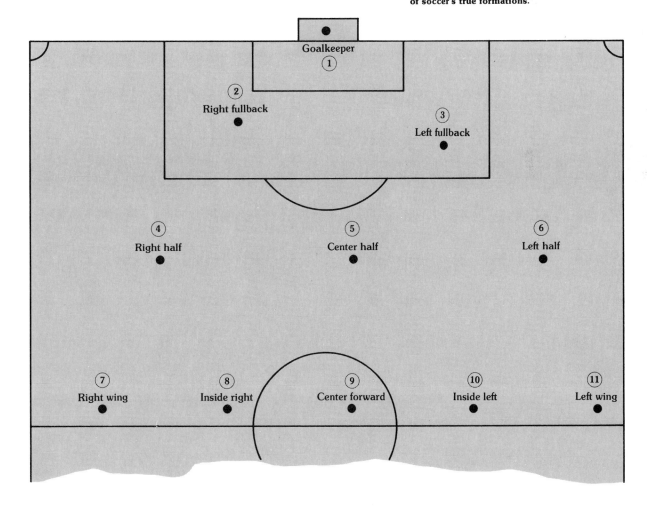

tions. Thus, in most parts of the world a right back wears the number 2. If the same player moves to right half in the next game, he will wear the number 4. And if the coach later discovers that the player is a born center forward, he will be given the number 9.

Modern systems began being developed in 1925, when the offside law was changed to require an attacker off the ball always to have 2, not 3, defenders between himself and the goal. Every system, however, has had one common ingredient: The players are divided into 3 categories; back players, midfield players, and forwards.

Systems of play are not always easily identified by the observer. A fan watching the 2-3-5, for example, should not expect to see a line of 5 forwards running parallel to each other, with 3 midfielders behind them and 2 fullbacks always the right distance farther back. Soccer is a game of fluidity, of constant motion, and there are players running all over the field, with or without the ball.

In addition to dribbling and "combination" play, or short passing, soccer developed a new weapon in 1883. The *long pass* was introduced by the English, and it forced players to learn new skills. The ball was in the air more frequently, and so heading and trapping it, especially with the upper parts of the body, became important. The long pass reigned supreme in English soccer because it proved effective; it seems that the English have still not changed their philosophy.

If you see a team that constantly kicks the ball long to the wings and then has the wings cross it high in front of the goal, you can be sure you are watching a team with a strong English influence. The odds are that the coach is English as well as most of the players. The English system is now old hat even to the newer soccer-playing nations. Thus, it is no surprise that the English did not reach the World Cup finals in 1974 and 1978.

Many students of systems and tactics feel that the long, high cross from the flanks constitutes the easiest system to defend against. There is no need for defenders with speed, quickness on the turn, or skill at dispossessing. All a team needs is a few tall players who can head the ball away. In the 1978 World Cup qualifying game between Italy and Finland, which Italy won 6 to 1, the only method of attack employed by Finland was the long, high cross from the flanks. Enzo Bearzot, the Italian coach, said, "If that is the type of attack a defense has to face, defenders can play until they are 100 years old."

There is some validity to this argument. For instance, the Tampa Bay Rowdies captured the NASL crown in 1975 by employing primarily the long, high cross from the flanks. However, things were slightly different in the NASL in those days. The caliber of play was not of the highest quality, and neither were the defenders, who could easily be beaten with the pinpoint crosses perfectly executed by the Rowdies. Strangely enough, their opponents in the final employed the same system. That team was the Portland Timbers, whose center forward, Peter Withe, could head the ball perhaps better than any forward in the League those days. The Timbers kept crossing the ball toward Withe, and without fail the center back of the Rowdies, Stewart Jump, kept heading it away.

It was not surprising that the Timbers, coached by Vic Crowe — an Englishman — did not change their tactics. When England played Brazil in the 1970 World Cup in Mexico, Carlos Alberto, Brazil's right fullback, patrolled the right side of the field as if it were his own backyard. The English coach, Sir

The English still employ the high cross pass in front of the goal. In the FA Cup final at Wembley in 1968, Everton goalkeeper West punches the ball clear from Clark and Lovett of West Bromwich Albion. *(English Football Association)*

Alf Ramsey, sat on the bench for 90 minutes and refused to make an adjustment. Some people claim that Ramsey had a game plan or system or formation and wanted to stick to it. Game plans, systems, or formations exist in modern soccer, but changes should be as easy to make as stretching a rubber band.

Modern Formations

With the introduction of the present offside rule in 1925, the 3-2-5, also known as the *W-M formation,* was developed in England and was soon adopted by the majority of teams around the world. Although there are 5 attackers listed, the 2 inside forwards, who usually wear numbers 8 and 10, actually play in the middle with the 2 midfielders, who wear numbers 4 and 6.

This may be confusing at first. Although this is the 3-2-5, the responsibilities of the players are such that there are 3 players on defense, 4 in midfield, and 3 attackers. The key to the success of the formation is, of course, the inside forwards, who must have defensive and offensive abilities. The inside forwards combine with the midfielders to form the W shape on attack and the M on defense (see below).

As with the 2-3-5 formation, the 3-2-5 is employed only by teams at soccer's lower levels. The professionals no longer think highly of these systems, but the USSF apparently does because it still refers to the 2-3-5 system as soccer's prime formation. No wonder youth and interscholastic leagues use these 2 formations so extensively. They are presented as the most effective formations in the USSF's rule book.

High school coaches have said that they employ the 2-3-5 because it gives their center half (who plays in the middle of the midfield) flexibility to attack and defend as the need arises. The average high school probably has only 1 exceptionally good player, and that's where he plays. A high school's leading scorer is often the center half, who is of course primarily a defender in modern pro soccer.

The conversion of the center half to strictly defensive duties came in 1925, when the offside rule was changed. That year an Englishman named Herbert Chapman took over as coach of Arsenal, a London-based team. Chapman was an example of an average player who turned into a brilliant coach. After losing his first game 7 to 0 to Newcastle, another first-division team in the

The 3-2-5 formation, or the W-M. The center half of the 2-3-5 has been withdrawn to become a third fullback, called a center back.

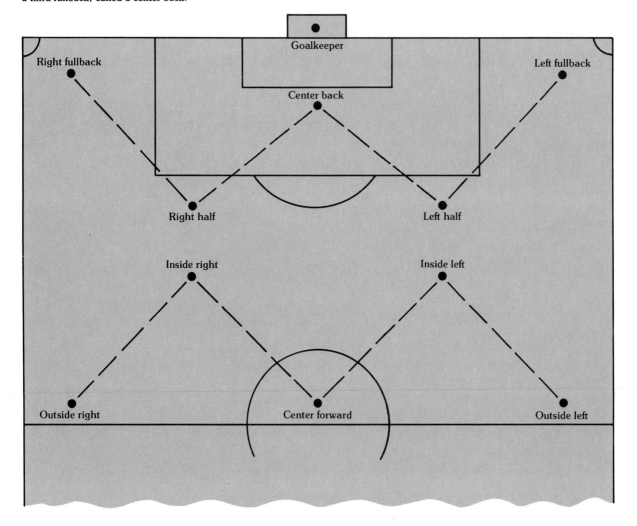

Goalkeeper

Right fullback

Left fullback

Center back

Right half

Left half

Inside right

Inside left

Outside right

Center forward

Outside left

English League, Chapman sat down with his captain, Charles Buchan, to evaluate the team's strengths (or weaknesses).

Chapman and Buchan decided that the team needed help on defense, and so they did something un-English—they made a change. They asked the center half to join the fullbacks and play as a *stopper*. Thus, the third back was born. His role was to plug holes on defense and cover the opposing center forward. This system proved so successful for Arsenal that other teams quickly adopted it.

In the 1950s a system using a fourth defender came into being. The Hungarians achieved great success in 1953 by using $3\frac{1}{2}$ fullbacks. With that system they defeated England 6 to 3 in London for England's first defeat to a foreign team on home soil. To prove that it was no fluke, the Hungarians trounced the English 7 to 2 in a return match in Budapest a few months later.

In the 1958 World Cup in Sweden, the Brazilians rounded off that figure of $3\frac{1}{2}$ by using 4 fullbacks. They also used 2 midfielders and 4 forwards, thus creating the 4-2-4 (see below). This system appeared at first to be defensive, but it was actually an offense-minded scheme.

The 2 outside fullbacks had instructions to move up to the middle of the field or beyond whenever Brazil was on attack. Suddenly, the apparently defensive alignment became powerfully offensive, with as many as 8 players

The 4-2-4 formation. This game plan was used effectively by Brazil against Sweden in the 1958 World Cup. Though at first glance it appears to be a defensive scheme, it is actually offense minded.

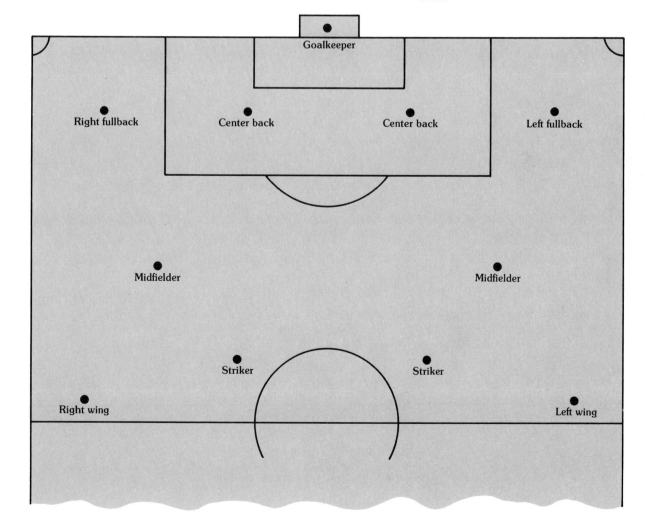

Goalkeeper

Right fullback   Center back   Center back   Left fullback

Midfielder   Midfielder

Striker   Striker

Right wing   Left wing

attacking. On attack, the Brazilians, who had Pelé for the first time, looked as if they were playing a 2-4-4. They won the World Cup that year and then repeated the feat in Chile in 1962, but with a basically different formation.

When Brazil's opponents in Sweden were on attack, 1 Brazilian wing, generally the left wing, Mario Zagalo (who later became coach of the national team), would move so that a 4-3-3 alignment was created. If the attack was sustained, Zagalo would fall further back into his own penalty area. Four years later in Chile, Zagalo spent most of his time in midfield. Thus the Brazilians played a 4-3-3 (see below) most of the time, and Zagalo's involvement on the attack became less frequent.

This was more of a defensive alignment, and for better or for worse it is used by most pro teams today. Certainly, a defensive mentality has reached epidemic proportions in some countries. In the 1974 World Cup in West Germany, the Brazilians paid more attention to defense and went home in fourth place behind Poland, the Netherlands, and West Germany.

Italy has been less prone to this overemphasis on defense than any other country. Nereo Rocco revived an old system invented by a Swiss. The system, called *Verrou* (a Swiss bolt), was originated by Karl Rappan. The formation did not at first receive the exposure or study it deserved because Switzerland was not a Mecca of soccer. As it developed, the system had a tremendous impact on contemporary soccer. One of the implications of *Verrou* was to have an extra defender playing "behind" the fullbacks. Rocco had his 3

The 4-3-3 formation. This system calls for only one winger, who can be used on either side.

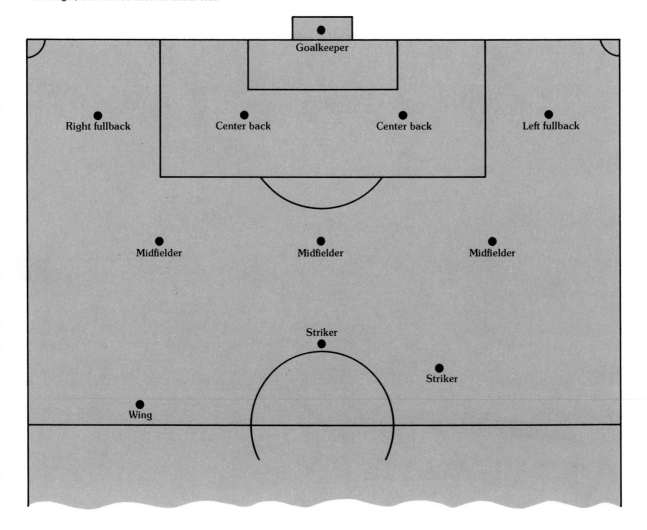

Playing for Team America in the Bicentennial Tournament, Pelé is surrounded by three Italian defenders. The Italians did not have to employ the catenaccio in this game as they won easily, 4-0, at RFK Stadium in Washington, D.C.
(George Tiedemann)

fullbacks play closer to each other and then placed another defender—now known worldwide as a *sweeper* or *libero*—behind the 3 fullbacks. His job was to stay back permanently and sweep up all the loose balls that got past his fellow defenders or were misplayed by the attackers.

Rocco's new formation was dubbed *catenaccio* (see diagram on page 208), which in Italian means "great chain." At first, the system was used in difficult games away from home, where the visiting teams were aiming for a tie. Teams then started using it at home, and a number of teams padded the defensive alignment by adding a fourth fullback in front of the libero.

Hellenio Herrera perfected the system with Inter-Milan, twice winner of the European Cup. Herrera's version of the *catenaccio,* however, was not strictly defensive. It called for the libero to break out and attack. Attacks by the libero were not common, however, until Franz Beckenbauer played the position and exploited its offensive potential to the fullest.

Beckenbauer and his West German teammates won the World Cup in 1974 by beating the Netherlands 2 to 1, but it would have been a wonderful achievement for the Netherlands to have won soccer's most prestigious prize. The Dutch played a brand of *total* soccer that thrilled the spectators and sent shock waves through the soccer world. Their attack was as intensive as any in history. Their fluid interpassing movements were brilliantly conceived and executed, often with 3 or 4 players rapidly interchanging and using accurate long or short passes at a slow tempo. Once the Dutch movement was flowing, the tempo quickened. Players regularly ran off the ball to create space, and as soon as the space appeared, the ball was pushed into it. The Dutch attacked and defended as a team. As soon as the ball was cleared from their penalty area, the defenders would move upfield.

Such massive attacking stretches the defense dangerously, but the Dutch had a way of making up for it. As soon as they lost possession of the ball, the Dutch forwards would turn back to harass and tackle their opponents. This

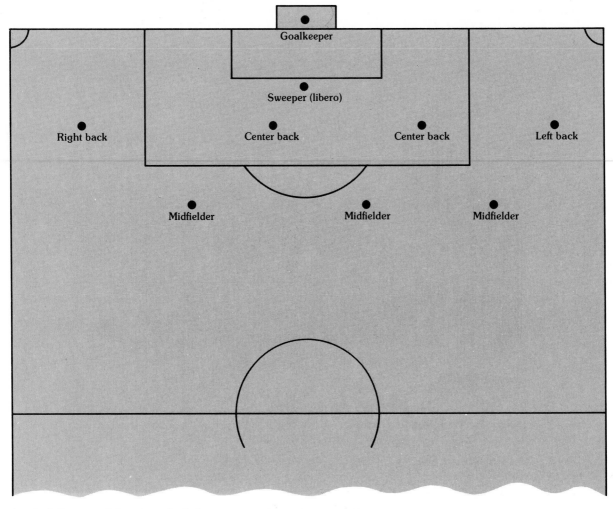

A typical alignment of the catenaccio. In its ultradefensive form, the two outside backs play closer to the middle and there is a fourth midfielder. This leaves only one player on attack. The sweeper is free to challenge any attacker or to move downfield on attack.

notable feature of the Dutch forwards' play helped defeat Brazil in the semifinals.

With very few exceptions, forwards in the NASL, ASL, and most parts of the world don't feel it's their responsibility to perform this duty. Most forwards are content to play defense by positioning themselves in front of the opponent with possession, thereby blocking his path and forcing him to pass. The Dutch forwards went a step or two beyond that—they immediately went into a tackle. Sometimes they won possession on the tackle, but more often they compelled the opponent to pass the ball with less than the usual accuracy and precision so that the passes were often intercepted. Their chances for interceptions were increased tremendously because 3 or 4 orange shirts were constantly swarming in the vicinity of the ball.

In a bar in Munich the night before the 1974 World Cup final, some journalists were contemplating the system the Dutch had been using in the World Cup or would use against West Germany the next day, Sunday, July 7.

Paul Wilcox of the prestigious *Manchester Guardian* couldn't make up his mind. He wasn't sure what system the Dutch were using, but he was sure of one thing: "If the Dutch don't win by four-nil, I am buying all the beer tomorrow night."

John Moynihan of the London *Daily Telegraph* was, I thought, partly correct in concluding that the Dutch were simultaneously playing the 4-2-4, 4-3-3, 2-3-5, and 3-2-5. My analysis was different; I came up with a unique formation. Everyone agreed that all the Dutch players except the goalkeeper attacked when they had the ball and defended when possession was lost, and so I said that they were playing the 1-10-10.

It's all very well to come up with names like the Swiss bolt, the pyramid, the whirl, or the *catenaccio* as well as all kinds of figure formations. But if the team's system does not call for all players to be involved on attack when in possession and to defend when possession is lost, that team is not playing what sophisticated observers call *total soccer*.

Evaluating a Player or Team

Whether you are a player, coach, dedicated fan, or occasional spectator, you should evaluate a performance in terms of 3 factors: *space, time,* and *support.* These are the keys to analyzing a game, assessing the all-around skill of individual players, and grading a team as a unit.

All players should be concerned about *space.* How much space do they need to utilize their skills? If they are denied space because of very close marking, do they have the ability to create the necessary space by deceiving their opponents? Are they equipped to create space for their teammates by drawing the opponents out of position?

Assume that a striker finds himself surrounded by several defenders in front of the goal and basically has only one choice—to put the ball into the net. Can he do it? Or take the player who has just beaten 2 defenders who attempted to barricade his way and now has only the goalkeeper as a last obstacle. Can he put the ball in the net despite the goalkeeper's coming out to narrow the angle of the inevitable shot?

Take the opposite case and consider the skills of a defender. Can he jump high enough and time the jump well enough to head the ball away before a striker knocks it into the goal? How closely can he mark that diminutive winger with the burning speed? Suppose the winger maneuvers behind him and heads for goal. Is the defender quick enough to catch him and gain another chance to knock the ball away without having to employ a sliding tackle, thus risking a foul?

Spectators who want to get more out of a soccer game and players, including goalkeepers, who want to win must try to constantly analyze the game. The goalkeeper in particular should never lose sight of the ball. Gordon Banks, England's goalkeeper in the 1960s, made contact with the ball only a few times in one particular game, yet when it was over he said, "I'm so exhausted!" Later, when he came to the United States to play in the NASL, I asked Banks for his analysis of a game from the viewpoint of the goalkeeper, who sees everything unfold in front of him.

Banks said: "Keep an eye on the ball at all times. Even if you don't make contact with the ball at all, you should be mentally tired at the end of the game. You should try to evaluate and analyze every move by the opposition. For example, after 10 minutes in a game, you should know whether the right wing can shoot with his left foot just as effectively as with his right. I am not going to tell you any more about it, because one day I will write my own book."

Players and spectators who take the game seriously know that soccer requires not only continuous analysis but also instant decision making. The

The goalkeeper has one of the best seats in the house for following the action. He tries to think a step or two ahead of the attackers so as to be ready for any shot at his net.

right moves, the good decisions, and the key plays are often simply a matter of timing. What was right 3 seconds ago may be wrong now.

Timing is crucial when passing the ball. A player should be ready to pass when his teammate is best positioned to receive the ball. If he wants to wait for the perfect time to pass, he must create time to hold it. The less skilled the player, the more valuable time and space he will require in order to perform. Ball skills are the foundation of success as a player.

Another key element for a soccer player is *support*, which involves a player doing things for his teammates when he doesn't actually have the ball. He must do everything he can to help them. He must be aware of their problems. A spectator can get an idea about a team by seeing if they shout instructions to each other or take positions where they can receive a pass. The more support a player with the ball receives, the more alternative moves he can make.

When a team can play the ball quickly, it is a sign that support is good. A team that supports well and plays the ball quickly cannot easily be put under pressure. A good supporting player usually tries to be about 10 yards from the man with the ball and always on an angle where he can receive a pass. Part of being a good supporting player is knowing when to provide support from behind the ball and when to move into position ahead of the ball.

Watch to see if a player can keep the ball when he is under pressure. Can he tap the ball easily with both feet? How well can he shield the ball? Can he trap it with any part of his body when an opponent is breathing down his back? How quickly can he turn?

When a player has the ball, he quarterbacks the play. You can judge a player with possession in terms of at least 5 important categories: passing, receiving, shooting, controlling, and judging. Keep an eye on the player while the ball is on the way to him. Does he bring it under control immediately within inches of his shoes, or does he bobble it and need 2 or 3 moves to bring it under full control?

It is easy for a spectator to be fooled by the distance of a player's passes. It is useless for a player to kick the ball from here to Paris when the intended receiver cannot readily bring it under control. A player should be judged by the accuracy of his passes, not their length. He should be judged by the ease of the receiver's control and whether the receiver was truly open when the pass was made.

Players often think that they can unburden themselves of responsibility by getting rid of the ball. The general rule is to move the ball as quickly as possible, but it is no good to pass it willy-nilly when no teammate is in position to receive it. The ball attracts players. A player instinctively runs toward the ball, which is not always the right move.

For example, a player who is caught between 2 opponents, 1 of whom has the ball, instinctively goes for the player with possession. Up to that point his instincts are right—he should by all means try to take the ball from his opponent. However, if the ball is passed a split second before the defender can get to it, his instinct is again to follow the ball. That's where instinct can lead a player astray. The defender should stay with the passer instead and let a teammate pick up the player with the ball.

A player's shooting ability is easier to judge than his passing capabilities. Whether a shot goes wide, goes over the crossbar, or ends up in the goal is one obvious way to judge, but there are other points to consider. Does the player get the shot off quickly? Can he shoot with both feet? Can he let fly from full stride, or does he have to stop and tee the ball up? Does he follow up his shots, ready to cash in when the goalkeeper lets the ball bounce off his chest, or does he just look on from a distance? Does he resist the urge to "kill" the ball when a simple tap would be more effective and accurate?

Gradually, you will learn that the shooter's best virtue is perhaps not his shooting ability but his ability to judge when to shoot and when to pass off to a teammate in a better position.

It is harder to appreciate the chores that defenders perform. See if you can judge whether a fullback should be paying more attention to his defensive duties or getting more involved in the attack. Can you tell when a defender "sells himself" by charging in for a ball he has only a slight chance of knocking away from an opposing forward? Don't be impressed when a defender

Unlike the relaxed attitude often found on a baseball team's bench, there is tension and intense concentration among all the players on a soccer bench. Everyone is trying to analyze the game's overall picture. *(Jerry Liebman)*

When evaluating a defender, it is important to know whether he is quick enough to catch up with an opponent after losing the initial battle. Here Stuart Pearson of Manchester United goes against Phil Thompson of Liverpool. *(Peter Robinson)*

saves on the line one moment and "sells himself" the next. The best defenders are in the right position to intercept the ball time after time.

One reason the Cosmos captured the NASL title in 1977 was Carlos Alberto. Alberto, captain of the Brazilian team that captured the 1970 World Cup in Mexico City, is a master of defensive positioning. He looked like just another sweeper when he joined the Cosmos in the middle of the 1977 season, but all of a sudden he would pick off a pass and start a counterattack. In the championship game against the Seattle Sounders in Portland, it seemed that Alberto intercepted more passes for the Cosmos than the other 3 fullbacks combined.

A sure indicator of a player's conditioning is his performance and temper in the later stages of a game. Loss of poise and unwillingness to run off the ball are giveaways.

In a game toward the end of the 1977 season, Steve Hunt made 4 long runs off the ball with a few minutes left. He didn't get the ball even once because his teammates had apparently chosen another route. Then Hunt gave the ball to Pelé and took off on a diagonal run of about 30 yards. A defender followed Hunt, and that opened up space for Pelé, who utilized it in the best possible way. He carried the ball about 20 yards and then blasted a shot that landed in the net. Pelé went right over to Hunt and congratulated him. Hunt appeared to be in condition to play another half.

You should judge a player's desire by how hard he fights for a loose ball. Every disputed ball should be claimed by a player. See how badly he *wants* the ball. The more he wants the ball, the more often he will save balls you thought were heading out of bounds.

A team is more than a bunch of talented soccer players, and assessing a team is much more difficult than evaluating a player. Does the team employ long or short passes? Long passes advance the ball quickly and methodically. With few exceptions, European teams favor long passes, while most South American teams prefer short passes. Most teams in the NASL employ the so-

One of the ways of judging a player is how hard he tries to get a loose ball. This is a neck-and-neck race between Franz St. Lot (dark jersey) and Steve Hunt. *(Harrison Funk)*

called *long ball,* but a few good teams like the Cosmos can use both.

When a team uses long passes, it usually means that the players like to run hard but may lack superior skills on the ground. When a team employs short passes and reaches the opposing penalty area after several players have made contact with the ball, it indicates that the players are more confident about themselves and their teammates. This method of attacking may be slower, but it is much more intricate and attractive to watch. Beauty and entertainment, however, come second to winning.

It may drive you crazy to watch a team play cautiously and wait for the breaks. There will be plenty of passing back and forth around the penalty area, with the goalkeeper often in the center of the action. A team that takes a lot of time with its goal kicks and free kicks and stalls every time it is awarded a throw-in can make things unpleasant for opponents and spectators alike. But if such a team gets a chance to sneak an extra man loose on the attack or suddenly counterattack and catch the other team off guard, it should indicate to you that the team's tactics are an honest attempt to stay in the game and that the team is not overwhelmed by the opposition.

After you have learned something about the tactical fundamentals, the next thing to look for is *flexibility* on both offense and defense. Actually, flexibility is not easy to spot because it is as much a state of mind as a physical maneuver. To fully appreciate flexibility, one must watch a team go through several tactics in one game and stick to the tactic that proves most effective. I forget who said it—it may have been me—"Learning soccer is like learning a foreign language. You discover that the more deeply you get into it, the less you know."

Before, During, and After the Game

You have parked the car, gotten the tickets, bought a program for the children, and found the way to your seats. Still standing, you glance down at a field that looks like a huge green bed sheet marked with white lines. You wish you could get down there and play with your kids. Or perhaps you wish you were one of the 22 men who will be playing before the huge crowd.

Imagine that you are one of the players. In the dressing room there is excitement, but the air is heavy with anxiety. Everyone seems to be aware that a life or two may be changed before the day is out. A player's behavior and thoughts before the game represent a caricature of his personality. Some players clown away the time; others retreat into private worlds and put a barrier around themselves. You can be sure of one thing, though—the tension is getting through to all. You can tell by the forced laughter that greets even the silliest remark or by the constant procession to the bathroom.

In the dressing room an hour before the game starts, the air is hot and smells of linament. Everybody is milling around. The room is almost full of naked bodies with massively developed thighs that have been rubbed over and over with oil by the trainer. Everybody is bending and stretching and windmilling, warming up in a way that seems simple but has been scientifically planned. No one says anything of substance, but everyone seems to argue and contest points of no significance. Strangely enough, there are hardly any game programs or newspapers, but there is enough tape on the floor to stretch the length of the Mississippi.

Once the game has begun, there's little time to think about anything except what is going to happen on the next play. The concentration displayed by the players here for Reading (striped jerseys) and Arsenal in the English First Division is typical of the game's intensity. *(UPI)*

In this two-on-two encounter between the old Baltimore (in dark) and St. Louis teams the players' intensity and determination show in every muscle. *(George Tiedemann)*

You have put on your shorts, and now you reach for your jersey and are glad you trained to exhaustion all week. You remember what the coach has told you time and again: "You will have a good time in the game if you worked hard in practice."

You are thirsty but know you are not supposed to drink before a game. You try hard to forget your thirst by putting on your socks, and then you pay another visit to the john. You don't want to see yourself in the mirror because you might be pale. Besides, that's where the sinks are, and you've felt like vomiting since you walked into the room 2 hours ago and saw your name posted in the starting line-up.

Suddenly, conversations get quieter, dropping almost to a whisper. When the coach comes out of his office to tell you to go out and warm up, it is so quiet you can almost hear a bandage fall to the floor. The minute you step on the field, the majority of fans in the stadium want to be in your shoes, but you wish you could get back to normal and return to your seat. You look at the opponents warming up at the other end and recall every detail the coach mentioned about their strengths and weaknesses.

Suddenly, the game is almost 30 minutes old and you don't even remember the singing of the "Star-Spangled Banner." Everything is going smoothly, the way the coach said it would. Your team is dominating in all categories, yet as you head for the locker room at halftime, you are losing. You run by the coach but don't look at him because he is staring at the asphalt. He is not thinking about last night's dinner.

The coach skips his office and walks directly into the dressing room. He is not happy, but he doesn't show it. He tolerates those who sit, those who lie down and elevate their legs, and those who keep moving. For the first few minutes he emulates the speechless players. Except for the trainer, who is giving instructions while rubbing someone's legs with alcohol, practically nobody says anything.

The coach breaks the silence. His talk is effective because it is succinct. He doesn't discuss what the disease is but how to cure it and how the team can take advantage of the opponents' weaknesses. The emphasis is on the positive, and the coach expresses confidence in the team's ability to handle the opposition. He appeals to the players' pride, telling them that with the time they have dedicated to their training, they should be able to overcome the opposition.

Individual criticism is avoided in the presence of the whole team. Even if the goalkeeper allowed the only goal by letting the ball go through his legs, the coach says nothing. He doesn't blame the forwards for not scoring while dominating the game. Substitutions are not made at this point, but you can tell that the coach has one or two in mind.

The team continues to dominate in the first half-hour of the second half but still has no goals. The coach realizes that this trend will not put anything on the scoreboard. If the team dominated without scoring for 75 minutes, chances are it will not score in the last 15 minutes. This is where the coach makes his move.

It is not as simple as putting in an extra forward in place of a defense-minded player. A coach must know precisely why the team has failed to score and take appropriate action. Perhaps the key is the simple advancement of a tall defender to the forward line because the wings have been putting the ball in front of the goal all afternoon, only to have the opposing defenders head it out.

Suddenly, the center forward scores twice within a few moments. You want to run over and hug him and kiss him, but something is holding you back. It's your son pulling your shirt. The next moment you find yourself trying to attract the attention of the ice cream vendor.

The Greatest of All Time

Here, in alphabetical order, are 100 players I consider the greatest of all time. Some emphasis has been put on players of the modern era, and 3 or 4 players were included because they have been bright stars in the NASL.

The Best One Hundred Players

FLÓRIÁN ALBERT (1941–) Hungarian forward. Albert played for Hungary's national team at the age of 17. He was European player of the year in 1967. One of the most dangerous forwards in the World Cup tournaments of 1962 and 1966, he played most of his career with Ferencvaros.

CARLOS ALBERTO (1944–) Brazilian defender. Alberto was captain of the national team in 1970 when Brazil captured its third World Cup. Extremely skillful and durable, he joined the Cosmos in 1977 and helped them to 2 consecutive championships.

JOSÉ ALTAFINI (1938–) Brazilian and Italian forward. Born in Brazil, Altafini played several years for that country before moving to Italy, where he spent 18 years in Division I, mostly with Milan and Juventus, in the 1960s and 1970s. Altafini played for Italy in the 1962 World Cup.

AMARO AMANCIO (1938–) Spanish forward. Amancio played 14 years for Real Madrid before retiring in 1976. Difficult to dispossess, he was an exhilarating player in every offensive position.

GIANCARLO ANTOGNONI (1954–) Italian forward-midfielder. An imaginative player with artistic ability, Antognoni joined Fiorentina in 1972 and has played consistently for the national team for the last decade.

GORDON BANKS (1938–) English goalkeeper. Banks was undeniably one of the best goalkeepers of all time. He played 73 games for England, helping the national team win the 1966 World Cup. A motor accident in 1972 cost him the sight in his right eye. He ended his career in the NASL with the Fort Lauderdale Strikers.

JIM BAXTER (1939–   )   Scottish forward. Baxter often played in midfield. At one time in 1963 he ridiculed the English defense. After breaking a leg in Vienna in 1964, he never regained form. Baxter bounced around the English league but played his best for the Glasgow Rangers.

FRANZ BECKENBAUER (1945–   )   West German defender. A star of 3 World Cups, Beckenbauer revolutionized the position of libero. He was captain of West Germany when it captured the European Championship (European Nations Cup) in 1972 and the World Cup in 1974 and captain of Bayern Munich, which won the European Cup in 1974, 1975, and 1976. Beckenbauer played 103 games for the national team of West Germany, where they call him the "Kaiser." Perhaps the most elegant player the game will ever see, he joined the Cosmos in 1977.

FERENC BENE (1944–   )   Hungarian forward. Bene led Hungary to the Olympic title in 1964, when he was 19. Small and incisive, he is always daring and dangerous near the goal.

GEORGE BEST (1946–   )   Northern Irish forward. Best's game features astonishing performances and magical goals. European player of the year in 1968, he has enjoyed being a celebrity and has displayed every quality of greatness except stability and concentration. In 1978, when Best was playing for Fort Lauderdale, he said, "If I had been born ugly, you would never have heard of Pelé."

OLEG BLOKHIN (1952–   )   Soviet forward. Blokhin is a good athlete who has run the 100 meters in 10.8 seconds. His mother was a hurdles champion. He was selected European player of the year in 1975. Playing primarily on the left side, Blokhin came into the limelight in the 1972 Olympic tournament. He has played most of his career with Dynamo Kiev.

STEVE BLOOMER (1874–1938)   English forward. Bloomer played the first of his 23 games for England in 1895. He scored 28 goals for the national team and 352 goals in the English League. He also coached in Germany.

GIAMPIERO BONIPERTI (1928–   )   Italian forward. One of the darlings of Italian soccer, Boniperti later became president of Juventus, which he had joined as a player in 1946. A member of the national team of Italy 38 times, he played on a world all-star team that faced England in 1953.

JOSEF BOZSIK (1925–   )   Hungarian midfielder. Bozsik was instrumental in Hungary's emergence as the world's best in the early 1950s. He played 100 times for the national team, helping it win the 1952 Olympic tournament.

PAUL BREITNER (1951–   )   West German defender. Breitner, perhaps the best attacking fullback I have ever seen, was a major factor in West Germany's success in the 1974 World Cup. After 2 years with Real Madrid, he returned to West Germany in 1977. In 1978 he rejoined Bayern Munich, where he had difficulties because of his left-wing politics.

BILLY BREMNER (1942–   )   Scottish midfielder. Bremner was Scotland's leader in the 1974 World Cup and starred for Leeds United in the English League for many years. A fierce competitor and motivator of other players, he was a dynamo in midfield.

JOHN CHARLES (1931–   )   Welsh defender-forward. Charles started as a defender but later became a formidable attacker, particularly when he went to Italy and played for Juventus. He became an idol in Turin and was called "King John." Charles played 38 games for the national team of Wales, including the 1958 World Cup.

BOBBY CHARLTON (1938–   )   English forward. Charlton joined Manchester United at 15 and later survived the 1958 air crash in which many of his teammates were killed. His stupendous left-footed shots have scared many goalkeepers around the world. He was European player of the year in 1966, when England won the World Cup with Bobby at center forward and his brother Jackie playing as a central defender. Bobby played for the national team of England 106 times, 2 short of the English record held by Bobby Moore.

GIORGIO CHINAGLIA (1947–   )   Italian and American forward. An explosive goal scorer with a ferocious right-footed shot, Chinaglia set an NASL record with 34 goals and 11 assists in 1978. He also led the NASL in scoring in 1976 with 19 goals and 11 assists despite missing 5 games.

MARIO COLUNA (1935–   )   Portuguese midfielder. Born in Mozambique, Coluna played for Benfica of Lisbon in the 1961 and 1962 European Cup finals, scoring goals on both occasions. He was the captain of Portugal's national team when it finished third in the 1966 World Cup tournament.

BOB CROMPTON (1879–1941)   English defender. Crompton played for Blackburn, where he was born, from 1896 to 1920. He played 42 times for the national team of England at a time when international games were infrequent.

JOHAN CRUYFF (1947–   )   Dutch forward. There can be no doubt about Cruyff's immense talent. Unbelievably quick, with an acceleration unmatched by defenders, he led Ajax to consecutive European Cup victories in 1971, 1972, and 1973 and was the captain of the Dutch national team when it reached the 1974 World Cup final. He was transferred to Barcelona after the 1974 World Cup for a record $2.2 million for 2 years. Along with Beckenbauer, he is considered the best after Pelé. He is certainly the richest soccer player as well as an excellent linguist.

TEÓFILO CUBILLAS (1949–   )   Peruvian forward. A player of limitless skill and initiative, Cubillas first played for the Peruvian national team in the 1970 World Cup when he was 20 years old. He has played in Switzerland, Spain, and the United States.

DIXIE DEAN (1907–1980)   English forward. Dean set a first-division record in the English League in the 1927–28 season by scoring 60 goals, raising his league total to 379. He also played 16 games for England's national team.

KAZIMIERZ DEYNA (1947–   )   Polish midfielder. Deyna was leader of Poland's national team for almost 10 years. His graceful control and impeccable cross-field passes helped lead Poland to third place in the 1974 World Cup.

DIDI (MALDYR PEREIRA; 1928–   )   Brazilian forward. A magnificent passer and splendid technician, Didi was the ideal inside forward for the 4-2-4 formation that the Brazilians introduced in the 1958 World Cup. He played 85 times for Brazil's national team and later coached the national team of Peru.

ALFREDO DI STÉFANO (1926–   )   Argentine and Spanish forward. Di Stéfano was the guiding genius of Real Madrid when they won the first 5 European Cups from 1956 to 1960. He also played in Colombia. Di Stéfano was one of the first forwards to display the ability to defend. He is one of the few men in the world to have played for 2 national teams: 7 games for his native Argentina and 31 games for Spain. Goalkeeping was his secret love.

DRAGAN DZAJIC (1946–)   Yugoslavian forward. A classic winger, Dzajic shone in the 1976 European Championship (formerly the European Nations Cup) and the 1974 World Cup. He played in Corsica in 1975 but returned to Belgrade and his original club, Red Star, in 1977.

DUNCAN EDWARDS (1937–1958)   English midfielder. One of the great lost talents, Edwards was only 21 when he died in the Manchester United air crash of 1958. He made his debut for Manchester United when he was 17 and played the first of his 18 games for England's national team in 1954.

EUSEBIO (EUSEBIO FERREIRA DA SILVA; 1942–)   Portuguese forward. Eusebio was a major figure in the 1966 World Cup, in which he led the scoring with 9 goals. A native of Mozambique, Eusebio joined Lisbon's Benfica when he was 19. His control, vision, fluidity, and tremendous acceleration made him second only to Pelé among the world's forwards. Knee injuries hurt his form in the 1970s, when he played for Boston, Toronto, Monterey, and later the New Jersey Americans of the ASL.

GIACINTO FACCHETTI (1942–)   Italian defender. Facchetti was Italy's top defender for about 15 years and in 3 World Cups, the last in 1974. He played about 90 times for the Italian national team, a record. Facchetti won several Italian titles, 2 European Cups, and 2 intercontinental titles with Inter, which he joined as a center forward in 1961. He was quickly converted to fullback and later to sweeper.

ELIAS FIGUEROA (1946–)   Chilean defender. Figueroa was South American player of the year three times. A dominating figure, he has also played in Uruguay and Brazil. At one time Brazil contemplated making him a citizen so that he could play for the national team.

TOM FINNEY (1922–)   English forward. Finney has been compared with Stanley Matthews as a dribbling wizard and master of accurate crosses from the wings. He played 76 games for England's national team over a period of 12 years and also played for Preston North End in the English League from 1940 to 1960. The national team played its best with Finney and Matthews on the wings.

JUSTE FONTAINE (1933–)   French forward. Fontaine scored 13 goals—still a record—in the 1958 World Cup in Sweden. Born in Morocco, he played for Nice and Reims in the French League and played 28 games for the French national team. Fontaine's career ended after he broke his leg twice.

GARRINCHA (MARBEL FRANCISCO DES SANTOS; 1933–),   Brazilian forward. Garrincha performed brilliantly in the World Cup tournaments of 1958, 1962, and 1966. Most Brazilian players use only one name, and his is the name of a small bird.

FRANCISCO GENTO (1933–),   Spanish forward. An instrumental part of Real Madrid when they won the first 5 European Cups, Gento helped the team capture a sixth European Cup in 1966. Short and dark, this left winger was a champion sprinter in his school days.

JIMMY GREAVES (1940–),   English forward. Greaves was one of the most dangerous strikers around the goal and away from it. He played for the English national team 58 times but never shone in World Cup play. He played briefly in Italy in

1961 and was transferred back to England for 99,999 pounds by Milan, which had paid 80,000 pounds to get him.

GUNNAR GREN (1920–   ),   Swedish forward. Gren made a career in Italy but also played for Sweden's national team in the 1940s and 1950s, including the team that lost the 1958 World Cup final to Brazil. In Italy he played for Milan, Fiorentina, and Genoa and coached Juventus.

AARIE HAAN (1948–   ),   Dutch defender. A versatile midfielder who has also played stopper-sweeper, Haan joined Ajax of Amsterdam as a schoolboy and played his first good game in the 1971 European Cup final against Panathinaikos of Greece. If Haan had played midfield in the 1974 World Cup final, perhaps the Netherlands would have defeated West Germany. He scored 2 unbelievable long-range goals in the 1978 World Cup in Argentina.

KURT HAMRIN (1934–   ),   Swedish forward. Like Gunnar Gren, Hamrin is a Swede who became rich in Italy. He was on the Swedish national team in 1958. In Italy he played for Juventus, Padova, Fiorentina, and Milan.

GERHARD HANAPPI (1929–   ),   Austrian defender. Eight times Austrian footballer of the year in the 1950s, Hanappi played 96 games for the Austrian national team. This versatile, sturdy player was a central defender who loved to attack, a right fullback who was keen to overlap and even a center forward.

EDDIE HAPGOOD (1909–1972),   English defender. Hapgood was captain of the national team of England 34 times in the 1930s and 1940s. He was an impeccable sportsman and perhaps the best left fullback of the interwar years. He was protegé of Herbert Chapman, manager of Arsenal, for which he played most of his career.

JOHNNY HAYNES (1934–   ),   English forward. Haynes played the first of his 56 games for the national team of England at age 15, opposing Scotland at Wembley in 1950. He played in the World Cup in 1958 and 1962 and also played for Milan in Italy. Haynes was an exceptionally good passer and shooter.

NANDOR HIDEGKUTI (1922–   ),   Hungarian forward. The center forward of the Magic Magyar team of the 1950s, Hidegkuti scored 3 goals in Hungary's 6 to 3 triumph over England in 1953 at Wembley. He was the perfect *withdrawn*, or deep-lying, center forward, capable of scoring as well as helping in midfield.

GEOFF HURST (1941–   ),   English forward. Hurst's record of 3 goals in a World Cup final, set in 1966, will perhaps remain forever. He played most of his career with West Ham United and had a brief stay with the Seattle Sounders of the NASL in 1976. Hurst was a powerful shooter and was good in the air.

ALEX JACKSON (1905–1946),   Scottish forward. Along with his brother Wattie, Alex played for Bethlehem Steel in the United States in the early 1920s. He returned to Scotland and became the hero of the Wembley Wizards when Scotland humiliated England 5 to 1 in 1928, scoring 3 of the goals. He died in an automobile crash while serving in the Army.

ALEX JAMES (1902–1957),   Scottish forward. A star of the great Arsenal team of the English League in the late 1920s and 1930s, James also played for Preston North End. An 8-time member of the national team of Scotland, he played with the 1928 Wembley Wizards team that scored 5 goals against England in London.

KEVIN KEEGAN (1951–   ),   English forward. Keegan joined Liverpool in 1971 and matured into a player of exceptional versatility. An intelligent player, he is very quick and has great acceleration. A member of the national team of England today, Keegan became one of the most sought-after players in the late 1970s.

MARIO KEMPES (1954–   ),   Argentine forward. Kempes emerged as the star of the 1978 World Cup, leading Argentina to its first world championship. He dominated the final game, scoring twice in the 3 to 1 overtime victory over the Netherlands. He was all over the field, playing a ''position'' that would defy tactical definition. He plays for Valencia in the Spanish League.

RAYMOND KOPA (1931–   ),   French forward. Born Raymond Kopaczewski, the son of a Polish miner, he was a key player for Real Madrid in the 1950s. Kopa played 45 games for the national team of France and ended his career with Reims of the French League.

LADISLAO KUBALA (1927–   ),   Hungarian, Czechoslavakian, and Spanish forward. A native of Hungary, Kubala played for the national teams of 3 countries in the 1950s and 1960s and made history again when he played alongside his son Branko in Toronto in 1967. An enormously powerful forward with a thumping right foot, he became coach of the Spanish national team in 1976.

ANGEL LABRUNA (1917–   ),   Argentine forward. Labruna was one of the few great Argentine players who did not move to Colombia in the late 1940s. He scored 457 goals in a long career with River Plate. Labruna played several years for the Argentine national team, the last time at the age of 41 in the 1958 World Cup.

GREGORZ LATO (1950–   ),   Polish forward. The leading scorer of the 1974 World Cup with 7 goals, Lato was one of the most effective members of the Polish squad that took third place, scoring the lone goal in the 1 to 0 victory over Brazil. A very fast right winger, Lato also played in the 1978 World Cup in Argentina.

DENIS LAW (1940–   ),   Scottish forward. An acrobatic shooter and superb header, Law played professionally at 15. He was bought by Manchester City for 55,000 pounds in 1960 and sold to Torino in Italy for 100,000 pounds a year later. He returned to England in 1962 to play for Manchester United. He played 54 games for the Scottish national team, but despite his immeasurable ability, Law never left his mark in World Cup competition.

TOMMY LAWTON (1919–   ),   English forward. Lawton became a professional at age 17. In 1938, at age 19, he played center forward for the national team of England. Perhaps the most effective striker of his era, Lawton had a tremendous shot with either foot and was excellent in the air.

WLODZIMIERZ LUBANSKI (1947–   ),   Polish forward. Lubanski played for the Polish national team 20 times before he was 20 years old. He helped Poland qualify for the 1974 World Cup but could not participate in the final because of an injury. He returned for the 1978 World Cup after an absence of almost 3 years from international competition. Lubanski might well be the best player Poland has produced.

RODNEY MARSH (1944–   ),   English forward. They call him the ''Clown Prince'' of British soccer, but Marsh is a charismatic player who can create miracles. Several times a member of the national team of England, he joined the Tampa Bay Rowdies of the NASL in 1976 and has already made his mark in the United States.

JOSEF MASOPUST (1931–   ),   Czechoslovakian midfielder. Masopust learned soccer from his father, a miner. Dukla Prague's most famous star, he often performed

in New York. A major in the Army at the peak of his career, Masopust was European
player of the year in 1962.

SIR STANLEY MATTHEWS (1915–   ),   English forward. Matthews was an
unmatched dribbler and played until he was 50 years old. A brilliant winger with exceptional skills, he was knighted for his service to soccer. His 1953 performance in
the FA Cup final with Blackpool was unforgettable, and Matthews was an attraction
even at age 49.

LADISLAO MAZURKIEWICZ (1945–   ),   Uruguayan goalkeeper. A star of 3
World Cups for Uruguay, Mazurkiewicz was recognized as a Spanish citizen despite his
Polish descent. Acrobatic and daring, he was one of the best goalkeepers of the 1960s
and 1970s.

SANDRINO MAZZOLA (1942–   ),   Italian forward. Extreme quickness of
thought and movement and admirable control compensated for Mazzola's spare phy-
sique. He made the first of his 70 appearances for the Italian national team in 1963
and helped Inter win the European Cup in 1964 and 1965. He has appeared in 3
World Cups and was perhaps the only Italian to play well against Argentina in 1974.
He is the son of Valentino Mazzola.

VALENTINO MAZZOLA (1919–1949),   Italian forward. Mazzola was captain of Torino and the Italian national team in the 1940s. Torino was on the verge of winning its
fifth consecutive Italian League title when the team plane crashed on the hillside at
Superga outside Turin in 1949 killing everyone on board.

GIUSEPPE MEAZZA (1910–   ),   Italian forward. Meazza scored 33 goals in 50
games with the Italian national team and 355 goals in the *Calcio*, or Italian League.
He was a brilliant center forward who played for the World Cup champion teams of
1934 and 1938.

BILLY MEREDITH (1877–1958),   Welsh forward. Along with Stanley Matthews,
Meredith has been the most durable winger in the history of British soccer. He was
close to 50 years old when he retired in 1925. Meredith played 51 games for the
Welsh national team from 1894 to 1920.

LUIS MONTI (1901–   ),   Argentine and Italian defender. Monti played for Argentina's Olympic teams in the 1920s and started in the 1930 World Cup final against
Uruguay in Montevideo. He moved to Italy in 1931 and played for Italy's national
team in the 1934 World Cup final. He is the only man to have played in World Cup
finals for 2 different countries.

BOBBY MOORE (1941–   ),   English defender. The "golden boy" of English
soccer in the 1960s, Moore played a record 108 times for the national team of England, which he captained in the World Cup triumph of 1966. An expert calculator
and reader of the game, Moore was renowned for his cool demeanor. He played for
West Ham United and had a brief stay in San Antonio and Seattle of the NASL.

STANLEY MORTENSEN (1921–   ),   English forward. Mortensen played 25
games for the national team of England, including the 1950 World Cup. He was an
opportunistic player, good in the air and famous for his acceleration and courage. He
is also remembered for his partnership with Stanley Matthews.

GERD MUELLER (1945–   ),   West German forward. Mueller has been a deadly striker inside the penalty area, scoring 69 goals in 62 games for the national team

of West Germany. He scored the winning goal in the 2 to 1 victory over the Netherlands in the 1974 World Cup final. In the quarter final round that year, he scored an amazing goal against Yugoslavia while flat on his back with 2 opposing players on him. Mueller is known for his timing and menacing positional sense.

IGOR NETTO (1930–   ),   Soviet midfielder. Netto was captain of the Soviet national team when it won the 1952 Olympic tournament. He played 59 times for the national team and later became a radio sports reporter in Moscow.

GUNTER NETZER (1944–   ),   West German midfielder. Netzer was the key player on the brilliant West German team that won the European Championship in 1972. A player of unlimited vision and imagination, he was capable of striking long cross-field passes with unbelievable accuracy. He later played for Real Madrid and in 1978 became general manager of Hamburg, one of the top teams in the Bundesliga.

GUNNAR NORDAHL (1921–   ),   Swedish forward. Nordahl scored 225 goals for Milan of the Italian League in the late 1940s and 1950s. Despite weighing over 200 pounds, he was a deft, skilled player. He played and scored for the European all-stars against the British all-stars in 1947.

ERNST OCWIRK (1926–1980),   Austrian defender. A powerful and delicate player, Ocwirk helped Austria take third place in the 1954 World Cup. He moved to Italy in 1956 and became a successful forward for Genoa and Sampdoria, which he later coached.

CARLO PAROLA (1920–   ),   Italian defender. Parola was the only Italian selected to play for the European all-stars against the British all-stars in 1947. He was famous for his overhead bicycle kicks. From 1938 to 1954 Parola played for Juventus, which he later coached to a championship.

PELÉ (EDSON ARANTES DO NASCIMENTO; 1940–   ),   Brazilian forward. Pelé first played for the national team of Brazil when he was only 17. He led Brazil to World Cup championships in 1958, 1962, and 1970. Pelé came to the United States to play for the Cosmos in 1975. His flashes of brilliance on the field and his modesty, ingenuity, and simplicity off the field made him a favorite with the American public. He was undeniably the greatest player of his generation and perhaps the best of all time.

SILVIO PIOLA (1913–   ),   Italian forward. Piola scored 356 goals in the defense-minded Italian League and was the best center forward in the 1938 World Cup. He played for Italy in 1952 at the age of 38, the last of his 33 games with the national team.

PIRRI (JOSÉ MARTINEZ SANCHEZ; 1945–   ),   Spanish defender. Pirri was born in North Africa. For a decade he provided Real Madrid and the national team of Spain with determination, mobility, and technique.

FRANTISEK PLANICKA (1904–   ),   Czechoslovakian goalkeeper. Planicka was born in 1904 but continued to play in "friendly" games into the 1970s. Perhaps the best goalkeeper in the 1934 World Cup, he was the captain of the national team of Czechoslovakia in the 1938 World Cup final and played 74 games for his country.

MICHEL PLATINI (1955–   ),   French forward. One of the stars of the 1978 World Cup, Platini is a schemer, a dribbler, and a goal scorer. Also a deadly free-kick specialist, he is destined to be a star of the 1980s.

FERENC PUSKÁS (1926–   ),   Hungarian and Spanish forward. Puskás was the
captain of the 1953 Magic Magyar team that handed England its first loss at home. He
played for Hungary when he was 18 and scored 85 goals in 84 games for the national team. He defected in 1956 and joined Real Madrid. Puskás played for Spain in the
1962 World Cup and has coached in many parts of the world.

ROB RENSENBRINK (1947–   ),   Dutch forward. Rensenbrink is extremely fast,
has superb skills, and is excellent in the air, as his opponents in the 1978 World Cup
can attest. He plays in Belgium but rarely misses games for the national team of the
Netherlands.

LUIGI RIVA (1944–   ),   Italian forward. Riva has been one of the most admired
and incisive Italian strikers since World War II. He was such a good player in the late
1960s and early 1970s that his countrymen expected him to win the World Cup
alone, although he suffered broken legs in 1967 and 1970. He helped Cagliari, an
obscure Sardinian club, win the Italian championship in 1970. Riva could have been
transferred for $3 million in 1973 but instead reaffirmed his loyalty to Cagliari.

ROBERTO RIVELINO (1946–   ),   Brazilian midfielder. Nobody can swerve the
ball with the left foot the way Rivelino does. Extremely skillful and tenacious, he has
already played in 3 World Cups for Brazil. He was a forward in the 1970 tournament
in Mexico and team captain in 1974 and 1978. By the time he retires, Rivelino will
probably have played more games for the national team of Brazil than anyone else.
He signed a contract to play in Saudi Arabia in 1978 for a reported $9 million.

GIANNI RIVERA (1943–   ),   Italian forward. Rivera was the "golden boy" of
Italian soccer for years after starting in Division I at the age of 15. He joined Milan in
1959 and was still playing for them in 1978. He became a controversial as well as a
celebrated player in Italy when he gained control of Milan in 1976, forcing the president of the team to leave. He has played 60 games for the Azzuri—the national team
of Italy—scoring 14 goals.

DJALMA SANTOS (1929–   ),   Brazilian defender. Djalma Santos played in 4
World Cups for Brazil from 1954 through 1966. A giant of a fullback, he loved to attack even when he was winding up his career at 37 years of age.

NILTON SANTOS (1926–   ),   Brazilian defender. Nilton Santos played his first
game for the national team of Brazil in 1949 at the age of 23 and was still with the
team in the 1962 World Cup final. He played his last game for Brazil when he was
40. Like Djalma Santos (no relation), he loved to attack at every opportunity.

JUAN SCHIAFFINO (1925–   ),   Uruguayan and Italian forward. Born in Montevideo, Schiaffino was allowed to play for Italy in 1954 after he joined Milan. Schiaffino was a frail man but a remarkable dribbler and superb passer. His biggest goal
was the tying goal against Brazil in the 1950 World Cup final, which Uruguay eventually won.

KARL-HEINZ SCHNELLINGER (1939–   ),   West German defender. An elegant
fullback, Schnellinger played in 4 World Cup tournaments from 1958 through 1970.
One of the first West Germans to make a career in Italy, he was also one of the few
defenders to be paid well in Italy. He helped Milan capture the European Cup in
1969 and the Cup Winners Cup in 1973.

UWE SEELER (1937–   ),   West German forward. Seeler made 4 successful
appearances in World Cup tournaments, playing his first game for the West German

national team at age 17. Along with Franz Beckenbauer and Gerd Mueller, he is the biggest name in West German soccer. He exemplified the mental attitude of West German players by competing on an artificial Achilles' tendon. Seeler retired from international soccer after the 1970 World Cup in Mexico.

ALAN SIMONSEN (1952–   ),   Danish forward. Simonsen was European player of the year in 1977. A diminutive striker, he has starred for Borussia Monchengladbach in West Germany and Barcelona in Spain. The Cosmos have pursued him feverishly because of his scoring ability and high work rate.

MATTHIAS SINDELAR (1903–1941),   Austrian forward. Sindelar was the main attacker on the *Wunderteam* in the 1930s. Despite his small size, he had a powerful shot and could penetrate defenses easily. He played in the 1934 World Cup. Sindelar killed himself after a teammate betrayed him to the Gestapo as being part Jewish.

LUIS SUAREZ (1935–   ),   Spanish forward. Suarez had great careers in Spain and Italy in the 1960s, playing for Barcelona and Inter. He signed his first pro contract at 18 and played his first game for the national team of Spain in 1957 at age 22. Suarez helped Barcelona reach the European Cup final in 1961 and was transferred to Inter for about $600,000 in 1962.

TOSTÃO (EDUARDO GONÇALVES DE ANDRADE; 1941–   ),   Brazilian forward. A player of fluency and balance, Tostão left Cruzeiro in 1973 to play for Vasco da Gama in Rio de Janeiro. He had to withdraw from Brazil's 1974 World Cup team because of an eye injury that had also almost kept him out of the 1970 World Cup.

PAUL VAN HIMST (1943–   ),   Belgian forward. Van Himst was only 17 when he was first chosen Belgium's player of the year; he had joined the Anderlecht team at about 10 years of age. Stars from around the world gathered in Brussels in 1974 to play in his testimonial game.

FRITZ WALTER (1920–   ),   West German forward. Walter played the first of his 61 games for the West German national team in 1940. He was on the team that beat Slovakia in 1942 in what was to be Germany's last international game for 8 years. Walter was the captain of the West German team that won the World Cup in 1954, and he also played in 1958 in Sweden.

BILLY WRIGHT (1924–   ),   English defender. Wright was picked as a forward in the first of his 105 games for the national team of England in 1946. He played in the World Cup in 1950, 1954, and 1958. Perhaps the greatest star ever to play for Wolverhampton, he also coached Arsenal briefly in the 1960s and then went into sports commentary for television.

LEV YASHIN (1929–   ),   Soviet goalkeeper. Yashin was one of the best goalkeepers of all time. Born in Moscow in 1929, he left school at 14 to join Moscow Dynamo and became coach of Dynamo after his retirement. He played in 3 World Cups and was the goalkeeper when the Soviet Union won the Olympic tournament in 1956. Yashin played superbly for the world all-stars that met England in London in 1963.

RICARDO ZAMORA (1901–1978),   Spanish goalkeeper. One of the best goalkeepers of all time, Zamora was a hero in the 1920, 1924, and 1928 Olympic tournaments as well as the 1934 World Cup. He played 47 games for the national team of Spain, 31 of them consecutively. In his first 34 games for Spain, Zamora allowed only 27 goals.

ZICO (ARTHUR ANTUNES COIMBRA; 1953–   ),   Brazilian forward. Brazilians considered Zico the heir apparent to Pelé, but he didn't fulfill their expectations in the 1978 World Cup. Small in size, with a ferocious shot and good distribution, he likes to play away from the goal.

ZITO (JOSÉ ELI MIRANDA; 1933–   ),   Brazilian midfielder. Strong and fluent, Zito was equally good at taking the ball away and distributing it. An intricate member of Brazil's 4-2-4 formation, he played most of his career with Pelé at Santos.

DINO ZOFF (1942–   ),   Italian goalkeeper. Zoff played for Udenese, Mandova, and Napoli before Juventus signed him in 1972. A dedicated and talented goalkeeper with sure hands, he did not allow a goal for 1143 minutes before the 1974 World Cup. Zoff has proved that a goalkeeper can become better late in his career.

The United States Hall of Fame

Past presidents of the USSF elect 2 to 6 individuals to their Hall of Fame each year. An exception was made in 1976 when all the members of the American national team that beat England 1 to 0 in the 1950 World Cup were installed. Nominations are usually made by the state associations, but a Hall of Fame Veterans Committee makes sure that no one who deserves nomination is overlooked. The USSF's efforts to find a home for the Hall of Fame intensified in 1978, with northern New Jersey and Oneonta, N.Y. as possible sites. Here is a list of the members of the Hall of Fame, which was instituted in 1950.

Electee	Elected	Electee	Elected
Abroncino, Uberto (Cal.)	1971	Cordery, Ted (Cal.)	1975
Ahrker, Albert (Pa.)	1979	Craddock, Robert (Pa.)	1959
Alonso, Julius (N.Y.)	1972	Craggs, Ed (Wash.)	1969
Andersen, William (N.Y.)	1956	Cummings, Wilfred R. (Ill.)	1953
Ardizzone, John (Cal.)	1971	DeLuca, Enzo (N.J.)	1979
Armstrong, James (N.Y.)	1952	Delach, Joseph (Pa.).	1973
Bahr, Walter (Pa.)	1976	DiOrio, Nick (Pa.)	1974
Barriskill, Joseph J. (N.Y.)	1953	Donaghy, Edward J. (N.Y.)	1951
Beardsworth, Fred (Mass.)	1965	Donelli, Aldo T. (Pa.)	1954
Bernabei, Dr. Raymond (Pa.)	1978	Douglas, James E. (N.J.)	1954
Birttan, Harold (Pa.)	1951	Dresmich, John (W. Penn.)	1968
Booth, Joseph (Conn.)	1952	Duff, Duncan (Cal.)	1972
Borghi, Frank (Mo.)	1976	Dugan, Thomas (N.J.)	1955
Boxer, Matthew (Calif.)	1961	Dunn, James (Mo.)	1974
Briggs, Lawrence (Conn.)	1978	Epperleim, Rudy (N.J.)	1951
Brock, John Dr. (Mass.)	1950	Fairfield, Harry (Pa.)	1951
Brown, Andrew M. (Ohio)	1950	Ferguson, John (Mass.)	1950
Brown, Dave (N.J.)	1951	Fernley, John A. (Mass.)	1951
Cahill, Thomas W. (N.J.)	1950	Ferro, Charles (N.Y.)	1958
Carrafi, Ralph (Ohio)	1959	Fishwick, George (Ill.)	1974
Chesney, Stanley (N.Y.)	1966	Flamhaft, Jack (N.Y.)	1964
Colombo, Charlie (Mo.)	1976	Fleming, Harry G. (Pa.)	1967
Collins, George M. (Mass.)	1951	Foulds, Powys A. L. (Mass.)	1953
Commander, Colin (Ohio)	1967	Foulds, Sam T. N. (Mass.)	1969

Fowler, Daniel W. (N.Y.)	1970	Morrison, Robert (Pa.)	1951
Fowler, Margaret (Peg) (N.Y.)	1979	Netto, Fred (Ill.)	1958
Fryer, William (N.J.)	1951	Niotis, Dimitrios J. (Ill.)	1963
Gaetjens, Joe (N.Y.)	1976	Olaff, Gene (N.J.)	1971
Garcia, Peter (Mo.)	1964	Oliver, Arnold (S. N.E.)	1968
Giesler, Walter (Mo.)	1962	Palmer, William (Pa.)	1952
Glover, Chas. E. (N.Y.)	1965	Pariani, Gino (Mo.)	1976
Gonsalves, Bill (Mass.)	1950	Patenaude, Bertrand A. (S. N.E.)	1971
Gould, David L. (Pa.)	1953	Peel, Peter J. (Ill.)	1951
Govier, Sheldon (Ill.)	1950	Peters, Wally (N.J.)	1967
Gryzik, Joseph (Ill.)	1973	Pisicopo, George (N.Y.)	1978
Healy, George (Mich.)	1951	Pomeroy, Edgar (Cal.)	1955
Hemmings, William (Ill.)	1961	Ramsden, Arnold (Texas)	1957
Hudson, Maurice (Cal.)	1966	Ratican, Harry (Mo.)	1950
Hynes, Jack (N.Y.)	1977	Reese, Vernon R. (Md.)	1957
Iglehart, Miss A. (Md.)	1951	Renzulli, Peter (N.Y.)	1951
Jaap, John (Pa.)	1953	Ringsdorf, Eugene J. (Md.)	1979
Jeffrey, Bill (Pa.)	1951	Rottenberg, Jack (N.J.)	1971
Johnson, Jack (Ill.)	1952	Ryan, John (Pa.)	1958
Kempton, George (Wash., D.C.)	1950	Sager, Tom (Pa.)	1968
Keough, Harry (Mo.)	1976	Schillinger, Emil (Pa.)	1960
Klein, Paul (N.J.)	1953	Schroeder, Elmer (Pa.)	1951
Kozma, Oscar (Cal.)	1964	Schwarcz, Erno (N.Y.)	1951
Kraus, Harry A. (N.Y.)	1963	Shields, F. (Zibikowski) (N.J.)	1968
Kuntner, Rudy (N.Y.)	1963	Smith, Alfred (Pa.)	1951
Lamm, Kurt (N.Y.)	1979	Souza, Eddie (Mass.)	1976
Lang, Millard (Md.)	1950	Souza, John (Mass.)	1976
Lewis, H. Edgar (Pa.)	1950	Spalding, Dick (Pa.)	1951
Maca, Joe (N.Y.)	1976	Stark, Archie (N.Y.)	1950
Magnozzi, Enzo (N.Y.)	1978	Steelint, Nicholas (Cal.)	1971
MacEwan, John J. (Mich.)	1953	Steur, August (N.Y.)	1969
McGrath, Frank (Mass.)	1978	Stewart, Douglas (Pa.)	1950
McGuire, James P. (N.Y.)	1951	Stone, Robert T. (Colo.)	1969
McGuire, John (N.Y.)	1951	Swords, Thomas (Mass.)	1951
McIllveny, Ed (Pa.)	1976	Tintle, George	1952
McLaughlin, Ben (Pa.)	1977	Triner, Joeph (Ill.)	1951
McLay, Allan (Mass.)	1968	Walder, James (Pa.)	1968
McSkimming, Den (Mo.)	1951	Wallace, Frank (Mo.)	1976
Maher, Jack (Ill.)	1970	Warshuer, Al (Cal.)	1977
Manning, Randolf R. (N.Y.)	1950	Weir, Alex (N.Y.)	1975
Marre, John (Mo.)	1953	Weston, Vic (Wash., D.C.)	1956
Mieth, Werner (N.J.)	1974	Wilson, Peter (N.J.)	1950
Millar, Robert (N.Y.)	1950	Woods, John W. (Ill.)	1952
Miller, Milt (N.Y.)	1971	Young, John (Calif.)	1958
Mills, James (Pa.)	1954	Zampini, Daniel (Pa.)	1963
Moore, James F. (Mo.)	1971	Zerhusen, Albert (Cal.)	1978
Morrissette, William (Mass.)	1967		

APPENDIX B

The Laws of the Game

This chapter is in four parts. It includes:

1. The Laws of the Game and Universal Guide for Referees
2. Questions and Answers
3. The Rules in the United States
4. The Rules for Indoor Soccer*

The Laws of the Game and Universal Guide for Referees

Notes

Provided the principles of these Laws be maintained, they may be modified in their application.

1. To players of school age, as follows: (a) size of playing pitch; (b) size, weight and material of ball; (c) width between the goal-posts and height of the cross-bar from the ground; (d) the duration of the periods of play.

2. For matches played by women: (a) size, weight and material of ball; (b) duration of the periods of play; (c) further modifications are only permissible with the consent of the International Football Association Board.

3. Recent changes in the Laws of the Game are indicated by a line in the margin.

*These rules are very similar to the rules used by the Major Indoor Soccer League.

LAW I. – THE FIELD OF PLAY

The Field of Play and appurtenances
shall be as shown in the following plan:

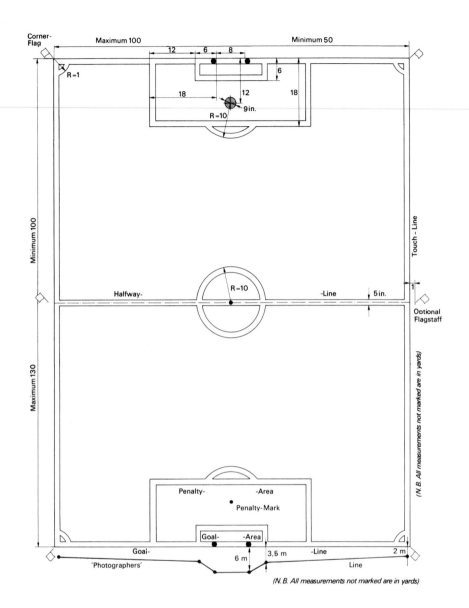

(N.B. All measurements not marked are in yards)

LAW I (continued)

(1) **Dimensions.** The field of play shall be rectangular, its length being not more than 130 yards nor less than 100 yards and its breadth not more than 100 yards nor less than 50 yards. (In International Matches the length shall be not more than 120 yards nor less than 110 yards and the breadth not more than 80 yards nor less than 70 yards.) The length shall in all cases exceed the breadth.

(2) **Marking.** The field of play shall be marked with distinctive lines, not more than 5 inches in width, not by a V-shaped rut, in accordance with the plan, the longer boundary lines being called the touch-lines and the shorter the goal-lines. A flag on a post not less than 5 ft. high and having a non-pointed top, shall be placed at each corner; a similar flag-post may be placed opposite the half-way line on each side of the field of play, not less than 1 yard outside the touch-line. A halfway-line shall be marked out across the field of play. The centre of the field of play shall be indicated by a suitable mark and a circle with a 10 yards radius shall be marked round it.

(3) **The Goal-Area.** At each end of the field of play two lines shall be drawn at right-angles to the goal-line, 6 yards from each goal-post. These shall extend into the field of play for a distance of 6 yards and shall be joined by a line drawn parallel with the goal-line. Each of the spaces enclosed by these lines and the goal-line shall be called a goal-area.

(4) **The Penalty-Area.** At each end of the field of play two lines shall be drawn at right-angles to the goal-line, 18 yards from each goal-post. These shall extend into the field of play for a distance of 18 yards and shall be joined by a line drawn parallel with the goal-line. Each of the spaces enclosed by these lines and the goal-line shall be called a penalty-area. A suitable mark shall be made within each penalty-area, 12 yards from the mid-point of the goal-line, measured along an undrawn line at right-angles thereto. These shall be the penalty-kick marks. From each penalty-kick mark an arc of a circle, having a radius of 10 yards, shall be drawn outside the penalty-area.

(5) **The Corner-Area.** From each corner-flag post a quarter circle, having a radius of 1 yard, shall be drawn inside the field of play.

(6) **The Goals.** The goals shall be placed on the centre of each goal-line and shall consist of two upright posts, equidistant from the corner-flags and 8 yards apart (inside measurement), joined by a horizontal cross-bar the lower edge of which shall be 8 ft. from the ground. The width and depth of the goal-posts and the width and depth of the cross-bars shall not exceed 5 inches (12 cm). The goal-posts and the cross-bars shall have the same width.

Nets may be attached to the posts, cross-bars and ground behind the goals. They should be appropriately supported and be so

(1) In International matches the dimensions of the field of play shall be: maximum 110 x 75 metres; minimum 100 x 64 metres.

(2) National Associations must adhere strictly to these dimensions. Each National Association organising an International Match must advise the visiting Association, before the match, of the place and the dimensions of the field of play.

(3) The Board has approved this table of measurements for the Laws of the Game:

130 yards	. . . . .	120 Metres
120 yards	. . . . .	110
110 yards	. . . . .	100
100 yards	. . . . .	90
80 yards	. . . . .	75
70 yards	. . . . .	64
50 yards	. . . . .	45
18 yards	. . . . .	16.50
12 yards	. . . . .	11
10 yards	. . . . .	9.15
8 yards	. . . . .	7.32
6 yards	. . . . .	5.50
1 yard	. . . . .	1
8 feet	. . . . .	2.44
5 feet	. . . . .	1.50
28 inches	. . . . .	0.71
27 inches	. . . . .	0.68
9 inches	. . . . .	0.22
5 inches	. . . . .	0.12
3/4 inch	. . . . .	0.019
1/2 inch	. . . . .	0.0127
3/8 inch	. . . . .	0.010
14 ounces	. . . . .	396 grams
16 ounces	. . . . .	453 grams
15 lb./sq.in.	. . . . .	1 kg/cm^2

(4) The goal-line shall be marked the same width as the depth of the goal-posts and the cross-bar, so that the goal-line and goal-posts will conform to the same interior and exterior edges.

(5) The 6 yards (for the outline of the goal-area) and the 18 yards (for the outline of the penalty-area) which have to be measured along the goal-line, must start from the inner sides of the goal-posts.

(6) The space within the inside areas of the field of play includes the width of the lines marking these areas.

(7) All Associations shall provide standard equipment, particularly in International Matches, when the Laws of the Game must be complied with in every respect and especially with regard to the size of the ball and other equipment which must conform to the regulations. All cases of failure to provide standard equipment must be reported to F.I.F.A.

(8) In a match played under the Rules of a Competition if the cross-bar becomes displaced or broken play shall be stopped and the match abandoned unless the cross-bar has been repaired and replaced in position or a new one provided without such being a danger to the players. A rope is not considered to be a satisfactory substitute for a cross-bar.

In a Friendly Match, by mutual consent, play may be resumed without the cross-bar provided it has been removed and no longer constitutes a danger to the players. In these circumstances, a rope may be used as a substitute for a cross-bar. If a rope is not used and the ball crosses the goal-line at a point which in the opinion of the Referee is below where

Laws of the Game

Decisions of the International Board

placed as to allow the goal-keeper ample room.

the cross-bar should have been he shall award a goal.

The game shall be restarted by the Referee dropping the ball at the place where it was when play was stopped.

(9) National Associations may specify such maximum and minimum dimensions for the cross-bars and goal-posts, within the limits laid down in Law I, as they consider appropriate.

(10) Goal-posts and cross-bars must be made of wood, metal or other approved material as decided from time to time by the International F.A. Board. They may be square, rectangular, round, half-round or elliptical in shape Goal-posts and cross-bars made of other materials and in other shapes are not permitted.

(11) 'Curtain-raisers' to International matches should only be played following agreement on the day of the match, and taking into account the condition of the field of play, between representatives of the two Associations and the Referee (of the International Match).

(12) National Associations, particularly in International Matches, should
— restrict the number of photographers around the field of play,
— have a line ("photographers' line") marked behind the goal-lines at least two metres from the corner flag going through a point situated at least 3.5 metres behind the intersection of the goal-line with the line marking the goal area to a point situated at least six metres behind the goal-posts,
— prohibit photographers from passing over these lines,
— forbid the use of artificial lighting in the form of "flashlights".

Footnote:

Goal nets. The use of nets made of hemp, jute or nylon is permitted. The nylon strings may, however, not be thinner than those made of hemp or jute.

LAW II. – THE BALL

The ball shall be spherical; the outer casing shall be of leather or other approved materials. No material shall be used in its construction which might prove dangerous to the players.

The circumference of the ball shall not be more than 28 in. and not less than 27 in. The weight of the ball at the start of the game shall not be more than 16 oz. nor less than 14 oz. The pressure shall be equal to 0.6-0.7 atmosphere, which equals 9.0-10.5 lb./sq.in. (= 600-700 gr/cm^2) at sea level. The ball shall not be changed during the game unless authorised by the Referee.

(1) The ball used in any match shall be considered the property of the Association or Club on whose ground the match is played, and at the close of play it must be returned to the Referee.

(2) The International Board, from time to time, shall decide what constitutes approved materials. Any approved material shall be certified as such by the International Board.

(3) The Board has approved these equivalents of the weights specified in the Law: 14 to 16 ounces = 396 to 453 grammes.

(4) If the ball bursts or becomes deflated during the course of a match, the game shall be stopped and restarted by dropping the new ball at the place where the first ball became defective.

(5) If this happens during a stoppage of the game (place-kick, goal-kick, corner-kick, free-kick, penalty-kick or throw-in) the game shall be restarted accordingly.

LAW III. – NUMBER OF PLAYERS

(1) A match shall be played by two teams, each consisting of not more than eleven players, one of whom shall be the goalkeeper.

(2) Substitutes may be used in any match played under the rules of an official competition at FIFA, Confederation or National Association level, subject to the following conditions:

(a) that the authority of the international association(s) or national association(s) concerned, has been obtained,

(b) that, subject to the restriction contained in the following paragraph (c) the rules of a competition shall state how many, if any, substitutes may be used, and

(c) that a team shall not be permitted to use more than two substitutes in any match.

(3) Substitutes may be used in any other match, provided that the two teams concerned reach agreement on a maximum number, not exceeding five, and that the terms of such agreement are intimated to the Referee, before the match. If the Referee is not informed, or if the teams fail to reach agreement, no more than two substitutes shall be permitted.

(4) Any of the other players may change places with the goalkeeper, provided that the Referee is informed before the change is made, and provided also, that the change is made during a stoppage in the game.

(5) When a goalkeeper or any other player is to be replaced by a substitute, the following conditions shall be observed:

(a) the Referee shall be informed of the proposed substitution, before it is made,

(b) the substitute shall not enter the field of play until the player he is replacing has left, and then only after having received a signal from the Referee,

(c) he shall enter the field during a stoppage in the game, and at the half-way line.

Punishment:

(a) Play shall not be stopped for an infringement of paragraph 4. The players concerned shall be cautioned immediately the ball goes out of play.

(b) For any other infringement of this law, the player concerned shall be cautioned, and if the game is stopped by the Referee, to administer the caution, it shall be re-started by an indirect free-kick, to be taken by a player of the opposing team, from the place where the ball was, when play was stopped. If the free-kick is awarded to a team within its own goal area, it may be taken from any point within that half of the goal area in which the ball was when play was stopped.

(1) The minimum number of players in a team is left to the discretion of National Associations.

(2) The Board is of the opinion that a match should not be considered valid if there are fewer than seven players in either of the teams.

(3) A competition may require that the referee shall be informed, before the start of the match, of the names of not more than five players, from whom the substitutes (if any) must be chosen.

(4) A player who has been ordered off before play begins may only be replaced by one of the named substitutes. The kick-off must not be delayed to allow the substitute to join his team.

A player who has been ordered off after play has started may not be replaced.

A named substitute who has been ordered off, either before or after play has started, may not be replaced (this decision only relates to players who are ordered off under Law XII. It does not apply to players who have infringed Law IV.)

(5) A player who has been replaced shall not take any further part in the game.

(6) A substitute shall be deemed to be a player and shall be subject to the authority and jurisdiction of the Referee whether called upon to play or not. For any offence committed on the field of play a substitute shall be subject to the same punishment as any other player whether called upon or not.

LAW IV. – PLAYERS' EQUIPMENT

(1) A player shall not wear anything which is dangerous to another player.

(2) Footwear (boots or shoes) must conform to the following standard:

(a) Bars shall be made of leather or rubber and shall be transverse and flat, not less

(1) The usual equipment of a player is a jersey or shirt, shorts, stockings and footwear. In a match played under the rules of a competition, players need not wear boots or shoes, but shall wear jersey or shirt, shorts, or track suit or similar trousers, and stockings.

(2) The Law does not insist that boots or

LAW IV *(continued)*

than half an inch in width and shall extend the total width of the sole and be rounded at the corners.

(b) Studs which are independently mounted on the sole and are replaceable shall be made of leather, rubber, aluminium, plastic or similar material and shall be solid. With the exception of that part of the stud forming the base, which shall not protrude from the sole more than one quarter of an inch, studs shall be round in plan and not less than half an inch in diameter. Where studs are tapered, the minimum diameter of any section of the stud must not be less than half an inch. Where metal seating for the screw type is used, this seating must be embedded in the sole of the footwear and any atachment screw shall be part of the stud. Other than the metal seating for the screw type of stud, no metal plates even though covered with leather or rubber shall be worn, neither studs which are threaded to allow them to be screwed on to a base screw that is fixed by nails or otherwise to the soles of footwear, nor studs which, apart from the base, have any form of protruding edge rim or relief marking or ornament, should be allowed.

(c) Studs which are moulded as an integral part of the sole and are not replaceable shall be made of rubber, plastic, polyurethene or similar soft materials. Provided that there are no fewer than ten studs on the sole, they shall have a minimum diameter of three eights of an inch (10 mm.). Additional supporting material to stabilise studs of soft materials, and ridges which shall not protrude more than 5 mm. from the sole and moulded to strengthen it, shall be permitted provided that they are in no way dangerous to other players. In all other respects they shall conform to the general requirements of this Law.

(d) Combined bars and studs may be worn, provided the whole conforms to the general requirements of this Law. Neither bars nor studs on the soles shall project more than three-quarters of an inch. If nails are used they shall be driven in flush with the surface.

(3) The goalkeeper shall wear colours which distinguish him from the other players and from the referee.

Punishment: For any infringement of this Law, the player at fault shall be sent off the field of play to adjust his equipment and he shall not return without first reporting to the Referee, who shall satisfy himself that the player's equipment is in order; the player shall only re-enter the game at a moment when the ball has ceased to be in play.

shoes must be worn. However, in competition matches Referees should not allow one or a few players to play without footwear when all the other players are so equipped.

(3) In International Matches, International Competitions, International Club Competitions and friendly matches between clubs of different National Associations, the Referee, prior to the start of the game, shall inspect the players' footwear, and prevent any player whose footwear does not conform to the requirements of this Law from playing until such time as it does comply.

The rules of any competition may include a similar provision.

(4) If the Referee finds that a player is wearing articles not permitted by the Laws and which may constitute a danger to other players, he shall order him to take them off. If he fails to carry out the Referee's instruction, the player shall not take part in the match.

(5) A player who has been prevented from taking part in the game or a player who has been sent off the field for infringing Law IV must report to the Referee during a stoppage of the game and may not enter or re-enter the field of play unless and until the Referee has satisfied himself that the player is no longer infringing Law IV.

(6) A player who has been prevented from taking part in a game or who has been sent off because of an infringement of Law IV, and who enters or re-enters the field of play to join or re-join his team, in breach of the conditions of Law XII, shall be cautioned. If the Referee stops the game to administer the caution, the game shall be restarted by an indirect free-kick, taken by a player of the opposing side, from the place where the ball was when the Referee stopped the game. If the free-kick is awarded to a team within its own goal area, it may be taken from any point within that half of the goal area in which the ball was when play was stopped.

LAW V. – REFEREES

A Referee shall be appointed to officiate in each game. His authority and the exercise of the powers granted to him by the Laws of the Game commence as soon as he enters the field of play.

(1) Referees in International Matches shall wear a blazer or blouse the colour of which is distinct from the colours worn by the contesting teams.

(2) Referees for International Matches will be selected from a neutral country unless

LAW V *(continued)*

His power of penalising shall extend to offences committed when play has been temporarily suspended, or when the ball is out of play. His decision on points of fact connected with the play shall be final, so far as the result of the game is concerned. He shall:

(a) Enforce the Laws.

(b) Refrain from penalising in cases where he is satisfied that, by doing so, he would be giving an advantage to the offending team.

(c) Keep a record of the game; act as timekeeper and allow the full or agreed time, adding thereto all time lost through accident or other cause.

(d) Have discretionary power to stop the game for any infringement of the Laws and to suspend or terminate the game whenever, by reason of the elements, interference by spectators, or other cause, he deems such stoppage necessary. In such a case he shall submit a detailed report to the competent authority, within the stipulated time, and in accordance with the provisions set up by the National Association under whose jurisdiction the match was played. Reports will be deemed to be made when received in the ordinary course of post.

(e) From the time he enters the field of play, caution any player guilty of misconduct or ungentlemanly behaviour and, if he persists, suspend him from further participation in the game. In such cases the Referee shall send the name of the offender to the competent authority, within the stipulated time, and in accordance with the provisions set up by the National Association under whose jurisdiction the match was played. Reports will be deemed to be made when received in the ordinary course of post.

(f) Allow no person other than the players and linesmen to enter the field of play without his permission.

(g) Stop the game if, in his opinion, a player has been seriously injured; have the player removed as soon as possible from the field of play, and immediately resume the game. If a player is slightly injured, the game shall not be stopped until the ball has ceased to be in play. A player who is able to go to the touch or goal-line for attention of any kind, shall not be treated on the field of play.

(h) Send off the field of play, any player who, in his opinion, is guilty of violent conduct, serious foul play, or the use of foul or abusive language.

(i) Signal for recommencement of the game after all stoppages.

(j) Decide that the ball provided for a match meets with the requirements of Law II.

the countries concerned agree to appoint their own officials.

(3) The Referee must be chosen from the official list of International Referees. This need not apply to Amateur and Youth International Matches.

(4) The Referee shall report to the appropriate authority misconduct or any misdemeanour on the part of spectators, officials, players, named substitutes or other persons which take place either on the field of play or in its vicinity at any time prior to, during, or after the match in question so that appropriate action can be taken by the Authority concerned.

(5) Linesmen are assistants of the Referee. In no case shall the Referee consider the intervention of a Linesman if he himself has seen the incident and from his position on the field, is better able to judge. With this reserve, and the Linesman neutral, the Referee can consider the intervention and if the information of the Linesman applies to that phase of the game immediately before the scoring of a goal, the Referee may act thereon and cancel the goal.

(6) The Referee, however, can only reverse his first decision so long as the game has not been restarted.

(7) If the Referee has decided to apply the advantage clause and to let the game proceed, he cannot revoke his decision if the presumed advantage has not been realised, even though he has not, by any gesture, indicated his decision. This does not exempt the offending player from being dealt with by the Referee.

(8) The Laws of the Game are intended to provide that games should be played with as little interference as possible, and in this view it is the duty of Referees to penalise only deliberate breaches of the Law. Constant whistling for trifling and doubtful breaches produces bad feeling and loss of temper on the part of the players and spoils the pleasure of spectators.

(9) By para. (d) of Law V the Referee is empowered to terminate a match in the event of grave disorder, but he has no power or right to decide, in such event, that either team is disqualified and thereby the loser of the match. He must send a detailed report to the proper authority who alone has power to deal further with this matter.

(10) If a player commits two infringements of a different nature at the same time, the Referee shall punish the more serious offence.

(11) It is the duty of the Referee to act upon the information of neutral Linesmen with regard to incidents that do not come under the personal notice of the Referee.

(12) The Referee shall not allow any person to enter the field until play has stopped, and only then, if he has given him a signal to do so, nor shall he allow coaching from the boundary lines.

LAW VI. – LINESMEN

Two Linesmen shall be appointed, whose duty (subject to the decision of the Referee) shall be to indicate when the ball is out of play and which side is entitled to the corner-kick, goal-kick or throw-in. They shall also assist the Referee to control the game in accordance with the Laws. In the event of undue interference or improper conduct by a Linesman, the Referee shall dispense with his services and arrange for a substitute to be appointed. (The matter shall be reported by the Referee to the competent authority.) The Linesmen should be equipped with flags by the Club on whose ground the match is played.

(1) Linesmen, where neutral, shall draw the Referee's attention to any breach of the Laws of the Game of which they become aware if they consider that the Referee may not have seen it, but the Referee shall always be the judge of the decision to be taken.

(2) National Associations are advised to appoint official Referees of neutral nationality to act as Linesmen in International Matches.

(3) In International Matches Linesmen's flags shall be of a vivid colour, bright reds and yellows. Such flags are recommended for use in all other matches.

(4) A Linesman may be subject to disciplinary action only upon a report of the Referee for unjustified interference or insufficient assistance.

LAW VII. – DURATION OF THE GAME

The duration of the game shall be two equal periods of 45 minutes, unless otherwise mutually agreed upon, subject to the following: (a) Allowance shall be made in either period for all time lost through accident or other cause, the amount of which shall be a matter for the discretion of the Referee; (b) Time shall be extended to permit a penalty-kick being taken at or after the expiration of the normal period in either half.

At half-time the interval shall not exceed five minutes except by consent of the Referee.

(1) If a match has been stopped by the Referee, before the completion of the time specified in the rules, for any reason stated in Law V it must be replayed in full unless the rules of the competition concerned provide for the result of the match at the time of such stoppage to stand.

(2) Players have a right to an interval at half-time.

LAW VIII. – THE START OF PLAY

(a) **At the beginning of the game,** choice of ends and the kick-off shall be decided by the toss of a coin. The team winning the toss shall have the option of choice of ends or the kick-off. The Referee having given a signal, the game shall be started by a player taking a place-kick (i.e., a kick at the ball while it is stationary on the ground in the centre of the field of play) into his opponents' half of the field of play. Every player shall be in his own half of the field and every player of the team opposing that of the kicker shall remain not less than 10 yards from the ball until it is kicked-off; it shall not be deemed in play until it has travelled the distance of its own circumference. The kicker shall not play the ball a second time until it has been touched or played by another player.

(b) **After a goal has scored,** the game shall be restarted in like manner by a player of the team losing the goal.

(c) **After half-time;** when restarting after half-time, ends shall be changed and the kick-off shall be taken by a player of the opposite team to that of the player who started the game.

Punishment. For any infringement of this Law, the kick-off shall be retaken, except in the case of the kicker playing the ball again

(1) If, when the Referee drops the ball, a player infringes any of the Laws before the ball has touched the ground, the player concerned shall be cautioned or sent off the field according to the seriousness of the offence, but a free-kick cannot be awarded to the opposing team because the ball was not in play at the time of the offence. The ball shall therefore be again dropped by the Referee.

(2) Kicking-off by persons other than the players competing in a match is prohibited.

before it has been touched or played by another player; for this offence, an indirect free-kick shall be taken by a player of the opposing team from the place where the infringement occurred, unless the offence is committed by a player in his opponents' goal area, in which case, the free-kick shall be taken from a point anywhere within that half of the goal area in which the offence occurred.

A goal shall not be scored direct from a kick-off.

(d) **After any other temporary suspension;** when restarting the game after a temporary suspension of play from any cause not mentioned elsewhere in these Laws, provided that immediately prior to the suspension the ball has not passed over the touch or goal-lines, the Referee shall drop the ball at the place where it was when play was suspended and it shall be deemed in play when it has touched the ground; if, however, it goes over the touch or goal-lines after it has been dropped by the Referee, but before it is touched by a player, the Referee shall again drop it. A player shall not play the ball until it has touched the ground. If this section of the Law is not complied with the Referee shall again drop the ball.

LAW IX. – BALL IN AND OUT OF PLAY

The ball is out of play:

(a) When it has wholly crossed the goal-line or touch-line, whether on the ground or in the air.

(b) When the game has been stopped by the Referee.

The ball is in play at all other times from the start of the match to the finish including:

(a) If it rebounds from a goal-post, cross-bar or corner-flag post into the field of play.

(b) If it rebounds off either the Referee or Linesmen when they are in the field of play.

(c) In the event of a supposed infringement of the Laws, until a decision is given.

(1) The lines belong to the areas of which they are the boundaries. In consequence, the touch-lines and the goal-lines belong to the field of play.

LAW X. – METHOD OF SCORING

Except as otherwise provided by these Laws, a goal is scored when the whole of the ball has passed over the goal-line, between the goal-posts and under the cross-bar, provided it has not been thrown, carried or intentionally propelled by hand or arm, by a player of the attacking side, except in the case of a goalkeeper, who is within his own penalty-area.

The team scoring the greater number of goals during a game shall be the winner; if no goals, or an equal number of goals are scored, the game shall be termed a "draw".

(1) Law X defines the only method according to which a match is won or drawn; no variation whatsoever can be authorised.

(2) A goal cannot in any case be allowed if the ball has been prevented by some outside agent from passing over the goal-line. If this happens in the normal course of play, other than at the taking of a penalty-kick: the game must be stopped and restarted by the Referee dropping the ball at the place where the ball came into contact with the interference.

(3) If, when the ball is going into goal, a spectator enters the field before it passes

wholly over the goal-line, and tries to prevent a score, a goal shall be allowed if the ball goes into goal unless the spectator has made contact with the ball or has interfered with play, in which case the Referee shall stop the game and restart it by dropping the ball at the place where the contact or interference occurred.

LAW XI. – OFF-SIDE

1. A player is in an off-side position if he is nearer to his opponents' goal-line than the ball, unless:
   (a) he is in his own half of the field of play, or
   (b) there are at least two of his opponents nearer their own goal-line than he is.
2. A player shall only be declared off-side and penalised for being in an off-side position, if, at the moment the ball touches, or is played by, one of his team, he is, in the opinion of the Referee
   (a) interfering with play or with an opponent, or
   (b) seeking to gain an advantage by being in that position.
3. A player shall not be declared off-side by the Referee
   (a) merely because of his being in an off-side position, or
   (b) if he receives the ball, direct, from a goal-kick, a corner-kick, a throw-in, or when it has been dropped by the Referee.
4. If a player is declared off-side, the Referee shall award an indirect free-kick, which shall be taken by a player of the opposing team from the place where the infringement occurred, unless the offence is committed by a player in his opponents' goal area, in which case, the free-kick shall be taken from a point anywhere within that half of the goal area in which the offence occurred.

(1) Off-side shall not be judged at the moment the player in question receives the ball, but at the moment when the ball is passed to him by one of his own side. A player who is not in an off-side position when one of his colleagues passes the ball to him or takes a free-kick, does not therefore become off-side if he goes forward during the flight of the ball.

LAW XII. – FOULS AND MISCONDUCT

A player who intentionally commits any of the following nine offences:
(a) Kicks or attempts to kick an opponent;
(b) Trips an opponent, i.e., throwing or attempting to throw him by the use of the legs or by stooping in front of or behind him;
(c) Jumps at an opponent;
(d) Charges an opponent in a violent or dangerous manner;
(e) Charges an opponent from behind unless the latter is obstructing;
(f) Strikes or attempts to strike an opponent;
(g) Holds an opponent;
(h) Pushes an opponent;

(1) If the goalkeeper either intentionally strikes an opponent by throwing the ball vigorously at him or pushes him with the ball while holding it, the Referee shall award a penalty-kick, if the offence took place within the penalty-area.
(2) If a player deliberately turns his back to an opponent when he is about to be tackled, he may be charged but not in a dangerous manner.
(3) In case of body-contact in the goal-area between an attacking player and the opposing goalkeeper not in possession of the ball, the Referee, as sole judge of intention, shall stop the game if, in his opinion, the action of the attacking player was intentional, and award an indirect free-kick.

Laws of the Game

Decisions of the International Board

LAW XII *(continued)*

(i) Handles the ball, i.e., carries, strikes or propels the ball with his hand or arm. (This does not apply to the goalkeeper within his own penalty-area);

shall be penalised by the award of a **direct free-kick** to be taken by the opposing team from the place where the offence occurred, unless the offence is committed by a player in his opponents' goal area, in which case, the free-kick shall be taken from a point anywhere within that half of the goal area in which the offence occurred.

Should a player of the defending team intentionally commit one of the above nine offences within the penalty-area he shall be penalised by a **penalty-kick.**

A penalty-kick can be awarded irrespective of the position of the ball, if in play, at the time an offence within the penalty-area is committed.

A player committing any of the five following offences:

1. Playing in a manner considered by the Referee to be dangerous, e.g., attempting to kick the ball while held by the goalkeeper;
2. Charging fairly, i.e., with the shoulder, when the ball is not within playing distance of the players concerned and they are definitely not trying to play it;
3. When not playing the ball, intentionally obstructing an opponent, i.e., running between the opponent and the ball, or interposing the body so as to form an obstacle to an opponent;
4. Charging the goalkeeper except when he
   (a) is holding the ball;
   (b) is obstructing an opponent;
   (c) has passed outside his goal-area;
5. When playing as goalkeeper,
   (a) takes more than 4 steps whilst holding, bouncing or throwing the ball in the air and catching it again without releasing it so that it is played by another player, or
   (b) indulges in tactics which, in the opinion of the Referee, are designed merely to hold up the game and thus waste time and so give an unfair advantage to his own team

shall be penalised by the award of an **indirect free-kick** to be taken by the opposing team from the place where the infringement occurred, unless the offence is committed by a player in his opponents' goal area, in which case, the free-kick shall be taken from a point anywhere within that half of the goal area in which the offence occurred.

A player shall be **cautioned** if:

(j) he enters or re-enters the field of play to join or rejoin his team after the game has commenced, or leaves the field of play during the progress of the game (except through accident) without, in either case, first having received a signal from the Referee showing him that he may do so. If the Referee stops the game to administer the caution the game shall be restarted by an indirect free-kick taken by a player of the

(4) If a player leans on the shoulders of another player of his own team in order to head the ball, the Referee shall stop the game, caution the player for ungentlemanly conduct and award an indirect free-kick to the opposing side.

(5) A player's obligation when joining or rejoining his team after the start of the match to 'report to the Referee' must be interpreted as meaning 'to draw the attention of the Referee from the touch-line'. The signal from the Referee shall be made by a definite gesture which makes the player understand that he may come into the field of play; it is not necessary for the Referee to wait until the game is stopped (this does not apply in respect of an infringement of Law IV), but the Referee is the sole judge of the moment in which he gives his signal of acknowledgement.

(6) The letter and spirit of Law XII do not oblige the Referee to stop a game to administer a caution. He may, if he chooses, apply the advantage. If he does apply the advantage, he shall caution the player when play stops.

(7) If a player covers up the ball without touching it in an endeavour not to have it played by an opponent, he obstructs but does not infringe Law XII para. 3 because he is already in possession of the ball and covers it for tactical reasons whilst the ball remains within playing distance. In fact, he is actually playing the ball and does not commit an infringement; in this case, the player may be charged because he is in fact playing the ball.

(8) If a player intentionally stretches his arms to obstruct an opponent and steps from one side to the other, moving his arms up and down to delay his opponent, forcing him to change course, but does not make "bodily contact" the Referee shall caution the player for ungentlemanly conduct and award an indirect free-kick.

(9) If a player intentionally obstructs the opposing goalkeeper, in an attempt to prevent him from putting the ball into play in accordance with Law XII, 5(a), the referee shall award an indirect free-kick.

(10) If after a Referee has awarded a free-kick a player protests violently by using abusive or foul language and is sent off the field, the free-kick should not be taken until the player has left the field.

(11) Any player, whether he is within or outside the field of play, whose conduct is ungentlemanly or violent, whether or not it is directed towards an opponent, a colleague, the Referee, a linesman or other person, or who uses foul or abusive language, is guilty of an offence, and shall be dealt with according to the nature of the offence committed.

(12) If, in the opinion of the Referee a goalkeeper intentionally lies on the ball longer than is necessary, he shall be penalised for ungentlemanly conduct and
(a) be cautioned and an indirect free-kick awarded to the opposing team;

LAW XII *(continued)*

opposing team from the place where the ball was when the Referee stopped the game. If the free-kick is awarded to a team within its own goal area it may be taken from any point within the half of the goal area in which the ball was when play was stopped. If, however, the offending player has committed a more serious offence he shall be penalised according to that section of the law he infringed;

(k) he persistently infringes the Laws of the Game;

(l) he shows by word or action, dissent from any decision given by the Referee;

(m) he is guilty of ungentlemanly conduct.

For any of these last three offences, in addition to the caution, an **indirect free-kick** shall also be awarded to the opposing team from the place where the offence occurred unless a more serious infringement of the Laws of the Game was committed. If the offence is committed by a player in his opponents' goal area, a free-kick shall be taken from a point anywhere within that half of the goal area in which the offence occurred.

A player shall be **sent off** the field of play, if:

(n) in the opinion of the Referee he is guilty of violent conduct or serious foul play;

(o) he uses foul or abusive language;

(p) he persists in misconduct after having received a caution.

If play be stopped by reason of a player being ordered from the field for an offence without a separate breach of the Law having been committed, the game shall be resumed by an **indirect free-kick** awarded to the opposing team from the place where the infringement occurred, unless the offence is committed by a player in his opponents' goal area, in which case, the free-kick shall be taken from a point anywhere within that half of the goal area in which the offence occurred.

(b) in case of repetition of the offence, be sent off the field.

(13) The offence of spitting at opponents, officials or other persons, or similar unseemly behaviour shall be considered as violent conduct within the meaning of section (n) of Law XII.

(14) If, when a Referee is about to caution a player, and before he has done so, the player commits another offence which merits a caution, the player shall be sent off the field of play.

LAW XIII. – FREE-KICK

Free-kicks shall be classified under two headings: "Direct" (from which a goal can be scored direct against the offending side), and "Indirect" (from which a goal cannot be scored unless the ball has been played or touched by a player other than the kicker before passing through the goal).

When a player is taking a direct or an indirect free-kick inside his own penalty-area, all of the opposing players shall remain outside the area, and shall be at least ten yards from the ball whilst the kick is being taken. The ball shall be in play immediately it has travelled the distance of its own circumference and is beyond the penalty-area. The goalkeeper shall not receive the ball into his hands, in order that he may thereafter kick it into play. If the ball is not

(1) In order to distinguish between a direct and an indirect free-kick, the Referee, when he awards an indirect free-kick, shall indicate accordingly by raising an arm above his head. He shall keep his arm in that position until the kick has been taken.

(2) Players who do not retire to the proper distance when a free-kick is taken must be cautioned and on any repetition be ordered off. It is particularly requested of Referees that attempts to delay the taking of a free-kick by encroaching should be treated as serious misconduct.

(3) If, when a free-kick is being taken, any of the players dance about or gesticulate in a way calculated to distract their opponents, it shall be deemed ungentlemanly conduct for which the offender(s) shall be cautioned.

LAW XIII *(continued)*

kicked direct into play, beyond the penalty-area, the kick shall be retaken.

When a player is taking a direct or an indirect free-kick outside his own penalty-area, all of the opposing players shall be at least ten yards from the ball, until it is in play, unless they are standing on their own goal-line, between the goal-posts. The ball shall be in play when it has travelled the distance of its own circumference.

If a player of the opposing side encroaches into the penalty-area, or within ten yards of the ball, as the case may be, before a free-kick is taken, the Referee shall delay the taking of the kick, until the Law is complied with.

The ball must be stationary when a free-kick is taken, and the kicker shall not play the ball a second time, until it has been touched or played by another player.

Notwithstanding any other reference in these Laws to the point from which a free-kick is to be taken, any free-kick awarded to the defending team, within its own goal area, may be taken from any point within that half of the goal area in which the free-kick has been awarded.

Punishment: If the kicker, after taking the free-kick, plays the ball a second time before it has been touched or played by another player an indirect free-kick shall be taken by a player of the opposing team from the spot where the infringement occurred, unless the offence is committed by a player in his opponents' goal area, in which case, the free-kick shall be taken from a point anywhere within that half of the goal area in which the offence occurred.

LAW XIV. – PENALTY-KICK

A penalty-kick shall be taken from the penalty-mark and, when it is being taken, all players with the exception of the player taking the kick, and the opposing goalkeeper, shall be within the field of play but outside the penalty-area, and at least 10 yards from the penalty-mark. The opposing goalkeeper must stand (without moving his feet) on his own goal-line, between the goal-posts, until the ball is kicked. The player taking the kick must kick the ball forward; he shall not play the ball a second time until it has been touched or played by another player. The ball shall be deemed in play directly it is kicked, i.e., when it has travelled the distance of its circumference, and a goal may be scored direct from such a penalty-kick. If the ball touches the goalkeeper before passing between the posts, when a penalty-kick is being taken at or after the expiration of half-time or full-time, it does not nullify a goal. If necessary, time of play shall be extended at half-time or full-time to allow a penalty-kick to be taken.

Punishment:

For any infringement of this Law:

(a) by the defending team, the kick shall be retaken if a goal has not resulted.

(1) When the Referee has awarded a penalty-kick, he shall not signal for it to be taken, until the players have taken up position in accordance with the Law.

(2) (a) If, after the kick has been taken, the ball is stopped in its course towards goal, by an outside agent, the kick shall be retaken.

(b) If, after the kick has been taken, the ball rebounds into play, from the goalkeeper, the cross-bar or a goal-post, and is then stopped in its course by an outside agent, the Referee shall stop play and restart it by dropping the ball at the place where it came into contact with the outside agent.

(3) (a) If, after having given the signal for a penalty-kick to be taken, the Referee sees that the goalkeeper is not in his right place on the goal-line, he shall, nevertheless, allow the kick to proceed. It shall be retaken, if a goal is not scored.

(b) If, after the Referee has given the signal for a penalty-kick to be taken, and before the ball has been kicked, the goalkeeper moves his feet, the Referee shall, nevertheless, allow the kick to proceed. It shall be retaken, if a goal is not scored.

(c) If, after the Referee has given the signal for a penalty-kick to be taken, and before the ball is in play, a player of the

(b) by the attacking team other than by the player taking the kick, if a goal is scored it shall be disallowed and the kick re-taken.

(c) by the player taking the penalty-kick, committed after the ball is in play, a player of the opposing team shall take an indirect free-kick from the spot where the infringement occurred.

If, in the case of paragraph (c), the offence is committed by the player in his opponents' goal area, the free-kick shall be taken from a point anywhere within that half of the goal area in which the offence occurred.

defending team encroaches into the penalty-area, or within ten yards of the penalty-mark, the Referee shall, nevertheless, allow the kick to proceed. It shall be retaken, if a goal is not scored.

The player concerned shall be cautioned.

(4) (a) If, when a penalty-kick is being taken, the player taking the kick is guilty of un-gentlemanly conduct, the kick, if already taken, shall be retaken, if a goal is scored.

The player concerned shall be cautioned.

(b) If, after the referee has given the signal for a penalty-kick to be taken, and before the ball is in play, a colleague of the player taking the kick encroaches into the penalty-area or within ten yards of the pen-alty-mark, the Referee shall, nevertheless, allow the kick to proceed. If a goal is scored, it shall be disallowed, and the kick retaken.

The player concerned shall be cautioned.

(c) If, in the circumstances described in the foregoing paragraph, the ball rebounds into play from the goalkeeper, the cross-bar or a goal-post, the Referee shall stop the game, caution the player and award an indirect free-kick to the opposing team from the place where the infringement occurred.

(5) (a) If, after the referee has given the signal for a penalty-kick to be taken, and before the ball is in play, the goalkeeper moves from his position on the goal-line, or moves his feet, and a colleague of the kicker encroaches into the penalty-area or within 10 yards of the penalty-mark, the kick, if taken, shall be retaken.

The colleague of the kicker shall be cau-tioned.

(b) If, after the Referee has given the signal for a penalty-kick to be taken, and before the ball is in play, a player of each team encroaches into the penalty-area, or within 10 yards of the penalty-mark, the kick, if taken, shall be retaken.

The players concerned shall be cautioned.

(6) When a match is extended, at half-time or full-time, to allow a penalty-kick to be taken or retaken, the extension shall last until the moment that the penalty-kick has been completed, i.e. until the Referee has decided whether or not a goal is scored.

A goal is scored when the ball passes wholly over the goal-line.

(a) direct from the penalty-kick,

(b) having rebounded from either goal-post or the cross-bar, or

(c) having touched or been played by the goalkeeper.

The game shall terminate immediately the Referee has made his decision.

(7) When a penalty-kick is being taken in extended time:

(a) the provisions of all of the foregoing paragraphs, except paragraphs (2) (b) and (4) (c) shall apply in the usual way, and

(b) in the circumstances described in paragraphs (2) (b) and (4) (c) the game shall terminate immediately the ball rebounds from the goalkeeper, the cross-bar or the goal-post.

LAW XV. – THROW-IN

When the whole of the ball passes over a touch-line, either on the ground or in the air, it shall be thrown in from the point where it crossed the line, in any direction, by a player of the team opposite to that of the player who last touched it. The thrower at the moment of delivering the ball must face the field of play and part of each foot shall be either on the touch-line or on the ground outside the touch-line. The thrower shall use both hands and shall deliver the ball from behind and over his head. The ball shall be in play immediately it enters the field of play, but the thrower shall not again play the ball until it has been touched or played by another player. A goal shall not be scored direct from a throw-in.

Punishment:

(a) If the ball is improperly thrown in the throw-in shall be taken by a player of the opposing team.

(b) If the thrower plays the ball a second time before it has been touched or played by another player, an indirect free-kick shall be taken by a player of the opposing team from the place where the infringement occurred, unless the offence is committed by a player in his opponents' goal area, in which case, the free-kick shall be taken from a point anywhere within that half of the goal area in which the offence occurred.

(1) If a player taking a throw-in, plays the ball a second time by handling it within the field of play before it has been touched or played by another player, the Referee shall award a direct free-kick.

(2) A player taking a throw-in must face the field of play with some part of his body.

(3) If, when a throw-in is being taken, any of the opposing players dance about or gesticulate in a way calculated to distract or impede the thrower, it shall be deemed ungentlemanly conduct, for which the offender(s) shall be cautioned.

LAW XVI. – GOAL-KICK

When the whole of the ball passes over the goal-line excluding that portion between the goal-posts, either in the air or on the ground, having last been played by one of the attacking team, it shall be kicked direct into play beyond the penalty-area from a point within that half of the goal-area nearest to where it crossed the line, by a player of the defending team. A goalkeeper shall not receive the ball into his hands from a goal-kick in order that he may thereafter kick it into play. If the ball is not kicked beyond the penalty-area, i.e., direct into play, the kick shall be retaken. The kicker shall not play the ball a second time until it has touched – or been played by – another player. A goal shall not be scored direct from such a kick. Players of the team opposing that of the player taking the goal-kick shall remain outside the penalty-area whilst the kick is being taken.

Punishment: If a player taking a goal-kick plays the ball a second time after it has passed beyond the penalty-area, but before it has touched or been played by another player, an indirect free-kick shall be awarded to the opposing team, to be taken from the place where the infringement occurred, unless the offence is committed by a player in his opponents' goal area, in which case, the free-kick shall be taken from a point anywhere within that half of the goal area in which the offence occurred.

(1) When a goal-kick has been taken and the player who has kicked the ball touches it again before it has left the penalty-area, the kick has not been taken in accordance with the Law and must be retaken.

LAW XVII. – CORNER-KICK

When the whole of the ball passes over the goal-line, excluding that portion between the goal-posts, either in the air or on the ground, having last been played by one of the defending team, a member of the attacking team shall take a corner-kick, i.e., the whole of the ball shall be placed within the quarter circle at the nearest corner-flag-post, which must not be moved, and it shall be kicked from that position. A goal may be scored direct from such a kick. Players of the team opposing that of the player taking the corner-kick shall not approach within 10 yards of the ball until it is in play, i.e., it has travelled the distance of its own circumference, nor shall the kicker play the ball a second time until it has been touched or played by another player.

Punishment:

(a) If the player who takes the kick plays the ball a second time before it has been touched or played by another player, the Referee shall award an indirect free-kick to the opposing team, to be taken from the place where the infringement occurred, unless the offence is committed by a player in his opponents' goal area, in which case, the free-kick shall be taken from a point anywhere within that half of the goal area in which the offence occurred.

(b) For any other infringement the kick shall be retaken.

The following questions have from time to time been submitted to the FIFA by National Associations. The answers given have been approved by The International F.A. Board.

Law I

1. Q. If the cross-bar becomes displaced through breakage or faulty construction in a competitive match and there are no available means of repairing and replacing it, should the match be abandoned ?
   A. *Yes. The cross-bar may not be substituted by a rope in order to finish the match.*

2. Q. Is it necessary for flags to be placed at the half-way line ?
   A. *No.*

Law III

1. Q. If a player passes accidentally over one of the boundary-lines of the field of play, is he considered to have left the field of play without the permission of the Referee ?
   A. *No.*

2. Q. If a player in possession of the ball passes over the touch-line or the goal-line without the ball in order to beat an opponent, should the Referee penalise him for leaving the field of play without permission ?
   A. *No. Going outside the field of play may be considered as part of a playing movement, but players are expected, as a general rule, to remain within the playing-area.*

3. Q. Is it permissible for a goalkeeper to take a throw-in ?
   A. *Yes.*

Law IV

1. Q. If a player, following doctor's orders, protects his elbow or any similar part of his body with a plaster bandage to prevent further injury, has the Referee power to decide if the bandage constitutes a danger to to other players ?
   A. *Yes.*

2. Q. Should a player be permitted to take part in a game when he is wearing ordinary kind of boots instead of the normal football boots ?
   A. *The Laws of the Game do not specify that a player should wear any particular type of boot; if, however, they are equipped with bars or studs, the bars or studs must conform with Law IV.*

Law V

1. Q. If a Referee is struck in the face by the ball which then enters the goal while he is temporarily incapacitated, should a goal be allowed although he has not seen it scored ?
   A. *Yes, if in the opinion of a neutral Linesman nearer to the incident the goal was properly scored.*

2. Q. A Linesman signals that the ball has passed over the touch-line, but before the Referee has given the ball out of play, a defending player inside the penalty-area strikes an attacking player. What action should the Referee take ?
   A. *After having taken the appropriate action in relation to the offence the Referee should re-start the game with a throw-in because the ball was out of play when the offence occurred.*

3. Q. What action should a Referee take against a player who lights a cigarette during the game ?
A. *Caution him for ungentlemanly conduct.*

4. Q. Can a captain send off one of his own team for serious misconduct ?
A. *No. Only a Referee can send a player off the field.*

5. Q. What should the Referee do if two Captains agree to forego the half-time interval and one of the players insists on his right to 5 minutes' rest ?
A. *Players have a right to 5 minutes' interval and the Referee must grant it.*

Law VI

1. Q. May a Referee ask a neutral Linesman to give an opinion as to whether or not the ball crossed the goal-line between the posts ?
A. *Yes.*

Law VIII

1. Q. May a game be started by a person, other than one of the players taking part in the match, kicking-off ?
A. *No. But if, in certain matches (e.g. charity or exhibition matches) a ceremony is arranged for a person not taking part in the game to kick the ball, it must be brought back to the centre of the field and kicked off in accordance with the Law.*

2. Q. When extra time is played, which team kicks off ?
A. *The Captains toss for the choice of ends or kick-off for the extra time period.*

3. Q. If the ball is kicked straight into the opponents' goal from the kick-off, what decision does the Referee give ?
A. *Goal-kick to the opposing team.*

Law IX

1. Q. Is the ball out of play if any part of the ball overlaps either the goal-line or the touch-line ?
A. *No, the whole of the ball must cross the line.*

2. Q. A player asks to leave the field and as he is walking off the ball comes towards him and he shoots a goal. What action should the Referee take ?
A. *The player shall be cautioned. The game shall be re-started by an indirect free-kick, taken by a player of the opposing team, from the place where infringement occurred.*

Law X

1. Q. If a Referee signals a goal before the ball has passed wholly over the goal-line and he immediately realises his error, is the goal valid ?
A. *No. The game should be re-started by dropping the ball at the place where it was when the Referee inadvertently stopped play.*

Law XI

1. Q. Does a player infringe the Law if he is in an off-side position and moves a little way beyond the boundary of the field of play to show clearly to the Referee that he is not interfering with play ?
A. *No, but if the Referee considers that such a movement has a tactical aim or is in any way a feint, and the player takes part in the game immediately after, the Referee should blow his whistle for off-side.*

2. Q. Is a team-mate allowed to stand in an off-side position at the taking of a penalty-kick ?
   A. *Yes, but he would be given off-side if the kicker failed to score directly and the player attempted to interfere with the game. The player would not be off-side if the goalkeeper had parried the ball and the ball went to him.*

APPENDIX B: THE LAWS OF THE GAME

Law XII

1. Q. Should a penalty be awarded, if while the ball is in play, a player intentionally trips or strikes an opponent who is in an off-side position in the penalty-area, but who is not attempting to play the ball nor interfere with play in any way ?
   A. *Yes.*

2. Q. What is the decision if a player, after receiving the approval of the Referee to leave the field of play because of slight injury or other cause, places himself near the touch-line and puts his foot into the field causing an opponent to fall ?
   A. *The player should be cautioned and the game re-started by a direct free-kick because the offence occurred within the field of play.*

3. Q. Should the Referee award a penalty-kick when a defending player is ordered off the field for kicking or striking an opponent within the penalty-area ?
   A. *Yes, provided the ball was in play at the moment when the offence was committed.*

4. Q. If a player intentionally lies on the ball for an unreasonable length of time, is he guilty of ungentlemanly conduct ?
   A. *Yes. He must be cautioned, and an indirect free-kick awarded to the opposing team. In case of repetition of the offence, he must be sent off the field.*

5. Q. How should the game be re-started if, when the ball is about to be dropped within the penalty-area, a defending player strikes an opponent before the ball touched the ground ?
   A. *After having taken the appropriate action in relation to the offence the Referee should drop the ball. If the misconduct took place inside the penalty-area he must not award a penalty-kick because the ball was not in play at the time the offence was committed.*

6. Q. What action should the Referee take if a player of the defending team, other than the goalkeeper, standing outside the penalty-area, intentionally handles the ball within the penalty-area ?
   A. *He should penalise the player by awarding a penalty-kick because the offence took place within the penalty-area.*

7. Q. What action should the Referee take if two players of the same team commit ungentlemanly or violent conduct towards each other on the field of play ?
   A. *The Referee should caution them or dismiss them from the field of play and re-start the game by an indirect free-kick.*

8. Q. If a player who enters or returns to the field of play without receiving a signal from the Referee to do so, and who, apart from this, commits another more serious infringement, e.g. handles the ball or strikes an opponent, how should he be penalised ?
   A. *1. The Referee shall caution the player for entering or returning to the field of play without having received a signal from the Referee.*
   2. The Referee shall furthermore punish the more serious infringement.

9. Q. If a Referee cautions a player who in turn apologises for his misconduct, can the Referee omit to report the incident ?
   A. *No, all cautions must be reported.*

Law XIII

1. Q. If a player takes a free-kick and then intentionally handles the ball before it has been played by another player, should the Referee punish the more serious offence and if so, how ?

A. *Yes, by a direct free-kick or by a penalty-kick if the offence took place in the penalty-area.*

2. Q. May a free-kick be passed backwards ?
   A. *Yes. The provisions of Law XIII must, however, be observed in respect of free-kicks taken by the defending side from within its own penalty-area.*

3. Q. A player is awarded a free-kick in his own half of the field of play and he passes it back to his own goalkeeper who misses it completely and the ball enters the net. Is it a goal or corner-kick ?
   A. *The Referee should award a corner-kick provided that, in the case of the free-kick in the penalty-area, the ball has already gone into play, otherwise the free-kick inside the penalty-area must be retaken.*

4. Q. If the ball from an indirect free-kick touches another player and enters the net, should a goal be awarded ?
   A. *Yes.*

Law XIV

1. Q. If a player intentionally goes beyond the boundary of the field of play at the taking of a penalty-kick, should the Referee caution him and if he repeats the offence, send him off ?
   A. *Yes.*

2. Q. If a penalty-kick is re-taken because the goalkeeper moved his leg, must the same player take the kick again or could another player do so ?
   A. *Another player could re-take the penalty-kick.*

3. Q. If a player taking a penalty-kick back-heels the ball to a colleague, who scores, should the goal be allowed ?
   A. *No. The goal should be disallowed and the penalty-kick re-taken.*

4. Q. Can a player taking a penalty-kick push the ball forward for a colleague to run to it and score ?
   A. *Yes, provided –*
   (a) all of the players, with the exception of the player taking the penalty-kick and the opposing goalkeeper, are outside the penalty-area and not within 10 yards of the penalty-mark, at the time the kick is taken.
   (b) the colleague to whom the ball is passed is not in an off-side position when it is kicked, and
   (c) the penalty-kick is taken in normal time and the requirements of the Law are satisfied.

5. Q. If a defender, whilst standing in his own penalty-area, strikes an opponent while the ball is in play in the opponents' penalty-area, should the Referee award a penalty-kick ?
   A. *Yes.*

6. Q. Is a player taking a penalty-kick allowed to place the ball elsewhere than on the penalty-spot owing to the water-logged state of the pitch ?
   A. *No.*

7. Q. What action does the Referee take if, at the taking of a penalty-kick, the ball strikes the goal-post and/or cross-bar and bursts ?
   A. (i) *He asks for another ball and re-starts the game by dropping the ball.*
   (ii) *If the penalty-kick is being taken in extended time (see Universal Guide – Law XIV, decision 7) and the ball strikes the goal-post and/or cross-bar and bursts, the game ends.*

8. Q. What are the decisions of the Referee if, the signal having been given, but before the ball is kicked, a colleague of the player taking the kick encroaches into the penalty-area and the Referee notices the offence but allows the kick to be taken and the ball rebounds from the goalkeeper, cross-bar or goal-posts to the player who has encroached and this player sends the ball into goal ?
   A. *The Referee shall disallow the goal, caution the player at fault for ungentlemanly conduct and re-start the game by an indirect free-kick.*

Law XV

1. Q. The ball is in touch, but before it is thrown in, a player deliberately kicks an opponent, what action should the Referee take ?
   A. *He should send him off the field of play and re-start the game by a throw-in.*

2. Q. If a player taking a throw-in, throws the ball so that it does not enter the field of play but passes outside the touche-line, what action should be taken ?
   A. *Throw should be re-taken.*

Law XVI

1. Q. If a player who has taken a goal-kick properly, intentionally plays the ball with the hand when the ball has left the penalty-area but before it has been touched by another player, what is the decision ?
   A. *A direct free-kick should be awarded to the opposite side.*

2. Q. Should the Referee award a penalty-kick if a player other than the goalkeeper takes a goal-kick and the ball passes out of the penalty-area into play but is blown back by a strong wind without any other player having touched it, and a player of the defending side other than the goalkeeper plays the ball with his hand within the penalty-area ?
   A. *Yes. If, in similar circumstances, the goalkeeper takes the goal-kick and he tries to stop the ball entering the goal and just touches the ball with his hand but fails to prevent it passing into goal, the Referee shall award an indirect free-kick.*

3. Q. If, at a goal-kick, when the ball has travelled the distance of its circumference towards leaving the penalty-area, an opponent then enters the penalty-area and is intentionally fouled by a defending player, can a penalty-kick be awarded ?
   A. *No, because the ball was not in play at the time the offence was committed. The offending player shall be cautioned or ordered off, according to the nature of the offence, and the goal-kick retaken. If the ball has passed outside the penalty-area before the game is stopped, a goal-kick should still be re-taken as the player of the attacking side has entered the penalty-area before the ball was in play.*

4. Q. If a player is intentionally tripped before the ball passes out of the penalty-area at the taking of a goal-kick, should a free-kick be awarded ?
   A. *No, the ball is not in play until it has been out of the penalty-area. The offender should be cautioned or sent off and the goal-kick retaken.*

The Rules in the United States

The rules of FIFA are followed in most countries and are observed in all international competitions. Some changes, however, have been introduced in the United States at the professional, collegiate, and interscholastic levels. A brief summary of the more important changes is given below. The NASL uses its own rules, colleges use the rules published by the NCAA, and high schools use the rules published by the National Federation of State High School Associations.

Rule I. The Field of Play

Dimensions

COLLEGE: Length may vary between 110 and 120 yards, width between 65 and 75 yards. Recommended size: 120 by 75 yards.

HIGH SCHOOL: Length may vary between 100 and 120 yards, width between 65 and 75 yards.

Markings

NASL: At each end of the field, a line across the full width of the field, 35 yards from the goal line. See Rule XI below.

COLLEGE AND HIGH SCHOOL The international rules call for a "suitable mark" to indicate the penalty-kick mark. Everywhere throughout the world this takes the form of a white circle 5 inches in diameter, except in the United States colleges and high schools, where a 2-foot-long line is used.

Rule III. Number of Players

The international rules state that in competitive soccer only 2 substitutes can be used, and that once a player has been removed from a game, he cannot reenter it.

NASL Allows 3 substitutes. No reentry permitted.

COLLEGE Five substitutes allowed, who can be resubstituted without limitation.

HIGH SCHOOL Allows teams to substitute and resubstitute "as many players as they wish."

Rule V. Referees

The universal practice, followed by the NASL, is to employ 1 referee aided by 2 linesmen. Again, the colleges and the high schools differ. High Schools recommend 2 referees and no linesmen. The NCAA soccer committee voted in 1979 to leave the 2-referee system optional.

By a decision of the International Board, coaching from the sidelines is banned under the international rules.

COLLEGE AND HIGH SCHOOL Coaching is permitted from the area of the bench.

Under international rules it is the referee who is the official timekeeper during games.

COLLEGE AND HIGH SCHOOL   Both employ an official timekeeper on the sidelines.

Rule VII. Duration of the Game

While the international rules allow the length of a game to be shortened from the regulation 90 minutes for boys' games, they still stipulate that the game shall be divided into 2 halves.

HIGH SCHOOL   Allows either "4 equal periods of not more than 18 minutes each or 2 equal halves of 35 minutes each."

Rule X. Method of Scoring

HIGH SCHOOL   When a defender deliberately handles the ball and so prevents it from entering the goal, the referee may *award* a goal to the attacking team. (Under all the other codes of rules goals must be scored. In the quoted example the referee would award the attacking team a penalty kick, not a goal.)

Rule XI. Offside

NASL   With the permission of FIFA, the NASL marks 2 extra lines on its fields, 35 yards in from each goal line. The lines run the full width of the field, and thus mark off a 35-yard zone at each end of the field. The application of the offside rule is limited to these 2 zones.

Rule XII. Fouls and Misconduct

COLLEGE AND HIGH SCHOOL   The referee shall remove without caution any player who intentionally charges the goalkeeper. Under international rules the goalkeeper can be shoulder charged when he is holding the ball.

Both college and high school rules single out a "hitch-kick or double-kick" as an example of dangerous play when performed within 6 feet of an opponent. It is not clear exactly what is meant by the terms, though presumably they include both the overhead volley (bicycle kick) and the full side volley (scissor kick). Both of these kicks are essential skills for any good soccer player, but the rule singling them out as examples of dangerous play has led to their virtual disappearance from college and high school play.

COLLEGE   Under international rules a player ejected from a game by the referee cannot be replaced. His team must continue play with only 10 men. If another player is ejected, the team must play on with 9 men. Under college rules an ejected player can take no further part in the game, but can be substituted for unless the player was ejected for physically assaulting a referee.

Rule XIV. Penalty Kick

COLLEGE AND HIGH SCHOOL   To take the kick, the ball can be placed anywhere along the 2-foot span of the penalty line.

The Rules for Indoor Soccer*

Law I—The Playing Field.
1. Length of the field: minimum of 175'; maximum of 210'
2. Width of the field: minimum of 75'; maximum of 100'
3. Goal: 12'x6'6"
4. Goal area: 16' wide x 5' from endline
5. Penalty area: 30'x25'
6. Penalty spot: 9" diameter; 24' perpendicular to endline and equidistant from goal posts
7. Penalty Arc: 10' arc measured from penalty spot
8. Corner Spot: 9" dot at the intersection of the touchline and an extension of the goal area line (See field of play diagram)
9. Center Circle: 20' diameter, to be placed in exact middle of the field
10. Touch Lines: dotted line 3' in from the perimeter wall between the corner spots on each side of the field

Law II—The Ball. 27"—28" circumference, 14-16 ounces, as used in the outdoor game (NASL-approved ball—Adidas).

Law III—Number of Players. A team can list a maximum of 14 players of which no more than 9 can be non-citizens on its lineup card for each game. The maximum number of players on the field at any time shall be 6 per team. The minimum number shall be no less than 4. One player shall be the goalkeeper. **Substitutions.** Substitutions may occur on an unlimited basis provided the player leaving the field arrives at the bench before his replacement enters the field. Play will be held up to allow for the completion of a substitution only on the following occasions: when the ball goes over the perimeter wall after a goal has been scored, after time penalty has been awarded or on an injury time out.

Law IV—Players' Equipment. Players must wear flat-sole shoes or molded-sole shoes with 10 or more studs. No shoes with removable cleats or shoes with less than 10 studs molded into the sole are to be worn. Goalkeeper must wear colors which distinguish him from the other players.

Law V—Referee. One referee shall be appointed to officiate each game. His authority and exercise of the powers granted to him by the Laws of the Game commence as soon as he enters the field of play.

Law VI—Assistant Referee and Other Game Officials. One assistant referee will assist the referee by notifying the referee of three-line-pass violations and illegal substitutions and will supervise the timekeeper, control the penalty box areas, and keep a record of all time penalties awarded. A timekeeper, two goal judges and two penalty box attendants are appointed to assist the referee.

Law VII—Duration of the Game. The duration of the game shall be 4 equal periods of 15 minutes. NASL games which remain tied at the end of regulation time will be extended by consecutive 15-minute periods of "sudden death" overtime until one team scores. **Stopping the Clock.** The clock will be stopped every time the ball is out of play which includes stoppages for fouls and misconduct and shall not be deemed in play until it has traveled half the distance of its circumference.

Law VIII—Start of Play. The visiting team will kick off in the first and third quarters; the home team will kick off in the second and fourth quarters. The home team has the choice of ends at the start of the game. The teams will change direction at each quarter interval. At the beginning of the first overtime period a flip of the coin will determine which team will kickoff.

Law IX—Ball In and Out of Play. Ball is out of play when (a) it has wholly crossed the goal line or when it has wholly crossed the perimeter wall or (b) when the game has been stopped by the referee. The ball is in play at all other times, even if it rebounds from the referee, perimeter wall, goal post, or corner flag.

Law X—Method of Scoring. A goal is scored when the whole of the ball passes completely over the goal line (between the goal posts and under the cross bar), provided no infraction of the law has been committed by the attacking team.

Law XI—Three-Line-Pass Violation. The outdoor offside law does not apply to indoor soccer, however the following shall apply: A three-line violation occurs when the ball passes over three lines (the two red lines and center line) in the air without touching the floor, the perimeter wall, or a player. The violation results in an indirect free kick from the point of the first red line passed. Any team playing with two players less than the opposing team due to time penalties shall not be penalized for this offense. However, at no time may the goalkeeper punch, throw, punt or drop kick the ball over the three lines.

Law XII—Fouls and Misconduct. Offenses committed during a game, and the disciplinary measures to be taken by the referee are categorized as follows:

1. **Technical Offenses** are those which do not involve body contact and include delay of game, illegal substitutions and three-line violations. For technical offenses, a referee may assess a two-minute time penalty which will not be considered in accumulating the total time penalties for purposes of ejection from the game except if the referee considers that an excessive number of technical time penalties have been served by a player which justifies the issuance of a yellow card for ungentlemanly conduct for persistent infringement of the laws.

2. **Ungentlemanly Conduct** includes such offenses as dissent in word or action, bench personnel interference with the game or persistent infringement of the laws including dangerous play, time wasting, obstruction and gamesmanship. A yellow card plus a two-minute time penalty will be issued by the referee on the field of play for misconduct considered by the referee to be ungentlemanly conduct.

3. **Penal Offenses** include the nine penalty offenses established in 11-a-side soccer plus boarding. Depending on the seriousness of the misconduct the referee can assess a two-minute time penalty with or without the issuance of a caution (yellow card). When a penalty kick is awarded however, the offending player will automatically be assessed a two-minute time penalty. The assessment of the second time penalty for a penal offense to a player will automatically result in the issuance of a yellow card at the bench area, and the third time penalty for a penal offense will automatically result in the ejection of the player from the game.

4. **Ejections** (a) **Violent Conduct.** For violent or serious foul play, and foul and abusive language the referee will eject the player from the game which will be indicated by the issuance of a red card by the referee at the point where the misconduct took place. The entire five-minute time penalty will be served in the penalty box by another player regardless of the number of goals scored by the opposing team. (b) **Accumulation of Time Penalties.** When a player receives two cautions (yellow cards) or is assessed his third two-minute time penalty for penal or ungentlemanly conduct, he will automatically be ejected from the game. A five-minute time penalty will be served in the penalty box by another player who will return to the game if and when the opponents score a goal during that time period. **Delayed Time Penalties.** A time penalty can only be suspended temporarily if it would reduce a team below 4 active players (including the goalkeeper) on the field. Under these circumstances, the offender must go into the Penalty Box immediately. He may be replaced on the field by a substitute until his team returns to an over-four player status. At this point his substitute will withdraw from the game and the offender will commence a full period of the allotted time penalty. **Power Play Return.** If one team is reduced to a lesser number of players on the field than its opponents by the time penalties and the team having more players scores a goal, then the penalized player on the team playing shorthanded who has served the longest amount of time can return to the game from the Penalty Box. Only one player can return on each goal. This rule does not apply to ejections for violent conduct, serious foul play or foul or abusive language. The

substitute player serving a five-minute ejection penalty for one of these three offenses shall not return until the full period of the time penalty served. If his ejection came as a result of a second caution (persisting in misconduct after being cautioned) his substitute shall be permitted to return if a goal is scored by the opposing team. **Time Penalty Awarded Against the Goalkeeper.** When a two-minute time penalty is awarded against a goalkeeper, the penalty shall be served by one of the other players on the field.

Law XIII—Free Kick. Free Kicks are classified into two categories: direct, from which a goal can be scored directly against the offending side; and indirect, from which a goal cannot be scored unless the ball has been touched by a player other than the kicker before entering the goal. For all free kicks the offending team must be at least 10 feet from the ball until it is kicked. The ball is not in play until it has traveled one-half of its circumference.

Law XIV—Penalty Kick. A Penalty Kick is a direct free kick taken from the penalty spot. All players except the kicker and goal-keeper must be outside the penalty area and penalty arc at the time of the kick. The goalkeeper may not move until the ball is played. The kicker may not play the ball a second time unless it rebounds from the goalkeeper or another player.

Law XV—Kick In. When the ball has passed over the perimeter wall at the sidelines (between the corner flags) it is put back in play with an indirect free kick from the spot along the dotted touch line where the ball left the playing surface by the opposite team to the one which played the ball out of play.

Law XVI—Goal Kick. When the ball has passed over the perimeter wall at the goal line after being last touched by a player from the attacking team, it is put back into play by an indirect free kick from within the goal area by the defending team.

Law XVII—Corner Kick. When the ball has passed over the perimeter wall at the goal line after being last touched by a player from the defending team, it is put back into play by a direct free kick by the attacking team from the corner spot closest to where the ball went out of play.

*Reproduced from the 1979/80 Official North American Soccer League Indoor Guide.

The World Cup

World Cup Winners

1930	Uruguay		1962	Brazil
1934	Italy		1966	England
1938	Italy		1970	Brazil
1950	Uruguay		1974	West Germany
1954	West Germany		1978	Argentina
1958	Brazil			

World Cup Final Round Games

First World Cup, Uruguay, 1930

Group 1

France 4	Mexico 1
Argentina 1	France 0
Chile 3	Mexico 0
Chile 1	France 0
Argentina 6	Mexico 3
Argentina 3	Chile 1
Winner Argentina	

Group 2

Yugoslavia 2	Brazil 1
Yugoslavia 4	Bolivia 0
Brazil 4	Bolivia 0
Winner Yugoslavia	

Group 3

Romania 3	Peru 1
Uruguay 1	Peru 0
Uruguay 4	Romania 0
Winner Uruguay	

Group 4

USA 3	Belgium 0
USA 3	Paraguay 0
Paraguay 1	Belgium 0
Winner USA	

Semifinals

Argentina 6	USA 1
Uruguay 6	Yugoslavia 1

Final

Uruguay 4	Argentina 2

Champion

URUGUAY

Second World Cup, Italy, 1934

First Round

Italy 7	USA 1
Czechoslovakia 2	Romania 1
Germany 5	Belgium 2
Austria 3	France 2
Switzerland 3	Netherlands 2
Sweden 3	Argentina 2
Hungary 4	Egypt 2

Second Round

Germany 2	Sweden 1
Austria 2	Hungary 1
Italy 1	Spain 1
Italy 1	Spain 0 (replay)
Czechoslovakia 3	Switzerland 2

Semifinals

Czechoslovakia 3	Germany 1
Italy 1	Austria 0

Third Place Game

Germany 3	Austria 2

Final

Italy 2	Czechoslovakia 1 (o/t)

Champion

ITALY

Third World Cup, France, 1938

First Round

Switzerland 1	Germany 1
Switzerland 4	Germany 2 (replay)
Cuba 3	Romania 3
Cuba 2	Romania 1 (replay)
Hungary 6	Dutch East Indies 0
France 3	Belgium 1
Czechoslovakia 3	Netherlands 0
Brazil 6	Poland 5
Italy 2	Norway 1

Second Round

Sweden 8	Cuba 0
Hungary 2	Switzerland 0
Italy 3	France 1
Brazil 1	Czechoslovakia 1
Brazil 2	Czechoslovakia 1 (replay)

Semifinals

Italy 2	Brazil 1
Hungary 5	Sweden 1

Third Place Game

Brazil 4	Sweden 2

Final

Italy 4	Hungary 2

Champion

ITALY

Fourth World Cup, Brazil, 1950

Pool 1

Brazil 4	Mexico 0
Yugoslavia 3	Switzerland 0
Yugoslavia 4	Mexico 1
Brazil 2	Switzerland 2
Brazil 2	Yugoslavia 0
Switzerland 2	Mexico 1
Winner Brazil	

Pool 2

Spain 3	USA 1
England 2	Chile 0
USA 1	England 0
Spain 2	Chile 0
Spain 1	England 0
Chile 5	USA 2
Winner Spain	

Pool 3

Sweden 3	Italy 2
Sweden 2	Paraguay 2
Italy 2	Paraguay 0
Winner Sweden	

Pool 4

Uruguay 8	Bolivia 0
Winner Uruguay	

Final Pool

Uruguay 2	Spain 2
Brazil 7	Sweden 1
Uruguay 3	Sweden 2
Brazil 6	Spain 1
Sweden 3	Spain 1
Uruguay 2	Brazil 1

Champion

URUGUAY

Fifth World Cup, Switzerland, 1954

Group 1

Yugoslavia 1	France 0
Brazil 5	Mexico 0
France 5	Mexico 2
Brazil 1	Yugoslavia 1
Qualifiers Brazil and Yugoslavia	

Group 2

Hungary 9	Korea 0
West Germany 4	Turkey 1
Hungary 8	West Germany 3
Turkey 7	Korea 0
West Germany 7	Turkey 2 (playoff)
Qualifiers Hungary and West Germany	

Group 3

Austria 1	Scotland 0
Uruguay 2	Czechoslovakia 0
Austria 5	Czechoslovakia 0
Uruguay 7	Scotland 0
Qualifiers Uruguay and Austria	

Group 4

England 4	Belgium 4
England 2	Switzerland 0
Switzerland 2	Italy 1
Italy 4	Belgium 1
Switzerland 4	Italy 1 (playoff)
Qualifiers England and Switzerland	

Quarterfinals

West Germany 2	Yugoslavia 0
Hungary 4	Brazil 2
Austria 7	Switzerland 5
Uruguay 4	England 2

Semifinals

West Germany 6	Austria 1
Hungary 4	Uruguay 2

Third Place Game

Austria 3	Uruguay 1

Final

West Germany 3	Hungary 2

Champion

WEST GERMANY

Sixth World Cup, Sweden, 1958

Group 1

West Germany 3	Argentina 1
Northern Ireland 1	Czechoslovakia 0
West Germany 2	Czechoslovakia 2
Argentina 3	Northern Ireland 1
West Germany 2	Northern Ireland 2
Czechoslovakia 6	Argentina 1
Northern Ireland 2	Czechoslovakia 1 (playoff)

Qualifiers   West Germany and Northern Ireland

Group 2

France 7	Paraguay 3
Yugoslavia 1	Scotland 1
Yugoslavia 3	France 2
Paraguay 3	Scotland 2
France 2	Scotland 1
Yugoslavia 3	Paraguay 3

Qualifiers   France and Yugoslavia

Group 3

Sweden 3	Mexico 0
Hungary 1	Wales 1
Wales 1	Mexico 1
Sweden 2	Hungary 1
Sweden 0	Wales 0
Hungary 4	Mexico 0
Wales 2	Hungary 1 (playoff)

Qualifiers   Sweden and Wales

Group 4

England 2	USSR 2
Brazil 3	Austria 0
England 0	Brazil 0
USSR 2	Austria 0
Brazil 2	USSR 0
England 2	Austria 2
USSR 1	England 0 (playoff)

Qualifiers   Brazil and USSR

Quarterfinals

France 4	Northern Ireland 0
West Germany 1	Yugoslavia 0
Sweden 2	USSR 0
Brazil 1	Wales 0

Semifinals

Brazil 5	France 2
Sweden 3	West Germany 1

Third Place Game

France 6	West Germany 3

Final

Brazil 5	Sweden 2

Champion

BRAZIL

Seventh World Cup, Chile, 1962

Group 1

Uruguay 2	Colombia 1
USSR 2	Yugoslavia 0
Yugoslavia 3	Uruguay 1
USSR 4	Colombia 4
USSR 2	Uruguay 1
Yugoslavia 5	Colombia 0

Qualifiers   USSR and Yugoslavia

Group 2

Chile 3	Switzerland 1
West Germany 0	Italy 0
Chile 2	Italy 0
West Germany 2	Switzerland 1
West Germany 2	Chile 0
Italy 3	Switzerland 0

Qualifiers   West Germany and Chile

Group 3

Brazil 2	Mexico 0
Czechoslovakia 1	Spain 0
Brazil 0	Czechoslovakia 0
Spain 1	Mexico 0
Brazil 2	Spain 1
Mexico 3	Czechoslovakia 1

Qualifiers   Brazil and Czechoslovakia

Group 4

Argentina 1	Bulgaria 0
Hungary 2	England 1
England 3	Argentina 1
Hungary 6	Bulgaria 1
Argentina 0	Hungary 0
England 0	Bulgaria 0

Qualifiers   Hungary and England

Quarterfinals

Yugoslavia 1	West Germany 0
Brazil 3	England 1
Chile 2	USSR 1
Czechoslovakia 1	Hungary 0

Semifinals

Brazil 4	Chile 2
Czechoslovakia 3	Yugoslavia 1

Third Place Game

Chile 1	Yugoslavia 0

Final

Brazil 3	Czechoslovakia 1

Champion

BRAZIL

Eighth World Cup, England, 1966

Group 1

England 0	Uruguay 0
France 1	Mexico 1
Uruguay 2	France 1
England 2	Mexico 0
Uruguay 0	Mexico 0
England 2	France 0

Qualifiers   Uruguay and England

Group 2

West Germany 5	Switzerland 0
Argentina 2	Spain 1
Spain 2	Switzerland 1
Argentina 0	West Germany 0
Argentina 2	Switzerland 0
West Germany 2	Spain 1

Qualifiers   West Germany and Argentina

Group 3

Brazil 2	Bulgaria 0
Portugal 3	Hungary 1
Hungary 3	Brazil 1
Portugal 3	Bulgaria 0
Portugal 3	Brazil 1
Hungary 3	Bulgaria 1

Qualifiers   Portugal and Hungary

Group 4

USSR 3	North Korea 0
Italy 2	Chile 0
Chile 1	North Korea 1
USSR 1	Italy 0
North Korea 1	Italy 0
USSR 2	Chile 1

Qualifiers   USSR and North Korea

Quarterfinals

England 1	Argentina 0
West Germany 4	Uruguay 0
Portugal 5	North Korea 2
USSR 2	Hungary 1

Semifinals

West Germany 2	USSR 1
England 2	Portugal 1

Third Place Game

Portugal 2	USSR 1

Final

England 4	West Germany 2 (o/t)

Champion

ENGLAND

Ninth World Cup, Mexico, 1970

Group 1

Mexico 0	USSR 0
Belgium 3	El Salvador 0
USSR 4	Belgium 1
Mexico 4	El Salvador 0
USSR 2	El Salvador 0
Mexico 1	Belgium 0
Qualifiers	USSR and Mexico

Group 2

Uruguay 2	Israel 0
Italy 1	Sweden 0
Uruguay 0	Italy 0
Israel 1	Sweden 1
Sweden 1	Uruguay 0
Israel 0	Italy 0
Qualifiers	Italy and Uruguay

Group 3

England 1	Romania 0
Brazil 4	Czechoslovakia 1
Romania 2	Czechoslovakia 1
Brazil 1	England 0
Brazil 3	Romania 2
England 1	Czechoslovakia 0
Qualifiers	Brazil and England

Group 4

Peru 3	Bulgaria 2
West Germany 2	Morocco 1
Peru 3	Morocco 0
West Germany 5	Bulgaria 2
West Germany 3	Peru 1
Bulgaria 1	Morocco 1
Qualifiers	West Germany and Peru

Quarterfinals

Uruguay 1	USSR 0
Italy 4	Mexico 1
Brazil 4	Peru 2
West Germany 3	England 2 (o/t)

Semifinals

Italy 4	West Germany 3 (o/t)
Brazil 3	Uruguay 1

Third Place Game

West Germany 1	Uruguay 0

Final

Brazil 4	Italy 1

Champion

BRAZIL

Tenth World Cup, West Germany, 1974

Group 1

West Germany 1	Chile 0
East Germany 2	Australia 0
West Germany 3	Australia 0
East Germany 1	Chile 1
East Germany 1	West Germany 0
Chile 0	Australia 0

Qualifiers   East Germany and West Germany

Group 2

Brazil 0	Yugoslavia 0
Scotland 2	Zaire 0
Brazil 0	Scotland 0
Yugoslavia 9	Zaire 0
Scotland 1	Yugoslavia 1
Brazil 3	Zaire 0

Qualifiers   Brazil and Yugoslavia

Group 3

Netherlands 2	Uruguay 0
Sweden 0	Bulgaria 0
Netherlands 0	Sweden 0
Bulgaria 1	Uruguay 1
Netherlands 4	Bulgaria 1
Sweden 3	Uruguay 0

Qualifiers   Netherlands and Sweden

Group 4

Italy 3	Haiti 1
Poland 3	Argentina 2
Argentina 1	Italy 1
Poland 7	Haiti 0
Argentina 4	Haiti 1
Poland 2	Italy 1

Qualifiers   Poland and Argentina

Semifinal, Group A

Brazil 1	East Germany 0
Netherlands 4	Argentina 0
Netherlands 2	East Germany 0
Brazil 2	Argentina 1
Netherlands 2	Brazil 0
Argentina 1	East Germany 1

Winner   Netherlands
Runner-up   Brazil

Semifinal, Group B

Poland 1	Sweden 0
West Germany 2	Yugoslavia 0
Poland 2	Yugoslavia 1
West Germany 4	Sweden 2
Sweden 2	Yugoslavia 1
West Germany 1	Poland 0

Winner   West Germany
Runner-up   Poland

Third Place Game

Poland 1	Brazil 0

Final

West Germany 2	Netherlands 1

Champion

WEST GERMANY

Eleventh World Cup, Argentina, 1978

Group 1

Argentina 2	Hungary 1
Italy 2	France 1
Argentina 2	France 1
Italy 3	Hungary 1
Italy 1	Argentina 0
France 3	Hungary 1

Qualifiers   Italy and Argentina

Group 2

West Germany 0	Poland 0
Tunisia 3	Mexico 1
Poland 1	Tunisia 0
West Germany 6	Mexico 0
Poland 3	Mexico 1
Tunisia 0	West Germany 0

Qualifiers   Poland and West Germany

Group 3

Austria 2	Spain 1
Sweden 1	Brazil 1
Austria 1	Sweden 0
Brazil 0	Spain 0
Spain 1	Sweden 0
Brazil 1	Austria 0

Qualifiers   Austria and Brazil

Group 4

Peru 3	Scotland 1
Netherlands 3	Iran 0
Scotland 1	Iran 1
Netherlands 0	Peru 0
Peru 4	Iran 1
Scotland 3	Netherlands 2

Qualifiers   Peru and Netherlands

Semifinal, Group A

West Germany 0	Italy 0
Netherlands 5	Austria 1
Italy 1	Austria 0
Netherlands 2	West Germany 2
Austria 3	West Germany 2
Netherlands 2	Italy 1

Winner   Netherlands
Runner-up   Italy

Semifinal, Group B

Argentina 2	Poland 0
Brazil 3	Peru 0
Argentina 0	Brazil 0
Poland 1	Peru 0
Brazil 3	Poland 1
Argentina 6	Peru 0

Winner   Argentina
Runner-up   Brazil

Third Place Game

Brazil 2	Italy 1

Final

Argentina 3	Netherlands 1 (overtime)

Champion

ARGENTINA

United States World Cup Record

1930

Final Round in Uruguay

USA 3	Belgium 0
USA 3	Paraguay 0

Semifinal

USA 1	Argentina 6

1934

Final Round in Italy

USA 4	Mexico 2
USA 1	Italy 7

1938

USA withdrew from tournament.

1950

Qualifying Round

USA 0	Mexico 6
USA 1	Cuba 1
USA 2	Mexico 6
USA 5	Cuba 2

USA qualified for final round.

Final Round in Brazil

USA 1	Spain 3
USA 1	England 0
USA 2	Chile 5

1954

Qualifying Round

USA 0	Mexico 4
USA 1	Mexico 3
USA 3	Haiti 2
USA 3	Haiti 0

USA failed to qualify for final round in Switzerland.

1958

Qualifying Round

USA 0	Mexico 6
USA 2	Mexico 7
USA 1	Canada 5
USA 2	Canada 3

USA failed to qualify for final round in Sweden.

1962

Qualifying Round

USA 3	Mexico 3
USA 0	Mexico 3

USA failed to qualify for final round in Chile.

1966

Qualifying Round

USA 0	Mexico 2
USA 2	Mexico 2
USA 1	Honduras 0
USA 1	Honduras 1

USA failed to qualify for final round in England.

1970

Qualifying Round

USA 2	Canada 4
USA 1	Canada 0
USA 6	Bermuda 2
USA 2	Bermuda 0
USA 0	Haiti 2
USA 0	Haiti 1

USA failed to qualify for final round in Mexico.

1974

Qualifying Round

USA 2	Canada 3
USA 2	Canada 2
USA 1	Mexico 3
USA 1	Mexico 2

USA failed to qualify for final round in West Germany.

1978

Qualifying Round

Canada 1	USA 1
USA 0	Mexico 0
Mexico 3	USA 0
USA 2	Canada 0

Playoff

Canada 3	USA 0

USA failed to qualify for final round in Argentina.

The Olympics and Other Competitions Among Nations

Olympic Games Winners

The 16 Olympic finalists are divided into groups of 4, with the group winners playing in the semifinals and the semifinal winners meeting in the final. Preliminary games are played on a regional basis as early as 2 years before the Olympic games. Here are the winners.

1900	Great Britain	1940	No competition
1904	Canada	1944	No competition
1908	Great Britain	1948	Sweden
1912	Great Britain	1952	Hungary
1916	No competition	1956	USSR
1920	Belgium	1960	Yugoslavia
1924	Uruguay	1964	Hungary
1928	Uruguay	1968	Hungary
1932	No competition	1972	Poland
1936	Italy	1976	East Germany

United States Olympic Record

The United States entered the Olympics for the first time in 1924, when not every country could afford to send a team to the site of the games. The system of regional qualifying games began in 1960.

1924 Paris

USA 1 Estonia 0
USA 0 Uruguay 3

1928 Amsterdam

USA 2 Argentina 11

1932   No soccer tournament

1936   Berlin

USA 0   Italy 1

1940 and 1944   Olympic games not held

1948   London

USA 0   Italy 9

1952   Helsinki

USA 0   Italy 8

1956   Melbourne, Australia

USA 1   Yugoslavia 9

1960

Qualifying Round

USA 0   Mexico 2
USA 1   Mexico 1
USA failed to qualify for final round in Rome, Italy.

1964

Qualifying Round

USA 0   Surinam 1
USA 4   Panama 2
USA 1   Mexico 2
USA failed to qualify for final round in Tokyo, Japan.

1968

Qualifying Round

USA 1   Bermuda 1
USA 0   Bermuda 1
USA failed to qualify for final round in Mexico City, Mexico.

1972

Qualifying Round   First Preliminary

USA 1   El Salvador 1
USA 3   Barbados 0
USA 1   El Salvador 1
USA 3   Barbados 1

Playoff Game

USA 1   El Salvador 1 (o/t)
(Game decided on penalty kicks, with the USA winning 6–5, and passing into the
2nd preliminary round.)

Qualifying Round   Second Preliminary

USA 1   Jamaica 1
USA 1   Mexico 1
USA 2   Guatemala 3
USA 2   Guatemala 1
USA 2   Mexico 2
USA 2   Jamaica 1
USA qualified for the final round in Munich, West Germany.

Final Round   Munich

USA 0   Morocco 0
USA 0   Malaysia 3
USA 0   West Germany 7

1976

Qualifying Round

USA 2   Bermuda 3
USA 2   Bermuda 0
USA 0   Mexico 8
USA 2   Mexico 4
USA failed to qualify for final round in Montreal, Canada.

The European Championship

This competition among the national teams of the 32 European countries was formerly known as the European Nations Cup. The trophy is known as the Henri Delaunay
Cup. The countries are divided by draw into 8 groups, the winners of which advance
to the quarterfinals, which are held on a home-and-home basis, with aggregate scores
deciding the winners. The semifinalists then travel to a previously selected site where,
within the space of about 7 days, the 2 semifinals, the third-place game, and the final
are held. Here are the winners of this competition, which started in 1960.

   1960   USSR
   1964   Spain
   1968   Italy
   1972   West Germany
   1976   Czechoslovakia

The South American Championship

The frequency of this competition among the nations in North, South, and Central
America and the Caribbean is irregular. The competition, known as Campeonato
Sudamericano du Fútbol, has fallen into hard times and has been staged only once

since 1967. This occurred in 1975, with Peru defeating Colombia. Here are the winners of the trophy.

Year	Winner	Year	Winner
1917	Uruguay	1942	Uruguay
1919	Brazil	1945	Argentina
1920	Uruguay	1946	Argentina
1921	Argentina	1947	Argentina
1922	Brazil	1949	Brazil
1923	Uruguay	1953	Paraguay
1924	Uruguay	1955	Argentina
1925	Argentina	1956	Uruguay
1926	Uruguay	1957	Argentina
1927	Argentina	1959	Argentina
1929	Argentina	1960	Uruguay
1935	Uruguay	1963	Bolivia
1937	Argentina	1967	Uruguay
1939	Peru	1975	Peru
1941	Argentina		

Champions in Europe and South America

The European Cup

The European Cup is the most prestigious of the 3 European competitions among clubs. The Cup Winners Cup and the UEFA Cup are the others. The holder of the trophy and the champion in each European country is eligible for this annual competition, the winner of which meets the winner of the Copa Libertadores for the World Club Championship.

Teams are drawn in pairs after each round of the knockout competition. The final is a 1-game affair that is normally held at a neutral site. Real Madrid captured the trophy the first 5 years after its inception in 1956. Here are the winning teams, with their countries in parentheses.

1956	Real Madrid (Spain)	1968	Manchester United (England)
1957	Real Madrid (Spain)	1969	Milan (Italy)
1958	Real Madrid (Spain)	1970	Feyenoord (Netherlands)
1959	Real Madrid (Spain)	1971	Ajax (Netherlands)
1960	Real Madrid (Spain)	1972	Ajax (Netherlands)
1961	Benfica (Portugal)	1973	Ajax (Netherlands)
1962	Benfica (Portugal)	1974	Bayern Munich (West Germany)
1963	Milan (Italy)	1975	Bayern Munich (West Germany)
1964	Internazionale (Italy)	1976	Bayern Munich (West Germany)
1965	Internazionale (Italy)	1977	Liverpool (England)
1966	Real Madrid (Spain)	1978	Liverpool (England)
1967	Celtic (Scotland)	1979	Nottingham Forest (England)

The European Cup Winners Cup

The defending champion and the cup winners from all European nations are eligible for this annual competition, which started in 1961. Here are the winning teams, with their countries in parentheses.

1961	Fiorentina (Italy)	1963	Tottenham Hotspur (England)
1962	Atlético Madrid (Spain)	1964	Sporting Portugal (Portugal)

1965	West Ham United (England)
1966	Borussia Dortmund (West Germany)
1967	Bayern Munich (West Germany)
1968	Milan (Italy)
1969	Slovan Bratislava (Czechoslovakia)
1970	Manchester City (England)
1971	Chelsea (England)
1972	Rangers (Scotland)
1973	Milan (Italy)
1974	FC Magdeburg (East Germany)
1975	Dynamo Kiev (USSR)
1976	Anderlecht (Belgium)
1977	Hamburg (West Germany)
1978	Anderlecht (Belgium)
1979	Barcelona (Spain)

The UEFA Cup

This competition is named after the Union of European Football Associations, although it was known from 1958 – the year of its inception – until 1971 as the Fairs Cup. The top clubs from each country, not including the champion or the cup winner, are chosen by a committee on the basis of their positions in the final standings of the national championship races. The committee can select more than 1 club from a country. The 1975 – 76 competition, for example, started with 64 clubs. Here are the winning teams, with their countries in parentheses.

1958	Barcelona (Spain)
1959	No competiion
1960	Barcelona (Spain)
1961	Roma (Italy)
1962	Valencia (Spain)
1963	Valencia (Spain)
1964	Real Zaragoza (Spain)
1965	Ferencvaros (Hungary)
1966	Barcelona (Spain)
1967	Dynamo Zagreb (Yugoslavia)
1968	Leeds United (England)
1969	Newcastle United (England)
1970	Arsenal (England)
1971	Leeds United (England)
1972	Tottenham Hotspur (England)
1973	Liverpool (England)
1974	Feyenoord (Netherlands)
1975	Borussia Monchengladbach (West Germany)
1976	Liverpool (England)
1977	Juventus (Italy)
1978	PSV Eindhoven (Netherlands)
1979	Borussia Monchengladbach (West Germany)

The European Player of the Year

Soccer journalists from as many as 30 countries in Europe vote for the top player each year.

Year	Winner	Club	National Team
1956	Stanley Matthews	Blackpool	England
1957	Alfredo di Stéfano	Real Madrid	Spain
1958	Raymond Kopa	Real Madrid	Spain
1959	Alfredo di Stéfano	Real Madrid	Spain
1960	Luis Suarez	Barcelona	Spain
1961	Omar Sivori	Juventus	Italy and Argentina
1962	Josef Masopust	Dukla Prague	Czechoslovakia
1963	Lev Yashin	Dynamo Moscow	USSR
1964	Denis Law	Manchester United	Scotland
1965	Eusebio	Benfica	Portugal
1966	Bobby Charlton	Manchester United	England
1967	Flórián Albert	Ferencvaros	Hungary
1968	George Best	Manchester United	England
1969	Gianni Rivera	Milan	Italy
1970	Gerd Mueller	Bayern Munich	West Germany
1971	Johan Cruyff	Ajax	Netherlands

1972	Franz Beckenbauer	Bayern Munich	West Germany
1973	Johan Cruyff	Barcelona	Netherlands
1974	Johan Cruyff	Barcelona	Netherlands
1975	Oleg Blokhin	Dynamo Kiev	USSR
1976	Franz Beckenbauer	Bayern Munich	West Germany
1977	Alan Simonsen	Borussia Monchengladbach	Denmark
1978	Kevin Keegan	Hamburg	England
1979	Kevin Keegan	Hamburg	England

The Copa Libertadores

This is the only major international competition for clubs staged within South America.
For South American clubs it is equivalent in prestige to the European Cup. Here are
the winning teams, with their countries in parentheses.

1960	Penarol (Uruguay)	1970	Estudiantes de la Plata (Argentina)
1961	Penarol (Uruguay)	1971	Nacional (Uruguay)
1962	Santos (Brazil)	1972	Independiente (Argentina)
1963	Santos (Brazil)	1973	Independiente (Argentina)
1964	Independiente (Argentina)	1974	Independiente (Argentina)
1965	Independiente (Argentina)	1975	Independiente (Argentina)
1966	Penarol (Uruguay)	1976	Cruzeiro (Brazil)
1967	Racing Club (Argentina)	1977	Boca Juniors (Argentina)
1968	Estaudiantes de la Plata (Argentina)	1978	Boca Juniors (Argentina)
1969	Estudiantes de la Plata (Argentina)	1979	Olimpia (Paraguay)

The Championship of Champions

This competition was organized for the leading clubs in North America, Central America, and the Caribbean, including the United States. The competition, unfortunately,
has met with all sorts of difficulties since its inception in 1967. The winners in the
NASL are supposed to represent the United States, but only 1 NASL team—the
Rochester Lancers in 1971—has entered the tournament. Unlike the European Cup
and the Copa Libertadores, this tournament is not very attractive or prestigious.
Here are the winning teams, with their countries in parentheses.

1967	Alianza (El Salvador)	1973	Transvaal (Surinam)
1968	Toluca (Mexico)	1974	Deportivo Municipal (Guatemala)
1969	Cruz Azul (Mexico)	1975	Atlético Español (Mexico)
1970	Final round not played	1976	Final round not played
1971	Cruz Azul (Mexico)	1977	America (Mexico)
1972	Olímpia (Honduras)	1978	Comunicaciones (Guatemala)

The World Club Championship

This competition is also called the Copa Intercontinentale. It involves the winners of
the European Cup and the Copa Libertadores, or South American Cup. This is a
true world club championship, but its image in recent years has been tarnished by
incidents of brutal play, particularly by teams from Argentina. It is an annual competi-

tion with variable dates, which must fall between September and December. Here are the winning teams, with their countries in parentheses.

Year	Team	Year	Team
1960	Real Madrid (Spain)	1970	Feyenoord (Netherlands)
1961	Penarol (Uruguay)	1971	Nacional (Uruguay)
1962	Santos (Brazil)	1972	Ajax (Netherlands)
1963	Santos (Brazil)	1973	Independiente (Argentina)
1964	Internazionale (Italy)	1974	Atlético Madrid (Spain)
1965	Internazionale (Italy)	1975	Not played
1966	Penarol (Uruguay)	1976	Bayern Munich (West Germany)
1967	Racing Club (Argentina)	1977	Boca Juniors (Argentina)
1968	Estudiantes de la Plata (Argentina)	1978	Boca Juniors (Argentina)
1969	Milan (Italy)	1979	Olimpia (Paraguay)

The South American Player of the Year

A poll of 17 top soccer journalists from South and Central America vote for this award, which was organized by *El Mundo,* a newspaper in Caracas. Here are the winners.

Year	Winner	Team	National team
1971	Tostão	Cruzeiro	Brazil
1972	Teófilo Cubillas	Alianza Lima	Peru
1973	Pelé	Santos	Brazil
1974	Elias Figueroa	Internacional (Brazil)	Chile
1975	Elias Figueroa	Internacional (Brazil)	Chile
1976	Elias Figueroa	Internacional (Brazil)	Chile
1977	Zico	Flamengo	Brazil
1978	Mario Kempes	Valencia (Spain)	Argentina
1979	Diego Maradona	Juniors	Argentina

Champions in the United States and Canada

National Challenge Cup Winners

1914	Brooklyn Field Club (Brooklyn, N.Y.)	1943	Brooklyn Hispano F.C. (Brooklyn, N.Y.)
1915	Bethlehem Steel F.C. (Bethlehem, Pa.)	1944	Brooklyn Hispano F.C. (Brooklyn, N.Y.)
1916	Bethlehem Steel F.C. (Bethlehem, Pa.)	1945	Brookhattan F.C. (New York, N.Y.)
1917	Fall River Rovers (Fall River, Mass.)	1946	Chicago Viking F.C. (Chicago, Ill.)
1918	Bethlehem Steel F.C. (Bethlehem, Pa.)	*1947	Ponta Delgada S.C. (Fall River, Mass.)
1919	Bethlehem Steel F.C. (Bethlehem, Pa.)	1948	Simpkins-Ford S.C. (St. Louis, Mo.)
1920	Ben Miller F.C. (St. Louis, Mo.)	1949	Morgan S.C. (Morgan, Pa.)
1921	Robbins Dry Dock F.C. (Brooklyn, N.Y.)	1950	Simpkins-Ford S.C. (St. Louis, Mo.)
1922	Scullin Steel F.C. (St. Louis, Mo.)	*1951	German Hungarian S.C. (New York, N.Y.)
1923	Paterson F.C. (Paterson, N.J.)	1952	Harmarville S.C. (Harmarville, Pa.)
1924	Fall River F.C. (Fall River, Mass.)	1953	Falcons S.C. (Chicago, Ill.)
1925	Shawsheen F.C. (Tiverton, R.I.)	1954	New York Americans (New York, N.Y.)
1926	Bethlehem Steel F.C. (Bethlehem, Pa.)	1955	Eintracht (New York, N.Y.)
1927	Fall River F.C. (Fall River, Mass.)	1956	Harmarville S.C. (Harmarville, Pa.)
1928	New York National S.C. (New York, N.Y.)	*1957	Kutis S.C. (St. Louis, Mo.)
1929	Hakoah All Star S.C. (New York, N.Y.)	1958	Los Angeles Kickers (Los Angeles, Cal.)
1930	Fall River F.C. (Fall River, Mass.)	1959	McIlwaine Canvasbaks (Los Angeles, Cal.)
1931	Fall River F.C. (Fall River, Mass.)	1960	National Ukrainian (Philadelphia, Pa.)
1932	New Bedford F.C. (New Bedford, Mass.)	1961	National Ukrainian (Philadelphia, Pa.)
1933	Stix, Baer & Fuller F.C. (St. Louis, Mo.)	1962	New York Hungaria (New York, N.Y.)
1934	Stix, Baer & Fuller F.C. (St. Louis, Mo.)	1963	National Ukrainian (Philadelphia, Pa.)
1935	Central Breweries F.C. (Chicago, Ill.)	1964	Lost Angeles Kickers (Los Angeles, Cal.)
1936	Philadelphia American S.C. (Philadelphia, Pa.)	1965	New York Ukrainian (New York, N.Y.)
1937	New York American F.C. (New York, N.Y.)	1966	National Ukrainian (Philadelphia, Pa.)
1938	Sparta A. & B. A. (Chicago, Ill.)	1967	Greek Americans (New York, N.Y.)
1939	St. Mary's Celtic S.C. (Brooklyn, N.Y.)	1968	Greek Americans (New York, N.Y.)
1940	No winner	1969	Greek Americans (New York, N.Y.)
1941	Pawtucket F C. (Pawtucket, R.I.)	1970	Elizabeth S.C. (Elizabeth, N.J.)
1942	Gallatin S.C. (Gallatin, Pa.)	1971	Hota S.C. (New York, N.Y.)

*Won both National Challenge Cup and Amateur Cup.

1972 Elizabeth S.C. (Elizabeth, N.J.)
1973 Maccabee S.C. (Los Angeles, Cal.)
1974 Greek Americans (New York, N.Y.)
1975 Maccabee S.C. (Los Angeles, Cal.)

1976 San Francisco Athletic Club (San Francisco, Cal.)
1977 Maccabee S.C. (Los Angeles, Cal.)
1978 Maccabee S.C. (Los Angeles, Cal.)
1979 Brooklyn Dodgers (New York)

National Amateur Cup Winners

1923 No winner
1924 Fleisher Yarn F.C. (Philadelphia, Pa.)
1925 Toledo F.C. (Toledo, Ohio)
1926 Defenders F.C. (Cleveland, Ohio)
1927 Heidelberg S.C. (Heidelberg, Pa.)
1928 Swedish American F.C. (Detroit, Mich.) and Powers Hudson Essex S.C. (Newark, N.J.) declared cochampions
1929 Heidelberg S.C. (Heidelberg, Pa.)
1930 Raffies F.C. (St. Louis, Mo.)
1931 Goodyear S.C. (Cleveland, Ohio)
1932 Shamrock S.C. (Cleveland, Ohio)
1933 German American S.C. (Philadelphia, Pa.)
1934 German American S.C. (Philadelphia, Pa.)
1935 W. W. Riehl S.C. (Pittsburgh, Pa.)
1936 Brooklyn German S.C. (Brooklyn, N.Y.)
1937 Trenton Highlander S.C. (Trenton, N.J.)
1938 Ponta Delgada S.C. (Fall River, Mass.)
1939 St. Michael's S.C. (Fall River, Mass.)
1940 Morgan Strasser S.C. (Morgan, Pa.)
1941 Fall River S.C. (Fall River, Mass.)
1942 Fall River S.C. (Fall River, Mass.)
1943 Morgan Strasser S.C. (Morgan, Pa.)
1944 Eintracht Sport Club (New York, N.Y.)
1945 Eintracht Sport Club (New York, N.Y.)
1946 Ponta Delgada S.C. (Fall River, Mass.)
*1947 Ponta Delgada S.C. (Fall River, Mass.)
1948 Ponta Delgada S.C. (Fall River, Mass.)
1949 Elizabeth Sport Club (Elizabeth, N.J.)
1950 Ponta Delgada S.C. (Fall River, Mass.)

*1951 German Hungarian S.C. (New York, N.Y.)
1952 Raiders S.C. (Rall River, Mass.)
1953 Ponta Delgada S.C. (Fall River, Mass.)
1954 Beadling of Beadling (Beadling, Pa.)
1955 Heidelberg S.C. (Heidelberg, Pa.)
1956 Kutis S.C. (St. Louis, Mo.)
*1957 Kutis S.C. (St. Louis, Mo.)
1958 Kutis S.C. (St. Louis, Mo.)
1959 Kutis S.C. (St. Louis, Mo.)
1960 Kutis S.C. (St. Louis, Mo.)
1961 Kutis S.C. (St. Louis, Mo.)
1962 Carpathia Kickers (Detroit, Mich.)
1963 Italian American (Rochester, N.Y.)
1964 Schwaben S.C. (Chicago, Ill.)
1965 German-Hungarian S.C. (Philadelphia, Pa.)
1966 Chicago Kickers S.C. (Chicago, Ill.)
1967 Hartford Italians S.C. (Hartford, Conn.)
1968 Chicago Kickers S.C. (Chicago, Ill.)
1969 British Lions S.C. (Washington, D.C.)
1970 Chicago Kickers S.C. (Chicago, Ill.)
1971 Kutis S.C. (St. Louis, Mo.)
1972 Busch S.C. (St. Louis, Mo.)
1973 Philadelphia Inter S.C. (Philadelphia, Pa.)
1974 Philadelphia Inter S.C. (Philadelphia, Pa.)
1975 Chicago Kickers S.C. (Chicago, Ill.)
1976 Bavarians (Milwaukee, Wisc.)
1977 Kickers (Denver, Colo.)
1978 Kickers (Denver, Colo.)
1979 Datagraphic S.C. (Atlanta, Ga.)

National Youth Cup Winners

1935 Reliable Juniors (New Bedford, Mass.)
1936 Hatikvoh Juniors (Brooklyn, N.Y.)
1937 Hatikvoh Juniors (Brooklyn, N.Y.)
1938 Lighthouse Boys' Club (Philadeophia, Pa.)
1939 Avella Juniors (Avella, Pa.)
1940 Avella Juniors (Avella, Pa.)
1941 Mercerville Juniors (Trenton, N.J.)
1942 1943–1944. No competition as travel was restricted because of war effort.

1945 Hornets (Chicago, Ill) and Pompei Juniors (Baltimore, Md.) declared cochampions.
1946 Schumacher Juniors (St. Louis, Mo.)
1947 Heidelberg Juniors (Heidelberg, Pa.)
1948 Lighthouse Boys' Club (Philadelphia, Pa.)
1949 Lighthouse Boys' Club (Philadelphia, Pa.)
1950 Harrison Juniors (Harrison, N.J.)
1951 Seco Juniors (St. Louis, Mo.)
1952 Kollsman S. C. (Brooklyn N.Y.)

*Won both National Challenge Cup and Amateur Cup.

1953	Hansa S. C. (Chicago, Ill.) (West)		1966	St. William (St. Louis, Mo.)
1953	Newark Boys Club (Newark, N.J.) (East)		1967	Lighthouse Boys' Club (Philadelphia, Pa.)
1954	Hansa S. C. (Chicago, Ill.)		1968	St. Philip Di Neri (St. Louis, Mo.)
1955	Gottschee S. C. (Brooklyn, N.Y.) (East)		1969	St. Philip Di Neri (St. Louis, Mo.)
1955	Schwaben (Chicago, Ill.) (West)		1970	St. Barts (St. Louis, Mo.)
1956	St. Singlebert (St. Louis, Mo.)		1971	Seco (St. Louis, Mo.)
1957	Lighthouse Boys' Club (Philadelphia, Pa.)		1972	Seco (St. Louis, Mo.)
1958	St. Paul (St. Louis, Mo.)		1973	St. Elizabeth S. C. (Baltimore, Md.)
1959	Ukrainian (New York, N.Y.)		1974	Florissant Celtics (St. Louis, Mo.)
1960	St. Paul (St. Louis, Mo.)		1975	Imo's Pizza (St. Louis, Mo.)
1961	Hakoah (San Francisco, Cal)		1976	Cavaliers (Annandals, Va.)
1962	Schumacher (St. Louis, Mo.)		1977	Broncos (Santa Clara, Cal.)
1963	Kutis (St. Louis, Mo.)		1978	Imo's Pizza (St. Louis, Mo.)
1964	Kutis (St. Louis, Mo.)		1979	Imo's Pizza (St. Louis, Mo.)
1965	I. M. Heart of Mary (St. Louis, Mo.)			

National Collegiate Athletic Association

Division I

Champion			*Runner-up*
1959	Saint Louis	5–2	Bridgeport
1960	Saint Louis	3–2	Maryland
1961	West Chester State	2–0	Saint Louis
1962	Saint Louis	4–3	Maryland
1963	Saint Louis	3–0	Navy
1964	Navy	1–0	Michigan State
1965	Saint Louis	1–0	Michigan State
1966	San Francisco	5–2	Long Island
1967	Michigan State	0–0	(cochampions, game called
	Saint Louis		because of bad weather)
1968	Maryland	2–2	(cochampions after
	Michigan State		2 overtimes)
1969	Saint Louis	4–0	San Francisco
1970	Saint Louis	1–0	U.C.L.A.
*1971	(Howard)	3–2	Saint Louis
1972	Saint Louis	4–2	U.C.L.A.
1973	Saint Louis	2–1 (o/t)	U.C.L.A.
1974	Howard	2–1 (o/t)	Saint Louis
1975	San Francisco	4–0	Southern Illinois
1976	San Francisco	1–0	Indiana
1977	Hartwick	2–1	San Francisco
1978	San Francisco	2–0	Indiana
1979	Southern Illinois	3–2	Clemson
	— Edwardsville		

Division II

Champion			*Runner-up*
1972	Southern Illinois	1–0	Oneonta State
1973	Missouri, St. Louis	3–0	Fullerton State
1974	Adelphi	3–2	Seattle Pacific
1975	Baltimore	3–1	Seattle Pacific

*Taken away because of alleged use of ineligible players.

1976	Loyola-Baltimore	2 – 0	New Haven
1977	Alabama A&M	2 – 1	Seattle Pacific
1978	Seattle Pacific	1 – 0	Alabama A&M
1979	Alabama A&M	2 – 0	Eastern Illinois

Division III

	Champion		Runner-up
1974	Brockport State	3 – 1	Swarthmore
1975	Babson College	1 – 0	Brockport St.
1976	Brandeis	2 – 1	Brockport St.
1977	Lock Haven	1 – 0	Cortland St.
1978	Lock Haven	3 – 0	Washington, Mo.
1979	Babson College	2 – 1	Glassboro St.

National Association of Intercollegiate Athletics

	Champion		Runner-up
1959	Pratt Institute	4 – 3 (o/t)	Elizabethtown
1960	Elizabethtown	2 – 2 (o/t)	(cochampions)
	Newark College of Engineering		
1961	Howard	3 – 0	Newark College of Engineering
1962	East Stroudsburg State	4 – 0	Pratt
1963	Earlham College		(cochampions; finals canceled
	Castleton State		because of snow)
1964	Trenton State	3 – 0	Lincoln
1965	Trenton State	5 – 2	Earlham
1966	Quincy	6 – 1	Trenton State
1967	Quincy	3 – 1	Rockhurst
1968	Davis and Elkins	2 – 1 (o/t)	Quincy
1969	Eastern Illinois	1 – 0 (o/t)	Davis and Elkins
1970	Davis and Elkins	2 – 0	Quincy
1971	Quincy	1 – 0	Davis and Elkins
1972	Westmont	2 – 1 (o/t)	Davis and Elkins
1973	Quincy	3 – 0	Rockhurst
1974	Quincy	6 – 0	Davis and Elkins
1975	Quincy	1 – 0	Simon Fraser
1976	Simon Fraser	1 – 0	Rockhurst
1977	Quincy	3 – 0	Keene St.
1978	Quincy	2 – 0	Alabama-Huntsville
1979	Quincy	1 – 0	Rockhurst

Hermann Trophy

The Hermann trophy is awarded to the collegiate soccer player of the year, who is chosen in a poll of college coaches conducted by *The Sporting News.* Many consider this trophy the equivalant of the Heisman Trophy in football. The trophy was instituted in 1967 in honor of Robert R. Hermann, owner of the NASL St. Louis Stars, who moved to Anaheim, California, in 1978. Here are the winners.

1967   Dov Markus (Long Island University)
1968   Mani Hernandez (San Jose State University)
1969   Al Trost (Saint Louis University)

1970   Al Trost (Saint Louis University)
1971   Mike Seerey (Saint Louis University)
1972   Mike Seerey (Saint Louis University)
1973   Dan Counce (Saint Louis University)
1974   Farrukh Quraishi (Oneonta State)
1975   Steve Ralbovsky (Brown University)
1976   Glenn Myernick (Hartwick College)
1977   Billy Gazonas (Hartwick College)
1978   Angelo DiBernardo (Indiana)
1979   Jim Stamatis (Penn State)

Canadian Challenge Cup Winners

This competition has been played in various formats over the years. Until 1956 the final was decided by a 3-game series, but since 1956 the final has been a 1-game affair. There have been times (such as the present) when this competition has been an all-amateur affair, but at other times pro teams have participated. Originally the teams played for the Connaught Cup, presented by the Duke of Connaught, but this has been replaced by a number of different trophies. The competition started in 1913. Here are the winners.

1913	Norwood Wanderers (Winnipeg)	1949	Vancouver North Shore United
1914	Norwood Wanderers (Winnipeg)	1950	Vancouver City
1915	Winnipeg Scottish	1951	Toronto Ulster United
1916	No competition	1952	Montreal Stelco
1917	No competition	1953	New Westminster Royals
1918	No competition	1954	A.N. & A.F. Scottish (Winnipeg)
1919	Montreal Grand Trunk	1955	New Westminster Royals
1920	Hamilton Westinghouse	1956	Vancouver Halecos
1921	Toronto Scottish	1957	Montreal Ukrainia
1922	Calgary Hillhursts	1958	New Westminster Royals
1923	Nanaimo	1959	Montreal Alouettes
1924	United Weston (Winnipeg)	1960	New Westminster Royals
1925	Toronto Ulster United	1961	Montreal Concordia
1926	United Weston (Winnipeg)	1962	No competition
1927	Nanaimo	1963	No competition
1928	New Westminster Royals	1964	Vancouver Columbus
1929	Canadian National (Montreal)	1965	Vancouver Firefighters
1930	New Westminster Royals	1966	Vancouver Under 23 All Stars
1931	New Westminster Royals	1967	Toronto Ballymena
1932	Toronto Scottish	1968	Toronto Royals
1933	Toronto Scottish	1969	Vancouver Columbus
1934	Montreal Verdun Park	1970	No competition
1935	Montreal Aldred Building	1971	Vancouver Eintract
1936	New Westminster Royals	1972	New Westminster Blues
1937	Vancouver Johnston National	1973	Vancouver Firefighters
1938	Vancouver North Shore United	1974	Calgary Kickers
1939	Vancouver Radials	1975	London Boxing Club (Victoria)
1940-1945	No competition	1976	Victoria West
1946	Toronto Ulster United	1977	Vancouver Columbus
1947	Vancouver St. Andrews	1978	Vancouver Columbus
1948	Montreal Carsteel	1979	Victoria West

American Professionals

1980 NASL Divisional Alignment

National Conference

Eastern Division	*Central Division*	*Western Division*
Toronto Blizzard	Minnesota Kicks	Vancouver Whitecaps
Rochester Lancers	Atlanta Chiefs	Seattle Sounders
New York Cosmos	Tulsa Roughnecks	Portland Timbers
Washington Diplomats	Dallas Tornado	Los Angeles Aztecs

American Conference

Eastern Division	*Central Division*	*Western Division*
New England Tea Men	Detroit Express	Edmonton Drillers
Philadelphia Fury	Chicago Sting	San Jose Earthquakes
Tampa Bay Rowdies	Memphis Rogues	California Surf
Fort Lauderdale Strikers	Houston Hurricane	San Diego Sockers

NASL Directory

ATLANTA CHIEFS
P.O. Box 5015
Atlanta, GA 30302
(404) 577 – 5425

CALIFORNIA SURF
P.O. Box 4449
Anaheim, CA 92803
(714) 634 – 8326

CHICAGO STING
Suite 1525
333 N. Michigan Ave.
Chicago, Il 60601
(312) 558 – 5425

DALLAS TORNADO
6166 North Central Expwy.
Dallas, TX 75206
(214) 750 – 0900

DETROIT EXPRESS
Pontiac Silverdome
1200 Featherstone Road
Pontiac, MI 48057
(393) 338 – 9100

EDMONTON DRILLERS
10039 Jaspen Ave.
Edmonton, Alberta
Canada T5J 1T4
(403) 428 – 8989

FORT LAUDERDALE STRIKERS
1350 North East 56th St.
Fort Lauderdale, FL 33334
(305) 491–5140

HOUSTON HURRICANE
P.O. Box 42999
Suite 569
Houston, TX 77042
(713) 960–8326

LOS ANGELES AZTECS
777 Rose Bowl Drive
Pasadena, CA 91103
(213) 681-6336

MEMPHIS ROGUES
2200 Union Ave.
Memphis, TN 38104
(901) 274–7861

MINNESOTA KICKS
7200 France Ave. So.
Minneapolis, MN 55435
(612) 831–8871

NEW ENGLAND TEA MEN
34 Mechanic Street
Foxboro, MA 12543
(617) 543–6100

NEW YORK COSMOS
75 Rockefeller Plaza
New York, NY 10019
(212) 265–7315

PHILADELPHIA FURY
Veterans Stadium
Broad St. & Pattison Ave.
Philadelphia, PA 19148
(215) 755–5400

PORTLAND TIMBERS
Suite 101 D
10151 Barbur Blvd.
Portland, OR 97219
(503) 245–6464

ROCHESTER LANCERS
812 Wilder Building
Rochester, NY 14614
(716) 232–2420

SAN DIEGO SOCKERS
San Diego Stadium
9449 Friars Road
San Diego, CA 92108
(714) 280–4265

SAN JOSE EARTHQUAKES
Suite 272
2025 Gateway Place
San Jose, CA 95110
(408) 998–5425

SEATTLE SOUNDERS
300 Metropole Bldg.
Seattle, WA 98104
(206) 628–3551

TAMPA BAY ROWDIES
Suite 109
1311 North West Shore Blvd.
Tampa, FL 33607
(813) 870–1122

TORONTO BLIZZARD
Pro Soccer Ltd.
1678 Bloor Street, West
Toronto, Ontario
Canada M6P 1A8

TULSA ROUGHNECKS
P.O. Box 35190
Tulsa, OK 74135
(918) 494–4625

VANCOUVER WHITECAPS
Suite 110
885 Dunsmuir Street
Vancouver, B.C.
Canada V6C IN5
(604) 682–0311

WASHINGTON DIPLOMATS
RFK Stadium
E. Capitol Sts & 22nd NE
Washington, DC 20003
(202) 544–5425

NASL Honor Roll

Champion		*Runnerup*	
1967	Oakland Clippers (NPSL)	1967	Baltimore Bays
1967	Los Angeles Wolves (USA)	1967	Washington Whips
1968	Atlanta Chiefs	1968	San Diego Toros
1969	Kansas City Spurs	1969	Atlanta Chiefs
1970	Rochester Lancers	1970	Washington Darts
1971	Dallas Tornado	1971	Atlanta Chiefs
1972	New York Cosmos	1972	St. Louis Stars
1973	Philadelphia Atoms	1973	Dallas Tornado
1974	Los Angeles Aztecs	1974	Miami Toros
1975	Tampa Bay Rowdies	1975	Portland Timbers
1976	Toronto Metros	1976	Minnesota Kicks
1977	New York Cosmos	1977	Seattle Sounders
1978	New York Cosmos	1978	Tampa Bay Rowdies
1979	Vancouver Whitecaps	1979	Tampa Bay Rowdies

Leading Scorer

Year	Player-Team	Games	Goals	Assists	Points
1967	Yanko Daucik (Toronto Falcons)	17	20	8	48
1968	John Kowalik (Chicago Mustangs)	28	30	9	69
1969	Kaizer Motaung (Atlanta Chiefs)	15	16	4	36
1970	Kirk Apostolidis (Dallas Tornado)	19	16	3	35
	Carlos Metidieri (Rochester Lancers)	22	14	7	35

1971	Carlos Metidieri (Rochester Lancers)	24	19	8	46
1972	Randy Horton (New York Cosmos)	13	9	4	22
1973	Kyle Rote, Jr. (Dallas Tornado)	18	10	10	30
1974	Paul Child (San Jose Earthquakes)	20	15	6	36
1975	Steve David (Miami Toros)	21	23	6	52
1976	Giorgio Chinaglia (New York Cosmos)	19	19	11	49
1977	Steve David (Los Angeles Aztecs)	24	26	6	58
1978	Giorgio Chinaglia (New York Cosmos)	30	34	11	79
1979	Oscar Fabbiani (Tampa Bay Rowdies)	26	25	8	58

Leading Goalkeeper

Year	Player-Team	Games	Saves	Goals	Shutouts	Average
1967	Mirko Stojanovic (Oakland Clippers)	29	N.A.	29	10	1.00
1968	Ataulfo Sanchez (San Diego Toros)	22	130	19	N.A.	0.93
1969	Manfred Kammerer (Atlanta Chiefs)	14	56	15	4	1.07
1970	Lincoln Phillips (Washington Darts)	22	96	21	12	0.95
		Minutes				
1971	Mirko Stojanovic (Dallas Tornado)	1359.00	91	11	8	0.79
1972	Ken Cooper (Dallas Tornado)	1260.00	107	12	6	0.86
1973	Bob Rigby (Philadelphia Atoms)	1157.00	78	8	6	0.62
1974	Barry Watling (Seattle Sounders)	1800.00	132	16	8	0.80
1975	Shep Messing (Boston Minutemen)	1639.32	140	17	6	0.93
1976	Tony Chursky (Seattle Sounders)	1981.00	135	20	9	0.91
1977	Ken Cooper (Dallas Tornado)	2100.00	120	21	8	0.90
1978	Phil Parkes (Vancouver Whitecaps)	2560.00	133	28	10	0.95
1979	Phil Parkes (Vancouver Whitecaps)	2704.00	99	29	7	0.96

Most Valuable Player

1967   Ruben Navarro (Philadelphia Spartans)
1968   John Kowalik (Chicago Mustangs)
1969   Cirilio Fernandez (Kansas City Spurs)
1970   Carlos Metidieri (Rochester Lancers)
1971   Carlos Metidieri (Rochester Lancers)
1972   Randy Horton (New York Cosmos)
1973   Warren Archibald (Miami Toros)
1974   Peter Silvester (Baltimore Comets)
1975   Steve David (Miami Toros)
1976   Pelé (New York Cosmos)
1977   Franz Beckenbauer (New York Cosmos)
1978   Mike Flanagan (New England Tea Men)
1979   Johan Cruyff (Los Angeles Aztecs)

Rookie of the Year

1967   Willy Roy (Chicago Spurs)
1968   Kaizer Motaung (Atlanta Chiefs)
1969   Siegfried Stritzl (Baltimore Bays)
1970   Jim Leeker (St. Louis Stars)
1971   Randy Horton (New York Cosmos)
1972   Mike Winter (St. Louis Stars)
1973   Kyle Rote, Jr. (Dallas Tornado)
1974   Douglas McMillan (Los Angeles Aztecs)
1975   Chris Bahr (Philadelphia Atoms)
1976   Steve Pecher (Dallas Tornado)

1977 Jim McAlister (Seattle Sounders)
1978 Gary Etherington (New York Cosmos)
1979 Larry Hulcer (Los Angeles Aztecs)

Coach of the Year

1968 Phil Woosnam (Atlanta Chiefs)
1969 No selection made
1970 No selection made
1971 No selection made
1972 Casey Frankiewicz (St. Louis Stars)
1973 Al Miller (Philadelphia Atoms)
1974 John Young (Miami Toros)
1975 John Sewell (St. Louis Stars)
1976 Eddie Firmani (Tampa Bay Rowdies)
1977 Ron Newman (Fort Lauderdale Strikers)
1978 Tony Waiters (Vancouver Whitecaps)
1979 Timo Liekoski (Houston Hurricane)

American Soccer League Honor Roll

Champions

1934	Kearny Irish	1957	New York Hakoah
1935	Philadelphia Germans	1958	New York Hakoah
1936	New York Americans	1959	New York Hakoah
1937	Kearny Scots	1060	Colombo
1938	Kearny Scots	1961	Ukrainian Nationals
1939	Kearny Scots	1962	Ukrainian Nationals
1940	Kearny Scots	1963	Ukrainian Nationals
1941	Kearny Scots	1964	Ukrainian Nationals
1942	Philadelphia Americans	1965	Hartford S.C.
1943	Brooklyn Hispano	1966	Roma S.C.
1944	Philadelphia Americans	1967	Baltimore St. Gerard's
1945	New York Brookhattan	1968	Ukrainian Nationals
1946	Baltimore Americans	1969	Washington Darts
1947	Philadelphia Americans	1970	Ukranian Nationals
1948	Philadelphia Americans	1971	New York Greeks
1949	Philadelphia Nationals	1972	Cincinnati Comets
1950	Philadelphia Nationals	1973	New York Apollo
1951	Philadelphia Nationals	1974	Rhode Island Oceaneers
1952	Philadelphia Americans	1975	Boston Astros/New York Apollo
1953	Philadelphia Nationals	1976	Los Angeles Skyhawks
1954	New York Americans	1977	New Jersey Americans
1955	Uhrik Truckers	1978	New York Apollo
1956	Uhrik Truckers	1979	Sacramento Gold

National Champions of the Top Twenty Countries

Argentina

1958	Racing	1966	Racing	1974	Newells Old Boys
1959	San Lorenzo	1967	Estudiantes	1975	River Plate
1960	Independiente	1968	San Lorenzo	1976	Boca Juniors
1961	Racing	1969	Chacarita Juniors	1977	River Plate
1962	Boca Juniors	1970	Independiente	1978	Boca Juniors
1963	Independiente	1971	Independiente	1979	River Plate
1964	Boca Juniors	1972	San Lorenzo		
1965	Boca Juniors	1973	Huracán		

Austria

1958	Wiener S.K.	1966	Admira-Energie	1974	Voest Linz
1959	Wiener S. K.	1967	Rapid Vienna	1975	Tirol-Svarowski
1960	Rapid	1968	Rapid Vienna	1976	Austria/WAC
1961	F.K. Austria	1969	F.K. Austria	1977	SW Innsbruck
1962	F.K. Austria	1970	F.K. Austria	1978	Austria Wien
1963	F.K. Austria	1971	Wacker Innsbruck	1979	Austria Wien
1964	Rapid Vienna	1972	Tirol-Svarowski		
1965	Linz ASK	1973	Tirol-Svarowski		

Brazil

Rio League

1958	Vasco de Gama	1966	Bangu	1974	Flamengo
1959	Fluminense	1967	Botafogo	1975	Fluminense
1960	America	1968	Botafogo	1976	Fluminense
1961	Botafogo	1969	Fluminense	1977	Vasco da Gama
1962	Botafogo	1970	Vasco da Gama	1978	Flamengo
1963	Flamengo	1971	Fluminense	1979	Flamengo
1964	Fluminense	1972	Flamengo		
1965	Flamengo	1973	Fluminense		

Brazil

São Paulo League

1958	Santos	1966	Palmeiras		Palmeiras (co-champions)
1959	Santos	1967	Santos	1974	Palmeiras
1960	Santos	1968	Santos	1975	São Paulo
1961	Santos	1969	Santos	1976	Palmeiras
1962	Santos	1970	São Paulo	1977	Corinthians
1963	Palmeiras	1971	São Paulo	1978	Santos
1964	Santos	1972	Palmeiras	1979	Corinthians
1965	Santos	1973	Santos and		

Chile

1958	Santiago Wanderers	1966	Universidad Católica	1974	Huachipato
1959	Universidad de Chile	1967	Universidad de Chile	1975	Unión Española
1960	Colo-Colo	1968	Wanderers Valparaiso	1976	Everton
1961	Universidad Católica	1969	Universidad de Chile	1977	Unión Española
1962	Universidad Católica	1970	Colo-Colo	1978	Palestino
1963	Colo-Colo	1971	Unión San Felipe	1979	Colo-Colo
1964	Universidad de Chile	1972	Colo-Colo		
1965	Universidad de Chile	1973	Unión Española		

Czechoslovakia

1958	Dukla Prague	1969	Spartak Trnava
1959	Red Star Bratislava	1970	Slovan Bratislava
1960	Spartak Hradec Kralove	1971	Spartak Trnava
1961	Dukla Prague	1972	Spartak Trnava
1962	Dukla Prague	1973	Spartak Trnava
1963	Dukla Prague	1974	Slovan Bratislava
1964	Dukla Prague	1975	Slovan Bratislava
1965	Sparta Prague	1976	Banik Ostrava
1966	Dukla Prague	1977	Dukla Prague
1967	Sparta Prague	1978	Dukla Prague
1968	Spartak Trnava	1979	Dukla Prague

England

1958	Wolverhampton Wanderers	1970	Everton
1959	Wolverhampton Wanderers	1971	Arsenal
1960	Burnley	1972	Derby County
1961	Tottenham Hotspur	1973	Liverpool
1962	Ipswich Town	1974	Leeds United
1963	Everton	1975	Derby County
1964	Liverpool	1976	Liverpool
1965	Manchester United	1977	Liverpool
1966	Liverpool	1978	Nottingham Forest
1967	Manchester United	1979	Liverpool
1968	Manchester City		
1969	Leeds United		

France

1958	Stade de Reims	1966	Nantes	1973	Nantes
1959	OGC Nice	1967	Saint-Étienne	1974	Saint-Étienne
1960	Stade de Reims	1968	Saint-Étienne	1975	Saint-Étienne
1961	AS Monaco	1969	Saint-Étienne	1976	Saint-Étienne
1962	Stade de Reims	1970	Saint-Étienne	1977	Nantes
1963	AS Monaco	1971	Olympique Marseille	1978	AS Monaco
1964	Saint-Étienne	1972	Olympique Marseille	1979	Strasbourg
1965	Nantes	1972	Olympique Marseille		

Hungary

1958	MTK	1966	Vasas Budapest	1974	Ujpest Dozsa
1959	Csepel	1967	Ferencvaros	1975	Ujpest Dozsa
1960	Ujpest Dozsa	1968	Ferencvaros	1976	Ferencvaros
1961	Vasas Budapest	1969	Ujpest Dozsa	1977	Vasa Budapest
1962	Vasas Budapest	1970	Ujpest Dozsa	1978	Ujpest Dozsa
1963	Ferencvaros	1971	Ujpest Dozsa	1979	Ujpest Dozsa
1964	Ferencvaros	1972	Ujpest Dozsa		
1965	Vasas Budapest	1973	Ujpest Dozsa		

Italy

1958	Juventus	1966	Internazionale Milan	1974	Lazio
1959	A.C. Milan	1967	Juventus	1975	Juventus
1960	Juventus	1968	A.C. Milan	1976	Torino
1961	Juventus	1969	Fiorentina	1977	Juventus
1962	A.C. Milan	1970	Cagliari	1978	Juventus
1963	Internazionale Milan	1971	Internazionale Milan	1979	A. C. Milan
1964	Bologna	1972	Juventus		
1965	Internazionale Milan	1973	Juventus		

Mexico

1958	Zacatepec	1966	America	1974	Cruz Azul
1959	Guadalajara	1967	Toluca	1975	Toluca
1960	Guadalajara	1968	Toluca	1976	Universidad de Guadalajara
1961	Guadalajara	1969	Guadalajara	1977	UNAM
1962	Guadalajara	1970	Cruz Azul	1978	Universitario de Nuevo Leon
1963	Oro Jalisco	1971	America	1979	Cruz Azul
1964	Guadalajara	1972	Cruz Azul		
1965	Guadalajara	1973	Cruz Azul		

The Netherlands

1958	DOS Utrecht	1966	Ajax	1974	Feyenoord
1959	Sparta	1967	Ajax	1975	PSV Eindhoven
1960	Ajax	1968	Ajax	1976	PSV Eindhoven
1961	Feyenoord	1969	Feyenoord	1977	Ajax
1962	Feyenoord	1970	Ajax	1978	PSV Eindhoven
1963	PSV Eindhoven	1971	Feyenoord	1979	Ajax
1964	DWS Amsterdam	1972	Ajax		
1965	Feyenoord	1973	Ajax		

Peru

1958	Sports Boys	1966	Universitaria	1974	Defensor Lima
1959	Universitaria	1967	Universitaria	1975	Universitaria
1960	Universitaria	1968	Sporting Cristal	1976	Union Huaral
1961	Sporting Cristal	1969	Universitaria	1977	Alianza Lima
1962	Alianza Lima	1970	Sporting Cristal	1978	Alianza Lima
1963	Alianza Lima	1971	Universitaria	1979	Sporting Cristal
1964	Universitaria	1972	Sporting Cristal		
1965	Alianza Lima	1973	Sporting Cristal		

Poland

1958	LKS Lodz	1966	Gornik Zabrze	1974	Ruch Chorzow
1959	Gornik Zabrze	1967	Gornik Zabrze	1975	Ruch Chorzow
1960	Ruch Chorzow	1968	Ruch Chorzow	1976	Stal Mielec
1961	Gornik Zabrze	1969	Legia Warsaw	1977	Slask Wroclaw
1962	Polonia Bytom	1970	Legia Warsaw	1978	Wisla Krakow
1963	Gornik Zabrze	1971	Gornik Zabrze	1979	Ruch Chorzow
1964	Gornik Zabrze	1972	Gornik Zabrze		
1965	Gornik Zabrze	1973	Stal Mielec		

Scotland

1958	Hearts	1966	Celtic	1974	Celtic
1959	Rangers	1967	Celtic	1975	Rangers
1960	Hearts	1968	Celtic	1976	Rangers
1961	Rangers	1969	Celtic	1977	Celtic
1962	Dundee	1970	Celtic	1978	Rangers
1963	Rangers	1971	Celtic	1979	Celtic
1964	Rangers	1972	Celtic		
1965	Kilmarnock	1973	Celtic		

The Soviet Union

1958	Spartak Moscow	1966	Dynamo Kiev	1974	Dynamo Kiev
1959	Dynamo Moscow	1967	Dynamo Kiev	1975	Dynamo Kiev
1960	Torpedo Moscow	1968	Dynamo Kiev	1976	Torpedo Moscow
1961	Dynamo Kiev	1969	Spartak Moscow	1977	Dynamo Kiev
1962	Spartak Moscow	1970	CSKA Moscow	1978	Dynamo Tbilisi
1963	Dynamo Moscow	1971	Dynamo Kiev	1979	Spartak Moscow
1964	Dynamo Tbilisi	1972	Saria Voroshilovgrad		
1965	Torpedo Moscow	1973	Ararat Erevan		

Spain

1958	Real Madrid	1966	Atlético Madrid	1974	Barcelona
1959	Barcelona	1967	Real Madrid	1975	Real Madrid
1960	Barcelona	1968	Real Madrid	1976	Real Madrid
1961	Real Madrid	1969	Real Madrid	1977	Atlético Madrid
1962	Real Madrid	1970	Atlético Madrid	1978	Real Madrid
1963	Real Madrid	1971	Valencia	1979	Real Madrid
1964	Real Madrid	1972	Real Madrid		
1965	Real Madrid	1973	Atlético Madrid		

Sweden

1958	IFK Gothenburg	1966	Djurgaarden	1974	Malmo
1959	Djurgaarden	1967	Malmo	1975	Malmo
1960	IFK Norrkoping	1968	Oester Vaexjoe	1976	IFK Halmstad
1961	IF Elfsborg	1969	IFK Gothenburg	1977	Malmo
1962	IFK Norrkoping	1970	Malmo	1978	Malmo
1963	IFK Norrkoping	1971	Malmo	1979	Oester Vaexjoe
1964	Djurgaarden	1972	Atvidaberg		
1965	Malmo	1973	Atvidaberg		

Uruguay

1958	Penarol	1966	Nacional	1974	Penarol
1959	Penarol	1967	Penarol	1975	Penarol
1960	Penarol	1968	Penarol	1976	Defensor
1961	Penarol	1969	Nacional	1977	Nacional
1962	Penarol	1970	Nacional	1978	Penarol
1963	Nacional	1971	Nacional	1979	Penarol
1964	Penarol	1972	Nacional		
1965	Penarol	1973	Penarol		

West Germany

1958	FC Shalke	1969	Bayern Munich
1959	Eintracht Frankfurt	1970	Borussia Monchengladbach
1960	Hamburg	1971	Borussia Monchengladbach
1961	Nuremberg	1972	Bayern Munich
1962	Cologne	1973	Bayern Munich
1963	Borussia Dortmund	1974	Bayern Munich
1964	Cologne	1975	Borussia Monchengladbach
1965	Werder Bremen	1976	Borussia Monchengladbach
1966	Munich 1860	1977	Borussia Monchengladbach
1967	Eintracht Brunswick	1978	Cologne
1968	Nuremberg	1979	Hamburg

Yugoslavia

1958	Dynamo Zagreb	1966	Vojvodina Novi Sad	1974	Hajduk Split
1959	Red Star Belgrade	1967	Sarajevo	1975	Hajduk Split
1960	Red Star Belgrade	1968	Red Star Belgrade	1976	Partizan Belgrade
1961	Red Star Belgrade	1969	Red Star Belgrade	1977	Red Star Belgrade
1962	Red Star Belgrade	1970	Red Star Belgrade	1978	Partizan Belgrade
1963	Red Star Belgrade	1971	Hajduk Split	1979	Hajduk Split
1964	Red Star Belgrade	1972	Zeljeznicar		
1965	Partizan Belgrade	1973	Red Star Belgrade		

National Participation in Soccer: Summary by Continents

AFRICA

Names of affiliated Associations (or belonging to that area) (40)	Population (Millions)	Clubs Affiliated			Teams taking part in Championships or Competitions				Players Registered						Registered Referees			
		Direct	Indirect	Total	General	Youth	Veteran	Total	Professional	Non-Amateur	Amateur	Youth	Veteran	Total	Superior	Average	Beginners	Total
ALGERIA	18.0	780	–	780	1,950	657	–	2,607	–	–	43,509	15,058	–	58,567	48	800	250	1,098
BENIN PR	3.5	31	–	31	10	9	–	19	–	–	4,965	200	–	5,165	12	18	31	61
BOTSWANA	(no information received)																	
BURUNDI	4.0	25	107	132	25	19	9	53	–	–	3,090	570	270	3,930	3	27	95	125
CAMEROON	7.1	62	138	200	179	16	69	264	–	–	4,786	3,256	1,286	9,328	48	200	200	448
CENTRAL AFRICA	3.0	256	–	256	256	25	2	283	–	1,500	4,000	1,500	200	7,200	7	50	35	92
CONGO	1.0	111	30	141	24	106	–	130	–	–	4,230	–	–	4,230	7	21	42	70
EGYPT AR	36.0	168	–	168	14	86	78	178	–	–	3,868	6,827	1,000	11,695	58	128	185	371
ETHIOPIA	29.4	305	–	305	244	76	–	320	–	–	11,200	2,225	–	13,425	85	611	709	1,405
GABON	0.6	275	–	275	265	–	10	275	–	–	8,086	–	–	8,086	15	36	77	128
GAMBIA	0.5	15	24	39	15	24	–	39	–	–	350	500	–	850	9	6	12	27
GHANA	10.5	150	150	300	16	200	–	216	–	2	1,000	4,000	–	5,002	44	175	85	304
GUINEA	5.0	42	264	306	42	42	–	84	–	–	5,508	3,600	–	9,108	8	24	106	138
IVORY COAST	4.0	48	30	78	85	20	–	105	–	–	3,255	–	–	3,255	10	15	35	60
KENYA	13.0	251	100	351	250	20	–	270	–	–	7,100	720	–	7,820	28	10	110	148
LESOTHO	1.5	62	26	88	62	36	–	98	–	–	1,200	876	–	2,076	4	26	40	70
LIBERIA	(no information received)																	
LIBYA	2.6	76	13	89	76	72	–	148	–	–	1,835	1,106	–	2,941	46	42	61	149
MADAGASCAR	8.0	775	–	775	310	–	–	310	–	–	23,536	–	–	23,536	6	40	161	207
MALAWI	4.0	24	34	58	30	22	–	52	–	127	594	22	–	744	5	21	5	31
MALI	6.6	128	–	128	128	52	–	180	1	–	4,630	850	–	5,480	7	45	50	102
MAURITANIA	1.5	44	15	59	44	10	10	64	–	–	1,080	250	600	1,930	1	12	30	43
MAURITIUS	0.9	40	357	397	363	34	–	397	–	–	10,500	12,000	–	22,500	5	21	11	37
MOROCCO	18.0	274	–	274	274	390	40	704	–	–	7,000	7,544	2,191	16,735	109	391	500	1,000
NIGER	4.5	45	–	45	–	–	–	–	–	–	–	–	–	–	30	20	50	100
NIGERIA	50.0	12	314	326	138	585	–	723	–	–	21,690	58,500	–	80,190	68	217	524	809
RHODESIA	5.1	545	60	605	396	24	–	420	–	704	10,455	525	–	11,684	73	87	90	250
RWANDA	(no information received)																	
SENEGAL	5.2	75	–	75	83	40	–	123	–	–	2,211	1,292	–	3,503	25	37	72	134
SIERRA LEONE	3.5	–	–	–	104	–	–	104	–	–	3,120	5,000	–	8,120	40	200	400	640
SOMALIA	3.0	8	8	16	8	20	1	29	132	44	176	440	24	816	9	6	22	37
SUDAN	15.0	400	350	750	400	350	21	771	–	–	23,500	12,500	840	36,840	42	120	393	555
SWAZILAND	(no information received)																	
TANZANIA	12.0	–	–	–	34	17	–	51	–	–	–	–	–	–	6	20	50	76
TOGO	2.0	144	–	144	124	18	2	144	–	–	3,500	750	90	4,340	5	10	70	85
TUNISIA	6.0	172	–	172	172	172	–	344	–	–	14,314	–	–	14,314	39	300	184	523
UGANDA	10.0	–	400	400	300	420	–	720	–	–	900	600	82	1,582	20	18	140	178
UPPER VOLTA	5.5	40	15	55	60	–	–	60	–	–	3,510	–	–	3,510	7	15	50	72
ZAIRE	21.0	2,100	300	2,400	1,500	700	–	2,200	–	52,627	–	–	–	52,627	75	1,800	–	1,875
ZAMBIA	4.1	10	10	20	194	68	18	280	330	–	1,610	1,360	800	4,100	146	80	64	290
TOTAL	325.6	7,493	2,745	10,238	8,175	4,330	260	12,765	463	55,004	232,222	142,071	7,383	445,229	1,150	5,649	4,939	11,738

CONCACAF — (America — North and Central and Caribbean = CONCACAF)

Names of affiliated Associations (or belonging to that area) (23)	Population Millions	Clubs Affiliated Direct	Indirect	Total	Teams taking part in Championships or Competitions General	Youth	Veteran	Total	Players Registered Professional	Non-Amateur	Amateur	Youth	Veteran	Total	Registered Referees Superior	Average	Beginners	Total
ANTIGUA	0.07	26	16	42	26	16	–	42	–	–	420	224	–	644	8	14	9	31
BAHAMAS	0.25	–	20	20	15	16	–	31	–	–	300	320	–	620	2	3	7	12
BARBADOS	0.26	8	74	82	48	18	–	66	–	–	600	350	–	950	14	36	23	73
BERMUDA	0.06	23	9	32	32	16	–	48	–	–	1,039	673	–	1,712	4	21	12	37
CANADA	22.0	1,300	–	1,300	1,300	6,600	–	7,900	36	336	19,500	99,000	–	118,872	45	638	304	987
COSTA RICA	2.0	431	–	431	359	62	–	421	–	504	10,375	1,550	–	12,429	12	12	102	126
CUBA	8.5	14	56	70	164	516	34	714	–	–	2,976	9,312	612	12,900	48	50	62	160
DOMINICAN REPUBLIC	4.6	12	60	72	261	44	4	309	–	–	9,185	880	100	10,165	7	8	10	25
GRENADA	0.1	15	–	15	15	–	–	15	–	–	200	–	–	200	3	5	7	15
GUATEMALA	6.0	1,521	90	1,611	606	1,356	–	1,962	–	352	12,300	30,864	–	43,516	28	50	187	265
GUYANA	0.8	71	32	103	85	40	1	126	–	–	857	748	60	1,665	6	12	18	36
HAITI	5.5	40	–	40	13	12	–	25	–	–	–	–	–	3,480	7	34	–	41
HONDURAS	3.0	452	–	452	322	128	–	450	–	300	8,050	3,200	–	11,550	67	147	209	423
JAMAICA	1.9	16	250	266	29	215	–	244	–	–	20,000	25,200	–	45,200	12	40	70	122
MEXICO	51.0	77	–	77	75,000	30,000	–	105,000	2,075	–	2,000,000	750,000	–	2,752,075	158	1,800	3,073	5,031
NETHERLANDS ANTILLES	0.16	–	85	85	85	20	–	105	–	320	3,000	500	–	3,820	15	35	20	70
NICARAGUA	2.0	16	15	31	8	–	–	8	–	–	160	–	–	160	6	4	4	14
PANAMA	(no información recibida)	–	–	–														
PUERTO RICO	3.2	16	50	66	20	216	–	236	–	–	800	2,400	–	3,200	25	30	50	105
EL SALVADOR	4.5	668	114	782	520	100	–	620	–	1,404	12,392	2,600	–	16,396	156	122	185	463
SURINAM	0.5	58	110	168	58	11	–	69	–	–	4,100	330	–	4,430	9	61	12	82
TRINIDAD AND TOBAGO	1.0	132	–	132	122	10	–	132	–	–	3,370	220	–	3,590	27	22	98	147
USA	217.7	–	–	–	300	1,396	–	1,696	3,000	–	70,000	252,000	–	325,000	–	–	–	4,900
TOTAL	335.1	4,896	981	5,877	79,388	40,792	39	120,219	5,111	3,216	2,179,624	1,180,371	772	3,372,574	659	3,144	4,462	13,165

AMERICA SOUTH – (Confederación Sudamericana de Fútbol – CONMEBOL)

Names of affiliated Associations (or belonging to that area) (10)	Population Millions	Clubs Affiliated			Teams taking part in Championships or Competitions				Players Registered						Registered Referees			
		Direct	Indirect	Total	General	Youth	Veteran	Total	Professional	Non-Amateur	Amateur	Youth	Veteran	Total	Superior	Average	Beginners	Total
ARGENTINA	25.5	88	2,625	2,713	5,713	9,015	–	14,728	2,650	61,320	72,455	163,470	–	299,895	867	1,530	875	3,272
BOLIVIA	5.8	305	–	305	295	23	2	320	–	895	10,658	207	29	11,789	6	76	120	202
BRAZIL	110.0	–	5,436	5,436	–	–	–	18,369	16,320	12	96,435	–	–	112,755	319	377	570	1,266
CHILE	8.9	–	5,615	5,615	8,095	5,525	–	13,620	835		243,580	79,995	–	324,422	30	90	5,400	5,520
COLOMBIA	25.7	–	3,685	3,685	4,250	1,200	460	5,910	460	490	126,000	24,200	900	152,050	163	1,261	616	2,040
ECUADOR	7.3	–	170	170	200	100	–	300	300	5,000	4,000	3,000	–	12,300	25	50	45	120
PARAGUAY	2.3	42	700	742	–	–	–	–	–	100,000	5,000	5,000	–	110,000	–	–	–	600
PERU	13.2	6,158	–	6,158	6,158	800	–	6,958	400	–	122,640	16,320	–	139,360	6	215	2,095	2,316
URUGUAY	2.6	60	910	970	406	564	–	970	550	12,000	72,000	17,000	650	101,550	20	31	89	140
VENEZUELA	13.0	12	976	988	501	1,202	32	1,735	260	50	10,034	24,053	–	35,047	50	203	108	361
TOTAL	214.3	6,665	20,117	26,782	25,618	18,429	494	62,910	21,775	179,767	762,802	333,245	1,579	1,299,168	1,486	3,833	9,918	15,837

ASIA

Names of affiliated Associations (or belonging to that area) (34)	Population (Millions)	Clubs Affiliated			Teams taking part in Championships or Competitions				Players Registered						Registered Referees			
		Direct	Indirect	Total	General	Youth	Veteran	Total	Professional	Non-Amateur	Amateur	Youth	Veteran	Total	Superior	Average	Beginners	Total
AFGHANISTAN	18.0	30	–	30	30	100	20	150	–	300	1,000	2,000	–	3,300	30	50	150	230
BAHRAIN	0.3	30	–	30	30	32	–	62	–	–	1,150	960	–	2,110	20	18	16	54
BANGLADESH	75.0	81	1,081	1,162	30	20	–	50	–	–	17,600	8,084	–	25,684	25	50	300	375
BRUNEI	0.2	12	10	22	12	8	5	25	–	–	35	30	18	83	–	6	8	14
BURMA	23.0	260	290	550	400	150	–	550	–	–	11,000	3,000	–	14,000	12	700	600	1,312
HONG KONG	4.7	50	22	72	64	120	–	184	–	263	1,285	2,256	–	3,804	14	30	118	162
INDIA	582.0	–	1,949	1,949	1,386	563	–	1,949	–	–	37,752	15,358	–	53,110	286	429	2,886	3,601
INDONESIA	135.0	2,880	–	2,880	288	180	–	468	–	–	72,000	25,000	–	97,000	7	150	300	457
IRAN	34.0	72	350	422	422	132	1,432	1,986	–	–	13,000	30,000	300	43,300	20	68	75	163
IRAQ	12.0	90	65	155	52	22	–	74	–	–	1,100	600	–	1,700	30	92	282	404
ISRAEL*	3.0	544	–	544	304	244	–	548	–	–	13,064	10,436	–	23,500	75	200	225	500
JAPAN	113.2	19,840	–	19,840	6,796	13,044	–	19,840	–	–	101,940	195,660	–	297,600	100	1,000	4,000	5,100
JORDAN	3.0	17	5	22	28	28	–	56	–	–	1,680	600	–	2,280	9	7	11	27
KHMER	7.5	23	7	30	14	16	2	32	–	–	400	200	50	650	7	10	25	42
KOREA DPR	14.0	45	40	85	20	35	13	68	–	–	1,607	850	250	2,707	17	80	500	597
KOREA REP.	31.1	113	363	476	41	72	–	113	–	–	750	1,297	–	2,047	10	20	20	50
KUWAIT	1.0	14	–	14	14	14	–	28	–	–	308	1,330	–	1,638	6	21	24	51
LAOS	3.0	20	73	93	112	30	10	152	–	–	1,953	606	253	2,812	5	24	57	86
LEBANON	3.0	105	–	105	105	36	–	141	–	–	5,500	2,625	–	8,125	4	20	60	84
MACAO	0.45	120	–	120	54	16	–	70	–	–	1,500	500	–	2,000	–	–	–	–
MALAYSIA	10.7	320	–	320	15	14	–	29	–	–	7,839	–	–	7,839	46	28	242	316
NEPAL	12.0	17	16	33	20	25	–	45	–	–	400	300	–	700	–	6	15	21
PAKISTAN	130.0	–	576	576	27	16	–	43	–	–	10,000	3,000	–	13,000	75	130	90	295
PHILIPPINES	44.0	420	–	420	330	490	–	820	–	–	7,400	9,400	–	16,800	4	30	150	184
QATAR	0.2	7	1	8	7	7	–	14	–	–	225	525	450	1,200	8	12	16	36
SAUDI ARABIA	9.0	66	30	96	66	30	54	150	–	–	2,970	2,370	2,260	7,600	24	36	57	117
SINGAPORE	2.3	41	131	172	30	40	–	70	–	–	6,000	2,000	–	8,000	26	17	109	152
SRI LANKA	13.0	–	600	600	73	41	–	114	–	–	16,525	2,300	–	18,825	17	80	250	347
SYRIA	7.5	53	49	102	–	–	–	–	–	–	15,300	5,100	10,200	30,600	29	65	115	209
THAILAND	43.2	145	–	145	145	40	–	185	–	–	6,000	3,000	–	9,000	37	34	56	127
UNITED ARAB EMIRATES	0.66	20	–	20	20	20	–	40	–	–	355	807	–	1,162	20	15	10	45
VIETNAM DPR	17.0	20	35	55	300	500	–	800	–	–	6,000	10,000	–	16,000	21	40	120	181
VIETNAM REP.	17.0	58	–	58	21	26	11	58	–	–	429	499	220	1,148	30	9	31	70
YEMEN PDR	1.5	–	–	–	24	12	–	36	–	–	1,000	700	–	1,700	8	12	20	40
TOTAL	1,371.5	25,513	5,693	31,206	11,280	16,123	1,547	28,950	–	563	365,067	341,393	14,001	721,024	1,022	3,489	10,938	15,449

* FIFA Member but not affiliated to Confederation

EUROPE

Names of affiliated Associations (or belonging to that area) (34)	Population (Millions)	Clubs Affiliated			Teams taking part in Championships or Competitions				Players Registered						Registered Referees			
		Direct	Indirect	Total	General	Youth	Veteran	Total	Professional	Non-Amateur	Amateur	Youth	Veteran	Total	Superior	Average	Beginners	Total
ALBANIA	2.4	42	–	42	–	–	–	215	–	–	3,014	1,716	–	4,730	–	–	–	265
AUSTRIA	7.5	–	2,041	2,041	3,696	2,770	–	6,466	–	468	254,657	–	–	255,125	289	1,385	261	1,935
BELGIUM	9.8	2,065	1,210	3,275	8,500	5,900	–	14,400	242	835	160,343	118,000	–	279,420	7	101	5,438	5,546
BULGARIA	9.0	983	2,940	3,923	4,821	880	36	5,737	–	–	104,000	12,340	940	117,280	138	840	2,130	3,108
CYPRUS	0.6	41	–	41	41	16	–	57	–	–	12,000	–	–	12,000	24	40	30	94
CZECHOSLOVAKIA	15.0	6,776	–	6,776	–	–	–	26,847	–	–	352,227	–	–	352,227	–	–	–	6,550
DENMARK	4.8	–	1,453	1,453	3,000	4,100	300	7,400	–	–	85,000	118,000	5,000	208,000	100	1,700	–	1,800
ENGLAND	56.0	254	37,461	37,715	32,226	4,678	–	36,904	5,000	–	1,500,000	–	–	1,505,000	5,000	4,500	–	9,500
FINLAND	4.7	900	–	900	1,322	1,115	–	2,437	–	–	24,111	20,219	–	44,330	150	850	1,500	2,500
FRANCE	52.0	18,285	–	18,285	–	–	–	52,000	447	674	980,887	162,636	49,545	1,194,189	56	2,629	12,222	14,907
GERMAN DR	17.1	4,981	–	4,981	10,851	14,192	–	25,043	–	–	308,098	238,957	10,000	557,055	36	14,036	4,015	18,087
GERMANY FR	61.5	17,549	–	17,549	48,659	66,486	–	115,145	1,000	–	2,310,431	1,300,000	–	3,611,431	126	34,874	5,000	40,000
GREECE	9.5	138	1,624	1,762	1,698	54	10	1,762	–	1,900	84,000	5,000	120	91,020	144	793	623	1,560
HUNGARY	10.5	–	2,440	2,440	2,837	2,489	–	5,326	–	–	86,192	52,269	–	138,461	97	2,920	1,643	4,660
ICELAND	0.2	20	47	67	310	117	–	427	–	–	7,756	6,100	–	13,856	35	133	105	273
IRELAND NORTH	1.5	740	–	740	740	135	–	875	185	–	14,800	2,700	–	17,685	16	220	116	352
IRELAND REP.	4.5	1,661	1,253	2,914	2,600	312	–	2,912	76	320	48,000	5,200	–	54,596	30	280	180	490
ITALY	54.1	11,689	10,156	21,845	11,116	11,016	–	22,132	4,609	19,341	614,037	195,577	–	833,564	102	183	13,164	13,449
LIECHTENSTEIN	0.02	7	–	7	20	32	8	60	–	–	400	650	150	1,200	–	7	4	11
LUXEMBURG	0.35	128	81	209	244	288	–	532	–	–	9,389	7,341	–	15,730	16	52	203	271
MALTA	0.3	61	170	231	290	72	–	362	350	10	5,010	2,090	–	7,460	23	36	8	67
NETHERLANDS	13.0	5,941	1,694	7,635	27,551	26,497	–	54,048	850	–	517,816	445,549	–	964,215	26	13,802	–	13,828
NORWAY	4.0	1,600	1,500	3,100	2,100	4,250	440	6,790	–	–	42,000	75,000	7,000	124,000	200	1,500	300	2,000
POLAND	34.5	–	5,334	5,334	8,107	3,236	–	11,343	–	–	234,052	–	–	234,052	83	4,971	2,106	7,160
PORTUGAL	8.7	690	190	880	112	112	–	224	710	16,263	12,564	11,278	–	40,815	359	751	40	1,150
RUMANIA	23.0	5,453	–	5,453	4,483	1,294	–	5,777	–	–	125,577	54,410	–	179,987	1,440	1,661	3,472	6,573
SCOTLAND	5.2	75	3,999	4,074	4,600	2,500	–	7,100	4,000	–	45,000	60,000	–	109,000	190	1,100	250	1,540
SPAIN	35.4	5,578	–	5,578	4,068	1,510	–	5,578	2,331	–	114,491	85,752	–	202,574	250	5,055	–	5,305
SWEDEN	8.3	3,220	–	3,220	4,208	1,803	–	6,011	–	128,197	–	24,351	–	152,548	600	4,500	1,000	6,100
SWITZERLAND	6.0	1,382	–	1,382	2,729	3,701	884	7,314	–	400	58,024	72,764	15,000	146,188	60	3,195	–	3,255
TURKEY	40.0	1,432	–	1,432	1,432	108	–	1,540	2,101	268	37,620	3,240	–	43,229	196	819	806	1,821
USSR	255.5	164	50,500	50,664	148	16	–	164	–	–	2,205,000	2,300,000	–	4,505,000	230	2,150	134,000	136,380
WALES	2.77	93	1,547	1,640	1,600	550	–	2,150	150	–	32,000	11,500	–	43,650	460	150	380	990
YUGOSLAVIA	20.5	4,289	–	4,289	2,719	1,570	–	4,289	540	–	115,337	56,348	–	172,225	421	4,834	1,286	6,541
TOTAL	778.2	96,237	125,640	221,877	196,828	161,799	1,678	439,305	22,591	168,676	10,151,606	5,448,987	87,755	16,231,842	10,904	110,067	190,282	318,068

OCEANIA

Names of affiliated Associations (or belonging to that area) (5)	Population Millions	Clubs Affiliated			Teams taking part in Championships or Competitions				Players Registered						Registered Referees			
		Direct	Indirect	Total	General	Youth	Veteran	Total	Professional	Non-Amateur	Amateur	Youth	Veteran	Total	Superior	Average	Beginners	Total
AUSTRALIA	14.0	14	6,500	6,514	2,266	12,000	–	14,266	–	6,000	28,000	180,000	–	214,000	110	400	1,600	2,110
CHINA REP.	17.0	36	–	36	263	462	117	842	–	–	5,470	8,505	2,594	16,569	80	120	165	365
FIJI	0.75	–	140	140	18	18	–	36	–	–	13,500	8,000	–	21,500	20	50	50	120
NEW ZEALAND	2.79	–	312	312	704	2,345	–	3,049	102	–	9,856	31,740	–	41,698	15	150	335	500
PAPUA–NEW GUINEA	2.0	–	–	320	320	48	–	368	–	–	4,500	1,200	–	5,700	5	15	120	140
TOTAL	36.5	50	6,952	7,322	3,571	14,873	117	18,561	102	6,000	61,326	229,445	2,594	299,467	230	735	2,270	3,235

SUMMARY BY TOTALS

Confederations (Number of Associations from which information is included)		Population Millions	Clubs Affiliated			Teams taking part in Championships or Competitions				Players Registered						Registered Referees			
			Direct	Indirect	Total	General	Youth	Veteran	Total	Professional	Non-Amateur	Amateur	Youth	Veteran	Total	Superior	Average	Beginners	Total
AFRICA	36	325.6	7,493	2,745	10,238	8,175	4,330	260	12,765	463	55,004	232,222	142,071	7,383	445,229	1,150	5,649	4,939	11,738
ASIA	34	1,371.5	25,513	5,693	31,206	11,280	16,123	1,547	28,950	–	563	365,067	341,393	14,001	721,024	1,022	3,489	10,938	15,449
CONCACAF	22	335.1	4,896	981	5,877	79,388	40,792	39	120,219	5,111	3,216	2,179,624	1,180,371	772	3,372,574	659	3,144	4,462	13,165
EUROPE	34	778.2	96,237	125,640	221,877	196,828	161,799	1,678	439,305	22,591	168,676	10,151,606	5,448,987	87,755	16,231,842	10,904	110,067	190,282	318,068
OCEANIA	5	36.5	50	6,952	7,322	3,571	14,873	117	18,561	102	6,000	61,326	229,445	2,594	299,467	230	735	2,270	3,235
SOUTH AMERICA	10	214.3	6,665	20,117	26,782	25,618	18,429	494	62,910	21,775	179,767	762,802	333,245	1,579	1,299,168	1,486	3,833	9,918	15,837
TOTAL	141	3,061.2	140,854	.162,128	303,302	324,860	256,346	4,135	682,710	50,042	413,226	13,752,647	7,675,512	114,084	22,369,304	15,451	126,917	222,809	377,492

Note:

The totals in the different columns do not necessarily add up to the grand total, as some
National Associations did not give breakdowns but only the total figures.

Index

References in italics are to illustrations.
Unless otherwise indicated, soccer teams are American or
Canadian.

304